P. Reilly OP

BUREAU OF INTERNATIONAL RESEARCH
HARVARD UNIVERSITY AND RADCLIFFE COLLEGE

WAR AND PEACE
IN
SOVIET DIPLOMACY

THE MACMILLAN COMPANY
NEW YORK · BOSTON · CHICAGO · DALLAS
ATLANTA · SAN FRANCISCO

MACMILLAN AND CO., Limited
LONDON · BOMBAY · CALCUTTA · MADRAS
MELBOURNE

THE MACMILLAN COMPANY
OF CANADA, Limited
TORONTO

WAR AND PEACE
IN
SOVIET DIPLOMACY

By
T. A. TARACOUZIO

NEW YORK
THE MACMILLAN COMPANY
1940

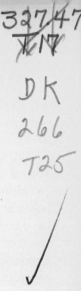
26934

MAY 9 1951

PREFACE

More than twenty years have passed since Russia became the political laboratory of Marxian experimentalists. Shelves of books have been written, and innumerable lives lost in an attempt to unveil the true workings and the actual results of the effort made by the Union of Socialist Soviet Republics to reconstruct human society according to the pattern designed by Marx, approved by Lenin, and followed by Stalin. Yet the enigma of the Red Kremlin still remains. The compatibility of the autocratic rule of a dictatorial régime with the democratic freedom allegedly prevailing in the Soviet Union, is still unexplained. In the field of revolutionary aspirations the mystery is even deeper, witness the continued coexistence of emphasis upon proletarian cosmopolitanism and stress upon Russian patriotism. The culminating evidence of this enigma, however, is to be found in the international relations of the U.S.S.R. Traditionally a champion of international peace, on August 23, 1939, the Soviet Union signed a Pact of Non-Aggression with the Third Reich and thereby became virtually a god-parent of the war now raging in Europe.

In the present study an attempt is made to explain the paradox of this Soviet-Nazi rapprochement. The Marxian dogmas on war and peace are analyzed, and the international relations of the Soviets are examined to determine the Marxian conceptions of war and peace and to indicate their reflections in the Soviet policy of peace.

Analytical rather than historical, the present study does not purport to censor in one way or another the Soviet records of yesterday, to appraise the Kremlin's outlook of today, or to forecast the international position of the U.S.S.R. for tomorrow. It is designed merely as an exposé of the fundamental principles of Marxism concerning the issues which have determined Soviet peace policies in the past, control the Kremlin's stand at the present, and will underlie the international relations of the U.S.S.R. in the future.

Being a study pertaining to the U.S.S.R., it is based primarily upon Russian materials. These may be broadly divided into those which furnish the theoretic background for Soviet conceptions of war and peace as social phenomena, and those which portray the practical application of these concepts by the U.S.S.R. in its intercourse with the non-communist world. To the former belong the writings of Marx, Lenin, and Stalin, as well as the records of the Communist International and of the All-Union Communist Party, made available through the reports of their meetings and congresses, and the comments found in the official Party organ, "Pravda." The latter group is comprised of official Soviet materials, including international treaties, diplomatic documents, enactments and articles in the official Soviet Government organ, "Izvestiia." Subsidiarily, works of Soviet authorities on the international relations of the U.S.S.R. and data from numerous Soviet periodicals have likewise been relied upon.

The author acknowledges his indebtedness to the Committee of the Bureau of International Research of Harvard University and Radcliffe College, under whose auspices this study has been carried out. He is especially grateful to the Chairman, Professor Sidney B. Fay, for his kind consideration and helpful encouragement both in regard to the substance and to the technique of the present study. The invaluable criticism and suggestions of Dr. Eleanor Wyllys Allen in the preparation of this book are acknowledged by the author with profound and sincere gratitude. So, also, is the kindness of Professor Eldon R. James of the Harvard Law School, whose readiness to coöperate with the Bureau has again enabled the author to devote part of his time to this work.

T. A. T.

April, 1940
Harvard Law School
Cambridge, Massachusetts

P. S. Many important changes have taken place in war-torn Europe and elsewhere since this book went to press. Hitler has become virtually the master of Western Europe by having succeeded in forcing into submission the Atlantic States from the Arctic coast of Murmansk to the sunny slopes of the Pyrenees in the Bay of Biscay. Italy entered the war on the side of Germany and is fighting Great Britain, once again hoping to materialize Mussolini's dream of *Mare Nostrum*. In the Balkans the merry-go-round of diplomatic wavering resulted in the dissection of Roumania and the further encroachment of the Axis Powers upon things Danubian. In the Far East it accelerated Japan's aspirations for expansion southward, ominously manifested, among other things, in the recent Rome-Berlin-Tokio Pact of Military Alliance. As to the Soviets, their gains have been by no means small: Bessarabia was incorporated in the Soviet Union, and the Baltic Republics of Estonia, Latvia and Lithuania were forced to become communist member-states of the U.S.S.R.

Under the circumstances, it may well seem that the present book is belated and no longer timely. Fortunately, this is not so, however, for the events of the last six months, far from contradicting the postulates advanced in this work, tend rather to substantiate them.

T. A. T.

October, 1940
Harvard Law School
Cambridge, Massachusetts

CONTENTS

x   CONTENTS

Chapter I

INTRODUCTION: FORGOTTEN FAILURES

CHAPTER I

INTRODUCTION: FORGOTTEN FAILURES

On September 3, 1939, peace in Western Europe came to an end, and the stimulating illusion of twenty-five years ago that the War of 1914–1918 was to bring to the world the coveted everlasting peace, was replaced by a painful disappointment—a pathetic price which the nations today have to pay for the luxury of their yesterday's folly: refusal to remember the forgotten failures of mankind to accomplish peace in the past.

If a complete world history could be written, it should, properly speaking, begin with the creation of the world itself. A complete record of human conceptions of war and peace should go back to mankind's first endeavors to establish a human society. Yet, incredible as it may appear, until as late as the middle of the last century many persons of Western civilization rested content in the belief that the year 4004 B.C., according to the first chapter of Genesis, was the date of the beginning of human history. Today Egyptologists and Assyriologists, speaking with a certain degree of confidence of the Pyramids and the Chaldean civilization, respectively, place the origin of the human race at 5000 or 7000 B.C., while astronomers and geologists do not hesitate to assert that hundreds of thousands, and even millions of years is not an impossible age for our globe. Tomorrow these figures may again be changed.

Obviously, the value of an individual opinion on the issue is of no account. Collectively, however, the variety of these theories justifies the suggestion of two basic facts. First, our notions of prehistoric events are nothing but speculations with illusory assumptions. Second, in concrete life as well as in abstract thinking, only facts proved by records or evidence in our possession constitute authentic history in the true sense of the term. This applies also to man's understanding of both war and peace.

It is superfluous to emphasize here that the present study does not envisage another history of the wars which mankind has seen in

the course of its existence. Nor does it intend to give a new, complete, chronological portrayal of human aspirations for peace. At
this point "war" and "peace" are to be understood neither in the
mechanical sense of these terms, connoting, respectively, the physical
conduct and the cessation of armed hostilities, nor as a legal concept or transaction, terminating, *mutatis mutandis,* peace or war
from the standpoint of international law.

For a better understanding of the Marxian conceptions of war
and peace and of the Soviet application of them in the international
life of the U.S.S.R., both war and peace must here be approached
merely as an expression of the political ambitions of humanity. As
such, each can be accepted only as an actual state or condition in
which, depending upon the circumstances, man, as a component of
organized society, prefers to find himself. Here no analysis will be
attempted of the everlasting argument as to whether war is the natural state of mankind based on the ancient adage *homo homini lupus,*
or peace the prevalent ideal of humanity in all ages. Historically,
however, it must be admitted that, while as a purely abstract phenomenon of interhuman relations, the origins of human notions of
war and peace are lost in the obscurity of the ages to which no
chronological measure of time can be applied, as a positive factor in
international relations, that is, as a historical concept, these notions
can be traced back to dates of antiquity now more or less definitely
established.

Whatever its causes, and regardless of its external manifestations or results, objectively, war is a social phenomenon natural to
some, inhuman to others, paradoxical to many, and unsolved to all.
Time is ineffective to alter this fundamental truism born in antiquity,
flourishing today, and destined to repeat itself in the future. The
only change which the past centuries were able to effect, which the
present can cause, and the future will bring, is in the ratio among the
groups into which the human mind falls regarding the issue. The history of mankind is proof of this.

WAR IN ANTIQUITY AND *Pax Romana*

To the ancient Hindu, a foreigner occupied a very lowly place
among things living. Ranking next to the wild animals and below
the elephant and the horse, he was one of the "impurs de moeurs et

de langage" [1] and hence a natural enemy. Even his gradual elevation to the social standing of a human being did not in principle
change his unfriendly status: he remained a barbarian to Egyptians,
Assyrians, Babylonians, Persians, Macedonians, Jews and Phoeni-
cians, who considered war against foreigners only natural. The aim
of their hostilities was sheer conquest and not the forcible compulsion of a foreign country to enter into peaceful intercourse.

In ancient Greece, too, the principle of equality was denied to
foreigners. There it was no longer the primitive instincts of the
earlier ages, but the admitted superiority of the Hellenic civilization
over the rest of mankind that prompted the Greeks to consider foreigners as barbarians and slaves and beyond the pale. Even the
greatest minds of that era subscribed to such a belief. The preachings of Isocrates that "Greeks are as much superior to the barbarians
as man is superior to an animal" were in full accord with the ideas
of his contemporary Plato, who did not hesitate to voice the opinion
that barbarians were "natural" enemies of the Greeks. Demosthenes'
admission, about five decades later, that the hatred of Greeks for
barbarians was "natural" coincided with the belief of his contemporary, Aristotle, that any war of Greece upon barbarians was nothing but "hunting wild animals." [2] Under these circumstances, there
is little ground for surprise that the relations of ancient Greece with
the non-Hellenic world were anything but peaceful. War reigned
supreme. Plato said four centuries before Christ that peace was
merely an "empty sound." So it continued through the lifetime of
Livy, who shortly before the beginning of the Christian era proclaimed from the shores of the Tiber that "Greece is conducting and
will continue eternal war with foreigners, because they are natural
enemies." [3]

The history of the wars waged by Rome, as well as the philosophy which sanctioned them, is too well known to warrant repetition
here. Suffice it to say that the slight consideration which Rome
showed for its neighbors while it was still a comparatively little-
known community in Latium, disappeared entirely after the fall of

[1] M. G. Fusinato, "Le droit international de la République Romaine," *Rev. de Dr. Int.*, 1885, XVII, p. 281; also Baron M. Taube, *Istoriia zarozhdeniia sovremennago mezhdunarodnago prava (Srednie Vieka)*, III, p. 11.

[2] *De permut.*, p. 293; *Rep.*, V, p. 470; *Mid.*, 530, 7, and *Polit.*, I, 3, 8, respectively (quoted in Taube, *op. cit.*, pp. 9–10).

[3] *Leges*, I, 625–626 and Lib. XXXI, p. 29 (*ibid.*, pp. 10–11), respectively.

Carthage. The requirement, "majestam populi Romani comiter conservare" became paramount, and the rule of Mars exlex "quidquid in hostibus feci, jus belli defendit," supreme.[4] With such an outlook, having replaced the Greek conception of foreigners as natural slaves with a recognition of its own superiority in things military, administrative and legal, Rome ordered its legions to heil "Vae victis," march out, and conquer the civilized world. This they did, accomplishing thus what Rome's predecessors had failed to achieve. The world was united in a single state.

The uniformity of this notion of militant state egoism throughout antiquity makes it seem paradoxical that ideas of international peace were not unknown to the ancients. Abstract aspirations for peace found in religion, philosophy, and even in poetry, as well as instances of concrete efforts in the field of politics, have now been historically proved.

Thus, Sakyamuni had already left to the Hindus a belief in a perfect peace.[5] In ancient Greek mythology, Ares, the god of war, personifying brute force and an unrestricted spirit of fighting, is surrounded with unfriendly Eris, fearful Deimos, and terrifying Phebos, while the goddess of peace is portrayed as a beautiful woman holding in her arms the infant Plutus, god of riches. The prophets of Judea raised their voices to glorify peace. It was fifteen centuries before the Christian era that Moses gave his Ten Commandments for the benefit of the generations to come—an imposing code of morals which even today guides humanity in its endeavors toward brotherly love and peace. Eight centuries later, in the midst of the disturbances which beset the peoples living in what is known today as Asia Minor, Isaiah appealed to mankind to march toward a new goal— peace among men on earth, a peace which was ultimately to transform itself into universal peace among all things natural.[6] The effect on human aspirations for peace of the dogma left to the world by the founder of Christianity is discussed elsewhere.[7]

The fact that the idea of peace occupied the minds of ancient philosophers needs no elaborate proof. Voluminous scholarly books

[4] Revon, *L'Arbitrage international*, p. 89 and Lib. XXXVI, p. 31.
[5] Bühler, G., *Grundriss der indo-arischen Philologie und Altertumskunde*, III, i, p. 63ff; *Cf.* also Sartorius, *Organon vollkommenen Friedens* (Zurich, 1873).
[6] Bk. II and XI, respectively.
[7] *Infra*, pp. 10ff.

have been written on the subject.[8] Here it may suffice to mention Plato, who, in one of his dialogues,[9] described the fantastic island of Atlantide—the utopian prototype of many later dreams envisaging a world of peace where kings and rulers are united in an ideal federation and capable of settling their conflicts not by war, but by resort to amicable means of mutual concession and friendly promises and understandings. The dean of ancient cynics, Juvenal, classed warring men below the status of animals, explaining that even the latter did not fight their own species.[10]

The same condemnation of war is found in ancient poetry, too. While Homer's Iliad and Odyssey, an epic of the Trojan wars, may appear to many as hardly convincing of its author's love of peace, no argument can prove that such a longing was alien to Horace, Virgil, and Ovid, who spared no effort to portray in their poems the blessings of peace in contrast to the horrors of war.[11]

So much for abstract human aspirations for peace. As to the inception of the idea of peace as a factor in international relations, it is obvious that, historically, practical manifestation of its workings could not appear before the establishment of such relations. According to some historians, the conquest of Syria by the Egyptian legions of Tutmos I, about seventeen centuries before Christ, marked the inauguration of international relations according to the modern understanding of the term.[12] Whatever the justification for this theory, it is significant that already in pre-Roman days the ancient world knew treaties envisaging both provisional and eternal peace.[13] To mention only the earliest one recorded thus far: about the year 1300 B.C. a treaty of peace was concluded between Rameses II of Egypt and Chatjzir of Chate, in which a promise was given to pre-

[8] Cf., for instance, Ritter, H., *Geschichte der Philosophie*, I–V; Zeller, ed., *Die Philosophie d. Griechen*, I–V; Lewes, G., *History of Philosophy* (IV ed., London, 1871). For a detailed bibliography, cf. Ueberweg, *Grundriss der Geschichte der Philosophie*, I, "Das Altertum."

[9] *Crit.*, pp. 119–120.

[10] Of other outstanding antagonists of war may be mentioned Hesiod, Herodotus, Pluto, Polybius, Cicero, Seneca.

[11] For others, *cf.* Pradier-Fodéré, *Traité du droit international public*, VI, n. 1, p. 37.

[12] "Avec l'entrée des Egyptiens en Syrie s'ouvre une nouvelle époque dans les déstinées des nations antiques: l'histoire du monde commence" (Maspero, *Histoire ancienne des peuples de l'Orient*, pp. 173–174).

[13] For texts of some of them, *cf.* Scala, *Staatsverträge des Altertums* (Leipzig, 1898).

serve perpetual peace between these states, and an understanding agreed upon to renounce mutually all aggression against each other in the future.[14]

Aside from these individual proofs of practical effort to approach peace as a political factor, in ancient Greece there were whole periods which bear a striking resemblance to modern times, whose notions of a political balance of power are nothing but a revival of the ancient effort for concerted preservation of international peace. Notable among these periods were the third and second centuries B.C., after the disintegration of the Macedonian empire of Alexander the Great. An epoch in itself, this period was characterized by political developments which had a profound influence on the events that followed. It was during these centuries that in the Eastern section of the then known world, ancient Greece and Persia were superseded by a new Hellenistic culture. Out of the ruins of Alexander's empire there sprang into being three strong states, Macedonia (what was left of it), Syria, and Egypt. In the Western regions of the Mediterranean, these three powers of Hellenic civilization were confronted with two equally strong antagonists: Rome and Carthage. In the struggle for survival, these states of the ancient "pentarchy" were induced to replace the never-realized idea of Alexander to secure world peace by the establishment of a single world empire, with the idea of accepting such a peace as the natural condition *among states*, and of establishing a workable balance of power as a means of achieving it.[15] The result of this change may bring to the statesmen and political theorists of modern times a considerable degree of consolation: neither the practical efforts nor the theoretical proof of the soundness of these ideas as exposed by Polybius,[16] were sufficient to prevent the doom of a decadent world.[17]

Within the comparatively short period of only two centuries of blood and iron, between the Second Punic War and the birth of Christ, all the states around the Mediterranean surrendered to Rome, and one by one ceased to exist as independent powers. By the first century B.C., "the joint wills of the ancient 'concert' states were dis-

[14] To quote in part a translation given by Scala: "welcher Frieden [und Bundniss] für ewig gewahren soll." (*Ibid.*, pp. 7–8).

[15] Walker, *A History of the Law of Nations*, I, pp. 50ff.

[16] Scala, *op. cit.*, pp. 156–305 and 319ff., and *Studien des Polybios;* also Laurent, *Études sur l'histoire de l'humanité* (2d ed.), III, pp. 412ff.

[17] *Cf.*, W. W. Tarn, *Hellenistic Civilization*, 1927.

solved in the single will of the Senate and the Roman people." [18]
With this change, all the earlier ideas of universal peace—abstract
glorifications, the unsuccessful attempt of the Alexandrine empire,
individual practical efforts in the form of treaties, and even the actual
"concert" of powers of the third and second centuries B.C.—
all found their materialization in the ancient world empire of
Rome.

That the peace thus secured differed from the modern conception of world peace is obvious. Indeed, the fusion of peoples by
Rome was achieved not as a result of the free union of free and independent states, but as a consequence of relentless armed compulsion.
Under such circumstances the idea of a democratic international
peace, the first suggestion of which has been traced to the post-Alex-
andrine epoch of the Hellenistic world, was absorbed by the idea of
universal *Pax romana* in the Roman *orbis terrarum*. Then, too, this
peace was not a world peace in the modern sense, for the Roman
empire though universal was geographically limited. Finally, it was
not peace even in the literal sense of the term, for along the boundaries of the Roman empire "eternal war" continued to rage with the
"barbarians." [19]

Barring all these limitations, the *Pax romana* is, nevertheless,
important, as it disclosed the Roman conception of world peace, and
gave rise to a school of political thought which for centuries influenced the various trends of human endeavor toward peace. As
expounded by the Stoics, the new theory proclaimed humanity to be
a single entity made up of its component members—men. The new
philosophy not only denounced the national differences admitted in
the international practice of the earlier centuries, but also deprived
the peoples of their right to equality, by clothing this real political
concept with an abstract, philosophical notion of the natural unity
of the world.[20] The "citizen of the world," who for the cynics, had
not yet lost his individuality, was made by the Stoics *civis totius
mundi quasi unius orbis*.[21] In other words, the principle of the international individuality of states was sacrificed not to prove the feasibility of peace by means of amicable relations among the various
peoples, but to justify the assertion that permanent peace could be

[18] M. Taube, *op. cit.*, III, pp. 16ff.
[19] Gibbon, *History of the Decline and Fall of the Roman Empire.*
[20] Scala, *Studien des Polybios*, pp. 304ff.
[21] Cicero, *De leges*, I, pp. 23 and 61.

made possible only through materialization of the idea of the political unity of the world.

Coupled with the practical results achieved by Rome, this theory brought to culmination the ancient search for peace both in the field of abstract thinking and in the domain of practical effort. Alone, each in its own right, neither the ideological vision of the preceding centuries, nor the earlier "world" monarchies could have resulted in what happened under Rome—a materialization of the abstract ideas of universal peace in a single world-wide state.

WAR AND CHRISTIAN *Pax Gentium*

There is no need for an elaborate explanation of why the pre-Hellenic theocracies and despotisms could not bring about universal peace. Such a peace could not be achieved by peoples who either ignored each other completely or almost invariably expressed their recognition of each other by waging merciless wars. The same was true in Greece, even at the height of its glory. Under the Roman Empire, on the other hand, the *Pax romana* could not last because it was based upon extreme regimentation completely disregarding man's natural desire and right to self-expression. It was only to be expected that the national egoism and force of the ancient Romans should fall before the human revolt against the autocratic supremacy of the social order established by the Caesars—the Christian idea of peace based on love, equality, and tolerance.

The beginning of the Christian era marked also the inauguration of the greatest of human paradoxes which has remained unsolved for almost two hundred decades, and which probably will continue to remain a mystery for generations to come—the concurrent indefatigability of the human mind in searching for new ways of happiness embodied in peace, and of the human body in enduring the sufferings wrought by wars. Upon a cursory comparison, it may well appear that the Christian ideals of peace among mankind and the brotherhood of nations are similar to the Roman conception of world peace and unity. Yet there is a vast difference between the two. With the advent of Christianity, the national ramifications of paganism were confronted with the cosmopolitan unity of God. Then, too, the original Christian indifference to any stamp of nationality, so frequently expressed in the all-embracing reply of the early martyrs—"Christianus sum"—must have been an unprecedented shock to the Romans who were trained to be proud of their right to say "civis romanus sum." Finally, the Roman conception of world unity and peace as an end in itself was now challenged by emphasis not upon the ideal but upon the means of achieving it.[22]

Historically, it is now admitted that all these differences contributed to the downfall of the Roman empire, and along with this, to the disappearance for many a century of the notions of world unity and peace based on the principles inherent in *Pax romana*. At the same time, it is evident that whatever change was wrought by Christianity, it did not include the abolition of war and did not bring about permanent peace. The history of the wars waged by mankind from the days of Christ and the record of simultaneous human efforts to attain peace are vivid illustrations of the failures and contributions made by Christianity in regard to war and peace. The accumulation of controversial philosophies which accompanied them is an eloquent commentary on this paradox.

It is superfluous here either to enumerate again the wars that the Christian world has suffered, or to elaborate upon their justifications or their reactions upon man's abstract thinking. Irrespective of time and kind, whether they were the suicidal wars of the early Dark Ages, the exalted crusades which lasted from the eleventh to the thirteenth century, the dynastic wars five hundred years later, or the French Revolutionary wars of one hundred and some decades ago, they all had their abstract counterparts: the philosophies of St. Augustine, St. Thomas Aquinas, Abbé de St. Pierre, and Kant. The World War of 1914–1918 was the culminating proof of this and its avowed purpose as a "war to end wars," a crowning illustration of the inventive ingenuity of the human mind. It would be futile to analyze in detail the reasons why the practical efforts for the preservation of peace have failed of fruition. Suffice it to say here that they have failed throughout history, whether it be the movement inaugurated by the French carpenter Durant in 1182, the kingly alliance of the Russian, Austrian, and Prussian monarchs, consummated in Vienna in 1815, or the twenty-year-old democratic League of Nations, which not so long ago proved helpless to quell wars in

---

[22] Instructing us to keep "the unity of Spirit in the bond of peace" (Paul, *Eph.*, IV, 3), and "if it be possible . . . live peaceably with men" (John, *Rom.*, XII, 18), the Gospel also teaches that "there is neither Greek nor Jew . . . Barbarian, Scythian, bond or free" (*Col.* III, 11), and that "faith without works is dead" (*Jas.*, II, 20, 26).

the Chaco Boreal, Ethiopia, and Spain, or to prevent bloodshed from the castled banks of the Rhine to the impoverished provinces of China.

The truth is that man is still far from having progressed sufficiently to be able to make the abstract Christian ideal a living reality on an international scale. Hence the ever-present friction between the Gospel and life, the coexisting tension of hope and disillusion, and the ever-repeating succession of wars and peace. Indeed, today, as heretofore, the teaching of the Gospel, "blessed are the peacemakers, for they shall be called the children of God," remains unchanged. But along with this, as heretofore, remains unchanged man's subjection to such social factors of communal life as the state, justice, law, and many other earthly concomitants of physical existence. The result of all this is that while abstract thinking continues to transform men into antagonists and protagonists of war, war continues, amid theories of peace, to make corpses of both its friends and foes.

Were it possible to reproduce the entire history of the Christian era, the early martyrs would prefer to die in the name of peace rather than carry arms in the name of war. The voice of Origen would repeat his belief that "being as we are, thanks to Jesus, sons of peace," we are to "change swords into ploughshares and lances into sickles." [23] In kaleidoscopic succession would pass the church fathers of the Dark Ages, the humanitarians of the succeeding generations, the rationalists of the eighteenth century, the positivists of the nineteenth, and the statesmen of the present. It would be another long and noble parade of the élite of the human mind in the fields of the legal, political, and social sciences who have preached good will among men. Their names may soon be again forgotten or confused, as also the place and the time in which they labored. Significant is the unison of their condemnation of war, which irrespective of its nature, whether just or unjust, legal or illegal, sanctioned by the law of nature or prohibited by the law of God, is an accumulation of human crimes for the commission of which the guilty, upon their return from the battlefields, "are led through the arch of triumph instead of to the guillotine." [24]

It has been said that with the advent of Christianity mankind entered into an era of paradox caused by the inevitability of wars in

[23] *Contra Celsum*, V, p. 33.
[24] Girardin, *Le Désarmement européen*, p. 23.

spite of the desire of humanity for peace. For an explanation for this, one must again go back to the time of primitive Christianity. Shocking as it may seem to many, the protagonists of war refer without reluctance to the very Gospel itself, and state with no small degree of justification that even Jesus, the Messiah, professed no objection to military service and, hence, to war.[25] Whatever the validity of such an extreme resort, it must be admitted that Christianity, though it was the antithesis of war in the apostolic period, was gradually forced to seek a compromise with the social demands of life, which, in turn, resulted in a synthesis between the Christian ideal of peace and the secular notion of war. As Christianity began to permeate society at an ever-increasing tempo, Christians found themselves forced to adjust their faith to the requirements of the State. One of these was the recognition of the legitimate authority of the State, to which Christianity soon consented. Once this first concession had been made, the next retreat of the Christians was only logical—the military profession was no longer incompatible with their religion and was henceforth held in esteem. In 314 A.D., Emperor Constantine ordered a synod to convene at Arles, where in the same year thirty-three bishops gave to war its first official Christian approval: anathema was to be the punishment for those who refused to carry arms for the military defense of their country. The philosophic utterances of St. Ambrose, St. Augustine, and St. Thomas Aquinas on war, written between that memorable date and the end of the thirteenth century, were only the natural sequence to such a sanction, as they were all concerned with the justification of the paradox thus created. It is perfectly understandable that their theories were focused mainly upon the issue of the just or unjust nature of war, rather than upon the Christian denunciation thereof. Respect for the teachings of the Gospel was preserved by them only in so far as humane charity is considered an essential feature of warfare.

The same problem concerned the Middle Ages, but the discovery of the New World gave an impulse to a more analytical treatment of the subject. While notions of religious truth and perfection remained the ideal of all mankind, scholars and philosophers saw the problem of war and peace becoming more and more inseparable from the steadily growing powers of the secular state. In the sixteenth century, Europe began its great political and military reor-

[25] Luke, VII, 1–10; Math., VIII, 5–13.

ganization. With this came also an infatuation for the Romans, who had in the past set the example *par excellence* of how great states could be built by properly organized armies and skilfully conducted wars. The writings of Vittoria, Suarez, and, later, of Hugo Grotius are documentary evidence that Christian morality became increasingly subordinated to state policies.

The seventeenth and eighteenth centuries witnessed the beginning of modern industry and commerce, and simultaneously the growth of state sovereignty, on the one hand, and Christian individualism on the other. The French Revolution, which marked the point of encounter of these cross-currents, gave birth to the humanitarianism of the last century. Representing a popularized version of Christianity, the liberalism of our great-grandfathers continued the process of fusing reverence for the sovereign state with the Christian conception of the sovereign individual. It accepted as normal the concurrent submission of man in his social behavior within the state to the moral code of Christian peace, and of states in their international existence within the family of nations to the rules of the ancient conception of war. Hence, it is only natural that against this background of the last two and a half centuries are to be seen the names of such protagonists of war as Bacon and Hobbes, De Maistre and Proudhon, Humboldt and Hegel, Arnold and Treitschke, Moltke and Dragomirov. It was only natural for them, in spite of being Christians, as most of them were, to glorify war as a means for the preservation of the moral unity of the world; to credit it with greater contributions to our progress than those made by love; to visualize it as an institution of good-will producing the blood needed as a fertilizer for growing the fruit of history—human civilization; and to accept it, finally, as the only condition under which the unity of individuals is possible, for it is only during wars that personal interests are sacrificed for the common good—the preservation of the state which protects them in time of peace.

Whatever the praise or criticism of Christianity in its relation to war and peace, and irrespective of one's preference, it cannot be denied that the influence of the Gospel has been and remains great. Indeed, it is to Christianity that mankind owes its gratitude for having brought about the compromise between our subconscious submission to religion and human morals, on the one hand, and our reasoned response to the demands of a material existence on the other.

It is due to Christianity that the enforced *Pax romana* of ancient Rome was replaced by the voluntary *Pax gentium,* manifested both in a free and world-wide fusion of peoples in a common bond of faith, and in the democratic blending of the independent states in the modern family of civilized nations. It is Christianity that has, finally, made it possible to endure the paradox of war and peace which it itself created. Having established a democratic union between our soul and body, and being democratically lenient in allowing men to interpret freely the words of Scripture, as well as in preserving for them the privilege of exercising their natural rights, Christianity has also found a way to console us with the idea that this disharmony between war and peace is by no means final. Yet, even in so doing, it remained true to its own paradoxism: almost simultaneously with the democratic League of Nations, there was established the State of the Dictatorial Proletariat.

INTRUDING ILLUSIONS: WAR AND PEACE
IN MARXISM

INTRUDING ILLUSIONS: WAR AND PEACE IN MARXISM

MARXIAN WAR AND *Pax Communa*

With the overthrow of Kerensky's Provisional Government in November, 1917, Russia became an experimental laboratory where the political philosophies of Marx and Engels were given practical application on a scale which exceeded the expectations of the leaders of the Bolshevist Revolution themselves, including Lenin. The political, economic and social experiments now being carried on in the former Empire of the Tsars are evidently being made with the same end in view as that pursued in the rest of the world by other means—to further man's progress. Hence, whatever new discoveries or benefits may result from the Soviet endeavors, they should not inure to the benefit of the U.S.S.R. exclusively, but are expected to affect the progress of nations outside the Red political boundaries. Hence the problem of the international relations of the Soviet Union. Hence also the need of an analysis of the Marxian understanding of war and peace.

Since the philosophical basis for the communist reconstruction of human society is utterly different from that upon which the social order rests in other countries, it follows that the Marxian concepts of war and peace cannot have much resemblance to the non-communist understanding of these terms.

In the realm of non-communist international politics, the problem of war and peace has always been the paramount issue. Whatever the changes in the outward manifestation of events or in abstract speculations regarding them, the basic contradiction between the two remains: they are incompatible. Accepted by some as a normal expression of the biological struggle for existence in the benevolent guise of "a perpetual rejuvenator which, like a mineral bath, stimulates new ambitions," [1] war, in the opinion of others, is merely an "enforced settlement of strained international relations which

[1] Banse, *Wehrwissenschaft*, p. 1.

cannot be solved otherwise." [2] Then, too, there are those who regard war as a relation in which there may lawfully be "a properly conducted contest of armed public forces." [3] To the great majority, however, it is merely a deviation from peace and, as such, connotes the destruction of the riches accumulated by mankind in the depository of civilization. It is immaterial whether or not this means that peace for them is, respectively, a state where human ambitions are doomed to succumb to the lethargy of nirvana, where the settlement of international controversies is left to the caprices of a policy of *laissez faire,* where the relations among the states may not lawfully be a properly conducted contest of armed public forces. The important fact is that to the great majority, peace is the norm—the only condition under which the well-being of mankind can be fostered.

Projected against this diversity of opinion, and in view of the turmoil with which the nations are again confronted, the query has become for the time being immaterial whether peace should connote assurance of lasting peace by conquest of arms or otherwise, or should be understood literally, *i.e.,* as merely a termination of war in the material sense of the term. To a student of Soviet affairs, however, the important fact is that Marxian notions of war and peace are not the same.

To understand the Marxian concept of war from the standpoint of ideological abstraction, a few remarks are necessary on the Marxian outlook on history in general. Widely though non-communist views of world history may differ from each other, none of them has anything in common with the concept envisaged by the fathers and disciples of communism. Preaching atheism and declaring religion to be opium to man, Marxism cannot accept history as a long process of gradual compromising between Christian morals and the laws of nature. Advocating the dictatorial authority of the proletarian class, it cannot conceive the democratic sovereignty of the individual as one of the few cherished products of history's achievements. Having discarded the juridical illusion that abstract principles and concepts of human duties must be taken *a priori* as the indisputable basis of all social phenomena, including war and peace,

[2] Bley, *Wehrpflicht des Geistes,* p. 83.
[3] Grotius, *"De Jure Belli ac Pacis,"* I, II, cited in Wilson, *International Law* (9th ed.), p. 45.

Marxism cannot credit history with being the result of human intellect, but visualizes it as a *summa summarum* of materialistic processes resulting from purely economic factors. History for a Marxist is not a chronological record of such world events as the collision between paganism and Christianity, the struggle between Church and State, the disappearance of by-gone sovereignties and the formation of modern democracies. Nor can a Marxist accept history merely as a political process consisting of an ever-recurrent succession of bloody wars and convalescing years of peace.

Marx discarded the old creed of rationalism that the social order depended upon the intellect and Christian morals of man, and that a man could invent an ideal of social order and then materialize it by the mere application of the necessary laws conceived for that purpose. He advanced a new, contrary doctrine in its stead: that history is regulated not by the abstract calculations of the human intellect, but by organic forces in man, and that the social order is shaped not by abstract inventions of the human intellect, but is the result of an elementary process reflecting the creative forces inherent in man. For Marx, these creative forces were labor and the returns of the working man, *i.e.,* an economic phenomenon. As Engels put it in 1870, these forces "are to be sought not *in a philosophy,* but *in the economics* of each particular epoch." [4]

Marx also rejected the principle of individualism, and viewed the community not as an agglomeration of individuals who by covenants can bring about a better social order, but as a complex organism *per se.* The protection of the organic creative forces collected in this communal organism, *i.e.,* safeguarding the compensation received by man, is considered a factor of basic importance. Hence, the grouping of men with common economic interests is to be viewed not as an abnormal phenomenon, jeopardizing the tranquillity of the social order, but as a natural outgrowth of the desire to ease the effort of the individual. Hence, also, the division and consolidation of mankind into economic factions is a normal phenomenon in the development of human society. Antagonistic to each other, and so incompatible that neither the Christian, "Render unto Caesar those things that are Caesar's," nor the communist, "Proletarians of the world, unite!" has been able thus far to bring about a lasting, amicable understanding, these classes continue to find no other alterna-

[4] Engels, *Socialism, Utopian and Scientific,* p. 94 (Italics his).

tive than to struggle with each other for the protection of their respective interests.

In other words, for Marx, history is a materialistic process, in which economic factors form the sole basis for all social phenomena, including war and peace. War and peace are only two different ways in which the collision of the material interests of different economic classes find their external manifestation. Since, therefore, to a Marxist the bloodiest war ever waged must appear merely as a particular phase of the class struggle, and the longest period of peace must be nothing but another phase of this class war, and whereas historically this struggle of classes has been claimed by the founders of Marxism to be a permanent and everlasting condition of human society,[5] a twofold conclusion is reached: while of equal importance as different phases of a single economic process, as non-economic phenomena, war and peace were non-existent problems in the past.

The same is true in regard to the social values of war and peace in the future. It is the firm belief of the Marxists that class distinction will be abolished in the future and that classes will disappear altogether when "the working class, in the course of its development, substitutes for the old order of civil society an association which will exclude classes and [their] antagonizers."[6]

Although Marx himself nowhere clearly stated it, the communist belief is that the state will disappear together with the classes, being, according to Engels, a dominating political instrumentality, superimposed upon the community by "whatever class happened at the time to be the exploiting class, for the purpose of forcibly keeping the exploited class in a condition of subjection":

"As soon as there is no longer any social class to be kept down; as soon as, together with class rule and the individual struggle for life founded in the previous anarchy of production, the conflicts and excesses that issued therefrom have been removed, there will no longer be any necessity for

[5] Marx declared in the opening sentences of his *Communist Manifesto* that "the whole history of mankind (since the dissolution of primitive tribal society, holding in common ownership) has been a history of class struggles, contests between exploiting and exploited, ruling and oppressed classes" (pp. 7–8) ; Engels, in his biography of Marx, repeats the same idea: "Marx has shown that all history down to the present day has been the history of class struggles" (Engels and others, *Karl Marx, Man, Thinker, and Revolutionist*, p. 28) ; cf., also, Lenin, who viewed the rebellion of slaves led by Spartacus in 73 B.C. as an illustration *par excellence* of one of the forms which the class struggle may take (*Works*, XXIV, 371).

[6] Marx, *Poverty of Philosophy*, p. 135.

applying such special means of repression as the State. The first act wherein the State appears as the real representative of the whole body social at the moment of seizing the means of production in the name of society is also its last independent act as the State. The interference of the State in social relations becomes superfluous in one domain after another, and falls of itself into desuetude. Government over persons is replaced by the administration of things and by the conduct of the processes of production. The State is not 'abolished,' it withers away." [7]

It is only logical to expect that with the disappearance of the classes themselves their struggle will come to an end, and that with the withering away of the state, the world will become an entity quite different from what it used to be and from what it is today. This, in turn, means that ultimately mankind will find itself blended into a single world-wide Marxian classless and stateless commonwealth which, while appealing seriously to many, to some may appear as an amusing Utopia, where the Christian ideals of brotherly love and world peace are evidently to find their materialization in the guise of economic *nirvana perpetua* and atheistic *pax communa*, Whatever the possibility of such a state in the future, it obviously renders inconceivable the continuance of the most common political phenomena of our day—international relations. With the disappearance of these, there will no longer be either war or peace, for the very notion of the two will become meaningless.

Such a picture of the future must obviously appear utopian for the present. Indeed, history itself furnishes proof that these conceptions are premature, to say the least. Century after century passed before the Roman absorption of the individual into the State, and before the cosmopolitanism of Christianity and the Germanic notion of individual sovereignty found a workable compromise in the idea of the modern state. It is quite possible that the present materialization of this idea in the coexistence of modern independent states is not the end of man's progress. Some time in the future the Marxian idea of universality may find its realization, and the present state be seen retrospectively as only a temporary medium, whose preliminary function was to consolidate individuals into political units which then will be combined into a single human body politic free of political boundaries, and worried neither by the prevention of wars nor by the preservation of peace.

[7] Engels, *Anti-Düring*, pp. 249–250. *Cf.*, also, Lenin, *The State and Revolution*, pp. 51, 86–87, 94ff., 108ff.

Desirable as such a world may be, centuries must pass before this ideal is reached. It is only in modern times that man has begun to realize the true significance of the rôle played by the state. Having accepted this form of communal division as the highest achievement of history, he treasures it to such a degree that even the greatest sacrifice—war—is justified.

Marxists, obviously, are no exception, nor is the Union of Socialist Soviet Republics, a state admittedly typifying the transition period from the world of capitalist individualism to the utopia of Marxian internationalism. The actual extent of Soviet progress up to date toward this communist goal is immaterial; the proletarian Fatherland is considered the greatest Marxian achievement thus far, an achievement for the safeguarding of which no sacrifice is too great. This, in turn, means that pragmatically war is not only conceivable, but, under certain circumstances, permissible and even obligatory to a Marxist.

Whatever the terms used to define or describe Marxism, it is first of all a historical phenomenon. Such being the case, Marxian pragmatics regarding war and peace apply to the past, the present, and the immediate future, that is, to the time preceding the advent of the Marxian world commonwealth. Concretely, the Marxian concepts of war and peace are derived from a particular interpretation of their historical significance in the past and a recognition of their inevitability in the pre-utopian future. In regard to the former, Lenin said that "one must clearly understand the historical conditions which caused the war, what classes are waging it, and what is its purpose," while one of the theses advanced at the Sixth Congress of the Communist International read as follows:

". . . The proletariat must carefully analyze the historical and political class significance of each given war, and must evaluate with particular care, from the standpoint of world revolution, the rôle of the dominating classes of all the countries participating in the war." [8]

Such an analysis is obviously a superhuman task, not only because of the volume of available historical material, but because of the difficulty of individual appraisal, whether it be in regard to the "class significance," "the standpoint of world revolution," or "its

[8] Lenin, XXX, 333, and *Kommunisticheskii Internatsional v Dokumentakh, 1919–1932,* p. 797, respectively.

purpose." Hence it is immaterial that non-communist justification of war as an unavoidable natural phenomenon, and attempts to abolish wars by meaningless phrases and treaties, are to a Marxist only the reactionary maneuvering of imperialists. Of like insignificance here is Marxian ridicule of the non-communist notion that the cause of wars is to be found in the forgotten or misinterpreted Christian doctrine of love, or in the poor policies of governments.

What is significant is the fact that to a Marxist, it is in capitalism, in the division of society into exploiting and exploited classes, that the cause of modern wars lies. It is also important that to a Marxist wars are neither exceptions nor contradictions to the principles of capitalism, or to the right of private property, or to the systems of competition and exploitation. They are the direct results thereof. Most important of all, however, is the fact that wars, being to a Marxist inseparable from capitalism, can be abolished only by destroying capitalism, and the overthrow of the latter is impossible without violence, *i.e.*, without armed uprisings and wars against the exploiting element of society. In other words, wars in the future are not excluded either by Marx or by his followers. Wars will continue, both just and unjust.[9]

It was Marx who said that the last word of social science would be war or death, bloody struggle or annihilation. It was also he who said that this war was not to be understood as limited to a conflict between classes, for "a theory of universal brotherhood *of nations* which does not take into consideration either the lessons of history, or the degree of cultural development of separate peoples, is merely a utopian dream." [10]

Said Lenin:

"We Marxists do not belong to the absolute opponents of any kind of war . . . Our aim is to bring about a socialist community, which, by abolishing the division of mankind into classes and by bringing to an end any exploitation of man by man and of one nation by another, will unavoidably preclude any possibility of wars in general. But in the war for achieving such a socialist community we are bound to find conditions under which the class struggle within a single nation may come into collision with a war

[9] Stalin divides wars into the just and the unjust. To the former belong wars having no imperialistic aims, wars for freedom, envisaging either protection of nationalities from enslavement or deliverance from the capitalist yoke, and, finally, wars waged by colonies for their independence. The unjust wars are those for conquest of foreign lands and peoples. (*Kratkii kurs istorii VKP (b)*, p. 161.)

[10] Karl Marx, *Literaturnoe nasledstvo*, III, 250 (Italics by author).

between different nations . . . Therefore, we cannot deny the possibility of revolutionary wars, *i.e.*, of wars resulting from class struggle, which are waged by the revolutionary classes and have a direct bearing upon revolutions . . ." [11]

In another place, again reminding his readers that they live in a class society and that there is no way of escaping from it but through the overthrow of the exploiting class, he said:

"Socialists cannot be opposed to any kind of wars without ceasing to be socialists. We are struggling against the very root of wars—capitalism. But inasmuch as capitalism has not yet been exterminated, we are struggling not against wars in general, but against reactionary wars, and [at the same time] for revolutionary wars." [12]

The theses advanced at the Sixth World Congress of the Communist International echo this inheritance from Lenin:

"The overthrow of capitalism is impossible without violence, *i.e.*, without armed uprisings and wars against the bourgeoisie. In our era of imperialistic wars and world revolution, revolutionary civil wars of the proletarian dictatorship against the bourgeoisie, wars of the proletariat against the bourgeois states and world capitalism, as well as national revolutionary wars of oppressed peoples against imperialism are unavoidable, as has been shown by Lenin." [13]

The admissibility of wars in the future was later indirectly recognized by the Soviets in their solemn constitutional declaration:

"Since the time of the formation of the Soviet Republics, the states of the world have been divided into two camps: the camp of capitalism and the camp of socialism." [14]

The inevitability of a collision and even a war between these two sets of social ideals was impliedly predicted by Stalin, when, at the Sixteenth Congress of the Communist Party, he came forth with this formula, which has now become a classic within the Kremlin and a gross misstatement in the outside world:

"We neither desire to gain even a single foot of foreign land, nor are we willing to lose even an inch of our own." [15]

[11] Lenin, XXX, 332–333.
[12] *Ibid.*, XIII, 453.
[13] *Kommunisticheskii Internatsional v Dokumentakh, 1919–1932*, p. 797.
[14] Constitution of 1924 (*Sist. Sobr. Deistv. Zak. S.S.S.R.*, I, p. 4). The Constitution of 1936 no longer contains this preamble.
[15] Stalin, *Voprosy Leninizma*, p. 361.

The possibility of wars for a communist state being thus admitted, it is only logical to determine next what is the concrete conception of war to a Marxist. The answer is to be found in the definition of war given by Clausewitz:

"Everybody knows that wars are caused by political relations between governments and peoples; usually, however, they are regarded as connoting a situation under which—from the very outbreak of hostilities—these relations cease to exist, and where this new condition of affairs is subject only to its own specific laws. We say on the contrary, war is nothing but a continuation of policy by the use of different means." [16]

This definition of war was sanctioned by Lenin, when he said that "war is a continuation of the same policies by using other [namely, *forcible*] means . . .," [17] and was subsequently endorsed at the Sixth Congress of the Communist International in 1928.[18] The flexibility of such a conception of war was duly appreciated by the communists. It was admirably adapted to their logical necessities, both pragmatic and doctrinal. It permitted war to appear in the guise of a mere extension of the class conflict beyond the confines of the U.S.S.R. As an integral part of Marxian state politics, which *ex principio* are not interrupted thereby, war becomes only a continuation of the domestic policies under conditions different from those prevailing in time of peace. In terms of war and peace, this blending of domestic and foreign politics is a logical prerequisite for Marxian revolutionary advance.[19]

This fusion of the two diametrically opposed political phenomena—war and peace—finds its logic as well as its justification in Marxian dogmatics also in regard to the future. As previously pointed out,[20] the problems of war and of peace are expected to disappear with the eventual establishment of the communist classless and stateless commonwealth. Therefore, these two concepts have in common their future fate. The fact of the ultimate disappearance of the whole problem of peace suggests that the attainment or preservation of peace as an international political phenomenon cannot be an end in itself to a Marxist. For him peace can only be a means to an end, one of the political means by which this

[16] Von Clausewitz, *Vom Kriege,* p. 28.
[17] Lenin, *Sobr. Soch.,* XVIII, p. 97 (Italics by author).
[18] *Kommunisticheskii Internatsional v Dokumentakh, 1919–1932,* p. 797.
[19] *Infra,* p. 132.
[20] *Supra,* p. 22.

problemless future is to be materialized. As such, peace must be ranked on a par with war, which has always been an instrumentality and never an end *per se*.

Having thus replaced the ancient duty of waging imperialistic wars and the Christian acceptance of wars as a necessary evil with communist condemnation of modern capitalistic wars, and having substituted the communist vision of a world-wide materialistic *Pax communa* for the geographically limited *Pax romana* and the universal abstraction of the Christian *Pax gentium*, Marxism has delegated to its own outgrowth—the Soviets—a self-imposed task well worth the purpose it envisages. In practice, this task is composed of safe piloting between war and peace, without losing sight of the dangers and benefits potentially inherent in both. For the better understanding of Soviet foreign relations in view of this task, an analysis of the Marxian classification of wars, of the proletarian duties in the event of war, and of the Soviet pragmatics of peace is next to be undertaken.

Communist Classification of Wars

The non-communist classifications of wars as offensive or defensive, lawful or unlawful, major or minor, do not fit the Marxian conception of war as an economic phenomenon. Indeed, the communist belief is that the cause of all wars is to be sought in capitalism. At the First All-Russian Congress of Soviets, Lenin said that the national policies pursued during war are determined by the same class which is in power in time of peace.[21] The Russian Revolution of November, 1917, divided the world into two camps, one of capitalism and one of communism.[22] In view of this, war to a communist is merely a phase in the class struggle, where arms have been taken up either to further capitalism or to promote revolution. In other words, wars can be only imperialistic and reactionary or revolutionary and progressive.

Inasmuch as the Soviet Union may rightly be considered to be still in its infancy, the attitude of the Soviets toward war must be examined not only from the point of view of the experience of the U.S.S.R., which is still in its initial stages, but also from the standpoint of proletarian application of Marxian theories on war in general.

[21] Lenin, XIV, 310.
[22] *Supra*, p. 26.

Of all communist writers, Lenin was by far the most explicit and at the same time the most authoritative interpreter of the Marxian outlook on war. In the U.S.S.R., at least, he is considered to be the man who extended the theories of Marx to present-day imperialism and to the proletarian dictatorship. Therefore, Lenin's words may well be taken as representative of Marxian thought on the matter.

It must be said at the outset that Lenin analyzed the various types of war not abstractly, but concretely, *i.e.*, from the standpoint of their effect upon the social structure of society at the time of the war. He never indulged in discussions of types of war that were "possible" in general, but rather approached the issue from the standpoint of the nature of wars germane to modern imperialism, and of their difference from wars in the past. This emphasis on imperialism makes it essential to mention briefly Lenin's understanding of the term.

Imperialism is defined by him as the monopolistic stage of capitalism, that is, a period when the world is divided into the political domains of the few larger capitalistic countries.[23] Historically, it is capitalism in its decline, which to Lenin meant a period of constantly growing antagonism between the bourgeoisie and the laboring classes, leading to proletarian revolutions. To state it in his own words:

"Imperialism is the dawn of the social revolution of the proletariat. Beginning from 1917, this is being proved on a world-wide scale." [24]

In other words, imperialism, to a Marxist, is a logically necessary stage in the development of capitalism, which differs economically and historically from the preceding period of progressive capitalism in that it signifies the approach of a new era which is to be permeated not only with new, unavoidable wars, but with revolutions as well. This political prognostication of the doom of the modern capitalist world is sufficient explanation of the fact that, to Lenin, as a revolutionary, there were only three types of wars possible in his day: imperialistic, national, and proletarian-revolutionary wars.[25] In revolutionary terminology, all reactionary wars waged by non-communist countries belong in the first category. Assumed to be a direct challenge to political tolerance, these wars may be further divided into three varieties, depending upon the parties to the war:

[23] Lenin, XIII, 305–306.
[24] *Ibid.*, p. 333.

If all the adversaries in the conflict are imperialist powers, such a war is to a Marxist a "classical" imperialistic war; if an imperialist power and an oppressed nation are involved in conflict, such a struggle is an imperialistic war of counter-revolution; finally, wars of this category are counter-revolutionary *par excellence* when fought against states where the proletarian régime prevails.

To national wars belong wars staged by colonial or semi-colonial peoples against their capitalist masters. Being, in fact, nothing but revolutionary movements and uprisings for national liberation, these wars are considered by communists to be the natural outgrowth of the imperialist policies of capitalism.

Finally, wars conducted by the proletarian classes for the ultimate materialization of communism are proletarian-revolutionary wars. Depending upon their immediate political purpose, and the revolutionary strategy and tactics followed, these wars may be either civil or international. That they need not always be defensive, however, was admitted by Lenin in 1915 when he wrote:

"We Marxists have always stood for revolutionary wars against counter-revolutionary peoples. If, for instance, socialism becomes victorious in America or Europe in 1920, and Japan together with China should then send against us their Bismarcks, we would be for an aggressive war against them." [26]

History has seen each of these three main types of war. One may consider the Napoleonic wars an example of military conquest, the wars inspired by Bismarck as typifying state craftsmanship, and the uprisings which lasted from the Lyon riots of a little more than a century ago to the Paris Commune of 1871 as outright revolution. To a Marxist, however, they were, respectively, imperialistic, national, and proletarian wars. Of the wars which have taken place during the present generation, the World War of 1914–1918, the war in China, and the Soviet war against intervention in 1918–1920 would be classified by an orthodox communist in the same way, namely, as imperialistic, national, and revolutionary, respectively.

[25] *Cf.*, however, the classification given by the Sixth Congress of the Communist International held at Moscow on August 17–September 1, 1928: wars among imperialist countries, wars of imperialist counter-revolution against proletarian revolution, and national-revolutionary wars (*Kommunisticheskii Internatsional v Dokumentakh, 1919–1932*, pp. 797ff).

[26] Lenin, XVIII, 250. Evidently in such cases the revolutionary wars waged by the proletariat are considered to be aggressive in the sense that they are fought to further socialism.

To Lenin, however, there was a great difference between such wars in the past and those of the present era. Indeed, irrespective of the former significance of each of these types, today the importance of imperialistic wars lies in the fact that they are no longer wars of mere capitalistic competition, but also wars for a new division of the world among the most powerful capitalist nations. Hence, national wars, in the present monopolistic stage of capitalism, have ceased to be mere wars against imperialism and have become an integral part of the proletarian revolution as well. Moreover, civil wars and proletarian wars against bourgeois states are not isolated instances of revolutionary attempts as they were in the past, but a means of inciting war between a coalition of proletarian states and the capitalist block.[27]

In view of the variety of types of wars, it is impossible either to outline a definite obligatory policy of the proletariat toward war in general, or to give a single formula for proletarian tactics during war. It must be noted that since war to a Marxist is merely a continuation of the policies carried out in time of peace, the war policies of the proletariat must be a continuation of its peacetime class policy. Hence, the proletarian war policy is conditioned by the peacetime class strategy and tactics of the proletariat.

From the aforesaid it follows that, *ex principio,* the proletariat must oppose imperialistic wars; it supports, sometimes even wages, national wars; and spares no effort in assisting the toiling masses in civil class wars against the bourgeoisie and in the revolutionary wars of a proletarian state against a non-communist foe. This does not determine the tactics of the proletariat in regard to each of these wars, however. Even if it be admitted that the basic principle remains the same in regard to imperialistic wars, the tactics will depend upon the nature of the contenders: whether both are imperialist powers, or one an oppressed nation or a proletarian state. The tactics may likewise be different in a national war, the decisive factors here being, on the one hand, the nature of the oppressor nation and, on the other hand, the class waging the nationalist war. Finally, in a proletarian revolutionary war, the tactics are determined by the class composition of the capitalist enemy state; different tactics are to be applied to different classes.

[27] Lenin, XVII, 245, and XIII, 133 and 440.

Proletariat and Imperialistic Wars

The proletarian tactics of opposition to imperialistic wars must be examined as regards the struggle against such wars before their inception, and in regard to the attitude during the conduct of actual warfare. The struggle of the communists against imperialistic wars differs basically from the non-communist struggle for peace. They make no distinction between the struggle against war and the class struggle. On the contrary, they accept the struggle against war as an integral part of the general class struggle of the proletariat, envisaging the inevitable overthrow of the bourgeoisie. At first sight, it may appear that communists, having subscribed to the pessimistic belief that war is inherent in the capitalistic order of things, are logically forced to concede that it is useless to carry on a special struggle against war. This would be grossly to misunderstand Marxian dialectics, however, for in spite of the force of such logic, communist opposition to imperialistic wars remains a dogma of permanent standing. In this opposition, emphasis is laid not upon the pacifist endeavors for world peace preached by non-communists, but upon communist propagation of revolutionary sentiments, preliminary to revolutionary action should such a war eventually come to pass. In practice this means that it is a primary duty of communists to unveil bourgeois preparations for war and to reveal to the masses at large the "hypocrisy" of non-communist politics. They must also gather around themselves the proletarian masses, so as to be able to transform the war, in case they cannot prevent it, into a civil war for the purpose of overthrowing the bourgeoisie. In terms of international relations, this means that first of all an intensive political struggle and propaganda must be carried on *against* pacifism, irrespective of whether it is (1) the official pacifism of capitalist governments, (2) the radical pacifism of revolutionary optimists who fail to conceive of wars of long duration, or of pessimists who do not believe in the transformation of capitalistic wars into civil ones, or, (3) the religious pacifism of the church.

In 1922 Lenin declared a boycott against war to be a meaningless gesture. "Communists," wrote he, "must take part in any reactionary war." [28] This was corroborated five years later by a resolution passed at the Eighth Plenary Session of the Executive Committee of the Comintern:

[28] Lenin, XX, pt. II, p. 530.

"As the struggle for actual peace and the liquidation of wars calls for the overthrow of bourgeois governments and the establishment of a Proletarian Dictatorship, pacifism is nothing but a cheating of the masses." [29]

Omitting for the time being any appraisal of non-communist hypocrisy in regard to their efforts for peace and of communist logic in regard to their struggle against pacifism, the tactics of the proletariat during the actual conduct of imperialistic wars are to be analyzed next. These tactics were worked out by the Communist Party under Lenin's leadership, and consist of a truly elaborate program of action, later formulated in the thesis advanced at the Sixth Congress of the Communist International held in Moscow from August 17 to September 1, 1928.

In brief, this program prescribes that communists must first explain to the workers and peasants the reactionary character of war, for imperialistic wars can be only such; then, an energetic struggle must be carried on against all kinds of labor movements which either openly or secretly justify the war; finally, the communists must spare no effort to transform the imperialistic war into a civil war of the proletariat against the bourgeoisie. Of these three lines of action, the last is obviously of paramount importance.

Lenin considered civil war as the most acute form of class struggle, and maintained that the dictatorship of the proletariat was the only logical sequence thereto. At the Sixth World Congress of the Comintern, the following theses were passed in regard to civil war of the proletariat against the bourgeoisie:

24. The imperialistic War of 1914–1918 was transformed in a number of countries in Eastern and Central Europe into civil war, which brought victory to the proletariat in Russia. The lessons of the October Revolution are of decisive importance from the standpoint of the proletarian attitude towards war. They show:

(1) that in imperialistic wars the bourgeoisie must itself hand over to the workers its arms, but that in defeat, etc., it loses its authority over massed armies;

(2) that an effective struggle against war calls for a preliminary revolutionizing of the enlisted masses, *i.e.*, for preparation for civil war, and

(3) that civil wars unconditionally call for a thorough preparation of the proletariat and of its party. . . .

[29] *Rezoliutsii VIII Plenuma Ispolkoma Kominterna,* pp. 78–85 and 95, respectively.

The proletarian uprisings in Shanghai in March, 1927, and in Canton in December, 1927, offer important lessons for the proletariat, particularly for the peoples of oppressed countries, colonies, and semi-colonies. . . .

25. These lessons are as follows:

(a) In regard to *conditions antecedent* to uprisings: there must exist a revolutionary situation, *i.e.*, a crisis for the power of the ruling class, brought about by military defeats.

There must be extraordinary aggravation in the conditions of the masses and in their oppression; increase in the activity of the masses and in their readiness to fight for the overthrow of the government by revolution; and the presence of an experienced communist party having strong influence upon the dominating elements within the proletariat.

(b) In regard to preparation for uprisings: Uprisings depend not only on the directing party, but on the working masses as well. . . . .

There must be intensive work purposing the disintegration of bourgeois armies, which, at the time of the uprisings, may result in a struggle for the preservation of the [revolutionized] army. . . .

(c) As regards the execution of the uprising, the rule must be that the uprising is not a pastime; once induced, it must be energetically continued until complete victory over the enemy is achieved.[30]

To achieve this transformation of imperialistic wars into civil, resort must be had to defeatism, which to a Marxist means assistance of the proletarian masses in the downfall of their own imperialistic government, with the purpose of the ultimate overthrow of the national bourgeoisie in general. The creation of an underground organization to lead the activities of the revolutionary-minded elements in this direction is essential.[31] Fraternization in the front lines must be given the widest possible application, so as to force a termination of the war, and thus signify the mainfest superiority of the proletarian will achieved through the mutual understanding and common solidarity with the lower ranks of the enemy. According to Lenin,

"fraternization must not be limited to conversations on peace in general; it must lead to discussions of a definite political program on how to end the war and how to overthrow the yoke of the capitalists who began the war and who continue to carry it on." [32]

[30] Lenin, XVIII, I, 291 and *Kommunisticheskii Internatsional v Dokumentakh, 1919–1932*, pp. 807–808, respectively; also Art. 19, cl. "d" (*ibid.*, p. 804); *cf.* also Taracouzio, *The Soviet Union and International Law*, Appendix XXIV, pp. 442–443.

[31] Lenin, XIII, 447.

[32] *Ibid.*, XIV, pt. 1, p. 131.

Finally, the transformation of an imperialistic war into a civil war is to be achieved through revolutionary mass uprisings. Communists must categorically not resort to methods of struggle against war which hinder the development of such uprisings. Consequently, those individual acts must likewise be denounced which bear no connection to revolutionary mass activities, which do not further their development, and which oppose any labor propaganda against the wars sponsored by petty-bourgeois elements. Such suggestions as, for instance, "refusal to carry arms," or "refusal to fire," are still widely made among the masses, and many workers seriously believe that by such means results can be achieved. The communist belief, however, is that actually they are meaningless and harmful. Communists should tell the workers that the struggle against war is not an individual undertaking, and that revolutionary mass uprisings of workers and poor peasants are the best means to that end.

While not so long ago such a transformation would have appeared to a non-communist as a mere revolutionary dream, to Lenin it meant the possibility of a civil war which would mark a partial proletarian victory, brought about, on the one hand, by defeatism, and, on the other hand, by the disintegration of the front through fraternization. Today this transformation may well connote to a non-communist the possibility of a revolution. To a communist, however, it is no longer a mere possibility, but the inevitability of the repetition in some other country of the experience of Russia in 1917.

In other words, Lenin's objective necessity for transforming imperialistic wars into civil wars of classes has become a definite communist program, the soundness of which has been illustrated to them by the events which took place toward the end of the World War. Today a fundamental communist dogma is that those who fail to see the possibility of defeat for all capitalist governments engaged in war are overlooking two facts: that in future imperialistic wars there will be active along with these governments a third force—the international revolutionary proletariat—and that the logical sequence of these wars will be the continuation of the proletarian class struggle "by other means"—civil war and revolution.[33]

In connection with the above, Lenin's attitude toward two specific revolutionary methods must be briefly analyzed, as they are

[33] Lenin, XIII, 79–80.

generally considered to be the most effective for this particular Marxian purpose. One is the general strike, and the other, refusal of military service.

The general strike, as a protest against war, is considered by communists from the standpoint of transforming an imperialistic war into a civil one. They cannot isolate the general walk-out as a means of struggle against war. As early as 1907, Lenin, opposing the viewpoint of Hervé, denounced the general strike as a "panacea" when isolated from the general class struggle waged by the proletariat.[34] Later, enlightened by the experience of the World War, he elaborated upon this viewpoint of his in the instructions which he gave to the Soviet delegates to the Hague Conference in 1922, and which remain fully in force, even today. In brief, the substance of the communist credo in this respect is that "it is just as impossible to reply to a war by a walk-out as to reply to a war by revolution in the simplest and most literal sense of these terms." [35] This, however, must be accepted *cum grano,* for, in spite of the communist denunciation of the watchword "a general walk-out is the reply to war," and irrespective of warnings to the workers that such illusions cause considerable damage to an effective struggle against war, communists can by no means oppose the general strike as one of the instrumentalities for transforming an imperialist war into a civil one, or categorically condemn the refusal to resort to such a method as an expression of opportunism. Indeed, it is hard to believe that communists overlook the fact that in comparison with other mass demonstrations, such as strikes in the factories working for defense, strikes in transport industries, and strikes in the field of food supplies, the general walk-out is a more important weapon, and that as a transitional stage to armed revolution, it is in itself an important phase in the transformation of imperialistic war into civil war. Therefore, it all depends upon the circumstances. Of the latter, three are considered prerequisite to effect the above method: the expressed will of the party, the presupposed existence of a general revolutionary situation, and the proved ability of the proletariat to carry out a mass uprising. Concretely, this means that there must be well-established leadership of the party nucleus, a growing wave of revolutionary mass activities, and persistent preparations on the

[34] Lenin, XI, pt. I, pp. 106–107.
[35] *Ibid.,* XX, pt. II, pp. 529ff.

part of the communists. Hence, whereas there is no doubt that a general strike will bring revolutionary results much quicker during a war than in time of peace, there should be no delusion as to the difficulty of revolutionary preparations in the field: the mobilization of industry by the state is to be expected as a natural countermeasure against the revolutionary behavior of the proletariat. Consequently, to meet this, communists must not be either limited to abstract propaganda for a general strike, or carried away by an uncontrolled enthusiasm for action. To transform an imperialistic war into a civil one, the working masses must patiently carry on their usual everyday revolutionary tasks in the professional unions, and defend the economic demands of the workers, simultaneously combining these activities with anti-war propaganda, the organization of revolutionary committees, and patient waiting for the signal of their leaders to act.

Lenin's attitude toward the problem of objection to military service finds an elaborate interpretation in the already mentioned theses of the Sixth World Congress of the Comintern:[36]

The slogan of *refusal of military service* (boycott of war), which is defended by some of the "radical" pacifists and "left" social-democrats, is also approached by communists from the same standpoint of the transformation of imperialistic war into a civil one. Communists oppose this slogan.

(a) The idea that imperialistic war can be rendered impossible by appealing to those of conscription age not to follow mobilization orders is just as illusory as the idea of "responding to war by a general walk-out." Propaganda by such a recipe only weakens serious revolutionary struggle against war.

(b) If such a "mass boycott" should partially succeed, the result would be that the most energetic and most class-conscious workers would not be in the army. [Hence] systematic revolutionary work in the army—which is one of the decisive factors in the struggle against war—would be rendered impossible.

Therefore, Lenin was perfectly right when, in 1922 he wrote: "To boycott war—is merely a stupid phrase. Communists must accept any reactionary war."

These directions of Lenin, however, regarding boycott (refusal to "perform military duty" as a means of struggle against war) do not mean that communists must agitate the working masses to join the bourgeois army. It simply means that communists must struggle with all their energy

[36] *Kommunisticheskii Internatsional v Dokumentakh, 1917–1932,* pp. 805–807.

against boycotts, which are harmful, for they create illusions; they must struggle for revolutionary work and organization in the bourgeois army, for armament of the proletariat, and for the transformation of imperialistic wars into civil wars.

Therefore, when any question arises about joining the bourgeois army, or about refusal to perform military service (boycott), communist parties must suggest to the workers and peasants that they denounce the slogan of refusal to perform military service, that they learn how to handle arms and how to carry on revolutionary work in the army, and how, at the proper moment, to turn their arms against the bourgeoisie.

In cases where, at the time of the declaration of war, an extensive mass movement of refusal to join the army takes place, it is necessary for communists to subscribe to this movement, to give it a revolutionary character, to set forth concrete demands and slogans of a revolutionary nature, protesting against imperialistic war, and to make the maximum use of it for revolutionizing the masses. . . .

The situation permitting, communists must take advantage of this kind of mass movement to form guerilla troops for the immediate instigation of civil war. This applies particularly to countries where a strong national-revolutionary sentiment is in evidence. In such countries, at the time of declaration of war (especially in case of war against the Soviet Union), or during it, the situation permitting, communists should proclaim slogans of national-revolutionary uprisings against imperialists and of the immediate formation of national-revolutionary guerilla units.

In countries where military service is not compulsory, the government will, at the beginning of war, carry on a wide campaign for enlistment in the army, and, in case of need, will declare general mobilization. Obviously, in these countries, too, communists must struggle to transform imperialistic war into civil war. . . .

Of the greatest importance for the transformation of an imperialistic war into a civil one is revolutionary work at the front. Here communists should not limit themselves to simple propaganda, but should prescribe slogans for action in accordance with the concrete situation prevailing.

(a) In connection with economic demands and complaints of the soldiers, it becomes necessary to look for collective refusal of service, or sabotage, as well as walk-outs of soldiers and sailors.

(b) The most important slogan for action at the front is that of fraternization. Its purpose is to unite soldiers, workers, and peasants from both sides of the trenches against bourgeois generals [sic]. The experience of the last war proved that mass fraternization inevitably leads to the class disintegration of armies and to armed conflict between soldiers and officers. Communists in the army must organize fraternization by giving it a definite political character, envisaging primarily peace and the organization of revolutionary forces in the army.[37]

[37] *Supra*, p. 34.

That the practical effect of the above doctrine may be of great significance was proved in Russia in 1917. To what extent the expectations of the Soviets will be justified in the future is a matter of conjecture: the new World War has only begun.

Proletariat in Wars for National Liberation

So much for proletarian tactics during imperialistic wars. The program of revolutionary tactics prescribed by Lenin for the proletariat during national wars has for its basis the communist view of national self-determination, and the lessons learned from the postwar developments in 1918 and thereafter. Lenin's attitude in regard to the former is the result of the paramount communist belief in the withering away of the state, whereupon the problem of nationalities as political entities will disappear together with political boundaries. Subscribing to the theory that a communist commonwealth can be reached only after the world has passed through a transition period in which the state is necessary in the guise of a Dictatorship of the Proletariat, Lenin declared that self-determination of nations during this period must be the basic principle for solving the nationality question. Hence his cardinal political doctrine, that the right of oppressed nations to self-determination, including complete independence, is paramount.

Whatever this right may mean to a non-communist, to a Marxist it signifies the application of Marx's teachings to present-day conditions. Marx had viewed the idea of national liberation as an integral part of the general democratic movement. Ever practical, Lenin did not hesitate to admit that times had changed. To him, modern imperialism had brought to the forefront of world issues the problems of proletarian revolution and of the materialization of socialism. In other words, Marx's limited vision of the national question had become for Lenin a paramount issue, in which national liberation was nothing less than an essential element of modern universal socialist advance, subject to the rules envisaging world revolution:

"Now, while opposing the unified and straightened front of the imperialistic powers, the imperialistic bourgeoisie, and the social-imperialists, for the sake of the socialist revolution [we must] make use of all the national movements against imperialism. The more defined the struggle of the proletariat against the unified imperialistic front becomes, the more needed is the principle of internationalism that a 'nation oppressing other nations cannot be free.' " [38]

Cherishing such convictions, Lenin could not but be a firm believer that wars of national liberation were not only possible but inevitable. In his arguments with Rosa Luxembourg, he vigorously attacked the criticism that such wars are dangerous because they may serve as an incentive to imperialistic wars; that notions of liberation may be drowned in sentiments of national patriotism and, finally, that such wars are impracticable for the simple reason that they are destined to meet with failure. With the full power of his logic he refers to the French Revolution and the Napoleonic Wars, and concludes that "only sophistry can deny that there is a difference between imperialistic and national wars from the fact that one may be transformed into the other.[39] Citing the Seven Years' War between England and France, the National War of Liberation of the United States, and the last World War, Lenin pugnaciously points out that only a standardized conception of imperialism denies the possibility of national wars. As to the hopelessness of wars for national liberation, the gist of his argument was that even hopeless wars are wars.[40]

In all his arguments, Lenin had in mind not only colonial or semi-colonial peoples, but European nations as well. Incredible as it may at first appear, he maintained that from the standpoint of wars for national liberation, there was no difference between Europe and the colonial possessions of European powers, and that such wars were possible in both. He saw two reasons why Europe could not be excluded: first, the national minorities on the continent were even more advanced culturally and politically; second, the competition of the imperialist powers and the ultimate war among them would incite such a liberation movement. In fact, Lenin went even so far as to say that "revolutionary movements of all types—including national—in Europe are more possible, more realizable, more insistent, more conscientious, and more difficult to suppress than in the colonies." [41]

A general summary of his attitude toward the whole issue states:

[38] Lenin, XIII, 419.
[39] *Ibid.*, XIII, 438–439.
[40] *Ibid.*, 440.
[41] *Ibid.*, XIII, 415.

"National wars against imperialistic powers are not only possible and probable, but unavoidable and progressive as well as revolutionary, although obviously, for their success there is necessary either the concerted effort of large masses of the population in the oppressed countries (hundreds of millions in India and China, for instance), or a particularly advantageous international situation (for instance, the impossibility of intervention by imperialistic powers caused by weakness, war, mutual antagonism, etc.), or a simultaneous uprising of the proletariat against the bourgeoisie in one of the large powers (this last condition is the most desirable and advantageous condition for proletarian victory)." [42]

This leads to an analysis of the proletarian tactics in national wars for liberation. Obviously, their tactics must be different from those used in imperialistic wars. The main reason for the difference is to be sought in the fact that the political aim of the proletariat in national revolutionary wars may differ, depending on such factors as the political situation in general, the rôle played by the bourgeois elements, the attitude of the peasants, etc. Therefore, it is difficult to outline a definite program or to give a general rule applicable to every war. All that can be done is to point out the basic principles upon which the proletariat must base its strategy and from which it should derive suggestions for action, not only in each individual war, but even in each phase of a given struggle. These principles are found in the theses formulated by Lenin in regard to the problem of nationalities, as accepted at the Second Congress of the Comintern:

"In the policies of the Comintern on national and colonial problems, the rapprochement of the proletarian and toiling masses of all nations and countries for common revolutionary struggle against and overthrow of landlords and bourgeoisie must be taken as the starting point." [43]

Whereas it is obvious that in national revolutionary wars the possibility is by no means excluded that national sentiment will engulf not only the proletarian but also the conservative elements, and since in such wars the proletariat must apply only such tactics as are determined on the basis of a concrete analysis of the rôle played by the separate classes, it follows that the national revolutionary policy in these wars must be determined by the attitude taken by the bourgeoisie. Says Lenin:

"The Communist International must enter into provisional agreements, and even into unions, with the bourgeois democracies of colonial and

[42] Lenin, XIII, 441–442.
[43] *Ibid.*, XVII, 212.

retarded countries, without becoming, however, fused therewith, but continuing unconditionally to preserve the integrity of the proletarian movement even if in the very primary stages . . ."

"Being communists, we must and shall support liberation movements of the bourgeoisie in colonies only when these movements are really revolutionary, and when their representatives are not going to hinder our education and organization of the peasantry and the exploited masses in the revolutionary spirit." [44]

A résumé of the above is found in the following thesis adopted at the Sixth Congress of the Comintern:

"37. From the teachings of Marx and Lenin, and from the experience of the national wars of recent years,[45] the following rules for proletarian tactics to be used during national-liberation wars may be deduced:

(a) The proletarian support of the war, and, in some instances, temporary coöperation with the bourgeoisie, must in no way signify renunciation of class struggle. Even in cases where the bourgeoisie, together with the proletariat, may oppose imperialism, it remains a foe of the proletariat and uses it only for furthering its own interests.

(b) Therefore, under no condition should the proletariat subscribe to the policy and tactics of the bourgeoisie, but should, without reservation, act independently, and by following its own program and slogans, establish revolutionary organizations (party, professional unions, workers' militia, proletarian army units, etc.). Communists must prepare the masses for the inevitable betrayal of the bourgeoisie; they must take every measure to safeguard the position gained by the proletariat; [finally] they must by all means hinder the bourgeoisie in struggling to gain its own ends, and [simultaneously] prepare to overthrow it.

(c) In national wars, where the bourgeoisie, or bourgeois government, plays a counter-revolutionary rôle (as in the struggle of Chinese laborers and peasants against the division of China by imperialists), communists must act to overthrow the bourgeois government, the revolutionary defense of the country being [in such cases] the slogan for their action." [46]

To conclude this analysis of the proletarian attitude toward national-liberation wars, a few words are pertinent in regard to the transformation of these wars into civil wars against the bourgeoisie. From what has been said, it follows that Marxism sets forth no

[44] Lenin, XVII, pp. 212 and 275, respectively.

[45] To one familiar with the Soviet literature, it is an open secret that the unrests in Ireland, uprisings in Morocco under Abd-el-Kemir in 1925–1926, Independents' movement in former Austria, Tyrolean problems in Italy, and other instances of national enthusiasm are classed by the communists as national wars.

[46] *Kommunisticheskii Internatsional v Dokumentakh, 1917–1932,* pp. 811–812.

standard recipe for such action. All will depend on the circumstances. Indeed, in wars where the proletariat has provisionally
joined the bourgeoisie for the common purpose of national liberation,
the possibility is rather remote that the toiling masses will rise in
opposition to the government which is leading them in such a war
against imperialism. At the same time, it would be erroneous to
assume that such possibilities are definitely excluded. History
affords an illustration of this during the Paris Commune of 1871,
when the bourgeoisie refused to take part in the struggle and the
national war became a civil war of the proletariat against the bourgeoisie. In modern times, the situation which prevailed in Germany
in 1923 may afford an analogy with the events in Paris fifteen decades ago. In other words, Lenin's dogmas in regard to imperialistic
wars are not applicable to wars for national liberation. National
wars differ also from revolutionary wars waged by countries where
the proletariat is the class in possession of political power, irrespective of whether such a war was forced upon the proletarian state or
instigated by it.

PROLETARIAT AND REVOLUTIONARY WARS

Of prime importance for the present study is an analysis of the
proletarian policy toward and tactics during revolutionary wars.
While it is true that the theoretical analysis of Lenin was made
before the Soviet power was firmly established, his interpretation
of their practical effects was made on the basis of the experience
of the Bolshevik Revolution. Then, too, since the U.S.S.R. still
remains the only country where the proletariat enjoys dictatorial
authority, the practical application of Marxian theories on this issue
can take place only in the Soviet Union. Hence, it is only logical
that in regard to proletarian wars, the abstract term "Marxism" is
synonymous with its material manifestation—the "Soviets," and
the practical tactics of the U.S.S.R. correspond to the theoretical
communist program.

In comparing a proletarian revolutionary war with a war of
national liberation, it must be remembered that the former is impossible before the proletariat has become the state power in some
country. It is the privilege of the proletariat to wage revolutionary
wars. Since the dictatorship of the proletariat is undoubtedly a

much higher form of class struggle than the political struggles of the toiling masses under the domination of non-communist authorities, revolutionary wars are logically a much more advanced form of proletarian war than civil wars.[47] Lenin's belief that only those are true Marxists who "extend the principle of the struggle of classes to the acceptance of the dictatorship of the proletariat," [48] may well be applied here, for by analogy it remains true not only in regard to economic and political struggles, but also in regard to civil and revolutionary wars as well.

When applied to the revolutionary war, which in fact is nothing but an integral part of the world revolution, this principle becomes even more important, for in such a light it becomes indicative of the conditions under which the proletariat can wage revolutionary wars. In this connection, it must be noted that Marxism does not deny the possibility that revolutionary wars may assume the guise of civil wars of the proletariat in capitalistic countries, or of national wars of oppressed peoples in the colonial possessions of the great powers. Yet it clearly suggests that while the proletariat, barring tactical limitations, can always conduct a civil war against its own bourgeoisie, a revolutionary war, *i.e.*, a war against the non-proletarian classes in a foreign country, is always subject to the principles of safeguarding the international solidarity of the working masses, based primarily upon the overthrow of the bourgeoisie. In April of 1917, Lenin enumerated the conditions under which such an undertaking might take place, when he said that "the conscientious proletariat may give its consent to a revolutionary war only under the following conditions:

"(a) The authority must pass into the hands of the proletariat and of the poorest peasantry sympathizing with it;

(b) Annexation must be denounced, not in words but in fact;

(c) All affiliation with capitalistic pursuits must be actually severed." [49]

The fact, however, that this was written at a time when the Russian bourgeoisie was still waging a war which to Lenin must obviously have been an imperialistic one, prompts the suggestion that there may be exceptions to this rule.

[47] On civil war, *cf. infra*, pp. 71ff.
[48] Lenin, XIV, pt. II, p. 323.
[49] *Ibid.*, XIV, pt. I, p. 17.

If the bourgeoisie is waging a war for national liberation, or if the toiling masses happen to be directly oppressed by the foreign bourgeoisie (as it may happen, for instance, during occupation), then the proletariat, even before taking over the state authority, may not only support the national war but instigate the revolutionary one.

In the preceding pages it was said that revolutionary wars are not only those started by proletarian states, but also those conducted by such states *ex necessitate*—wars in which the latter find themselves on the defensive.[50] The U.S.S.R. is thus far the only country where the proletariat rules. Therefore, it may prove of interest to analyze briefly the proletarian tactics in the defense of the Soviet Union against imperialism, for it will at the same time reveal the Marxian theory regarding the proletarian defense of any proletarian country.

There is no better way to do this than to quote once again from the resolutions passed at the Sixth World Congress of the Communist International:

26. An imperialistic war against the Soviet Union is an openly counter-revolutionary class war of the bourgeoisie against the proletariat. Its main purpose is the overthrow of the dictatorship of the proletariat, and the establishment of the White Terror over the working classes of the world. The basis for the tactics of the proletarian masses in capitalist countries against such a war is the communist program for struggle against imperialistic war: its transformation into a civil war. However, the methods and aim of this struggle, both prior to and during the war, must be adjusted to the concrete conditions of its preparation, as well as of its class character. Tactics undergo important changes, inasmuch as the "enemy" is an imperialistic country and not under proletarian dictatorship.

27. Concretely, in connection with the problem of propaganda during an imperialistic war and during the preparation of war against the Soviet Union, the following must be noted:

(a) Pacifism—a screen for military preparation—will become the most important weapon. Therefore, it becomes necessary to increase the struggle against pacifism and its specific slogans; against the League of Nations, which will conduct the coming war against the Soviet Union in the name of "civilization" and "peace"; against "realistic pacifism" which considers the Soviet Union and proletarian and colonial revolutions dangerous for "peace"; against "radical pacifism," which, in the

[50] *Supra* p. 30. For the Marxian theory regarding defense of "fatherland," *cf. infra*, pp. 48ff.

guise of struggle against "any war," wishes to discredit the idea of defending Soviet power. . . .[51]

28. International [ly organized] working classes and working masses at large see in the Soviet Union their protector and are increasingly sympathetic to it. Taking into consideration the fact that the aim of imperialistic war against the Soviet Union will be understood by the working masses much more readily than in 1914 . . . it may be said that the possibilities of the struggle against war have since grown considerably, and that there now exist data for carrying out much more important tactics.

(a) There is a possibility of preventing the inception of war by increasing class struggle, including revolutionary mass uprisings against the government, even prior to the declaration of war. . . .

(b) There is a possibility that the proletariat of the bourgeois country will transform the imperialistic war against the U.S.S.R. into a civil war against its own bourgeoisie much more quickly than in a war among imperialists.

(c) Therefore, in spite of the fact that communists in the capitalist countries, in case of a war against the U.S.S.R., may denounce the slogan "reply by a general walk-out," they must not overlook the possibility of taking advantage of the mass walk-out, even during mobilization, i.e., prior to the declaration of war.

(d) In case of armed attack upon the Soviet Union, communists in oppressed nations and in imperialistic countries must do all in their power to bring about uprisings of national minorities in Europe and in colonial and semicolonial territories, and to organize the imperialistic enemies of the Soviets.

29. Inasmuch as the imperialistic war would be directed against the Soviet Union, the fatherland of the international proletariat, the tactics, as compared with those used in a "purely" imperialistic war, should be changed as follows:

(a) The proletariat in imperialistic countries must not only struggle for the defeat of its own government in this war, but also actively pursue the victory of the Soviet Government.

(b) Therefore, its tactics and the selection of the means for this struggle are determined not only by the interests of the struggle of classes in its own country, but also by the interests of the warfare at the front, which is nothing but a class war of the bourgeoisie against the proletarian state.

(c) The Red Army is not an "enemy" army, but an army of the international proletariat. During a war against the Union of Socialist Soviet Republics, the proletariat in capitalistic countries will not permit itself to become frightened by the bourgeoisie accusing it of national

[51] Cf. supra, p. 26.

betrayal, and will not refuse to support this army and to help it in its struggle against its own bourgeoisie as well.[52]

It is immaterial whether such an explanation of proletarian revolutionary wars is or is not convincing as to these wars being wars of the toiling masses for their own economic, political, and social interests. Nor is it important that such wars must be preceded by considerable revolutionary preparations. Significant is the fact that

"no revolutionary class can denounce revolutionary war, for it would mean condemnation to a ridiculous pacifism . . . It is impossible to denounce such a war. This would mean Tolstoiism and the pitifulness of the bourgeoisie; it would mean forgetting all the science of Marxism, all the experience of European revolutions." [53]

Of even greater importance is the not unintentional omission of any differentiation between "offensive" and "defensive" operations. Such wars need not always be either in theory or in practice defensive wars. Lenin himself admitted the possibility that military and political changes in the international situation might force a defensive war of the proletariat to become an aggressive revolutionary war for socialism:

"Socialism cannot be victorious simultaneously in every country. It will win at first in one or several countries, while the others for some time will remain bourgeois or semi-bourgeois. This will not only cause friction, but an outright desire of the bourgeoisie in other countries to overthrow the victorious proletariat of the socialist state . . . A war [which would thus result] would be a war for socialism, [i.e.] for the liberation of other peoples from the yoke of the bourgeoisie." [54]

Thus revolutionary wars not only differ from national wars but have even less in common with imperialist wars. In the latter, the cardinal point in proletarian tactics is the transformation of the imperialistic war into a civil one, achieved through revolutionary defeatism in the rear and fraternization at the front; in a war between capitalistic and communist states the proletarian tactics are fundamentally changed. Here the need for overthrowing one's own government and the resort to fraternization no longer apply to both

[52] *Kommunisticheskii Internatsional v Dokumentakh, 1917–1932*, pp. 809–810.
[53] Lenin, XIV, pt. I, p. 309.
[54] *Zapiski Instituta Lenina,* No. 2, 1927.

parties; they remain compulsory only for the proletariat of the imperialistic power. The proletariat of the proletarian state, on the contrary, is expected to support its own government with all available means and instead of sowing seeds of disloyalty in the army, must cement its ranks with revolutionary enthusiasm. In an imperialistic war, the aim of the international proletariat is to give birth to a proletarian state; in a revolutionary war the aim is to secure victory for such a state. This difference in aim is the reason for the difference in tactics, which must be borne in mind by every communist, particularly in the country or countries which find themselves at war with a proletarian state, which thus far has meant at war with the U.S.S.R.

Proletarian Problem of Self-Defense

In a discussion of war and peace, be it an academic abstraction or an analysis of concrete politics, it has become a commonplace to touch upon the issue of self-defense. It has enough sophistry to suit philosophers; it is elastic enough to accommodate diplomats; it affords ample material to support both antagonistic and protagonistic contentions in regard to war. All this applies also to Marxian theory and Soviet practice.

As to the Marxian attitude toward self-defense in an imperialistic war, the substance of this attitude is to be found in the resolutions passed at the congresses of the Second International in Stuttgart in 1907, and Basel, in 1912, and in the criticism launched by Lenin against the socialists who, at the beginning of the World War, were overcome by sentiments of patriotism and joined their respective French, German, British, and other armies to take part in the imperialistic war.[55]

Denying to the patriotic motto "defense of the 'fatherland' " any academic characteristic bearing upon economics or politics, Lenin dismisses it merely as an expression ordinarily used to justify war.[56] He remains firm in his uncompromising attitude regarding generalizations, and again warns that proletarian policies must depend on the nature of each individual war. From what has been said in regard to Marxian tactics in imperialistic wars, Lenin's attitude must

[55] Lenin, XIII, 342.
[56] *Ibid.*, XIII, 343.

be obvious: the proletariat must denounce the principle of "defense of the fatherland," [57] for in such wars, the proletariat has no "fatherland" to defend.[58] There are only governments to be overthrown. At the Sixth World Congress of the Comintern in 1927, this idea was made formally binding upon every communist:

"18. The political program of communists during an imperialistic war . . . consists of the following basic principles:

(a) Refusal to defend the imperialistic fatherland in this war; explaining to the workers and peasants the reactionary character of the war; a most energetic struggle against all kinds of labor movements which either openly or secretly justify such war.

30. While in imperialistic countries [the proletarian masses] are forbidden to defend their country, in the state of the proletarian dictatorship this defense is a revolutionary duty." [59]

So much for the Marxian duty of national defense in imperialistic wars. Confused as may appear the issue when applied to wars of national liberation, the above categorical formula does not apply to them. Lenin left to his disciples an explanation of the complex and delicate interrelation of such factors bearing upon the problem as the proletarian concept of a war for national liberation, the substance of class struggle, and the meaning of national uprisings. Prior to his clarification, even in communist ranks there had been a great deal of uncertainty in regard to the proletarian defense of the fatherland in a war for national liberation. Some were of the opinion that this defense could never take place, while others were inclined to accept it as obligatory, but only after the proletariat had gained the authority and the power. Pointing out that Marx and Engels themselves admitted the proletarian duty of defending the fatherland in national wars even before the power had been taken over by the proletariat, Lenin brought this uncertainty to an end when he ruled that communists "are not against the defense of the fatherland in a truly national war." [60] What constitutes a "truly national" war is still a matter of individual opinion, witness the contention of many

[57] Lenin, XIII, 408.

[58] This was in full accord with the earlier, now out of date though still proverbial, motto that the proletariat has "nothing to lose but their chains" (From *The Programme of the Communist International*, p. 65 (London, 1932)).

[59] *Kommunisticheskii Internatsional v Dokumentakh, 1919–1932*, pp. 804 and 810, respectively.

[60] *Ibid.*, XIII, 342.

socialists that even the World War was in a sense a war of national liberation when it came to the issues of national self-determination and annexation, yet, in spite of this, proletarian defense was considered not the proper behavior for the proletariat. Criticizing the arguments advanced in 1914 by German radicals against the support of national wars, Lenin did not hesitate to write:

"In such arguments there is not a single ounce of Marxism or of revolution. To remain loyal to socialism we must support any uprising against our main enemy—the bourgeoisie of great powers, provided this uprising is not one of the reactionary class. It is precisely in the era of imperialism, which is nothing but an era of the beginning of social revolution, that the proletariat must support with particular energy uprisings in annexed territories so that either simultaneously with them, or some time later, an attack can be made on the thus weakened bourgeoisie of the great power." [61]

The importance of this is two-fold. First, communists must remember that there is a great difference between national wars and proletarian revolt. While closely connected with each other, they remain two distinct problems. Second, communists are thus warned that in a national war the proletariat must support the liberation movement and, therefore, must be on the defensive against the encroachment of the capitalist powers.

The theoretical problem regarding the proletarian duty to defend a proletarian state became an actual issue at Brest-Litovsk in 1918, when Marxian theories on proletarian revolutionary war had a chance to be applied in practice for the first time.[62] With the coming into existence of the first state under the Dictatorship of the Proletariat, the problem of its defense was a logical sequence. It was during the crucial Brest-Litovsk negotiations between Germany and the Soviets that a proletarian state for the first time was faced with the concrete problem of how to apply Marxian dogmas in real life. The ultra-revolutionary enthusiasm of Trotzky was in favor of waging an aggressive revolutionary war, while the dialectics of Lenin insisted on finding a way to defend the country which only a few weeks before had become the proletarian fatherland. Hence, it is from Lenin's solution of the situation which confronted the Soviets in the

---

[61] Lenin, XIII, 409–410.

[62] For Lenin's denial of any analogy between the situation which prevailed in 1918 and the French revolutionary wars of the end of the eighteenth century, cf., Lenin, *Works*, XV.

Spring of 1918 that the communist theory on the issue can best be deduced.

What happened at Brest-Litovsk in regard to the outward settlement of the armed conflict between the two countries is common knowledge. Few, however, are aware of Lenin's true conception of the proletarian defense of the proletarian fatherland. In a technical military sense, an offense is the best defense. Translated into the field of Marxian dialectics, this would mean that Trotzky's idea of waging an aggressive revolutionary war would be the best way for the proletariat to defend their newly acquired fatherland. Yet, history has shown that when it came to putting it into practice, Lenin disagreed with such a policy. Firm in his belief that war, revolutionary or otherwise, is merely a continuation of old policies by a different means, he maintained that resort to such a means can be made only under the following two conditions: first, there must be a definite end to justify revolutionary war, and second, there must be a political situation which makes the resort to such a means mandatory. Neither of these two conditions prevailed at the time of the Brest-Litovsk negotiations, according to Lenin:

"At the present time a truly revolutionary war would be a war waged by a socialist republic against bourgeois countries, provided that the overthrow of the bourgeoisie in other countries be the definitely expressed aim approved by the socialist army. No such end is possible at the present." [63]

That the political situation in Europe was not yet ripe for revolution, calls for no comment.

Protection of the proletarian dictatorship by physical defense of the country was declared to be of much greater importance for the time being than revolutionary aggression by war. This did not mean that the idea of a revolutionary war was to be abandoned altogether, but merely that the time was not opportune for engaging in such an undertaking. While the preparations for such a war were to go on, the primary task for the newly established Soviets was "to restore order and to generate energy which [some day] was bound to produce the best that can be offered by a revolution." [64]

As will be shown elsewhere,[65] later events proved not only the soundness of the position taken by Lenin, but also that the physical

[63] Lenin, XV, 64.
[64] *Ibid.*, pp. 62 and 131, respectively.
[65] *Infra*, pp. 71ff.

defense of the proletarian fatherland, necessary as it is *per se* to the communists, is at the same time a political issue of paramount importance. To quote Lenin:

"When we represented the oppressed class, we took the problem of the defense of the fatherland in imperialistic wars seriously—we denied such defense in principle. When we became the representatives of the ruling class which commenced to organize socialism, we demanded that everyone take national defense [likewise] seriously." [66]

In practice this means a thorough preparation for such defense and an exact calculation of the forces that may become involved. In regard to the latter, the basic principle is that defending a country of the dictatorship of the proletariat is the paramount duty of the proletariat the world over:

"30. While in imperialistic countries the defense of its fatherland is not permitted [to the proletariat], in a state of proletarian dictatorship this defense is a revolutionary duty. Here the defense rests with the armed proletariat of the Union of Socialist Soviet Republics. The victory of the October Revolution gave to the workers of all the world a socialistic fatherland—the Soviet Union. The defense of the Union of Socialist Soviet Republics against the international bourgeoisie concurs with the class interests [of the proletariat] and is, for the international proletariat, a matter of honor." [67]

At the Sixth World Congress of the Comintern, the rules on the communist attitude toward national defense in various wars were formulated as follows:

"Upon the attitude taken by the proletariat towards a given war depends *ex principio* its position in regard to the 'defense of the fatherland.' The proletariat has no fatherland until it wins the political power and takes over the means of production from the hands of the exploiters. The expression 'defense of the fatherland' is the most commonly used expression in justification of war. In wars waged by the proletariat or by a proletarian state against imperialism, the proletariat must defend its socialistic fatherland. In national-revolutionary wars, the proletariat defends the country against imperialism. In imperialistic wars, however, it must most emphatically condemn the idea of 'defense of the fatherland,' which idea serves to protect exploitation and to betray socialism." [68]

In summarizing the practical communist evaluation of imperialistic, national and revolutionary wars, the following statement by

[66] Lenin, XV, 240.
[67] *Kommunicheskii Internatsional v Dokumentakh, 1919–1932*, p. 810.
[68] *Ibid.*, pp. 798–799.

Lenin regarding the pragmatics of war may well be taken as the starting point:

"War is a great disaster. But a social-democrat cannot analyze war apart from its historic importance. For him there can be no such thing as absolute disaster, or absolute welfare and absolute truth. He must analyze and evaluate the importance of war from the point of view of the interests of his class—the proletariat . . . He must evaluate war not by the number of its casualties, but by its political consequences. Above the interests of the individuals perishing and suffering from war must stand the interests of the class. And if the war serves the interests of the proletariat, as a class and *in toto,* and secures for it liberation from the [capitalist] yoke, and freedom for struggle and development,—such a war is progress, irrespective of the victims and the suffering it entails." [69]

Three principles stand out prominently in this none too common approach to war, namely, that human conceptions are not conclusive but relative, that class interests of the toiling masses must be the guiding spirit of the proletariat, and that war is progress when it serves the interests of the toilers. The first of these may be discarded for the present, as it may readily lead to a pointless sophistry; the principle of the predominance of the class interest, however, is worthy of note. Indeed, the transformation of imperialistic wars into civil wars certainly is nothing but an important phase in the class struggle, one serving to further the interests of the proletarian class. The basic idea of wars for national liberation, struggle against oppression, would lose all its revolutionary significance if such wars were not to serve the interests of proletarian world revolution. In revolutionary wars, the aim of the proletariat, the rôle played by it, and the means resorted to, are self-evident.

Worthy of note also is the significance attached by the communists to the revolutionary progressiveness of wars. Indeed, Marxists share the non-communist belief that progress consists of everything that leads to a definite goal. To them this goal is a warless and peaceless commonwealth of mankind. They accept war and peace as means of equal value to reach this goal.[70] In other words, to a Marxist, wars, like peace, are an advance toward the ultimate proletarian end—the World Union of Socialist Soviet Republics. Inasmuch as any advance toward a goal, however limited and whatever the nature of the goal, is progress *per se,* it must follow that

[69] Lenin, VI, 457.
[70] *Supra,* pp. 27–28.

even in the case of very slight advantage to the proletariat, wars (imperialistic wars again not excluded) must represent progress. This inclusion of imperialistic wars leaves the impression, apparently paradoxical from the Marxian point of view, that they should be welcomed rather than opposed by the toiling masses. That this inconsistency is not illusory, however, but is to be accepted as one of the illustrations of the workings of Lenin's pragmatics has been already substantiated by the revolutionary parity of war and peace. A further proof of this is to be found in the communist pursuit of war and peace, as reflected in the foreign relations of the Soviet Union.

CHAPTER III

RED RETREAT: SOVIETS IN TURMOIL,
1917–1921

CHAPTER III

RED RETREAT: SOVIETS IN TURMOIL, 1917–1921

PEACE AND REVOLUTION

Peace has been from the outset the cardinal objective of formal Soviet foreign policy. Inaugurated on the morrow of the Bolshevist Revolution by the promulgation of the first Soviet decree, the Decree "On Peace," [1] this policy has been prominent in the persistent peace notes and proposals of the earlier months, in the indefatigable espousals of disarmament in later years, and in the numerous non-aggression and neutrality pacts of the more recent period. The efforts of the Soviets for the actual attainment of world peace may in some instances have differed from the usually accepted methods of modern diplomacy; in others, they may have been inopportune under the circumstances; they may even have had an air of obviously impracticable bravado. At no time prior to the fall of 1939, however, had they deviated from the course charted by the new communist masters of the former Russian Empire. The solemn declarations made by Litvinov in 1928 that the Soviet Government had been interested in the preservation of world peace "from the very day of taking over authority," [2] and by Molotov, in 1935, that the Soviets "always have struggled and are continuing to struggle for the preservation of peace," [3] are typical of Bolshevist statements to that effect throughout the almost quarter century of their régime—statements too numerous and too often repeated to warrant further illustration here. To deny this would mean either the admission of a biased attitude, or a profession of a complete unfamiliarity with Soviet records.

[1] *Sobr. Uzak. i Rasp. R.S.F.S.R.*, 1917–1918, I. pp. 2–3. English text in *The Soviet Union and Peace*, pp. 22–23. For Soviet efforts for peace, *cf.*, also, Taracouzio, *op. cit.*, pp. 302ff.

[2] Speech on March 22, 1928, at the Fifth Session of the Preliminary Disarmament Conference (Litvinov, *Vneshniaia Politika S.S.S.R.*, p. 131).

[3] From the Report made to the VII Congress of Soviets of the U.S.S.R. on January 28, 1935 (Molotov, *Otchetnyi doklad o rabote pravitel'stva VII S'ezdu Sovetov S.S.S.R. 28 ianvaria 1935g.*, p. 26).

At the same time, however, to accept these assertions without analyzing the underlying motives of the Soviet peace policy would mean to manifest dangerous superficiality in the appraisal of such a vital issue. For an evaluation based solely on a realistic manifestation of the Soviet peace policy, divorced from a dogmatic interpretation in terms of Marxian principles, may readily lead to erroneous conclusions as to the nature both of the ultimate world peace envisaged by Marx and of the international peace championed by the Soviets. It is precisely to prevent this possibility that the continuity of the Soviet pursuit of peace must be analyzed not only from the standpoint of official diplomatic records, but also from the imprint which these records leave on Soviet adherence to the Marxian understanding of the term "peace." The clarification of the difference between the ideological concept of Marxian peace and the pragmatic substance of peace for the Soviets is the issue in point.

In the preceding pages the Marxian abstraction of ultimate world peace has already been discussed. Likewise, it has been shown that it is from the communist concept of the origin of wars that the way to such peace is to be found. At the First Enlarged Plenary Session of the Communist International in March, 1922, it was resolved that "the proletarian revolution, by overthrowing capitalism, is the only effective means to prevent the danger of war." [4] This suggestion of achieving world peace by world revolution is merely a repetition of Lenin's formula of Marx's belief that the cause of all wars lies in capitalism.[5]

Dogmatically, to a communist, ultimate world peace must spell the downfall of capitalism and the establishment of a homogeneous classless and stateless society of men, and to the Soviets, a political rearrangement, to be achieved in times yet to come, where in the revolutionary nirvana of the World Union of Socialist Soviet Republics the problems of war and peace will be non-existent. Pragmatically, to the Marxist, peace must be a provisional social *status quo* in which the class war between the proletariat and capitalism must go on, while to the Soviet Union, it must connote outward international tranquility. Whether it be an actual cessation of armed warfare, with or without the sanction of formal treaties of peace, or a legal *status quo* characterized by the amicable conduct of foreign

---

[4] *Kommunisticheskii Internatsional v Dokumentakh, 1919–1932,* pp. 267–268.
[5] *Supra,* p. 25.

relations, irrespective of the means by which these are maintained, whether by solemn agreements or sheer fear of force—from the standpoint of the immediate expediency of the U.S.S.R., this international tranquility encompasses concrete measures for assuring *de facto* international peace in the present communist and non-communist worlds.

Irrespective of the assertions that only the proletariat will be capable of eliminating wars in the future, and without regard to the likelihood of actual materialization of the communist ultimate world peace, it is evident that concretely the issue is limited to finding a way for the practical attainment of this peace, *i.e.*, to the formulation of a peace policy to be followed. In this policy, "peace" is to be understood not as an ultimate end in itself, but as a provisional means to an end. It is also evident that this peace policy, like any other, is bound to have its continuation by "other means," that is, to the Soviets, by war.[6] When, at the Seventh Party Congress, speaking of the Brest-Litovsk Treaty, Lenin said that peace is nothing but a breathing spell for the preparation for new wars, he referred not only to the Brest-Litovsk Treaty, but also to the formal peace policy of the Soviets, which is bound to terminate in war which will involve also the Soviet Union.

It was Lenin who in the summer of 1915 wrote that the struggle of classes within a country at war is inseparable from war itself.[7] In other words, the ideological analogies between Marxian war and peace find their practical parallelism in the fact that international wars and the formal peace policy of the U.S.S.R. are fused into an informal communist policy of revolutionary advance, a policy which, if carried out in accordance with the dictates of Marxism, is expected to terminate in *Pax communa*—the final permanent well-being of the world proletariat under the blessings of the warless and peaceless future.

In comparison with proletarian policies in regard to war, Marxian dogmas relative to practical peace efforts not only occupy much less space in communist writings, but also are much less definite. As a matter of fact, before the Russian Revolution, Lenin limited himself mainly to hypothetical possibilities germane to the World War.

[6] *Cf.*, Lenin's modification of Clausewitz's definition of war, which he visualizes as a "continuation of the same policies by using other (namely *forcible*) means" (Lenin, XVIII, 97), *supra*, p. 27.

[7] Lenin, XIII, 93.

Thus, to his own question as to what would be the action of the proletariat in case they came to power during the War, he answered in 1915 that the proletariat would offer peace to all warring nations, but with the proviso that all colonies and all oppressed peoples be freed and given an opportunity of untrammelled national self-expression.[8]

About a year later he elaborated upon his vision of peace in 1915, and formulated a revolutionary program of peace:

"The peace program of the social-democrats first of all must consist of unveiling bourgeois hypocrisy . . . Without this we would become willing or unwilling sponsors of cheating the masses. Our 'peace program' demands that the focal point in this problem—the denunciation of annexations— must be put into practice actually and not in words only, and be made to serve international propaganda and not national hypocrisy . . . Our 'peace program,' finally, must consist of an explanation of the fact that imperialistic powers and the bourgeoisie cannot give a democratic peace."[9]

His vision of the proletarian peace policy grew broader and broader with the onrush of events. His revolutionary specifications grew *pari passu*. In April of 1917, only a month after the Russian Empire became the Russian Socialist Republic, he wrote that "it is impossible to get out of an imperialistic war and to have a democratic, non-rapacious, peace without the overthrow of capitalism, and the transfer of state authority to another class—the proletariat."[10] The intrinsic idea of the outwardly prosaic French proverb *"l'appetit vient en mangeant"* found its revolutionary application seven months later. In November, 1917, the proletariat became the ruling authority of the Bolshevist State, and thereupon the communist peace policy was extended still further. From now on, it was to embrace the interests not alone of the first proletarian state, but of the world proletariat *in toto*. As such, it was to take into account not only the immediate necessities of the Soviets, but the position of the toiling masses in capitalist countries, as well as the ambitions of oppressed nations, and the rights of colonial peoples. Tactical coördination among these factors, and their theoretical fusion in a

[8] Lenin, XV, 14. This the Soviets actually did, as will be shown later (*infra*, p. 65).

[9] *Ibid.*, XIII, 239; *cf.*, also, Appeal of the Soviet People's Commissar for Foreign Affairs of Dec. 19, 1917, to the workers of Europe (*Sovetskii Soiuz v Bor'be za Mir*, p. 33).

[10] *Ibid.*, XIV, 45.

common revolutionary cause became the materialist credo of communist peace worshipers. In other words, the concrete efforts of the Soviets toward peace became the embodiment of Marxian peace dogmas.

It is a matter of conjecture whether the reverse is correct, namely, that this Soviet peace policy is the result of the repeatedly claimed never-failing adherence of the Red Kremlin to Marxian ideology. Two facts are important: First, the materialization of these dogmas in practice was ordered to be carried out not only in the international relations of the Soviets with non-communist powers, but also in the field of the political intercourse of the imperialistic powers among themselves. Second, it became the duty of the Soviets to see that the revolutionary "peace" tactics of the proletariat were carried out in each of these domains.

The international relations of the Soviet Union during the last quarter century are a matter of history recorded both in the official documents preserved in various foreign offices all over the world, and in voluminous writings of historians, economists, political scientists, and scholars in many other fields. From the standpoint of war and peace, these relations will be analyzed later; here it may be noted *de limine* that the basic principles upon which they must rest were outlined by Lenin long before the Soviets were sure of their own survival. Thus, in September of 1917, when he became convinced of the forthcoming overthrow of Kerensky's government, he wrote that

"we have all the prerequisites for a successful uprising . . . in which our victory will cut short all flirtation with the notions of a separatist peace as a means against revolution, by proposing a more complete peace, a peace that would be more just and of more service to revolution." [11]

Early in 1920, he continued in the same vein, reminding his disciples that for the Soviets peace was possible, provided, however, that the communist efforts toward it "are accompanied by the utmost military preparedness, [*i.e.*] by absolute prevention of the disarmament of our army." [12]

[11] Lenin, XIV, pt. II, p. 138. Referring to a separatist peace to stop revolution, Lenin evidently had in mind, among other things, the plans expounded by some on the Emperor's staff during the abdication and later in Petrograd during the Kerensky régime, that peace should be concluded with Germany for the purpose of suppressing the revolution with her aid.

[12] *Ibid.*, XVII, 71.

From these commitments it is not difficult to detect the principles which were henceforth to guide Soviet foreign policies. First, every communist must bear in mind that it is perfectly conceivable for a proletarian state to conclude a peace with imperialistic powers for revolutionary purposes. Second, such an outward peace is to remain to a communist a potential political battlefield of classes, for to a Marxist it would be utterly unrevolutionary to accept such a peace as a *de facto* cessation of the struggle waged by the proletarian state against non-communist powers.

The international pursuit of peace by the U.S.S.R. as regards the political intercourse of the non-communist powers among themselves is subject to different considerations. Obviously, here the peace policy of the Soviets cannot follow the same pattern, at least formally, because the preservation of *de facto* peace does not fall within the province of the immediate control of the Kremlin. On the one hand, the dictatorship of the proletariat *ex principio* cannot prevent wars by coöperating with its foes, *i.e.*, with imperialistic nations, in such conciliatory procedures as arbitration, or instrumentalities such as the Permanent Court of International Justice, or the League of Nations.[13] On the other hand, if the idea of world revolution was not to be forced into stagnation, the Soviets could not remain mere disinterested onlookers in the competition going on among the non-communist countries. Under the circumstances, the only way to prove the applicability of Marxian dogmatics to actual life was to formulate the proletarian peace program in this respect in such a fashion that it would afford sufficient elasticity in interpreting its meaning to suit the immediate necessities of the Soviet Union. This was ingeniously achieved by ruling that the proletarian peace policy as regards the international relations of the imperialistic states must consist of strenuous opposition to all imperialistic wars and of the unmasking of bourgeois pacifism, which is nothing but a convenient camouflage for imperialistic political designs.[14]

However vague and self-contradictory this Marx-Lenin rule pre-

---

[13] This was proved by the attitude of the Soviets in the Eastern Karelian case in 1923 (*Publications of the Permanent Court of International Justice*, Series C, No. 3, v. I, p. 69, as cited in Taracouzio, *The Soviet Union and International Law*, p. 297), and by Litvinov's reply to Commander Hilton Young at The Hague in 1922, respectively (*Conference at The Hague, June 26–July 20, 1922. Minutes and Documents*, p. 126, as cited in *ibid.*, p. 296). For the later change in the Soviet attitude toward the League of Nations, *cf.*, *infra*, pp. 187ff.

[14] *Cf.*, *supra*, p. 33.

scribing an uncompromising struggle against imperialistic wars, even if they are unavoidable and objectively advantageous for world revolution,[15] when combined with the Soviet peace tactics in the field of the formal international relations of the U.S.S.R., it becomes indicative of its true purpose. Designed to serve solely the interests of the proletariat, the peace policy of the Soviets is expected to bring several advantages to the proletarian cause in the field of concrete politics. Indeed, through it, a closer rapprochement can be effected between the Russian proletariat and the toiling masses in other countries; then, under the banners of peace, a greater advantage can be taken of the discontent of smaller and oppressed nations; finally, this policy affords the tactical advantage of gaining time in which to prepare for the decisive revolutionary action against capitalism when conditions are ripe enough to warrant it. Above all these immediate interests and tactics the ultimate aim stands out: the disintegration of standing armies and the consequent disappearance of wars.

Blitzrevolution vs. Brest-Litovsk

While practical efforts for the assurance of peace were initiated by the Bolsheviks simultaneously with the Revolution in November, 1917, the notion of the peace to be pursued by them had been voiced much earlier. Indeed, the hypothetical problem of the relationship between a communist state and the capitalist world had been important items on the agenda at Kienthal and Zimmerwald in 1915 and 1916. The resolutions adopted at these Communist Congresses had already advanced a revolutionary program for peace. Without going into detail, it may be briefly pointed out here that the renunciation of former treaties, the abrogation of secret agreements, an immediate armistice, the liberations of colonies, and the repudiation of all debts were declared to be the basic principles of this program. It was not until November, 1917, however, that this abstract program became a practical issue for its authors, who now found themselves not in neutral Switzerland, but in warring, exhausted, revolutionary Russia.

Accepted thus as a factual execution of a definite Marxian program, the Soviet peace policy falls into four successive phases. In military parlance these are: retreat, entrenchment, reconnaissance,

[15] *Infra*, pp. 241ff.

and attack. Similarly, the tactics prescribed by Marx and Lenin for achieving communist peace are correspondingly different. The first initial phase had its beginning on the morrow of the Bolshevist coup d'état and lasted until the end of the civil war. As in many a warfare the Kremlin's retreat commenced with the failure to solidify the original advance, which to Moscow meant bringing about the world revolution. Surprised at their own initial success, ill-equipped with a realistic understanding of concrete situations, and confronted with the overpowering difficulties inherent in every sudden political change, particularly when the latter takes place on a scale encompassing one-sixth of the globe, the new rulers of Russia found themselves in a condition verging upon despair. Unquestionably, the preservation of the régime which they had succeeded in establishing was their dominating concern. At the same time, the mission of Marxism which fell upon their shoulders could not be neglected. Ironically enough, it was precisely in the abstract Marxian instructions regarding world revolution that they placed their hope of finding relief, if not salvation, for their concrete revolutionary achievement in Russia. Under the circumstances, it did not matter that their idea of a sudden expansion of revolution was utterly inconsistent with the teachings of the founder of communism. Nor were they disturbed by the fact that no instructions could be found in Marxian literature as to the exact procedure in such an emergency, and that the circumstantial details were necessarily vague, to say the least. Of importance only was the realization of the necessity of finding outside support for their revolutionary undertaking.

In theory, the collapse of capitalism would have been the greatest possible aid. In practice, a socialist revolution in at least some of the most advanced countries would have served the purpose for the time being, and the immediate cessation of hostilities was considered the first step necessary in this direction. The general exhaustion of the masses at home and of the armies at the front afforded a fertile field. The theoretical knowledge of the revolutionary possibilities in the transformation of imperialistic wars into civil ones, now enriched by their own experience, served as the infallible spiritual guide. Finally, the actual existence of the proletarian state, unique as it was then and still remains today, was by no means ill-adapted to the scheme of things vital for the necessary revolutionary expansion.

The very first act of the new Soviet Government was also the first practical step in the Soviet endeavor to bring about world peace: the Peace Decree, passed on October 28 (November 8), 1917. Rather a political declaration than a decree in the literal sense of the word, it invited "all belligerent nations and their governments to begin immediate negotiations for a just and democratic peace." [16] Losing no time, the People's Commissariat for Foreign Affairs two weeks later sent a note to the ambassadors of the Allied countries informing them officially of the change in the Russian Government. Simultaneously, the note called their attention to the above-mentioned Soviet Peace Decree, asked them to accept this note as a formal proposal to their respective Governments to commence negotiations for immediate peace, and expressed the Soviets' revolutionary hope that these nations could not "but long for peace." [17]

Revolutionary, indeed, as it was, and pursuing revolutionary ends as they obviously were, the Soviet Government proved itself revolutionary also in its method of conducting the Kremlin's international policies. Along with these formal communiqués through the ordinary diplomatic channels, the Soviet leaders also resorted to the non-conventional method of appeal to the masses abroad, over the heads of their respective governments. Such, for instance, was the appeal sent on November 28, 1917, by the Council of Peoples' Commissars of the R.S.F.S.R. to the peoples of the belligerent countries, asking them to join in the negotiations for an armistice. The Appeal to All Mohammedan Workers in Russia and the East, of December 7, 1917, to the Toiling, Oppressed, and Exhausted Peoples of Europe, of December 19, 1917, and to the Peoples and Governments of the Allied Countries, of December 29, 1917, are other illustrations of Soviet unconventionality, which some may excuse as a literal adherence to Marxian tactics, and which others, with equal justice, consider as a sign of sheer despair.[18]

These political overtures were supplemented by the threats of a separatist peace with Germany, by the exemplary Decree of the Council of Peoples' Commissars of November 15, 1917, recognizing the equality, and sovereignty, of the peoples in Russia and their right to complete independence, and supported by the theoret-

[16] *Sborn. Dekretov 1917–1918 gg.*, pp. 1–3. For the translated text, *cf.*, Taracouzio, *op. cit.*, Appendix XIII.

[17] *Sovetskii Soiuz v Bor'be za Mir*, p. 29.

[18] *Cf.* Taracouzio, *op. cit.*, pp. 302ff.

ical arguments of Lenin.[19] These all envisaged national self-determination, the abrogation of all secret treaties, and an immediate peace without annexations or indemnities.

It would be utterly erroneous to accept today such a formulation of the early Soviet peace policy as an altruistic *beau geste* of the first communist dictators in Russia. It was rather a policy of direct incitement to world revolution. To Lenin as a statesman, it was dictated by the immediate expediency resulting from the complete isolation in which the Soviets found themselves at the outset; to Lenin as a Marxist, it was a policy of communist logic and doctrinary considerations.

The claim prevailing today in the U.S.S.R. that in launching their peace policy the Bolshevik leaders did not anticipate an easy victory as to world revolution may appear gratifying to the casual reader. Yet the fact is that in the enjoyment of the original success in Russia, the hope was openly voiced that a series of civil wars would evolve from the termination of the war on the other fronts. This, in turn, was expected to result in the establishment of proletarian dictatorships everywhere. In other words, ushered in by the Decree of Peace on October 28, 1917, the offers of armistice and peace made by the Bolsheviks in the very first month of their rule were intended primarily as instrumentalities for the sudden transformation of the World War into a series of civil, revolutionary wars.[20] It was expected that, if successful, these "wars" would bring about communist "peace" by the extension of social revolution to new areas without delay. In other words the original peace policy of the Soviets envisaged the attainment of Marxian peace in Europe by a short-cut method, *i.e.*, by immediate world revolution, without the preliminary stages prescribed by Marx.[21] The event proved, however, that this *Blitzrevolution* was not destined to take place.

The fact is that the Bolshevist revolutionary invitation to other nations into their peace "camp" could not be limited to the Allies alone. The Central Powers, which continued to remain Russia's enemies *de jure,* could not be left out of consideration, in spite of the fact that from a revolutionary standpoint the bulk of their armies

[19] *Cf.,* respectively, *Sovetskii Soiuz v Bor'be za Mir,* and Bunyan and Fisher, *The Bolshevik Revolution,* 1917–1918; *Sobr. Uzak. i Rasp. R.S.F.S.R.,* 1917–1918, p. 21; and Lenin, *Works,* XV.

[20] *Supra,* pp. 34–35.

[21] Marx only in exceptional cases admits the possibility of revolutionary *salti.*

were no longer considered to be foes of the Russian soldiers and workers. In other words, the need of revolutions abroad became concurrent with the need of terminating war at home.

Paradoxical as it may appear, the peace negotiations which the Soviets conducted at Brest-Litovsk, aside from their purely technical aspects, did not differ in spirit from the revolutionary aims found in the peace proposals made to the Allies. The belief in the imminence of the world revolution, so pronounced in the peace proposals, was manifest also in the decision of the Soviet plenipotentiaries to use the Brest-Litovsk negotiations as a vehicle for revolutionary propaganda. What actually happened at these sessions of Soviet bargaining is well known.[22] However, for a better understanding of the Soviet attitude toward war and peace at the time, mention must be made of the dissension in this regard which arose during these crucial weeks among the communist leaders themselves.

Spurred by the success in Russia, some communists took the attitude that the Marxian program of world revolution should be put into practice without delay. To the considerations of general exhaustion and of the existence of proletarian Russia [23] was added the belief that the situation then prevailing in Europe was exceedingly favorable for revolutionary outbreaks. In fact, it was considered more than ripe: the strikes which were taking place in Austria and Germany were considered to be the first steps of the proletarian uprising preliminary to a *de facto* world revolution. In this enthusiasm, the possibility was overlooked that the defeat of Germany might have had on the Allies an effect quite different from the revolutionary expectations of the Kremlin. So the idea of furthering world revolution through defeated Germany was placed on the revolutionary agenda. This meant that war with the Central Powers must continue. The full realization of Russia's weakness as a fighting unit was overbalanced by the unmarred belief in the power of fraternization on the front lines. To these extremists a proletarian victory over Imperial Germany and her allies was not only the most certain, but the only way of gaining the true objective of Marx; a separatist peace would, in their opinion, result in the failure of both the Russian and the world revolutions.

[22] Cf., *Mirnye peregovory v Brest-Litovske* (Moscow, 1920), Bunyan and Fisher, *op. cit.*, and Wheeler-Bennett, *The Forgotten Peace: March, 1918* (New York, 1939).
[23] *Supra*, pp. 50ff.

A modification of this extreme optimism of the left-wing communists was introduced by Trotzky, who based his ideas on the subject on the belief that the Germans would not dare to advance into Russia. Subscribing to the general idea of world-wide *Blitz-revolution,* and believing with the others that in case of need the immediate interests of the Russian revolution must be sacrificed to those of world revolution, Trotzky did not consider the survival of the proletarian authority in Russia essential to that end. Bukharin, who sided with him, went even further when he said that "by saving our socialist republic we are losing the chance of promoting world revolution." [24] While the comparatively recent trials in Moscow which sealed the fate of most of these "opportunists" is now recorded evidence of their gross error, in passing, it may be said that Trotzky's unprecedented formula "no war, no peace" throws light upon the variety of forms which the communist notion of war and peace took in the days of the inaugural revolutionary efforts of the dictatorial proletariat.

Opposed to these uncompromising views of the extremists and of Trotzky was Lenin's more cautious program. Under the circumstances, he did not see any possibility for Russia to go on with the war against Germany. Nor did he share Trotzky's illusions in regard to the timidity of the German armies. [25]

To him it was evident that the Soviet appeals for peace were without effect abroad, and that a continuation of the war with Germany, a foe at the time infinitely superior, would be suicidal. It would mean not only the dismemberment of Russia, but would jeopardize the very existence of the newly established communist state, the state which was to serve as a base for the ultimate revolution on a world-wide scale. The only possibility of preventing this from coming to pass was to limit their designs for peace to Russia alone, that is, bring the war between Russia and the Central Powers to an end at any cost.

The original idea of a short-cut to world revolution had to be discarded. In its stead new tactics in Soviet peace policy were ordered. To justify this step dogmatically, a new theory was conceived by Lenin, which he later formulated as follows:

[24] *Cf.* Louis Fischer, *op. cit.*, pp. 60ff.
[25] *Cf.* his report to the Seventh Congress of the Russian Communist Party (Lenin, XV, 115ff.).

"To wait until the toiling classes bring about the revolution on an international scale is to condemn oneself to a state of inactivity and mere waiting. This is nonsense. The difficulties of revolution are well known. Having started as a spectacular success in one country, revolution may have to go through periods of trials because the final victory is possible only on a world-wide scale and through the united efforts of workers in all countries. Our task is to exercise tact and caution; we must maneuver and retreat until reinforcements come to our aid." [26]

Displaying thus a much keener sense of political realism, Lenin preferred to see the original triumph suffer a humiliating set-back rather than to have it ultimately nullified by blind enthusiasm. Soberly, he preferred to "accept peace when the army was in flight, and could not but be in flight without losing thousands of men, in order to prevent things from getting worse." [27] Cognizant of his revolutionary authority, he argued that the need of the moment was not an aggressive proletarian revolutionary war but revolutionary defense of the country of the proletarian dictatorship. To negotiate a peace was the best way to meet this need. "We are now signing a peace treaty," said he, "we have a respite, we are taking advantage of it to defend our fatherland better." [28]

That the cessation of armed hostilities was the immediate internal and external necessity for the Soviets after they came into power was admitted later by Stalin at the Sixth Party Congress, when he said that in those days Russia was facing two possibilities:

"Either the war was to be ended, all economic ties with the capitalist world severed, revolution pushed ahead . . . or the war was to be continued, which meant subordination to Allied capital and the triumph of the counter revolution. There was no third way out." [29]

The expectation of Lenin proved not ill-founded: internally the appeal for peace helped the Bolsheviks in mobilizing not only the Russian standing army, but also the workers and peasants for the purpose of solidifying the new revolutionary régime. The external repercussions, however, were disappointing. The first sign of the the difficulties which were to follow became evident at Brest-Litovsk.

[26] Speech at the Plenary Session of the Centr. Exec. Com., the Moscow Soviet of Workers' Deputies and the Representatives of Trade Unions and Factory Communities, May 14, 1918 (*Protokoly Zasedanii Vserossiiskogo Tsentral'nogo Komiteta 4-go Sozyva*, pp. 265ff.).

[27] Lenin, XV, 128.

[28] *Ibid.*, p. 127.

[29] Lenin and Stalin, *Sbornik proizvedenii k izucheniiu istorii VKP (b)*, I, p. 847.

The Soviet proposals at the opening session of the Brest-Litovsk Conference consisted of the following six major points: (1) the renunciation of forcible annexations and the evacuation of occupied areas; (2) the restoration of full political independence to peoples who had lost it during the war; (3) the granting of the right of self-determination to peoples who had not enjoyed political independence before; (4) a full guaranty of cultural independence and administrative autonomy for minorities; (5) the renunciation of war indemnities; and (6) an agreement that colonial questions be decided on the basis of the first four points.

While outwardly these proposals may appear as concrete bases for a just peace, which would effectively terminate the "imperialist" war, intrinsically they were vanguard tactics of revolutionaries contemplating a rapid conquest of the world. To one familiar with the arguments which took place between Kühlmann and Joffe, the reason why the latter and his colleagues had to leave Brest-Litovsk on December 29th, without carrying home the desired peace, is quite understandable: the Plenipotentiaries of Imperial Germany could not endorse the principles in the form in which they were presented by the delegates of proletarian Russia.

On January 5, 1918, Joffe was replaced by Trotzky who left Petrograd for Brest-Litovsk to continue peace negotiations. On February 10th, he terminated them when he refused to attach "the signature of the Russian revolution to terms which carry with them oppression, sorrow, and misery for millions of human lives," and pronounced his now celebrated formula "we are out of the war but we refuse to sign the peace treaty." [30]

Irritated though it must have been, the Soviet Government at first sanctioned, over Lenin's objections, this notion of "no war, no peace." The result of this disregard of Lenin's warning was that German troops commenced an immediate and rapid advance in the direction of Petrograd. This brought about a realization that neither the policy of the extreme leftists nor that of Trotzky was practical. The continuation of the war no longer promised the defeat of Germany, advocated by the former, and the German Generalkommando did not see fit to accept the cataclysmal status of "no war, no peace," proposed by Trotzky. The war policy was abandoned, and Lenin's insistence that the demands of the enemy be complied with was now

[30] *Sovetskii Soiuz v Bor'be za Mir,* p. 41.

considered the only course possible if the Bolshevist revolution was to survive. The price which the Soviets paid for Trotzky's error is well known: instead of the Brest-Litovsk Peace desired by Lenin, communist Russia fell prey to the Brest-Litovsk dictates of General Hoffmann.

The signing of the Peace Treaty with Germany on March 3, 1918, marked the end of the initial phase of the first period of Soviet aspirations for peace, and was a milestone in communist interpretation of peace. Under the spell of the rapid success at home, the revolutionary hopes of the Soviets soared high that the coveted ideal of the Marxian world was well within practical reach. Even the compelling necessity of the Brest-Litovsk surrender did not seem to indicate a long postponement of the ultimate coming of the warless and peaceless commonwealth of stateless and classless nations. To the new masters of Russia, it was merely a subsidiary tactical move. In other words, while the war during these few months was for Russian communists simultaneously a theoretical condemnable imperialistic outrage and a welcome revolutionary prerequisite, concretely, peace was to them synonymous with immediate world revolution, *i.e.*, to the undelayed materialization of the Marxian ideology.

CIVIL WAR AND FOREIGN INTERVENTION

Induced by this halt of the communist hope for an immediate world revolution, the actual retreat of the Soviet peace policy commenced with the signing of the Brest-Litovsk Treaty. From the standpoint of Lenin's revolutionary tactics, this treaty was a vehicle designed to overcome the need for a strategic material peace to safeguard the revolution at home. To put it again in the words of Lenin:

"Under the circumstances, the only way out was the temporary breathing spell which we secured by signing the Brest Peace, a breathing spell which . . . enabled the majority of Russian soldiers to return to their homes, to take advantage of the conquest of the revolution, to take over the land, to look around, and to gather new strength for the sacrifices that were ahead of them." [31]

[31] That this treaty was actually a temporary "retreat" was proved on November 13, 1918. When, after the defeat, Germany was going through the turmoil of her own revolution, and when the events there indicated that she would follow the footsteps of the Russian Empire, the Soviets no longer considered her dangerous. The Brest-Litovsk Treaty was annulled. *(Sobr. Uzak. i Rasp. R.S.F.S.R., 1917–1918,* p. 1207).

He also admitted that events had placed the Soviets in an extraordinarily difficult position. In fact, the cause of the Bolshevist revolution was considered hopeless if there were no revolutionary movements in other countries, and Lenin warned his comrades that they must be ready to suffer a number of humiliating defeats. True, these defeats were not considered to be the convulsions of a dying organism, but rather strategic retreats in an unprecedented revolutionary battle. The solution was to be sought not in the extent of the retreat but in the calmness of its execution. That the situation was indeed far from promising can be judged from Lenin's own resort to the help of God, when, atheist though he was, he said: "God grant that we retreat in perfect order. If we cannot retreat in perfect order, then God grant that we retreat in semi-order." [32]

The trials thus predicted by Lenin, which the Soviets had to face during this retreat, were not limited to the need of peace with Germany alone. The Brest-Litovsk "episode" over, the communist rulers of Russia were confronted with a new danger, likewise calling for the necessity of peace in the material sense of the term.

The independent withdrawal of the Soviet Union from the war, the open revolt of the conservative elements against the Red rule so ruthlessly imposed upon them, and the opportunities for independence which the various nationalities in Russia saw in the situation, all resulted in unprecedented turmoil which presented the Soviets with a three-fold task, a struggle for the protection of their own revolutionary achievements, for the prevention of further disintegration of the communist empire, and for the propagation of the revolutionary cause beyond the political boundaries of Russia, which item was still on their agenda, in spite of the lesson of Brest-Litovsk. Civil war, foreign intervention, and the struggle with the neighboring peoples in the west were the new trial, while revolutionary appeals, individual peace treaties and attempts at collective bargaining were the outward manifestations of the Soviet longing for peace during the next few years.

Numerous volumes have been written on the Russian Civil War. Memoirs, scholarly treatises, and official documents are now available on the subject. Their ample information precludes the necessity of repeating here the substance of the non-communist opposition to the Soviets, or the circumstances under which the anti-Bolshevik armies

[32] Lenin, XV, 120.

came into being; the sequence of events on the various fronts to the north, west, south, and east of the Kremlin where the respective armies of Generals Miller, Yudenich, Denikin, and Vrangel, and of Admiral Kolchak fought the Red forces of Lenin and Trotzky, Voroshilov and Stalin; or the reasons which caused the failure of the armed counter-revolution. Nor is it necessary to enumerate here the places at the four corners of the world to which the remnants of the "whites" were led on their *via dolorosa* after the ultimate triumph of the dictatorial proletariat of the R.S.F.S.R.

Strictly speaking, enormous as was the sacrifice of human life, the armed conflicts between the two Russian factions, separated from each other by the political abyss of communism, could readily be considered a purely domestic Soviet problem. As such, the Russian Civil War actually had no bearing upon the communist conception of international war and peace.

The actual reason for the Soviet victory matters little. Procommunists may well argue that Lenin's promise of a glorious future had a stronger appeal than his opponents' references to the record of the past, or that communist propaganda was a much more effective weapon than the strategic superiority of the anti-Bolshevik leaders in things military. Their opponents can with no less justification say that the geographical dissemination of the White forces was no match for the Bolshevist unity of command, or that the Allied help given to the anti-communist cause, coincident as it was with simultaneous overtures of Paris and London to the Kremlin, could hardly be as effective as the Soviet independent reliance on their own resources.[33]

The importance of the civil war lies in the fact that it induced the intervention of the foreign powers and brought about the Baltic wars for national independence. It goes without saying that these factors transformed the domestic Soviet armed conflict of 1918–1922 into an international conflict affording another instance in which the Marxian theoretical conception of war and peace and its application in practice can be further studied.

The foreign intervention calls for three separate brief studies: the German intervention, the participation of the Allies in the Rus-

[33] For bibliographies on the civil war in Russia, *cf.* Bunyan, *Intervention, Civil War, and Communism in Russia* (Baltimore, 1936), and Stewart, *The White Armies of Russia* (New York, 1933).

sian civil war, and the Soviet continuation of revolutionary appeals to the masses beyond the political boundaries of the R.S.F.S.R.

In the pandemonium of the revolutionary confusion which reigned supreme, it was not long before unpleasant news began to reach Moscow. The Japanese regiments landed at Vladivostok. The Don Cossacks had arisen against the Soviets. The Czechoslovak regiments, formed as fighting units against Germany, had turned against the Kremlin and refused to surrender their arms. The Transcaucasian Republic was dissolved. Tomsk had been captured by the "whites"; Omsk, Samara, and Vladivostok, by the Czechoslovaks. The Orenburg Cossacks had started an offensive against the Bolsheviks. So had the Volunteer Army in the Northern Caucasus. Siberia had separated from Moscow by declaring itself an independent republic. Simbirsk had been captured by the volunteers of the Samara Government. The Allied forces had landed at Archangel. American troops had arrived at the same port, and at Vladivostok. Baku had been taken by the Turks. With the growing success of the revolt against the Kremlin, an All-Russian, anti-Bolshevist provisional government had been elected at the Ufa conference. The death of General Alexeev in the South was a signal for General Denikin to take his place and to give new vigor to the anti-Bolshevist cause.

Such was the succession of alarming events which took place in the regions free from German control during the first eight months of Russia's peace with Germany. Having anticipated them, however, on purely theoretical grounds, the Soviet masters of new Russia were hardly surprised at all this.

Developments in the west, however, caused a different reaction. The point is that the Brest-Litovsk Treaty did not stop the German advance beyond the line of demarcation fixed by that treaty. In addition to the occupation of Finland, the Baltic Provinces, Poland, Lithuania, and White Russia, the German penetration extended southward to the Don region and Crimea, as well as northward into Kursk and Voronezh provinces.

With an indignation both just and revolutionary, Chicherin, the Soviet People's Commissar for Foreign Affairs, on April 27, 1918, dispatched a protest against such violation of the Brest-Litovsk Treaty,[34] but it proved of no avail. Instead of stopping military

[34] *Svoboda Rossii*, No. 15, April 28, 1918, p. 2 (quoted in Bunyan, *Intervention, Civil War and Communism in Russia*, p. 114). *Cf.* also his earlier protest of April 21, 1918, against German occupation of Crimea (*Izvestiia*, April 25, 1918).

operations, the Germans launched an even more aggressive policy toward the Bolsheviks. On the very next day the Ukrainian Rada was overthrown, and twenty-four hours later General Skoropadsky was proclaimed Hetman of the Ukraine. This was soon followed by a demand to cede to Finland Fort Ino, important for the defense of Petrograd.[35] This Russia did.

The strained situation between the Soviets and the German Empire continued for some time without any signs of improvement. Powerless, communist diplomats were compelled to adopt a waiting policy and "to gain as much time as possible in order to allow the growing proletarian movement in other countries to mature," [36] while the German Generalkommando remained unwilling to yield the advantages derived from their penetration into the richest regions of Russia.

On October 4, 1918, *i.e.*, at the time when Ludendorff was on the verge of admitting the imminence of Germany's collapse, Lenin was penning his letter to the All-Russian Central Executive Committee in which he said that a political crisis indicating a trend toward revolution was taking place in Germany. In this message he also says that the Russian proletariat is "not only watching these developments intently and jubilantly, but is discussing the problem of how to gather forces to help the German workers, who are bound to face . . . a most intensive struggle against their own [German] and British imperialism." [37] The tenor of his statements suggests and later events proved that he was more than hoping at the time. Lenin knew what was taking place in Germany, and the source of his information was none other than Joffe, Soviet Ambassador at the Imperial Court in Berlin. Acting in "perfect" bad faith, Joffe worked zealously against the Government to which he was accredited. Propaganda through tons of printed matter and political pressure through bribery were the evidence submitted by him to prove that "in the preparation of the German Revolution, the Russian Embassy worked all the time in close contact with the German Socialists." [38] The inevitable result came only too soon. The *Drang nach Vaterland* which preoccupied the minds of the tired German soldiers in the

[35] Within shelling distance of the Fortress of Kronstadt.
[36] Chicherin's report to the Fifth Congress of Soviets, July 5, 1918 (*Izvestiia*, July 5, 1918, p. 6).
[37] Lenin, XV, 389–390.
[38] Fischer, *op. cit.*, p. 75.

Baltic, Poland, and the Ukraine found its counterpart in the *Drang aus Vaterland* which was being prepared for the Soviet Representative Plenipotentiary by their not less tired compatriot diplomats in Berlin.[39] On November 5, 1918, Joffe and his ambassadorial staff received orders to evacuate the Berlin Embassy. Soon after that the trains carrying German troops and Joffe must have met somewhere:[40] The former were on their way back to their Deutschland. Joffe, to his R.S.F.S.R.

While the German Revolution brought renewed hopes,[41] in the field of communist revolutionary aspirations, the relief which the Soviets expected from it in regard to peace proved a mere illusion. True, Hetman Skoropadsky had to leave the Ukraine simultaneously with the withdrawal of the German and Austrian divisions.[42] In Finland, General Mannerheim was left to find new sources of aid and support. The few volunteers who saw no prospects in their revolutionary Germany, and preferred to remain in the Baltic countries to fight the virus which wrought havoc in their own fatherland, presented no real military force.[43] In reality, however, the change in Germany could not have much effect on the Soviet situation, as the German occupation of Russian provinces was a minor incident in the much greater problem which confronted the Kremlin. Aside from the civil war itself, the Allied intervention was the main issue in point.

It has already been pointed out that the Allied troops had appeared in Russia long before the November events in Germany. With war silenced at home, it did not take long for them to cut short the relief which the Soviets enjoyed on the western and southern fronts of their civil war after the German exodus from the Baltic Provinces, Poland, and the Ukraine.

[39] On the abolition of the customary diplomatic ranks by the Soviets, *cf.* Taracouzio, *op. cit.*, p. 165.

[40] On November 5, 1918, Joffe and his staff received orders to evacuate the Berlin Embassy and return to Russia. This was reported by Chicherin a year later to the Seventh Congress of Soviets in the following statement, rather paradoxical from a revolutionary standpoint: "The rising revolutionary wave in Germany gradually forced the technical diplomatic work into the background. On November 5 . . . our Embassy, including the different commissions, was expelled from Germany" (*Izvestiia,* Nov. 6, 1919). The relations between the two countries were resumed only in 1922 (*infra,* p. 115).

[41] *Cf. Izvestiia,* Nov. 10, 1918, and ff. On German occupation and its end, *cf. Krakh Germanskoi Okkupatsii na Ukraine* (Moscow, 1936).

[42] On opportunities missed by the Soviets in this connection, *cf. infra.,* pp. 88ff.

[43] Most of them joined Bermondt' troops in Mitau.

It was on November 26, 1918, *i.e.,* within less than ten days after the Armistice, that the French detachments found their way to the northwestern shores of the Black Sea, and the British forces arrived to help Denikin in the southeastern regions of Russia as well as their own troops already in Archangel and Vladivostok. The end of the German intervention simply meant the consolidation of the intervention by the Allies.

For a better understanding of this, a skeleton review of the Allied rôle in the Russian Civil War may be permitted. Usually, the very notion of intervention suggests unfriendliness. Much as there was of animosity between the Kremlin and the Allies, the latter came to Russia at first not as enemies but as Allies in the Great War. Two factors contributed to this original friendliness soon after the November Revolution between the Bolsheviks and their ultimate foes. On the one hand, after the downfall of Kerensky, the powers at war with Germany were reluctant to lose Russia as a fighting force in the east. On the other hand, the uncertainty of the Brest-Litovsk negotiations prompted the Soviets not to disregard completely Allied help in case Germany should continue her march of conquest eastward.

Early in March, 1918, a small British detachment landed at Murmansk, soon to be reinforced by others at Archangel and Vladivostok, and by former Czechoslovak prisoners of war who by that time had been released to be transported from Russia to the western front by way of the latter city. The readiness of the Soviets to collaborate with the British in their plans to reëstablish the eastern front in Russia was not so innocent, however, as it appeared on the surface. It must be remembered that the old Imperial Army had by this time ceased to exist; its officers had been persecuted by their former soldiers who were hurrying home to divide the land of the dispossessed landlords. It should not be forgotten either that Lenin foresaw the struggle that lay ahead and was more than concerned with the problem of forming a new army, a Red Army, to protect the gains of the Revolution. Hence there is room for skepticism, as to whether the real reason for the early rapprochement of the "proletarian" revolutionaries with the bourgeois Allies was the formal assurance of friendship or the Soviet desire to secure the assistance of Allied military experts in the organization of the Red Army.[44]

[44] For Lenin's viewpoint of this, *cf., infra,* p. 265.

The further developments proved discouraging for peace, though at first the Soviets had good reasons to be satisfied. The Allies became involved in discord in handling the Russian situation: Great Britain was in favor of intervention against Germany; France and Japan wanted intervention against the Bolsheviks; while the United States, for obvious reasons, was keeping its troops in Archangel and was opposed to any intervention in the Far East.[45] The Germans, at this time, after having secured peace on the eastern front, were too busy on the western front to disturb the Kremlin with annihilation of the Soviet régime. Soon, however, the Soviets not only learned that harmony had been restored among the Allies, but that the latter were making additional landings in Archangel and Vladivostok—a help no longer wanted under the circumstances. These arrivals were interpreted by the Soviets as the beginning of an intervention directed against themselves. The flow of protests in the form of official diplomatic communiqués and informal revolutionary appeals to the masses abroad commenced at once. Inaugurated with the proclamation of the Council of Peoples' Commissars of April 5, 1918, protesting against the Japanese landing at Vladivostok, and inviting the "workers and peasants, [and] honest citizens" to resist the imperialistic "attack" from the east, it was followed by Chicherin's note to the French Government demanding the recall of the French Ambassador, Noulens.[46]

The complications which arose in connection with the disposition of the Czechoslovak legions [47] resulted in open warfare between

[45] For a brief outline of the Allied intervention and selected documents, cf. Bunyan, op. cit., pp. 60ff.

[46] Full English text of both documents, in Bunyan, op. cit., pp. 68–70 and 72, respectively.

[47] The chronological outline of these events is as follows: On March 16, 1918, the Soviet Commander in Chief granted permission to the Czechoslovaks to leave the Ukraine. On the 22nd day of the same month, the Omsk Soviet ordered the stopping of their echelons. On the 26th, the Soviet Government repealed the order of the Omsk Soviet and granted passage to Vladivostok. On April 12th, a confirmatory order was issued. Disappointed by the slow progress of their transportation, the Czechoslovaks threatened resistance to Soviet obstructions (April 14, 1918). One week later, Chicherin wired to the Siberian Soviets that the Soviet Government had ordered the Czech eastward movement stopped. On April 26th, the French proposed to hasten the transportation. On May 20th, the Council of Peoples' Commissars ordered the Czechoslovak units to disband. On the 21st, their own delegates at Moscow ordered them to surrender arms. On May 22nd, the Czech decision was not to comply with the orders. On May 25th, Trotzky, then People's Commissar for War, issued his orders to have the Czechoslovaks disarmed. The reply to this was that the Czechs became the confrères of the Whites in arms, fighting on the side of the anti-Bolsheviks and their sponsors, the Allies (ibid., pp. 75–100).

them and the Soviets. This clash may be considered the direct cause of the official break between the Soviets and the Allies. To Trotzky's orders of May 25, 1918, to disarm the Czechoslovak troops, the Allies replied by lodging a formal protest against the Soviet attempts to do so. To this, Chicherin, on June 12, 1918, responded with a note to the Allied diplomatic representatives, stating, among other things that "the Czechoslovaks acted in coöperation with the White Guards." [48] Trotzky, who only three months earlier had welcomed the British at Murmansk, on June 22, 1918, came out with an open denunciation of the Allied intervention saying that the Soviets "cannot regard the intervention of the Allied imperialists in any other light than as a hostile attempt against the freedom and independence of Soviet Russia." [49]

By now events were moving rapidly. On July 2, 1918, the Supreme War Council decided formally in favor of intervention in Russia.[50] On July 12, Chicherin lodged the Soviet protest against British intervention and assured the Allies that the Red Army was ready to "meet foreign invasion with the most determined resistance." [51] As this had no effect, on the 29th day of the same month, Lenin, speaking before a joint session of the Central Executive Committee, the Moscow Soviet, and the representatives of trade unions, declared a state of war to exist between Soviet Russia and "Anglo-French imperialism," while the Central Executive Committee resolved to consider "the socialist fatherland in danger." [52] Lenin's declaration was repudiated by Chicherin on the following day on the ground that it was not a formal declaration of a war *de jure*.[53] The Soviet appeal, issued on August 1, 1918, to the Toiling Masses of England, America, France, Italy, and Japan leaves little doubt, however, that the relations between the Allies and the Kremlin had become nothing short of war *de facto*.[54] This was substantiated, furthermore, by the appeals which the Soviets sent in rapid succes-

[48] Kliuchnikov i Sabanin, *Mezhdunarodnaia politika noveishogo vremeni v dogovorakh, notakh i deklaratsiiakh*, II, pp. 144–146.

[49] Trotzky, *Kak vooruzhalas' revoliutsiia*, I, p. 199.

[50] *U. S. Foreign Relations*, 1918, II, pp. 245–246.

[51] *Izvestiia*, July 13, 1918.

[52] Lenin, XXIII, 163, and *Piatyi Sozyv Vserossiiskogo Tsentral'nago Ispol'nitel'nogo Komiteta Sovetov Rabochikh, Krest'ianskikh, Kazach'ikh i Krasnoarmeiskikh Deputatov*, pp. 8–9, respectively.

[53] *Cf.* a note of Aug. 6, 1918, from Chicherin to D. C. Poole, the U. S. Consul in Moscow (*Sovetskii Soiuz v Bor'be za Mir*, pp. 47ff.).

[54] Kliuchnikov i Sabanin, *op. cit.*, II, pp. 158–161.

sion to the Allied Governments, asking them to bring peace to the peoples of Europe and Russia.[55] These ranged from accusations that the Allies desired to reinstate the "worst tyranny in the world—the detested Tsarist Government" to suggestions that the Soviets, in order to "avert the further ruining of Russia which must result from continuation of internal and external fighting," were "prepared to go to any length in making concessions, as far as the interests of their country are concerned, if they can thereby secure conditions enabling them peacefully to work out their social schemes." [56] Persistent though they were, these diplomatic efforts proved of no avail. Relief from the Allied intervention was secured to the R.S.F.S.R. not by pleas or threats. Nor was it the result of Red superiority over British and French soldiers in the field. Developments in Europe forced the Allies to terminate their intervention of their own accord.

It has been said that the withdrawal of the German and Austrian divisions from Russia merely meant consolidation of Allied aggression there. However, the plans of the Allies for intervention were to suffer an unforeseen set-back almost from the very beginning of their taking over complete control of the destinies of their Russian anti-Bolshevist confrères.

Indeed, there is no doubt that the first three months of 1919 were the most trying for the victorious Allies in Europe. The worries of the Peace Conference over the settlement with Germany rivaled the worries of the governments over the threat of social upheaval caused by general disillusionment and fatigue. The fear of Lloyd George that intervention might drive Germany into the hands of the R.S.F.S.R. equalled the fear of Churchill that Bolshevism might

[55] Of these outstanding were the already mentioned note (F. N. 53) of Chicherin to Mr. Poole, of Aug. 6, 1918; the Soviet note to President Wilson, of Oct. 24, 1918; the formal proposal of peace made by the Soviets to the Entente Powers through their representation remaining in Moscow, Nov. 4, 1918; the confirmation of this proposal by the special resolution of the Extraordinary Congress of Soviets on Nov. 8, 1918; Litvinov's exhaustive note of Dec. 24, 1918, to President Wilson; Chicherin's peace proposal of Jan. 12, 1919, to the United States; similar proposals to the Allies made through Stockholm on Jan. 14 and 17; finally, the proposal of immediate peace made by the Seventh All-Russian Congress of Soviets on Dec. 5, 1919. (*Sovetskii Soiuz v Bor'be za Mir*, pp. 84ff.). On the Prinkipo Conference and the Bullitt mission, *cf.*, *infra*, p. 90. For other documents, see Kliuchnikov i Sabanin, *op. cit.*

[56] Chicherin's note to Poole of Aug. 6, 1918, and Litvinov's note to Woodrow Wilson of Dec. 24, 1918, respectively (*ibid.*, pp. 47 and 60, respectively). *Cf.* also accusations made against the Allied diplomatic representatives by the Council of Peoples' Commissars on Sept. 2, 1918 (*Izvestiia*, Sept. 3, 1918).

become an immediate issue in the British realm. With British and French troops actually in Russia, the tendency of Paris to limit its "cordon sanitaire" to the mere supplying of gold and guns to the Russian White armies, was paralleled by London's lack of interest in operations of actual warfare against the Bolsheviks, due to the pressure of labor and liberals. The result of all this indecision was that early in April, 1919, the French support of anti-Bolshevists in Russia came to an end. Odessa was evacuated and French troops were withdrawn from the shores infected with revolutionary unrest, but not before the Red flag had been raised on French warships which necessitated the disarming of the revolutionized white French contingents by their own more stable Senegalese units and Greek battalions.[57] Simultaneously, British plans for withdrawal from South Russia and the Caucasus began to mature.

The peace which the Soviets might have expected, under the circumstances, was not yet to become an actuality, however. The successful advances of Admiral Kolchak from Siberia changed the situation. The position of the anti-Bolsheviks no longer appeared hopeless, in spite of the reverses suffered by Denikin in the south, for in addition to the communist retreat on the Ural front, Yudenich was now ready to launch his first offensive against Petrograd. Then, on May 7, 1919, the Peace Treaty between the Allies and Germany was completed, and the peace-makers at Versailles were now free to look into the Russian problem more thoroughly. Intervention gained renewed momentum and the communists had another year and a half ahead of them before the issue was settled by a definite victory for the Red cause.[58]

Soviet efforts to make peace with the anti-Bolshevik Russians and with the intervening Allies were not restricted to actual resistance by arms. There was another method which the Soviets expected to be of use—revolutionary propaganda. This was applicable equally to the German occupation,[59] to the Russian counter-revolutionaries, and to the Allied intervention.

The appeal of the Soviet Government of August 1, 1918, to the Toilers of the Allied countries has been already mentioned.[60] There

[57] B. Vinogradov, *Miravoi proletariat i S.S.S.R.*, pp. 57ff.

[58] For a bibliography on Russian Civil War and the Allied intervention, *cf.* Stewart, *The White Armies of Russia*, N. Y., 1933.

[59] *Supra*, p. 75.

[60] *Supra*, p. 79.

can be no two meanings as to the Soviet conviction expressed therein that

"every measure taken against those who are hatching conspiracies on Russian soil against the Russian Revolution will meet with your sincere sympathy because these conspiracies are directed against us." [61]

Nor is there any mystery as to the meaning of the appeal made in the concluding paragraph of this document addressed to the workers of the world to unite for the sake of overthrowing the "bandits of international imperialism."

The diplomatic correspondence in regard to the White and Red Terror, from September 5 to 12, 1918; [62] the above-mentioned resolutions of support to the German revolutionaries; [63] the official Soviet greeting to the Communist government of Hungary, April 9, 1919; Chicherin's appeal to the toiling masses of Persia, August 30, 1919; a similar appeal to the workers of Turkey, September 13, 1919; Chicherin's appeal to the workers in the Allied countries calling for their protest against the blockade of the R.S.F.S.R., April 19, 1919; the resolutions of the Seventh All-Russian Congress of Soviets, adopted on December 5, 1919; [64] and, finally, the concrete form which the Soviet propaganda took in September, 1920, when the first Congress of the Peoples of the East convened at Baku, [65] —are only a few of the documentary evidences that the Soviet search for peace was not limited to fighting by military forces or through diplomatic channels. Leading the Soviets and the world toward peace by means of international revolution was another of the Kremlin's tactics, the sanction for which was found not only in concrete expediency, but also in the appearance in Moscow of the Third International. If expediency can rightly be considered as the determinant in the field of concrete revolutionary policies of the Soviets, the Comintern, formed on March 4, 1919, became their spiritual sponsor.

Convoked in the midst of the civil war, the Comintern based its work on the theoretical theses read by Lenin before the Eighth Congress of the Russian Communist Party.[66] By issuing a Manifesto

---

[61] *Sovetskii Soiuz v Bor'be za Mir,* pp. 60ff.

[62] Kliuchnikov i Sabanin, *op. cit.,* pp. 167ff.

[63] *Supra,* p. 75.

[64] Kliuchnikov i Sabanin, *op. cit.,* pp. 341, 384, 238, and 420, respectively.

[65] *Pervyi S'ezd Narodov Vostoka. Baku 1–8 sentiabria 1920* (Petrograd, 1920).

[66] *Kommunisticheskii Internatsional v Dokumentakh, 1919–1932* (Moscow, 1933) and *Rossiiskaia Kommunisticheskaia Partiia (b). Vos'moi S'ezd. 18–23 Marta 1919g. Resoliutsii i Postanovleniia* (Moscow, 1920).

to the proletariat of the world in which it pledged the allegiance of the communists to the principles of world revolution as laid down in 1847 by Marx in his Communist Manifesto, the Third International became actually a society for revolutionary propaganda.[67] That its immediate aim was not limited to the teaching of abstract ideologies but included also peace for the Soviets is evident from the instructions which it issued to the toiling masses of the world. In brief, these instructions were that the following demands should be made by the workers abroad upon their respective governments: (a) termination of the intervention in Russia, (b) non-interference in Russia's domestic affairs, (c) immediate withdrawal of the Allied troops from the R.S.F.S.R., (d) recognition of the Soviets and resumption of diplomatic relations, (e) the invitation of the Soviets to the Peace Conference, (f) lifting of the economic blockade, and (g) resumption of trade with the Soviets.[68]

No great difference in regard to Soviet aspirations for peace is found either in the work of the Second Congress of the Comintern which took place from July 19 to August 7, 1920. Amid lengthy discussions and resolutions bearing upon the various aspects of world revolution, the idea of securing peace for the R.S.F.S.R. by way of revolutions in other countries was by no means forgotten. In fact, it was formally admitted that the "Communist International had declared the cause of Soviet Russia to be its own cause, [and that] the international proletariat will not lay down its arms until Soviet Russia had become a member of a World Federation of Soviet Republics." [69] A suggestion as to how peace, which is the prerequisite for such a federation, can be achieved by the Soviets may be deduced from the solemn declaration that "civil war in the whole world has become the issue of the day, the Soviet Government being its symbol." [70] A much more concrete appeal for peace was made at this Second Congress in the resolutions adopted in regard to the Soviet war with Poland. The world proletariat was solemnly urged to exert all its influence, even through revolution if necessary, that the aid of the Allies to Poland should cease and that the peace between Moscow and Warsaw might enable the transformation of

---

[67] For Zinov'ev's admission of this at the Second Congress of the Comintern, cf., 2–i Kongress Kommunisticheskogo Internatsionala, Stenograficheskii Otchet, p. 193. Cf. also, Lenin XXIV, 25ff.

[68] Kommunisticheskii Internatsional v Dokumentakh, 1919–1932, pp. 87–88.

[69] Ibid., p. 152.

[70] Ibid., p. 152.

non-communist Polonia Restituta to the Polish Socialist Soviet Republic.[71]

The grand total of the Allied intervention is well known; it was unique in that there were virtually no losers in the struggle. The Allies had their victory: the Red flag was never hoisted in Western European capitals,[72] Russia was conveniently made weaker so as not to be in a position to have her voice heard at the Peace Conference, and a solid belt of buffer states from the Baltic to the Black Sea was set up as a *cordon politique* against Red influences. The Soviets had theirs: the Red flag was not hauled down from the Kremlin and continues to fly there.

Wars against Limitrophe Neighbors

So much for the Allied intervention. The Soviet wars with the Baltic States, with Finland and with Poland was the other aspect of the civil war which became an international problem for the Kremlin. The revolution in Germany and the Armistice not only resulted in the ultimate replacement of the German and Austrian divisions in the Baltic, Poland, and the Ukraine by the Allies, but offered the Bolsheviks an opportunity to extend their proletarian domain westward. The dilemma with which these countries were confronted and the failure of the Soviets to take advantage of the opportunity now belong to history.

Two facts must be recalled. First, the Treaty of Versailles, which abrogated the Brest-Litovsk Treaty, did not force upon Germany an immediate withdrawal of its troops from the occupied territories. This was to take place "as soon as the governments of the Principal and Associated Powers shall think suitable, having regard to the internal situation of these territories." [73] Second, the Baltic Governments, formed under German occupation, could remain in power only as long as they were protected by some greater power. Their size, the absence of any military force of their own to speak of,[74] and the peculiar Soviet procedure of effecting national self-determination were against them.

[71] *Kommunisticheskii Internatsional v. Dokumentakh, 1919–1932*, pp. 161–162.

[72] The communist régimes of Bela Kun in Hungary and Kurt Eisner in Munich were short-lived.

[73] Article 433.

[74] Only Latvia had its own army, but it was a Red Army. Drawn from the Latvian communists in Russia and commanded by Vazetis, it was a foe of the non-communist Letts rather than a welcome protection for their national interests.

The situation became ambiguous indeed. Anxious to have a belt of non-communist states to separate them from the Soviets, the Allies at the same time were in no position to send their own troops to protect these limitrophe states. A solution was found by giving practical application to the above-mentioned provision of Article 433 of the Versailles Treaty of Peace. The German troops were permitted to remain for a while in the Baltic. Berlin was only too glad to take political advantage of Allied short-sightedness. Its enjoyment was short-lived, however, for soon pressure was brought to bear to halt the operations of German troops in these states. General von der Goltz and his forces were ordered to withdraw. By the time this took place, however, the Baltic States had had their "breathing spell": the Red forces were now confronted not only with their national non-communist forces, but also with Yudenich's battalions in Estonia, a mixture of Russian and German volunteers in Latvia and Lithuania, and Poles in White Russia.[75] The Soviet wars with their western neighbors started.

While the Versailles Treaty, in abrogating the Brest-Litovsk Treaty, permitted the Germans to stay in the Baltics, Soviet abrogation of the same, particularly of the clauses regarding the transfer of territories, was followed by an appeal to the toiling masses of Estonia, Latvia, Lithuania, Finland, and Poland, "freed from the yoke of an oppressive treaty dictated by German militarists" to decide their own fate. The real meaning of this Soviet magnanimity was made clear six weeks later, when, on December 23, 1918, as a farewell to the now "revolutionary" German regiments returning to their fatherland from the Baltic provinces, the Central Executive Committee of the R.S.F.S.R. recognized Estonia, Latvia, and Lithuania as independent Soviet Republics,[76] and offered their communist governments [77] "all necessary aid and support."

[75] Finland, at this juncture, had its well-established government recognized by the Allies. For Soviet-Polish war, cf., infra, pp. 88ff.

[76] Kliuchnikov i Sabanin, *Mezhdunarodnaia Politika noveishogo vremeni v dogovorakh, rotakh ideklaratsiiakh,* II, pp. 208–209. Their independence was recognized by the Council of Peoples' Commissars a few days earlier: Estonia, on Dec. 8, 1918, and Latvia and Lithuania, on Dec. 22, 1918 (*ibid.,* p. 206, and *Sobr. Uzak. i Rasp. R.S.F.S.R.,* 1917–1918, II, pp. 1267–1268, respectively). Independence of Finland was recognized on Jan. 4, 1918 (*ibid.,* 1917–1918, I, p. 166). In accord with the Soviet political ambitions expressed in these recognitions is the Soviet refusal to recognize the independence of Georgia (Decree of Dec. 24, 1918, *ibid.,* II, p. 1272).

[77] This policy of the Soviets to form "Soviet" governments for other countries was repeated twenty-two years later, when in December, 1939, the Finnish communist government of Kuussinen was brought into being in Moscow and promptly recognized as the legitimate authority of Finland.

Indicative as it was of communist expansionist designs, this recognition was not only belated, but somewhat paradoxical. The population of these former Russian provinces at that time was not only opposed to any form of Sovietism, but was taking up arms to defend its own destinies, and giving shelter to the anti-Bolshevist units of Yudenich, Bermondt, and others whom they considered as needed and welcome allies in the forthcoming struggle against the Red invasion.

The new danger which this turn of events added to the already precarious situation of the Soviets was only too obvious: troops had to be rushed to this section from other fronts where they were needed more than ever, as the anti-Bolshevist front itself was gradually moving toward Moscow, circling closer and closer to the Kremlin and what was left of the proletarian R.S.F.S.R.

When, after alternate successes on both sides during the nine months of the struggle, General Yudenich launched his last drive on Petrograd in October, 1919, the gravity of the Soviet situation was admitted by Lenin himself, who addressed the workers of Petrograd saying, October 17, that "the decisive moment had arrived," and that in a few days "the fate of Petrograd, one of the citadels of Soviet authority in Russia," [78] was to be decided. As is well known, Yudenich never reached his goal, and soon was forced to abandon the cause altogether.

Individual sentiment may picture different reasons for the Soviet victory. Extreme nationalists may think that the capture of Petrograd by the "Whites" was inopportune and not in the scheme of things planned by the Allies. Communists may well advance a revolutionary theory, namely, that the real cause is to be sought in the fear of the Baltic peoples that non-communist Russia was going to force upon them the pre-war *status quo*,[79] while military strategists are ready to argue that tactical errors, suggestive even of actual treason, were at the bottom of the reverses suffered by the anti-Bolshevist forces.[80]

This, however, is not the point. The fact is that although peace was needed by the Soviets more than ever, it was needed not for the mere sake of bringing to an end the actual physical struggle as

[78] Oct. 17, 1919.

[79] *Cf.* Margulies, *God interventsii*, II, 193.

[80] *Cf.*, for instance, the failure of Gen. Vetrenko to cut through the railroad connecting Petrograd and Moscow, contrary to the orders received (*ibid.*, III, 111).

was the case in the civil war proper. Here much more important considerations came into play, which prompted the Soviets to seek for peace in spite of the fact that the general situation might have suggested an opposite course in regard to the "Soviet" republics in the Baltic.

Indeed, by the time Petrograd had been saved, the Soviets had met with partial successes on their other fronts also. Denikin was forced to commence his retreat to the Black Sea. By the end of January, 1920, Archangel was taken by the Red Army, and on February 7, Admiral Kolchak met his death by a Soviet firing squad, with his army in full retreat to the shores of the Pacific. Notwithstanding this, however, vigorous efforts were made by the Kremlin to shorten the crisis, and treaties of peace were chosen as the means to accomplish this.

These were ushered in by the Treaty of Tartu signed on February 2, 1920, which terminated the hostilities between Russia and Estonia.[81] Timely for the latter, this treaty proved outstanding for the Soviets also as it was a turning point in communist tactics for assuring the desired peace on a much wider scale. Becoming more and more disillusioned in the possibility of immediate world revolution, from this time on the Soviets focused their efforts on effecting the second stage of the retreat predicted by Lenin, namely on coming to terms with neighboring states as an introduction to peaceful existence with the rest of the world. What these terms were can readily be seen from the content of the Treaty of Tartu: Neutrality, non-intervention, non-recognition of pretender governments, and guaranties of non-aggression.

The treaties with Lithuania, Latvia, and Finland followed in rapid succession. The treaty of July 12, 1920,[82] relieved the Soviet troops from their war duties on the Lithuanian front, and freed Lithuania of her fear that the Allies might force her into subjugation to Poland. The war between Latvia and the Soviets was stilled thirty days later, on August 11, 1920, when the Treaty between these two countries led to the immediate resumption of peaceful diplomatic relations.[83] The territorial ambitions of Finland caused a slight delay, and it was not until October 14, 1920, that peace was

[81] *Sborn. Deistv. Dogov.*, I, 1921, No. 17, p. 100. Also, Taracouzio, *op. cit.*, pp. 253–254, and Appendix XXIV.

[82] *Sborn. Deistv. Dogov.*, I–II, 1928, No. 22, p. 59.

[83] *Ibid.*, No. 20, p. 37.

restored, the Finnish Government consenting to give up Eastern Karelia, and Lenin rejoicing at the progress of his peace program.[84]

There is no need to recount here in detail the provisions of these treaties. Patterned after those of the Treaty of Peace with Estonia, they not only embodied the same principles for securing the material peace so badly needed by the Russian Socialist Federated Soviet Republic, but they were by no means ill-adopted to such fundamental revolutionary objectives of Lenin as renunciation of forcible annexations and self-determination for minor nationalities.[85]

The war of Soviet Russia with Poland was an affair of much larger proportions. The withdrawal of the German army of occupation from Volyniia and Chelm permitted the Russians to advance there without much resistance on the part of Poland. Preoccupied, however, with war on all sides, the Soviets were in no position to take advantage of the situation. The result was that the year 1919 saw the Poles pushing forward into Soviet territory. On April 19, 1919, Vilna, claimed to be the capital of Soviet Lithuania, was occupied by Polish troops, and three and a half months later, the same fate befell Minsk, the center of Soviet White Russia.[86] In October, the Soviets suggested an armistice. The negotiations lasted almost three months, bringing no results. On December 22, 1919, Chicherin sent to Warsaw a peace offer in which he said that peace between Poland and Russia was a "life necessity for both countries." [87] Re-

[84] *Sbozn. Deistv. Dogov.*, I–II, 1928, No. 35, p. 130.

[85] It is hardly necessary here to analyze at length the treaties which the R.S.F.S.R. signed at approximately the same time with Georgia (May 7, 1920), Persia (Feb. 26, 1921), Afghanistan (Feb. 28, 1921), and Turkey (Mar. 16, 1921). Inasmuch as the hostilities between the Soviets and these countries were not formal wars, and since the military operations were very limited, these treaties actually cannot be considered as treaties of peace. However, they all elaborated, in varying degrees, the provisions which the Soviets considered essential not only for preventing a renewal of open hostilities against them by these countries, but also to forestall and limit the aid which could be forthcoming from these quarters to the organizations hostile to the Bolshevik régime (*Sborn. Deistv. Dogov.*, I, 1921, p. 27; II, 1921, p. 36; I, 1924, p. 40; and II, 1921, p. 72, respectively. Also, Taracouzio, *op. cit.*, Appendix XXIV). Nor is there any need here to scrutinize the treaties of the R.S.F.S.R. with Khorezm, Azerbaidjan, the Ukraine, Bukhara, Mongolia, and, finally, with the Far-Eastern Republic. Drawn chiefly in terms of proletarian bounds of amity, they provided more for constitutional union than anything else. (*Sborn. Deistv. Dogov.*, I, 1921, p. 12; I, 1921, p. 1; I, 1921, p. 15; II, 1921, p. 7; II, 1921, p. 28; and III, 1922, p. 21, respectively. Also, Taracouzio, *op. cit.*, Appendix XXIV). The same is true in regard to the treaties concluded between the various component Soviet Republics and the limitrophe states bordering the Soviet Empire (*cf.* Taracouzio, *op. cit.*, Appendix XXIV).

[86] *Cf.* Kakurin i Melikov, *op. cit.*

[87] *Krasnaia Kniga, Sbornik diplomaticheskikh dokumentov v Russko-Pol'skikh otnosheniiakh s 1918 po 1920g*, p. 82.

ceiving no reply, Lenin on January 20, 1920, issued a declaration in the name of the Council of Peoples' Commissars in which, along with a warning that the Allies were driving Poland into "a senseless and criminal war with Soviet Russia," he again reassured Poland of the Soviet desire for peace.[88] Two more notes were dispatched, on February 2, and March 6, 1920, before Poland consented to listen to Moscow's plight. The conditions proposed by Poland, however, were inacceptable to the Kremlin. Therefore, on April 26, 1920, while the Russians were still occupied with the retreating forces of Denikin, Polish troops started their offensive. On May 8, Kiev fell. Whatever the reasons that prompted the Poles to bide their time during the last months in 1919, they lost their real opportunity.[89] True, in the spring of 1920, the Polish offensive took the Soviets unprepared. On the other hand, however, by now Moscow had managed to finish with Admiral Kolchak in Siberia, and with General Denikin in the south. The Soviets could now throw their forces against Pilsudski. The result was disastrous for Poland: by July, the Red Army was at the gates of Warsaw. It was Poland's turn now to beg for peace. Refusing to negotiate peace in a conference composed of representatives of Russia, Poland, and the Baltic States, as proposed by the Allies, Lenin preferred direct negotiations with Warsaw. Meanwhile the Allies became perturbed by the successes of the Red Army, and sent to Warsaw a French mission under General Weygand to assist the Polish General Staff. On August 14, 1920, a counter offensive was launched by Pilsudski, and the Red forces were driven back. Exhausted, and in need of peace, both the R.S.F.S.R. and Poland signed an armistice in Moscow on October 12, 1920. On March 18, 1921, at Riga, the Treaty of Peace was signed by Dombski for Poland and Joffe for Soviet Russia.[90]

Onerous as it was from the Soviet standpoint, this peace was the last link in the Soviet chain of international agreements reflecting Lenin's efforts for the attainment of a concrete peace between the R.S.F.S.R. and its neighbors.

[88] *Kzasnaia Kniga* . . ., p. 82.

[89] Louis Fischer suggests that it was France, with her idea of *cordon sanitaire*, which prevented the termination of hostilities between Poland and the Soviets. He also quotes the concurring opinions of Soviet Commander Kakurin (*Kak borolas' revolutsiia*, II, p. 321) and Count Alexander Skrzynski (*Poland and Peace*, p. 39), that the reestablishment of a reactionary Russia constituted a danger to Poland (Louis Fischer, *The Soviets in World Affairs*, I, 240 and 238, respectively).

[90] *Sborn. Deistv. Dogov.*, I, 1921, p. 63, and I, 1924, p. 121, respectively.

PEACE FOR THE EXHAUSTED

These bilateral negotiations with Estonia, Latvia, Lithuania, Finland, and Poland were one way to pursue the needed peace. Collective bargaining was the other method. The Conference of Prinkipo, proposed by the Allies, and the Litvinov-Bullitt negotiations were the outstanding diplomatic efforts of this kind conducted by the Soviets during these years. The idea of the Prinkipo meeting, to which the regional anti-Bolshevik governments formed on the territory of Russia were also invited, was conceived at the Peace Conference of Paris in January, 1919, and envisaged bringing the civil war in Russia to an end. Eager to grasp at every opportunity for peace, the Soviets took up the suggestion of convening a Russian truce parley contained in an unaddressed news broadcast and on February 4, 1919, the People's Commissar for Foreign Affairs wired Soviet acceptance of the plan. It assured the powers that the Soviets were ready to go any length in granting concessions, provided they "can secure thereby conditions enabling them to work out their social schemes peacefully." Concretely, to secure peace, the Soviets were ready to repay privately held debts, to guarantee payment of interest on government loans, to grant concessions of mines, forests, and other resources, so long as these involved no violation of the new Soviet economic order. They were willing even to make territorial concessions if necessary, and to promise, in a general agreement with the Allied powers, not to interfere in their internal affairs.[91]

A mere glance at the civil-war map of Russia will readily reveal that the acceptance of these promises by the other parties to the Conference would have meant Soviet renunciation of sovereignty over most of Siberia, northern Russia, parts of the Ukraine, the Crimea, parts of the Don region, and all of the Caucasus. In Lenin's words, Soviet readiness to buy peace at such a price was "a repetition of many things that were done at Brest-Litovsk."[92] One may rightfully add, however, that there was now a significant difference from 1918. The Soviets were more experienced and could better foresee the advantages to be derived from another "breathing spell."

[91] For English texts, cf. The Soviet Union and Peace, pp. 63ff. For history, cf. Winston S. Churchill, The Aftermath, pp. 172ff.; also Fischer, op. cit., pp. 166ff.

[92] Lenin, XVI, 96–98.

However, peace assured in this way meant also the dismemberment of Russia. President Wilson and Mr. Lloyd George were ready to pay this price for stopping the turmoil. Opposed to them was Winston Churchill, who probably cherished the not unsound idea that a strong non-communist Russia was of much greater advantage to Great Britain, and favored suppression of the Red menace by direct action. This difference of opinion found its solution when President Wilson departed for the United States and Mr. Lloyd George had to go to London. Winston Churchill won; the Prinkipo Conference did not take place, and the Soviets had to continue their wars.

When this opportunity to bring about peace between the Kremlin and its antagonists proved a failure, another far more significant event in the Soviet pursuit of the same end—peace—took place. The new opportunity for them came in March, 1919, when Mr. Bullitt went secretly to Moscow, as an unofficial representative of President Wilson, to reach an understanding with Lenin regarding the possibility of coming to terms with the anti-Bolshevik forces. Anxious for peace, the Soviets willingly took up this new possibility. Litvinov, with the approval of Lenin, drafted the text of a general convention. Of its seven articles, noteworthy were those providing for a reciprocal pledge "not to attempt to upset by force existing *de facto* governments" (Art. 1), to refrain from propaganda, *i.e.*, from "interference in the domestic politics of the respective countries" (Art. 4), and to consider "simultaneous reduction of armies" (Art. 6).[93]

When Mr. Bullitt brought this message of peace back to Paris, the eagerness of those who had sent him to Moscow was checked by various considerations. To quote Louis Fischer:

"Wilson was not inclined to take a committing step. Lloyd George stood in terror of his voters. On the one hand, labor opposed intervention. On the other hand, the bourgeois parties opposed a pact with the Communists. April 2, just a day or two after Bullitt had submitted his written report, the London *Times* warned that the Council of Ten contemplated a deal with Bolshevism, and, acting on this and similar information, a group of members of Parliament telegraphed Lloyd George their protest against any agreement with the Lenin régime." [94]

[93] *Sovetskii Soiuz v Bor'be za Mir,* pp. 66ff.
[94] Fischer, *op. cit.,* p. 173.

Like the Prinkipo Conference, this attempt also failed to bring the desired results.

While the failures of Prinkipo and of the Bullitt-Litvinov proposals to secure peace left the Soviets to their own resources for the time being, the limit to which the Bolshevik authorities were willing to go for the sake of peace is significant. Peace for them was more than ever essential. Having failed to obtain a collective peace, the Soviets concentrated their efforts, as has been shown, on the termination of hostilities by bilateral agreements. Here they succeeded admirably, witness the already mentioned treaties with the Baltic States, Finland and Poland, as well as with their neighbors to the southeast.

By the spring of 1921, it became clear that the Soviets had succeeded in bringing about the much-sought-for *de facto* cessation of open hostilities in Russia. Indeed, the civil war had come to an end: with the defeat of the White armies and their expulsion from Russia, the aggressive defense by arms was over.[95] The Allied intervention had terminated: their troops were being withdrawn from Archangel and Odessa, the Caucasus and Vladivostok.[96] Peaceful relations with neighboring states became normal from the standpoint of international formality: treaties of peace were signed and placed in the files of the People's Commissariat for Foreign Affairs.

Their revolutionary world peace, however, still remained far from materialization. Amid the many troublesome problems which now occupied the minds of the Soviet leaders, the most disturbing was their disillusion in that the transition to socialism had proved more difficult than had been anticipated. This pessimism was by no means ill-founded, for in spite of their revolutionary appeals to the peoples of Europe, and nothwithstanding their "no less than twenty peace proposals to different Powers" made between 1918 and 1921,[97] the

---

[95] *Cf.* Stewart, *The White Armies of Russia;* Fischer, *op. cit.,* Denikin, *Ocherki Russkoi Smuty,* 5 vols., Berlin, 1924–1926; Lampe, A, von, ed., *Bieloe Dielo. Letopis' bieloi voiny,* I–VII, Berlin, 1926–1933, and Bibliography. The anti-Bolshevist movement in the Far East and the "White" government of Merkulovs' in Vladivostok (May 26, 1921 to Oct. 22, 1922) must be disregarded here: far away and entirely dependent on the Japanese support, then the only one available, it was rightfully considered by Moscow as a minor issue.

[96] The economic blockade, declared soon after the Armistice, was cancelled by the Allied Supreme Council much earlier, namely on Jan. 16, 1920. Of the Allied troops, only the Japanese units in the Maritime Province remained on Russian soil for another year and a half (*cf.,* preceding foot-note).

[97] Litvinov, in *Pravda,* Nov. 30, 1922.

Soviets had to console themselves with the mere fact that they themselves had survived for a much longer period than had been expected, and with making believe that this survival was adequate
compensation for the failure of the workers in other European countries to follow the revolutionary call of the Bolsheviks.

Indeed, disappointments were coming in rapid succession. The
short-lived communist rule of Bela-Kun in Hungary collapsed in the
summer of 1919. The socialist-democratic leaders of the German
Revolution, instead of enthusiastically joining Lenin in his scheming
for world revolution, preferred to occupy themselves with finding a
modus vivendi on the basis of friendly coexistence with their former
enemies in the west.[98] Zinoviev's optimistic hope expressed as late
as October, 1920, that socialist revolutions were ready to take place
in Italy, Austria, the Balkans, and even in England, soon proved to
have been mere illusory speculations of the militant head of the
Third International, since executed for his revolutionary enthusiasm
by his own "comrade"—Stalin.[99] The very first signs of social disturbances in Italy promptly resulted in the establishment of Fascism,
the antithesis of Marxism. Austria, whose regiments had not so long
ago brought home first-hand information about the blessings of the
new proletarian régime in Russia, refused to enjoy them under the
dictatorship of its own proletariat. The Balkan peoples failed to
exchange their status of Imperial Russia's "Brother Slavs" for that
of the Soviets' "communist comrades." As to the British Isles, the
would-be new government—the English Council of Action—never
became a *de jure* competitor of the British Parliament.[100]

SOVIET WARS IN REVIEW

To conclude this review of the first period in the Soviet struggle
for peace, the question remains to be answered from the Marxian
standpoint: What were the wars that the Soviets were waging during
these two years and what was the Soviet revolutionary conception
of the peace which the Bolsheviks finally secured for themselves?

[98] *Cf.*, f.i., the German radiogram of Dec. 3, 1918, declining the Soviet request
(after the denunciation of the Brest-Litovsk Treaty) to resume diplomatic relations
with the R.S.F.S.R. The bad faith expressed in carrying on revolutionary propaganda,
was the charge against the former Soviet Embassy (*Izvestiia*, Dec. 6, 1918).

[99] G. Zinov'ev, *Mirovaia revoliutsiia i Kommunisticheskii Internatsional*, pp. 10ff.
Zinoviev was executed in August, 1936.

[100] *Cf.* Bjarne Braatoy, *Labour and War*, London, 1934.

In view of the variety of aspects to be considered, no summary reply, particularly in regard to war, will suffice. An analysis must be made: first, in regard to the civil war and intervention proper, and, second, in regard to the Soviet wars with neighboring states.

If the overthrow of the Soviet régime be accepted as an indisputable aim of the anti-Bolshevist movement, then the nature of the civil war of the Soviets against the White armies depends upon whether the Kremlin and Lenin be viewed as representatives of government and state officialdom, or whether they be accepted as symbols of the proletarian fatherland and revolution. In the former case, as with any government finding itself in danger of mass rebellion, the armed conflict of 1918–1921 was nothing but a necessary suppression of domestic disturbances which, in the case of the Soviets, took the form of a violent and prolonged life-and-death struggle for existence. As such, it has no bearing on either Marxian dogmas or Lenin's pragmatics. If, however, the Soviets and Lenin be viewed as symbols of the proletarian fatherland and Marxian revolt, then the Soviet struggle of 1918–1921 was a revolutionary war in more than one way. It was a revolutionary war because it served the interest of the toiling masses not only in Russia, but the world over. A war for self-preservation though it was, it was also an obligatory revolutionary defense of the proletarian fatherland, *i.e.*, a war exemplifying the way in which the proletariat of such a fatherland performs its duty of protecting it and fighting for its preservation, even if the toiling masses in other countries fail to lend their revolutionary assistance as prescribed by Lenin.[101] In support of this, his explanation of the gallantry shown by the Red Army and his assertions that the cause defended by the R.S.F.S.R. was duly appreciated by the proletariat in other countries may be pointed out.

On March 13, 1919, in his speech on "The Success and Difficulties of the Soviets" he said:

"We are able to carry on the war because the masses know what they are fighting for, and [because] they want to fight . . . defending their socialist cause and struggling side by side with those workers in other countries who have begun to understand our position." [102]

[101] On the tactics of the proletariat in revolutionary war, *cf., supra*, pp. 43ff.
[102] Lenin, XVI, 69.

Ten days later, at the Eighth Congress of the Communist Party, he elaborated this by saying that

". . . if this war is waged with much greater energy and with exalted gallantry, it is only because for the first time in history an army has been created which knows what it is fighting for [because it is] for the first time in the world that the workers and peasants, amidst unprecedented sacrifices, clearly understand that they are defending a Soviet Socialist Republic, the supremacy of the toiling masses over the capitalists, and the cause of the world socialist revolution of the proletariat." [103]

As to the Soviet struggle against the intervention, it was a revolutionary war against the Allies. True, neither France nor England, nor the United States nor Japan, and still less Serbia had any designs for a concrete conquest of Russia. Since, however, the reason for the presence of their respective forces there was support of political philosophies antagonistic to the régime of the proletarian dictatorship, the Soviet war against the Allies was a revolutionary war against imperialism *ex principio*. It was again Lenin, who, in his reference to the Allied intervention, said that the Soviets had to defeat "not only the White guard but also world imperialism." [104] A fortnight later, celebrating the first anniversary of the Soviet régime, at the Sixth All-Russian Congress of Soviets, he showed how this was to be achieved:

"We survived during this year and have achieved certain success. This is not enough, however, in comparison with the formidable foe that is marching against us. This foe is the universal English and French imperialism which has conquered the whole world. We are ready for war with it not because we think that we are able to compare with the advanced countries of Europe, technically or politically . . . No . . . We know that each step toward the strengthening of our army will be echoed by ten steps toward disintegration and revolution in [the countries of] this outwardly strong enemy." [105]

His explanation of the reasons for the withdrawal of the Allies from Archangel and Odessa in 1919 is also the Soviet interpretation of the workings of their revolutionary strategy. Mercilessly criticizing the complaints of the Mensheviks that the foreign proletariat

[103] Lenin, XVI, 155. *Cf.* also his speech at the Eighth Congress of Soviets, Dec. 22, 1922 (*ibid.*, XVIII, pt. I, 291).

[104] Speech on the Joint Session of the Central Executive Committee, Moscow Soviet and the Professional Unions, Oct. 22, 1918 (*ibid.*, XV, 409).

[105] *Ibid.*, pp. 518–519.

were failing in their duty, Lenin bluntly declared that the Soviets were victorious not because the Red Army was stronger but because "the proletariat in the Allied countries proved to be closer to us than to their own governments." [106] That the correctness of his statement was evidenced not only by disturbances and sabotage abroad, but by direct revolt in the expeditionary forces themselves, he implied in his report to the Seventh Congress of Soviets in December of the same year:

"The victory which we achieved when we forced the French and British troops to withdraw was the most important victory over the Allies which we have ever had: we took away from them their soldiers; to the incalculable military and technical supremacy of the Allies we responded by robbing them of this supremacy through the solidarity of the workers against the imperialistic governments." [107]

While it cannot be denied that the Russian civil war was for the Soviets a defensive revolutionary war against counter-revolution, the question whether it was a defensive or an offensive revolutionary war against the Allies, is a matter of conjecture. It may well be called both.

Somewhat more controversial are the considerations in regard to the wars waged by the Soviets against the Baltic States, Finland and Poland. The fact that the population in these countries is of non-Russian nationality subjects the whole issue to Marx's theories on wars for national liberation. According to Lenin's theory, oppressed nationalities were divided into three categories. To the first belong the peoples who were oppressed under Tsarism, and who now, through the acceptance of the Soviet régime, enjoy complete national freedom. The second group is composed of nationalities who were freed through revolution, but who with the help of the imperialistic powers became independent bourgeois republics. Finally, there remain peoples who continue to stay in subjugation to and remain exploited by the Great Powers. Inasmuch as the first of these groups obviously comprised only various nationalities

[106] Lenin, XVII, 5–6.

[107] *Ibid.*, XVI, 405–406. *Cf.* also his speech on the All-Russian Congress of Transport Workers in March, 1921 (*ibid.*, XVIII, pt. I, 161–162). How much trust can be placed in these assertions can be seen from the disappointments which the Soviets had to endure in regard to the actual revolutionary progress in foreign countries (*supra,* p. 93). On the difficulties of the Allies in regard to their expeditionary forces, *cf. supra,* p. 81.

already incorporated into the country of the Soviets, and since the last group evidently refers to colonial and semi-colonial peoples, the Baltic neighbors of the R.S.F.S.R. must belong to the second group.[108] In other words, to Lenin these former Baltic provinces have become bourgeois republics taking orders from their capitalistic sponsors and at the same time oppressing their own proletariat.

The fact that these countries took up arms against the R.S.F.S.R. and coöperated with the anti-Bolshevik units formed within their territories, suggests three possibilities: first, that these peoples had imperialistic designs for the conquest of Russia; second, that they desired the suppression of communism in Russia on purely ideological grounds; and, third, that they were fighting for their own national liberty. To charge the states bordering on the U.S.S.R. to the west with having entertained any plans for conquering Russia would be just as ridiculous as to accuse Finland in the recent Soviet-Finnish war of having had aggressive designs against the Soviets and to insist upon the justice of the Soviet *casus belli*.

Nor is the second of these possibilities substantiated, that the paramount desire of these countries was the suppression of communism in Russia. Whatever the true reasons, their coöperation with the White units within their territories did not signify a determination to march on Leningrad or Moscow to overthrow the Red régime and then to return to their own lands. True, they fought the Bolsheviks and fought well. They also welcomed help from Mannerheim and were glad to have Yudenich's divisions fighting side by side with their own troops. This did not mean, however, that the Baltic republics were ambitious to undertake altruistic crusades eastward for the purpose of liberating the Russians from the communist régime. Lenin himself admitted the impossibility of such ideological designs when he said that even the bourgeoisie of these countries refused to go against the Soviets: "We managed to lure to our side not only the workers of all countries, but also the bourgeoisie of the smaller nations." [109] Concretely, this meant that the downfall of the Soviet régime appeared by no means advantageous to the limitrophe states, as such a change in Russia might well mean

[108] Lenin, XVIII, 83 ff. and XIX, 270 ff.

[109] Speech at the Ninth Congress of the Russian Communist Party, Mar. 20, 1920 (*ibid.*, XVII, 63). *Cf.* also his report to the Seventh Congress of Soviets, Dec. 6, 1919 (*ibid.*, XVI, 408–409).

the end of independence for the Baltic republics themselves. To substantiate this, one may recall the admissions of the Red commander Kakurin and of Count Skrzynski,[110] or the distrust of the Estonians in Yudenich, or, finally, the advance of Bermondt's troops against Riga in October, 1919, instead of going in the direction of Dvinsk to afford a flanking movement on the right of Yudenich's forces, who at the time were advancing toward Petrograd from Estonia.[111]

The elimination of these two possibilities means that in spite of communist claims to the contrary, the Soviet wars against the Baltic States, Finland and Poland, strictly speaking were not only proletarian wars of revolutionary self-defense, and not merely a struggle against the White armies sheltered in these former Russian provinces, but also an armed conflict with the peoples of countries fighting for their national liberation. An obvious question follows: how did this fit in with the Marxian philosophy and Soviet aggression?

Extending full credit, for the sake of argument, to the generally known Soviet contention that the national freedom of these countries actually was a non-proletarian régime, originally established with the aid of German bayonets, and later saved by Allied tanks, it must also be admitted that if this was the case, then the Soviets should not have made any distinction between their immediate western neighbors and the capitalistic powers farther to the West. Yet Lenin himself insisted that a difference should be made. In fact, speaking of frequent national distrusts, he left precise directions to the effect that the proletariat in all countries must be very careful to pay particular attention to the national sentiments of peoples who have been oppressed for a long time, and that it must even show lenience toward them in certain respects.[112] The communist belief that this theory of his was actually put into practice in the Baltic can be seen from his own statement made on February 27, 1921, that the Soviets were lenient with the Baltic States in their peace terms, and that they were ready to give in before Poland's demands so as to alienate Polish workers and peasants from the influence of the Allies.[113]

---

[110] Footnote 89, *supra*, p. 89.

[111] Margulies, *op. cit.*, III, 30ff.

[112] This he formulated in his thesis on colonial problems, advanced at the Second Congress of the Comintern (Lenin, XIX, 270–271).

[113] *Ibid.*, XVIII, pt. I, 83–84.

These admissions of Lenin can mean only one thing, namely, that the wars of the R.S.F.S.R. against Estonia, Latvia, Lithuania, Finland, and Poland, were for these countries wars for national liberation. In this connection it must be borne in mind that such wars may be both of national concern to the peoples involved and of revolutionary concern to the proletariat in general. It does not follow, however, that liberation must result in an immediate Dictatorship of the Proletariat. Quite the contrary, as has been pointed out; in such wars coöperation of the proletariat with their own bourgeoisie is perfectly permissible for a Marxist.[114]

Therefore, it logically follows that from a theoretical standpoint there was neither reason nor ground for the Soviet wars against these countries. Instead, the Soviets should rather have extended their assistance to these peoples in their struggle for freedom and independence, irrespective of the form of the governments chosen and regardless of the class in power.[115] Granting, again for the sake of argument, that the Red troops that invaded Estonia, Latvia, and Poland were not enemy forces but friendly revolutionaries, then the Soviet wars with these countries were not wars but something else. This raises two possibilities.

Had the Soviets fought these peoples merely as coincidental allies of the anti-Bolsheviks, who had voluntarily retreated, after the defeat of the latter, beyond the national boundaries of their respective countries, these wars of the R.S.F.S.R. would have been merely revolutionary interventions on behalf of the "oppressed" Estonians, Latvians, etc. It goes without saying that in such a case the Soviets would have played the same rôle as the Allies did, only on the other side of the political fence, and would have been exposed to the same charges as they themselves preferred against the Allies. The substance was the same; only the color differed. In one case it was White, in the other Red. The fact, however, is that these nationalities were not the "allies" of the Whites, but peoples opposed to the Communist régime within their own respective national boundaries, and the Soviet troops did not retreat of their own free will but were driven back—witness the treaties of peace, concluded under the pressure of fatigue on both sides, and at a time when the opposing forces found themselves on lines corresponding approximately to

[114] *Supra,* pp. 41–42.
[115] *Cf.* the Declaration on Peoples' Rights, signed by Lenin and Stalin on Nov. 15, 1917 (*Dekrety Oktiabr'skoi Revoliutsii,* I, p. 30). For an analysis of Marxism on national problems, *Marksizm i natsional'no kolonial'nyi vopros,* 1939 ed.

the present national boundaries. Hence, the conclusion that the Red advances could hardly have been accompanied by friendly intentions, at least from the viewpoint of those whom they were "helping" and fighting at the same time. This in turn, means that the war of the R.S.F.S.R. against their neighbors in the west not only was not a revolutionary defense of the proletarian fatherland of the Russians, but was not a communist intervention in revolutionary affairs either.

There remains one more possibility, namely, that the Soviet war against these countries was a revoluntionary war of aggression. That it could be nothing but a revolutionary war is obvious, as it was waged by a revolutionary country, conducted for revolutionary purposes, and fought by a revolutionary army.[116] That it was a war of aggression is likewise true. When, by the end of December, 1918, only a small region around Tallinn was left unoccupied by the Red forces, the revolutionary friendship of the Soviets toward the Estonians found expression in a peculiarly revolutionary way: the Estonians were presented with a Soviet government of their own, prefabricated on Russian soil in anticipation of the success of the Red invasion. The same took place when Riga fell and only an insignificant portion of Latvia remained non-communist. Needless to say, in none of these instances was the population in the occupied territory, now supposedly freed from the yoke of capitalism, given the benefit of the right usually enjoyed by free peoples—the right of political self-expression.

Communists may well consider this as gross slander purposing to discredit the régime which they established in Russia. They may also argue that the proletarian régimes set up in these countries under Soviet occupation were the results of the freely expressed desire of the masses. Be that as it may, the facts speak for themselves. Simple and condemning, yet convincing facts they are: The war continued, the population of the regions occupied by the Red forces rejoiced at their repulsion to Soviet borders, and the régimes which they finally chose for themselves were not patterned after

---

[116] Lenin always considered the Red Army as a revolutionary force which is "guided by the ideas of the struggle for liberation of the exploited masses" (Lenin, XV, 74). That this remains true also for the Soviets, is proved by the innumerable instances of the glorification of its growth, spirit, and purpose, recorded in the resolutions of various Party meetings, minutes of different Congresses, and proceedings of the military parades.

the dictatorial government of the Russian proletariat. The argument that under the circumstances these countries had to fall victims to their capitalistic sponsors does not hold. Two decades have since passed, but the peoples in these countries have not yet changed their minds. Even as recently as 1939, when the Red detachments arrived in Estonia, Latvia, and Lithuania in fulfillment of the military concessions "granted" to the Soviet Union by these countries, the population did not welcome them with jubilant manifestations but rather with grave concern: the Soviets will continue their "peaceful" conquest and will not stop until the Red flag of the U.S.S.R. flies over Tallinn, Riga, and Kaunas.

The three-month war between the Soviet Union and Finland in the winter of 1939–1940 is *prima facie* evidence that in 1918–1921 the Soviets greatly overestimated Finnish sympathy for the régime which the Red Army was then bringing them.

As to the war with Poland, its aggressive purpose was admitted by Lenin himself. To quote:

"By attacking Poland, we are attacking also the Allies; by destroying the Polish Army, we are destroying the Versailles Peace upon which rests the whole system of present international relations.

"Had Poland become sovietized . . . the Versailles Peace would have been terminated, and the system built on victory over Germany would have been destroyed likewise." [117]

In other words, not only from the political standpoint but from the military as well, the Soviet war against the Poles became a *de facto* aggressive war against Poland, against the imperialistic powers, and against the Versailles Treaty of Peace.

In concluding this analysis of the Soviet wars of 1918–1921, it must be admitted that opinions may differ in accordance with individual taste and preference. Pro-communists are apt to call these wars a glorious revolutionary epic. Their antagonists will brand them as Red imperialism. Those who have read Lenin will probably expatiate by applying the flexible Marxian formula of war to the Soviets, and say with perfect right, yet without committing themselves, that these wars were simply a continuation of the Soviet policy only by "using different (namely *forcible*) means." [118]

So much for war. The Soviet concept of peace during these diffi-

[117] Speech at the Tannery Congress, Oct. 8, 1920 (Lenin, XVII, 334).
[118] Lenin, XVIII, 97 (italics by author).

cult years must likewise be analyzed in two aspects: pragmatically and as to the ideological Marxian peace of the world.

In regard to peace in the material sense of the term, it may be recalled that the essence of the original Soviet peace policy during the Brest-Litovsk negotiations was the readiness of the communists to sacrifice the immediate interests of the Russian revolution for the sake of spreading revolution abroad. As has been said, however, the final peace terms reflected a change in this attitude; hopes for a successful, sanguinary exportation of revolution proved premature and the national revolution in Russia had to be safeguarded first. The events which followed proved that Lenin's logic, calling for a "breathing spell," was sound, and that the price demanded of the Soviets for this opportunity was not a luxurious waste. Today, there is no longer any doubt that the retreat made by the Soviets at Brest-Litovsk, the sacrifice of life suffered by them in the civil war and in the war against the Allied intervention, and their surrender of the limitrophe states to the control of the capitalistic powers were only difficulties incidental to the struggle for the only possible means of survival—peace. Analyzed from the pragmatic standpoint of self-preservation, this peace obviously meant first of all peace at home, without armed conflict with the outside world.

Great as was the importance attached to the achievement of such a condition, this pragmatic peace did not force into complete oblivion Soviet aspirations for the ideological revolutionary peace of the world. Evidence of this is to be found in the already cited Soviet appeals to the workers and toiling masses in other countries, as well as in the enthusiasm shown by the Russian revolutionaries at the social unrest which the western nations experienced immediately after the World War.

Further proof to the same effect is found in the optimism which continued to possess Lenin and his lieutenants during these years of turmoil. Lenin admitted his hope for international revolution when he confessed to Clara Zetkin that the failure of the Soviet campaign against Poland was due to "false political reckoning," namely "hope for a Polish revolution." [119]

Zinoviev was more romantic in his exultation over the imminence of immediate world revolution. To him there was no doubt that "old Europe was dashing at mad speed towards the proletarian revo-

[119] Fischer, *op. cit.*, p. 271.

lution," *i.e.*, much more rapidly than was anticipated even by the greatest optimists in Moscow. Firm in his convictions, he did not hesitate to share his illusions openly:

"The [revolutionary] movement is proceeding at such terrific speed that we may say with full confidence, within a year we shall already forget that there was a struggle for communism in Europe, because in a year the whole of Europe will be communist. And the struggle for communism will be transferred to America, perhaps to Asia, and to other parts of the world." [120]

In a more reserved way this outlook was shared by Bukharin when he said, without referring to the calendar, however, that "there can be no great revolution that will not affect the whole world, enlist the sympathy of the proletariat, bring upon itself the forces of world imperialism, and develop into a world revolution." [121] Even Stalin, whose opinions at that time did not carry much weight, did not escape the exaltation of hope for the relief soon to be brought about by the revolutionary successes of the Soviets beyond their own boundaries.[122]

Finally, the fact that Marxian peace via world revolution had not been discarded from Soviet military strategy is substantiated by the debates which took place at the first two Congresses of the Communist International and by the resolutions adopted. Having declared that the speedy victory of communism was the purpose of the newly born Third International, the First Congress limited its proceedings to the problem of revolutionary propaganda. It optimistically assured the workers of the world that it was a matter of not more than twelve months before Europe would follow the footsteps of the Russian proletariat. Denouncing the League of Nations, then in its formative stage, as "the Holy Alliance of the bourgeoisie for the suppression of the proletarian revolution," it pointed out that the Soviets were the only means for transforming the world into a Marxian community of men, and ruled that there could be no compromise between the workers and their exploiters. The class war must go on to the end.[123]

[120] G. Zinov'ev, "Perspektivy proletarskoi revoliutsii," *Kommunisticheskii International*, No. 1, pp. 37ff. (cited in Florinsky, *World Revolution and the U.S.S.R.*, pp. 41–43).

[121] N. Bukharin, "Diktatura proletariata v Rossii i mirovaia revoliutsiia," *ibid.*, No. 4, pp. 491–492 (cited in *ibid.*, p. 45).

[122] *Cf.* also, *Lenin i Stalin*, II, pp. 281–282.

[123] *Kommunisticheskii Internatsional v Dokumentakh, 1919–1932*, p. 80.

The Second Congress of the Comintern displayed similar optimism. It met at the time of the Soviet advance on Warsaw, which
fact must have added greatly to the revolutionary enthusiasm of the
delegates assembled in Moscow. Even Lenin was not unaffected by
the prevailing sentiment. At one of the meetings he advanced his
new theory that backward countries need not pass through a capitalist stage of development if the Soviet governments in other countries would come to their assistance with all their resources.[124] This
contradiction of the Marxian theory of evolutionary sequence can
be explained only by the optimism which he entertained at the
time.[125] The militant enthusiasm of Zinoviev continued to vitalize
the imagination of others when he proclaimed that "the working
class has been waiting long enough," and that "the time for the
decisive struggle has now arrived." [126] The resolutions and particularly the Statute of the Third International which this Congress
adopted were in the same vein. True, neither the First nor the
Second Congress heralded the advance of world revolution as unreservedly as many would have liked. The fact, however, that they
met in 1919 and 1920, *i.e.*, at a time when the Soviets were at the
peak of their difficulties, is good ground for the belief that optimism
was one of the factors which guided their proceedings.

Yet this optimism was no longer the exaltation of the period
which ended with the Treaty of Brest-Litovsk. Indeed, it was during his above-mentioned speech of May 14, 1918, that Lenin admitted
the difficulties which the R.S.F.S.R. had to face in connection with
world revolution:

"The difficulties of revolutions are well known. Having started as a
spectacular success in one country, revolution may have to go through periods of trial because final victory is possible only on a world scale and through
the united efforts of the workers in all countries. Our task is to exercise tact
and caution; we must manoeuver and retreat until reinforcements come to
our aid." [127]

The same sober attitude toward realities, unpleasant as they were
from a revolutionary standpoint, is seen in his warnings voiced in

[124] *Kommunisticheskii Internatsional v Dokumentakh, 1919–1932*, p. 131.
[125] *2-i Kongress Kommunisticheskogo Internatsionala, Stenograficheskii Otchet*
(Petrograd, 1921).
[126] *Ibid.*, p. 324.
[127] *Protokoly zasedanii Vscrossiiskogo Tsentral'nogo Ispoilntel'nogo Komiteta 4-go
sozyva*, pp. 263–270.

1919 that the capitalist world was not yet enthusiastic to follow the Soviets in the reconstruction of society.[128] The actual revolutionary failures abroad were material evidence supporting his contention.[129] Nor was his general international outlook for world revolution by any means brighter in 1920. Speaking in Moscow on March 6, 1920, he expressed his opinion that while the revolutionary situation had been extremely promising at the end of the war, the communists now had to admit the failure of their hopes to see the immediate transformation of Western Europe into a Marxian comity of nations.[130] The same disillusion was also admitted by Zinoviev who, in contradiction to his own earlier enthusiasm, at the Second Congress of the Comintern admitted overindulgence in optimism and was now willing to extend the time limit for world revolution to two or "perhaps even three years more." [131]

By the time of the signing of the peace treaty with Poland on March 18, 1921, the hope for an immediate world revolution had been abandoned altogether. At the Tenth Congress of the Russian Communist Party, which met at Moscow on March 8–16, 1921, Lenin admitted that to entertain any illusions of such a revolution at that time would "verge upon being afflicted with lunacy." "We have learned in the course of the last three years," said he, "that our [having a] stake in international revolution does not mean that we expect it to materialize within a definite period of time . . . and that therefore we must coördinate our activities with the relationships existing among the various classes in our own country and abroad in order thereby to maintain for a protracted period the dictatorship of the proletariat and to free ourselves, even if gradually, of all the misfortunes and the effects of the crisis which has befallen us." [132]

Without going into a further analysis of Soviet reactions toward Marxian plans for world revolution, it may suffice here to say that in comparison with the revolutionary *Sturm und Drang* of the first few months, the years of civil war and intervention were years of

[128] Lenin, "Tretii internatsional i ego mesto v istorii," *Kommunisticheskii Internatsional,* 1919, No. 1, pp. 35ff.

[129] *Supra,* p. 93.

[130] Lenin, *op. cit., ibid.,* 1920, No. 10, p. 1453.

[131] *2-i Kongress Kommunisticheskogo Internatsionala, Stenograficheskii Otchet,* p. 16.

[132] *Desiatyi S'ezd Rossiiskoi Kommunisticheskoi Partii, Stenograficheskii Otchet,* pp. 20ff.

further retreat in the field of concrete diplomacy and of the inauguration of capitulation in the realm of communist doctrinism.

In summarizing this period of retreat, extending from 1917 to 1921, it must be admitted that to the Soviets the Brest-Litovsk Treaty was a revolutionary necessity, while wars with the Baltic states and Poland were an armed struggle signifying the possibility of practical application for the Marxian ideology regarding revolutionary wars and wars for national liberation, their defensive and aggressive nature, and, finally, their transformation from one into the other. Peace also ceased to be a synonym with immediate world revolution. Pragmatically, connoting primarily the actual cessation of physical warfare, during the years from 1918 to 1921, it became a paramount, practical necessity. Ideologically, its place on the revolutionary agenda of the Kremlin was after the immediate problems, as a goal "once removed."

CHAPTER IV

ENFORCED ENTRENCHMENT: TRANQUIL
INTERLUDE, 1921–1933

ENFORCED ENTRENCHMENT: TRANQUIL
INTERLUDE, 1921–1933

Red Halt

The new era into which the Soviets now entered proved to be not only complex but of long duration. In fact, it continued until December, 1939, when for the first time since the Treaty of Riga in 1921, the Soviets again became engaged in an international war, this time against Finland. The basic principles of international conduct remained the same, however. Peace continued to be the paramount concern of the Bolshevik leaders, but proletarian methodology underwent certain changes. From 1921 to the Soviet entrance into the League of Nations, in 1934, the Soviet peace policy became that of revolutionary entrenchment.

Having relieved themselves from the Allied intervention and having come to terms with the bourgeois border countries, the Soviets found themselves in a state of peace. That this was by no means an enviable peace, however, calls for no elaborate explanation. Exhausted economically by war and famine, with a disorganized governmental machinery functioning on the principle of terrorism, and facing the disintegration of whatever was left of the social morale inherent in man, Russia was virtually in ruins. No bright outlook for an immediate future either in the field of domestic affairs or in regard to the international position of the R.S.F.S.R. was visible. Yet today, even the antagonists of the communist régime are forced to admit that from this desperate situation of two decades ago Russia has emerged victorious.

It does not fall within the scope of the present study either to analyze the Soviet recovery in things domestic, or to emphasize the vast and complex exertions to that end. Suffice it to say that peace was considered essential for survival, and that every possible effort, often even at great sacrifice of life, was made to preserve it in order to bring to materialization the ultimate designs of the Kremlin. Concretely, this meant that in 1921 the general policies of the Soviets were reoriented along lines to afford the R.S.F.S.R. another breathing spell during which the entrenchment could be carried out effectively and without further endangering the existence of the régime established in November, 1917. In the field of domestic affairs this was to be achieved by economic reconstruction through industrialization of the country and collectivization of rural economy, and by the solidification of political gains in an area restricted geographically by the political boundaries of Soviet Russia. The principle which now guided the Soviets in their domestic policies and which became the point of departure for their crusade for peace was posited on realization of the fact that hope for revolutionary assistance from the workers of other countries had to be abandoned, and that world revolution was not to be a *Blitzrevolution* but a slow and painful process of establishing socialism at home before attempting to establish it elsewhere. Alone in their political ideology, the Soviets were also left to their own resources in the concrete execution of this unprecedented task.

Nor is it possible here to appraise the actual results achieved by them in the reconstruction of social life in the U.S.S.R. The Soviet estimate is illustrated by Stalin's summary of the results of the First Five-Year Plan, in which he said that had there been no progress in recovery, the Soviets

"would have had an armed intervention, and instead of non-aggression pacts—a war, a dangerous, bloody, and disastrous war, as we would have been almost disarmed as compared with our enemies who have at their disposal all the modern means for attack." [1]

What the actual political, economic, and military growth of the Soviets was is a matter of conjecture. As has been said elsewhere, "partisans of the communist cause would vigorously insist that Soviet data are conclusive proof of the results," while their opponents "would insist with no less vigor that the evidence is far from being conclusive precisely for the reason that it is based upon Soviet data." [2]

Whatever one's preference, to Lenin the successful outcome of this new trial at home meant, among other things, gain of revolu-

[1] Stalin, *Voprosy Leninizma*, p. 492.
[2] Taracouzio, *Soviets in the Arctic*, p. 367.

tionary prestige abroad, because the precedent set by the Socialist Soviet Republic in Russia was to "stand out as a vivid example for peoples the world over," and "the effect of the revolutionary propaganda which this example will have was going to be gigantic." [3] At one with this was his warning that the primary duty of the Soviets in Russia was to serve merely as a vanguard of world revolution. To this end, peace was of prime importance, for, according to him, it would "open a hundred times more easily and widely the way for our influence." [4]

The disillusion in bringing about immediate world revolution which prompted the reorientation of the domestic policies of the Soviets was also instrumental in the change in their foreign diplomacy. True, their longing for peace had not diminished. On the contrary, it may have even increased. In this the Soviets remained consistent. What did change was the revolutionary strategy in the Soviet conduct of relations with other states: instead of militant antagonism against the non-Soviet scheme of things, the irreconcilable contrast between the communist and capitalist orders of society was accepted as a phenomenon that must be endured. While it was solemnly admitted in the Declaration of Union of 1922, that "all the countries in the world had become divided into two camps: the camp of capitalism and the camp of socialism," the expediency which now dictated the international conduct of the Soviets was manifested in the realization that these two camps were destined to coexist for an undetermined time. Witness the constitutional confirmation of this in the same Declaration:

"On the other hand, the instability of the international situation and the danger of new attacks render inevitable the creation of a common front by the Soviet Republics against capitalist encirclement . . . The new united State . . . shall stand as the firm bulwark against world capitalism and form a decisive step toward the union of the workers of all countries into one World Socialist Soviet Republic." [5]

An endorsement of this idea is found in Stalin's report to the Fourteenth Party Congress, where he said that Soviet relations with the capitalist countries were based on the acceptance of the co-existence

[3] Lenin, XV, 63.
[4] *Ibid.*, XVII, 70.
[5] Taracouzio, *The Soviet Union and International Law*, Appendix I, p. 355. It is of interest to note that the Constitution of 1936 no longer mentions this division.

of two opposing systems.[6] The explanation of this acceptance, in turn, is found in the statement he made on May 9, 1925, when, referring to the years 1923 and 1924, he said:

"characteristic of this time was not only the fact that capitalism and the Soviet régime became stabilized, but also the fact that the strength of these two camps reached a sort of temporary equilibrium." [7]

In the field of concrete diplomatic endeavor, this reorganization of foreign policy meant the admission of Soviet Russia as a full-fledged member in the community of nations, which was to be achieved through economic coöperation with the outside world and reduction of the danger of new aggression from abroad. Today, the membership of the Soviet Union in the family of the Great Powers is an established fact; the development of economic ties between the U.S.S.R. and capitalistic nations has had a long and varied history, and its constant fear of war may rightly appear as a "perfectly grotesque obsession." [8] Ironically enough, today, these Soviet achievements may well result in war, but in 1921 and the years immediately thereafter, endeavors to these ends were undertaken solely to assure peace.

Before proceeding further, two things must be pointed out by way of explanation. In an attempt to analyze the Soviet attitude toward war and peace as reflected in the foreign relations of the U.S.S.R., a detailed history of Soviet economic foreign policy and of the diplomatic relations of the Soviet Union may well appear logically indispensable. At this juncture, however, neither the immediate purpose of the present study nor space admit of such an undertaking. Hence, the background for this analysis must be limited to a mere skeleton picture of Soviet international life from the time of the signing of the Treaty of Peace with Poland.

It has already been said that from the standpoint of war and peace, the era which was ushered in by this peace treaty continued until December, 1939. Of the various events which took place in the course of these years, the entrance of the Soviets into the League of Nations stands out not only as a milestone in the formal international diplomacy of the Kremlin, but as a signal of the change in communist evaluation of the intrinsic purpose of peace. Hence, the

[6] *Stenogr. Otchet XIV Parts'ezda*, 1926, p. 8.
[7] Stalin, *Voprosy Leninizma*, p. 155.
[8] Florinsky, *op. cit.*, pp. 211–212.

era of the peaceful coexistence of the Soviets and the non-Marxian nations actually falls into two divisions: the pre-League period, and the years of the Soviets' membership in the League of Nations.

Since there were no international wars from 1921 to 1933 to which the Soviets were a party *de jure,* and as all their efforts were concentrated on the preservation of international peace, the record of the Soviet endeavors for and attitude toward peace will be analyzed first.

Whatever the particulars of the Soviet ambition to enter into economic and political intercourse with the outside world, the international security of the proletarian régime in Russia was the paramount concern of the U.S.S.R. Peace was rightly considered to be the important condition essential for building up this security, and diplomatic maneuvering the necessary means. This involved constant efforts at making the co-existence of the Soviet and capitalist states possible and adjusting the international bargaining accordingly.

IN SEARCH OF SECURITY

While disarmament and non-aggression were the cardinal points on the agenda of the Soviet foreign policy during this period, Soviet diplomats did not disregard the possibility that the respect of other nations for the U.S.S.R. as a great power might also contribute to the establishment of this security. Nor did they wait for long to put this conviction to a practical test. Scarcely four months had passed from the day on which the peace with Poland was signed, when, on July 19, 1921, the Soviet Government, after having learned through the press of the proposed Washington Conference of the Pacific Powers and Powers with Specific Interest in the Pacific, sent a protest against its exclusion from this conference.[9] Maintaining that Russia was one of such powers, the Soviet Government stated that in the interests of peace, it considered it a duty to participate in all international conferences which were aimed at the solution of questions involving the interests of Soviet Russia.

The warning that "the policy tending to leave Russia outside the collective decisions of various powers on questions concerning it not

---

[9] Text in Taracouzio, *op. cit.,* Appendix XV, pp. 411–413. *Cf.* also, *Vashingtonskaia Konferentsiia po ogranicheniiu vooruzhenii i tikhookeanskim i dal'nevostochnym delam 1919–1922g.,* Moskva, 1922.

only cannot assist the settlement of the conflicts at present disturbing the world, but can only render them more acute and more complicated," was ignored by the Powers. So also was a second protest which the Soviets forwarded on November 2, 1921.[10] The Conference took place without the delegates from the R.S.F.S.R. The Soviet diplomats were forced to admit their failure and to wait for better opportunities. These, however, were soon forthcoming.

Indeed, before long, at Cannes, the Great Powers realized that the communist and non-communist régimes were to coexist for some time, and that the political and economic problems confronting postwar Europe could not be solved without the participation of the Soviets. The result was that on January 7, 1922, a memorandum was sent to Moscow, inviting the Soviet Government to attend the Genoa Conference.[11] By accepting this invitation the next day,[12] the Soviets became drawn into the discussions concerning the postwar settlement of international affairs. Their importance thus recognized, it was only logical for them to proceed with other plans to solidify their security. Of these, disarmament came first on their schedule.

Spurred by the pleasant realization of Europe's need for things Russian, and still anxious about their own security, the Soviets went to Genoa in a dual capacity. Speaking of this conference, Lenin made a pointed remark:

"It is obvious that we are going to Genoa not as communists, but as business men. We must sell, and so must they. We wish to trade so that the benefit be ours, and they wish that it be theirs." [13]

In the light of such an admission, peace-makers though they were, the Soviet plenipotentiaries were first of all political merchants of Moscow.

De jure recognition was the Soviet price for Russia's coöperation with other powers in making life tolerable under universal peace.[14]

---

[10] For text, *cf. The Soviet Union and Peace*, pp. 80–81.

[11] *Cf. Materialy Genuezskoi Konferentsii*, Moscow, 1922.

[12] Text in *The Soviet Union and Peace*, pp. 81–82.

[13] Lenin, XVIII, 21.

[14] In the opinion of the Soviet delegation there were three principles fundamental to agreement on controversial post-war problems that retarded the stabilization of world peace. These principles were:

"(1) Recognition of the full sovereignty of every nation, entailing [recognition of] its own system of property, economy, and administration; (2) the legal, juridical, and administrative guarantee of personal and property rights of those foreign-

The proposal for disarmament, inserted unexpectedly by the Soviet delegates in the agenda of the Conference, which was limited to the economic and financial restoration of Europe, was the trial *coup* of Soviet diplomacy in the field of concrete measures for the security of the R.S.F.S.R. The refusal of the Great Powers to deal with the Soviets on the conditions proposed is well known, and calls for no elaborate comment. Notwithstanding the fact that active participation in international unions and technical commissions, and even an implicit pledge to participate in the League of Nations at a later date were considered as possible concessions on the part of the Soviets, the differences between the communist political philosophy and that of the non-communist states proved too great. The answer to the Soviet proposal of disarmament was the emphatic "No!" of Mr. Barthou.[15] The Genoa Conference proved disappointing to European diplomats and failed to materialize the hopes of the Soviets. Balked entirely at Genoa, and having gained no headway at the resumed discussions at The Hague,[16] the Soviets realized that a concerted agreement with the Western Powers was impossible. Their only source of solace was the Treaty of Rapallo, signed on April 16, 1922, which was negotiated outside the Genoa Conference and which brought Germany and Soviet Russia to an understanding amounting virtually to an alliance.[17]

After their experience at Genoa, the Soviets, objecting to political participation in the larger institutions of international government, distrustful of any arbitration machinery,[18] and enthusiastic over their success in separate dealings with Germany, retreated to their policy of individual understandings, testing out their immediate neighbors first. The outcome of this change was that the Soviet Foreign Office proposed the convocation in Moscow, under its own auspices, of a conference of the Baltic States to discuss the limita-

---

ers desiring to visit Russia for economic activities, and (3) the recognition of the principle of reciprocity in the execution by all Governments of their obligations and in the compensation for losses suffered by foreign citizens." (*Sovetskii Soiuz v Bor'be za Mir,* p. 138).

[15] *Materialy Genuezskoi Konferentsii,* p. 83.

[16] *Gaagskaia Konferentsiia,* Moscow, 1922.

[17] *Sborn. Deistv. Dogov.,* I, 1924, pp. 58ff.

[18] *Cf.* Litvinov's statement of July 12, 1922, regarding the Soviet attitude toward the League of Nations that "only an angel could be unbiased in judging Russian affairs," and the Soviet refusal to coöperate with the Permanent Court of International Justice in the Eastern Karelian case on the ground that this Court cannot be considered "as impartial in this matter" (Taracouzio, *op. cit.,* pp. 296 and 297, respectively).

tion of armaments. Poland, Finland, Latvia, and Estonia responded, and in December, 1922, the Moscow Disarmament Conference met.[19] It is well known that this conference also failed: the Soviets refused to agree to the "moral disarmament" proposed by these states, and the latter, in turn, did not see fit to accept the drastic proposals of concrete disarmament made by the Soviets.[20] Nevertheless, it proved of importance as it not only committed the Soviet Government to the idea of pacific settlement of international disputes,[21] but disclosed more clearly the basic Soviet conception of provisional, non-communist world peace. This involved abstention from every act of armed aggression, refusal of support to any third, non-signatory, aggressor on the territory of any of the contracting parties, refusal of support to any signatory violating the convention through an act of aggression, the settlement of all differences by pacific means, and the acceptance of arbitral procedure in problems not covered by treaty provisions. This ideological consensus of the Soviet peace policy found its manifestation in subsequent Soviet agreements in the non-aggression, anti-coalition, neutrality, and conciliation clauses of the various security pacts.

In spite of the failure of this Moscow Conference, the Soviet Government continued to believe in the ultimate value of disarmament, and at every conference for the limitation of armaments consistently advanced its desire for universal disarmament, as well as its general appeal for world peace. While it is impossible to enter here into a detailed analysis of other Soviet efforts in this direction,[22] the extent of the Soviet disarmament program can be seen most clearly in the Declaration of the U.S.S.R., delivered by Litvinov at the Session of the Preparatory Disarmament Commission of November 30, 1927, at Geneva, which unreservedly suggested complete disarmament.[23] The principles outlined therein were advanced

[19] *Conférence de Moscow pour la limitations des armaments.*

[20] The idea of proportional disarmament, suggested at this Conference, never materialized because the delegates of the limitrophe states refused at the last moment to sign the agreement.

[21] *Ibid.*, p. 7.

[22] For a list of Soviet documents, *cf.*, Taracouzio, *op. cit.*, p. 306, fn. 41.

[23] For text see, Taracouzio, *op. cit.*, Appendix XX. Of interest in this respect is the speech by Litvinov, the Soviet delegate, delivered on Nov. 22, 1927, at this Conference, in which the hope for universal peace through disarmament, cherished by the Soviets, was opposed by the fear of another war: ". . . We live in times when the outbreak of new wars is not a theoretical, but a real threat. This is not only our opinion, but this fear has been expressed lately also by many authoritative statesmen in capitalistic countries.

numerous times from 1928 to 1931. In April, 1932, when the General Disarmament Conference resumed its work, Litvinov once again emphasized the fact that in principle the Soviet Union stood by its original proposal for complete disarmament, and set forth the following three fundamental principles, by adherence to which the work of the Conference might, in Soviet opinion, result in at least a partial reduction of armaments: (1) a change of the term "limitation" of armaments, to "reduction" of armaments, which would mean, in his estimation, the reduction of existing armed forces; (2) application of this reduction to all kinds of war materials and munitions; (3) the discussion of the whole problem, not from the point of view of the safety of states, but on the basis of a ratio of reduction in proportion to the actual military strength of the nations.[24]

PAPER RAMPARTS

Prior to taking up the second aspect of the Soviet security policy, agreements of non-aggression, it must be pointed out that Soviet Russia was gradually being drawn further and further into the cross currents of European politics. A number of trade agreements were concluded between the Soviets and the Western Powers which brought considerable comfort to the Kremlin, not only from the standpoint of the economic possibilities which they envisaged but also as indicating the *de facto* recognition of Russia as a new socialist state.[25] In their relations with the countries in the Near East, the Soviets successfully played upon the sentiment of liberation of colonial and semi-colonial countries, with the result that *de jure* recognition was accorded them in a series of treaties with Turkey, Persia, Afghanistan, and Mongolia.[26]

The air of the approaching war is felt everywhere." (*Sovetskii Soiuz v Bor'be za Mir*, p. 193). Likewise significant is the fact that this project was submitted with an *a priori* assurance that it would not be accepted by non-communist countries. (*Cf.*, the Theses of the Sixth Congress of the Comintern, Aug. 17 to Sept. 1, 1928, *Kommunisticheskii Internatsional v Dokumentakh, 1919–1932*, p. 825). These admissions call for no further comment regarding the conflict between the theoretic value of the Soviet idea of complete disarmament, and the concrete impossibility of its realization, as proved later.

[24] *Cf.* also Korovin, "The U.S.S.R. and Disarmament" (*International Conciliation*, Sept., 1933, No. 292).

[25] These were inaugurated by the Economic Agreement with Great Britain of Mar. 16, 1921 (*cf.* Taracouzio, *op. cit.*, pp. 258ff). For other treaties, *cf.* Appendix.

[26] *Cf., ibid.*, Appendix XXIV, pp. 450ff, also: Graham, "The Soviet Security Treaties" (*AJIL*, XXII, 332ff); and *Sborn. Deistv. Dogov.*, v. I.

In 1922 the various independent Soviet republics became consolidated into a single Union of Socialist Soviet Republics. As the guardian of communist interests at home and abroad, the U.S.S.R. was soon given an opportunity to prove its efficiency. Mussolini's march on Rome in 1922, Curzon's ultimatum of 1923 indicating clearly that he preferred trading with India rather than Russia,[27] not to mention the Ruhr disturbance of the same year, and Lenin's death in January, 1924, were only some of the events which called for both determination and skill on the part of Soviet statesmen and diplomats. The outcome was not to their discredit; witness the *de jure* recognition which the Soviets netted in their dealings with England, France, Italy, and the Scandinavian countries.[28]

Confronted at the very outset with a fiasco in their attempts at disarmament, the Soviets endeavored to seek the desired security of peace by resorting for the time being to less drastic measures than actual disarmament. To this end, they were now ready to substitute for the latter certain guaranties of non-aggression. Distrustful as ever of the League of Nations, they sought a solution in non-aggression pacts signed with individual countries independently of the institutions of Geneva, on an ostensibly anti-League basis. The signing of the Geneva Protocol and of the Locarno treaties made this change imperative.[29] The Geneva Protocol sanctioned unlimited boycott and blockade against an offending country, while the Locarno treaties indicated a strengthening of the war-torn powers of Western Europe. Obviously, when taken together, they could mean only one thing to the Soviets: the possibility of another aggression against the U.S.S.R. To forestall this, new devices had to be invented. To Soviet diplomacy this meant the establishment of its foreign relations on a definitely permanent basis, and treaties of non-intervention, non-aggression, and neutrality were used for building a political barrier against the feared capitalist designs upon Russia.

At this point a brief explanation of Soviet emphasis on neutrality

[27] On the latter, cf. *Correspondence between His Majesty's Government and the Soviet Government Respecting the Relations between the Two Governments,* London, 1923, Cmd. 1869, and *A Selection of Papers Dealing with the Relations between His Majesty's Government and the Soviet Government, 1921–1927,* London, 1927. Cmd. 2895.

[28] England, France, Italy, Sweden, Norway, Denmark, and China accorded *de jure* recognition in 1924, Japan in 1925 (cf. Taracouzio, *op. cit.,* Appendix XXIV, pp. 450ff).

[29] *Lausanne Conference on Near Eastern Affairs, 1922–23.* London, 1923. Cmd. 1814. *Cf.,* also, Graham, *op. cit.,* pp. 338–339.

is pertinent. It must be recalled that while in the days of civil war and Allied intervention, neutrality to the Soviets was merely a technical device to terminate warfare, now, when the illusion of a new aggression against the U.S.S.R. was made to appear a real danger, neutrality for the Soviets became an instrumentality for the prevention of hostilities. Embodied in conventional form, neutrality was now viewed by the Kremlin as an explicit *a priori* avowal of conduct and "as the only possible, tangible, [and] legal guarantee of safety from attack or intervention . . . It laid the basis for permanent security by permitting the discounting of eventual hostilities against the pledged word of the nation; it formed the completing counterpart to a system of non-aggression pure and simple, by furnishing guarantees of inaction in the event of aggression or hostility in some other quarter. Finally, neutrality was the only formula capable of reconciling the fact of the absence of any higher tribunal, any functioning center of reference or ultimate jurisdiction to which communist and non-communist states might appeal." [30]

During the proceedings at Locarno, it became evident to the Soviets that they were confronted with a new problem, namely that of checking the extending influence of the capitalist Powers in the Near and Middle East. Hence, Soviet attention was immediately turned in that direction. The reverses which Moscow and Ankara had suffered at Locarno and The Hague,[31] respectively, paved the way for the Soviets to make the advances which were to serve the end secretly cherished by the U.S.S.R. The first of the Soviet treaties envisaging the security of the U.S.S.R. was the Treaty of Paris signed by the U.S.S.R. and Turkey on December 17, 1925.[32] Brief as it was, this treaty was of importance, although not so much as an actual counter-blast at the Powers which had come to an understanding at Locarno, as in the guise of a moral victory of Soviet diplomacy, and as a practical basis for the continuity of this policy. Similar treaties were later signed with Afghanistan, Persia, and Yemen.[33] To fuse these bilateral efforts at peace into a system of

[30] Graham, "The Soviet Security System," *International Conciliation,* 1929, pp. 360–361.

[31] On the Mosul case the Permanent Court of International Justice rendered its decision against Turkey *(Publications of the Permanent Court of International Justice. Series B. No. 12).*

[32] *Sborn. Deistv. Dogov.,* III, 1927, p. 9.

[33] Aug. 31, 1926, Oct. 1, 1927, and Nov. 1, 1928 *(ibid.,* IV, 1928, p. 11; IV, 1928, p. 23, and VI, 1931, p. 6, respectively). For other treaties of Soviet Russia with the Levant Countries, *cf.,* Taracouzio, *op. cit.,* Appendix XXIV.

mutually binding obligations, numerous analogous treaties were signed among these Levant countries, not without the influence of the Kremlin.[34]

The initial success of the negotiations with Turkey was sufficient for the Soviets to realize that they would succeed in building in the Near East a united front against the Western Powers and that it was merely a question of time before the U.S.S.R. would find itself securely protected, in case of danger from that direction, by a cordon of neutral Near Eastern states. Relieved, thus, from worries in this direction, the Soviets busied themselves with further barricading against the possibilities of aggression from the west. In the Soviet People's Commissariat for Foreign Affairs, negotiations with Germany and the Baltic states were placed on the agenda of problems calling for immediate action.

The relations of the U.S.S.R. with Germany had been very friendly since the signing of the Treaty of Rapallo in 1922.[35] Locarno had brought Germany to the doors of the League of Nations. Anxious to salvage what was left of the rapprochement consummated in 1922, the Soviets were by no means willing to abandon Germany without a struggle. Circumstances intrinsically similar to those which had helped the Soviets in their dealings with Turkey were to help the Kremlin once again. It will be recalled that at first the Locarno Powers had failed to procure the admittance of Germany to the League of Nations. The Soviets seized the opportunity to take advantage of the resentment which this refusal caused in Germany. On April 24, 1926, a Treaty patterned after that signed by the Soviet and Turkey in 1925, was concluded between the Soviets, anxious at least to divide Germany's allegiance between Locarno and Moscow, and Germany, humiliatingly left waiting before Geneva.[36]

Negotiations with the Baltic States proved successful only in part. Disappointed in the earlier proposals made to Poland in 1924 and 1925, Chicherin now directed his *aggression diplomatique*

---

[34] Thus, Turkey and Persia signed a Treaty of Friendship and Neutrality on Apr. 22, 1926; Afghanistan and Persia signed a similar Treaty on Nov. 27, 1927, and Turkey and Afghanistan on May 25, 1928. (*L.N.T.S.*, CVI, 247, CVII, 433, and Wheeler-Bennett, *Disarmament and Security since Locarno*, pp. 332 and 324, respectively).

[35] *Supra*, p. 115. For the relations between Germany and the U.S.S.R., *cf.*, *infra*, pp. 180ff. and 240ff.

[36] *Sborn. Deistv. Dogov.*, IV, 1928, p. 16. For English text, see *The Soviet Union and Peace*, p. 280.

toward Finland, Estonia, Latvia, and Lithuania. Finland preferred to pursue its customary policy of aloofness in regard to the U.S.S.R., and only Lithuania was inclined favorably to the Soviet proposals. Bitterness over the loss of Vilna, which had been seized by the Polish General Zeligovsky in 1920,[37] coupled with a fear of Poland, outweighed the warnings of Latvia and Estonia, and on September 28, 1926, a Treaty of Neutrality and Non-Aggression, along the lines of that already concluded with Germany, was signed by Lithuania and the U.S.S.R.[38] Aware as they were of the fact that Soviet eagerness for such treaties was nothing but a political maneuver, the Latvian and Estonian governments found themselves forced to seek a compromise with the Soviets. A solution satisfactory to all concerned was found in agreements regarding the settlement of conflicts in the frontier zones. Such agreement was entered into by the U.S.S.R. with Latvia[39] on July 19, 1926, and with Estonia, on August 18, 1927.[40] Substitutes for treaties of non-aggression, these agreements served the practical need of the U.S.S.R., for they tended to remove elements of friction between the Soviets and these Baltic neighbors.

The general principles underlying the Soviet pacts of non-aggression are both significant and simple. In brief, they comprise mutual pledges of neutrality, similar pledges to abstain from attack upon one another, promises of non-participation in any alliance or agreement of a political, military, or economic character, or any hostile act directed against the other party, and, finally, promises to negotiate for a method of settling differences between them.

These efforts of the Soviets can be appreciated much better if it be recalled that the difficulties surrounding them were not only numerous but complicated. Indeed, the international situation in Europe by this time had become threatening to the maintenance of peace. Germany had been admitted to the League of Nations, which, to the Soviets, meant that for proper remuneration "in a showdown she might well be aligned with the enemies."[41] Pilsudski became the dictatorial master of Poland in 1926. Conservative governments

---

[37] Cf. *Sovetskaia Rossiia i Pol'sha* and *Krasnaia Kniga;* also, Taracouzio, *op. cit.,* p. 317.

[38] *Sborn. Deistv. Dogov.,* IV, 1928, p. 19.

[39] *Ibid.,* p. 38. On June 2, 1927, a Treaty of Commerce was additionally signed between the U.S.S.R. and Latvia (*ibid.,* p. 61).

[40] *Ibid.,* p. 49.

[41] *VKP (b) v rezoliutsiakh,* II, pp. 179ff.

in England, France, and Japan replaced their liberal predecessors. It was a severe blow to the Soviets when Great Britain broke off relations with the Kremlin in May, 1927.[42] The Japanese designs on the mainland of Asia brought war clouds to the Far East. Finally, the struggle between the Stalinists and Trotzkyists within the Russian Communist Party itself had to be handled.[43]

Under the circumstances it was only natural that the Soviet desire for peace by means of rapid rapprochement with other nations grew more and more intense. At the world Economic Conference which met in Geneva in 1927, the Soviet delegation solemnly proclaimed the necessity of coöperation between the capitalist and the communist worlds. On November 30, of the same year, as said, at a meeting of the League's Preparatory Commission on Disarmament, Litvinov voiced a spectacular demand for an immediate, complete, and general disarmament.[44] Amid these appeals of little practical value, the concrete efforts of the Soviets to safeguard the needed peace were continued. An excellent opportunity to further the success which Soviet diplomacy had had with the treaties of non-aggression came in 1928 when the Briand-Kellogg Pact was signed, and in 1929 when the Litvinov Protocol made this Pact a workable instrument, at least formally.

It will be recalled that the above-mentioned Soviet treaties of neutrality and non-aggression contained nothing which precluded the accession thereto of states members of the League of Nations. From this standpoint, the ingenuity of Soviet diplomacy must be admitted, as it was left to the discretion of other non-communist states to decide whether or not to subscribe to the principles of good will embodied in their provisions. As has been said, the Briand-Kellogg Pact afforded the Soviets another opportunity to add considerably to the armor of their international security. True, at first this Pact was considered as another unfriendly gesture of the Great Powers toward the U.S.S.R., for to Chicherin, the Soviet Commissar, it appeared as "an instrument for the isolation of and struggle with the U.S.S.R." [45] Its advantages were soon realized, however, and on August 27, 1928, the Soviet Government informed the French

---

[42] The Anglo-Soviet relations were resumed only in 1929 (Valerin, *Ot rasryva do vosstanovleniia Anglo-Sovetskikh otnoshenii*, pp. 102ff).

[43] This resulted in the spectacular trials staged in Moscow in 1928–1931.

[44] *The Soviet Union and Peace*, pp. 137ff.

[45] *Cf.* Interview with him of Aug. 7, 1928 (*The Soviet Union and Peace*, p. 246).

Ambassador in Moscow that "inasmuch as the Paris Pact imposes on the Powers some external obligations before public opinion and gives the Soviet Government another opportunity to place before all participators in the Pact the most important question for peace— the question of disarmament, the solution of which is the only guarantee for averting war, the Soviet Government declares its consent to subscribe to the Paris Pact." [46] It is of minor importance whether the desire for promoting disarmament was the real reason for Soviet haste, or whether being the first to adhere was an ingenious *coup diplomatique* which inscribed yet another item on the credit sheet of their Foreign Office ledger. It must be remembered that the Soviets were still busy erecting around the U.S.S.R. an anti-aggression barrier of international treaties, promises, and understandings, and that in the final analysis this Pact was nothing but another link in the Soviet scheme of international bargaining.

The Litvinov Protocol of 1929 was a sequel to the Briand-Kellogg Pact. Unforeseen by the non-communist signatories to the latter, it evolved as the result of the never-ceasing Soviet ambition to be the foremost formal sponsor of peace. Outwardly disappointed at the slowness which the fifteen signatory powers displayed in ratifying the Pact, and consistent in their policy of trying out their immediate neighbors on the west first, the Soviets invited Poland, the only original signatory bordering the U.S.S.R. on the west, to sign a "Protocol according to which the Paris Treaty for the prohibition of war should come into force between the Soviet Union and Poland immediately after the ratification of it by the two States, regardless of the condition stipulated in Article III of the Pact." [47] The note furthermore informed the Polish Government that a similar proposal had been made to Lithuania, the only Baltic State which had so far adhered to the Kellogg Pact. The proposal placed Poland in a rather difficult position. The Polish Government did not see any real reason why the proposal should not be accepted, yet it was reluctant to have the Baltic states brought into the sphere of the Pact under the auspices of the Kremlin. The Soviets, however, succeeded in ironing out this difficulty with remarkable speed. Polish objection to the participation of Lithuania, which had no

---

[46] *The Soviet Union and Peace*, p. 225; for the Soviet Decree, *cf.*, *Sobr. Zak. i Rasp. U.S.S.R.* 1929, II, p. 525.
[47] *Ibid.*, p. 257.

common frontier with the U.S.S.R. and no diplomatic relations with Poland, as well as Polish commitments to Roumania,[48] with whom, in turn, the Soviet Union had no diplomatic relations, proved no obstacle to final understanding: Poland's suggestion of a multilateral protocol to include Finland, Estonia, Latvia, and Roumania was readily accepted by the Soviets who in return raised no objection to the omission of Lithuania.[49] On February 9, 1929, the Protocol was signed by the U.S.S.R., Poland, Latvia, Estonia, and even Roumania.[50] While Finland cautiously remained entirely aloof from security arrangements, and attempts to bring her into the scope of the Protocol failed, Lithuania eventually adhered on April 1, 1929. The Free City of Danzig, Turkey, and Persia were soon listed among Litvinov's diplomatic successes, following suit on April 30, July 1, and July 4, 1929, respectively.[51] The earlier failures of Soviet diplomacy were, to a certain extent, corrected.

To the Soviets, this Protocol, which now united by a bond of common aversion to war every one of their neighbor states from Estonia to Persia, was primarily "a link in the long chain of the Soviet Government's efforts toward universal peace and especially peace in Eastern Europe." [52] It must be remembered, however, that the renunciation formula of both the Briand-Kellogg Pact and the Litvinov Protocol applied only to allegedly offensive wars. In other words, this Protocol assured the Soviets security only against certain types of aggression and did not relieve them from the need of negotiating non-aggression pacts in the strictest sense of the term with neighboring states not yet bound by such treaties.

There were two factors which, paradoxical as it may appear at first, helped the Soviets to complete their entrenchment. One was the economic crisis which befell the world. The other was the appearance of the National Socialists as the second largest political

---

[48] *Cf.* Treaty of Guaranty signed by Poland and Roumania on March 26, 1926 (*L.N.T.S.*, LX, 163ff).

[49] This omission was quite wisely considered as unimportant under the circumstances, since Lithuania had already met the Soviet proposals in 1926 (*supra*, p. 121) and had announced her readiness to adhere to the Litvinov Protocol afterward.

[50] For text, *cf.*, *ibid.*, pp. 258–260.

[51] On Jan. 25, 1925, the U.S.S.R. signed also a Convention with Germany regarding conciliation procedure, realizing thus the pledge of signing a special treaty on the pacific settlement of disputes given in the Treaty of Berlin of 1926 (*Sborn. Deistv. Dogov.*, V, 1930, p. 10).

[52] From Litvinov's speech at Signing the Protocol (*The Soviet Union and Peace*, p. 268).

party in the Reichstag after the elections of September, 1930. The former brought about noticeable discord in the evaluation of the basic issues controlling relations between the capitalist and communist worlds; the appearance of the Nazis was an unpleasant surprise for the Allies, who saw that the movement threatened one of the pillars of the peace structure of Versailles. The combination of these two events meant to the Soviets the fomentation of open conflict, for now the ideological antagonism between the two worlds was augmented by impulses of a purely economic nature. To the frightened powers of Western Europe this rapid sequence of events spelled the need for securing their own well-being by placing around Germany a *cordon politique* after the fashion of pre-World War days. As a result of the new situation, a summary alarm was sounded in the U.S.S.R. that it was being encircled anew with aggressive unfriendliness both from the west and from the east,[53] and the Soviet authorities busied themselves with averting this new "danger." At the same time the Western Powers were working laboriously to find ways for a closer rapprochement with Moscow, thereby assisting the Soviet diplomats in their efforts to prevent both an aggression against the U.S.S.R. and war in Western Europe, which they were not yet in a position either to withstand successfully or to witness advantageously.

As a result of all this the Soviets have to their credit the securing of non-aggression conciliation conventions with Afghanistan, Turkey, and Lithuania in 1931,[54] with the other Baltic States and with France in 1932,[55] and with Italy in 1933.[56] Basically similar to the treaties of 1925 to 1928,[57] as regards the pledges of neutrality, non-aggression, pacific settlement of disputes, and the covenant of non-participation, they contained two new features, namely: provision for the immediate liberation of the signatories from their obligations if the other contracting party commits an act of aggression, and the preservation of their legal rights under agreements

[53] For Soviet relations with the Far-Eastern Powers, *cf., infra,* pp. 207ff.

[54] Treaty with Afghanistan was signed on June 24, 1931 (*Sobr. Zak. i Rasp. S.S.S.R.,* 1932, II, p. 75). Agreements with Turkey and Lithuania signed on Mar. 7, 1931, and May 6, 1931, respectively, were not treaties but protocols renewing the earlier treaties. (*Ibid.,* 1931, II, pp. 480 and 477, respectively.)

[55] These were: with Finland, of Jan. 21, 1932; with Estonia, May 4, 1932; Latvia, Feb. 5, 1932; Poland, July 15, 1932; and France, Nov. 29, 1932 (*Sborn. Deistv. Dogov.,* VII, pp. 21, 32, 6, 12, and 27, respectively).

[56] *Ibid.,* VIII, p. 8.

[57] *Supra,* p. 119.

concluded "before the coming into force of the present Pact, so far as the said agreements contain no aggressive elements."

At this point a few words must be said regarding Soviet attempts to safeguard their frontiers in the Far East. The relations of the U.S.S.R. with China and Japan had only complications in common. On May 21, 1924, the U.S.S.R. and China signed a treaty by which the Soviet Government was recognized *de jure* and diplomatic relations between the two countries were established.[58] A similar understanding was reached between the Soviets and Japan on January 20, 1925.[59] Here the analogy ends, however. The interest of Moscow in Chinese affairs was focused mainly on the revolutionary possibilities, whereas Soviet relations with the Empire of the Rising Sun were perforce mainly directed toward preventing Japan from becoming uncontrollable in her ambitious designs in Asia. The history of these relations is yet to be written, but it may be said here that whatever disappointment was suffered by the Kremlin in regard to revolutionary failures in China, the Soviets were satisfied that there was no real danger of war as far as China was concerned.

The situation as to Japan was different, for here the possibilities of an open conflict were much greater. The trouble over the fishery and mining concessions, the problem of Sakhalin Island, of the Eastern Chinese Railway, and of Manchuria are only a few of the well-known complications which characterized and which continue to characterize Soviet relations with Japan. It must suffice to say that to the Soviets the success of Japan in its dealings with China mean not only a set-back to the penetration of communism into the Far East but the strengthening of a formidable and uncompromising foe as well. Hence, it is only natural that Soviet effort was concentrated on securing from Japan some kind of an arrangement analogous to the pacts of neutrality and non-aggression concluded with the powers in the West. The Soviet Government had repeatedly expressed its readiness to enter into such an agreement with Japan, but the Kremlin's efforts proved of no avail; not even the negotiations launched by Litvinov in 1931 when Yoshizawa stopped at Moscow on his way from Paris to Tokio to assume his duties of Foreign Minister had been successful. Even the sale of the Chinese Eastern Railway and the yearly renewals of economic concessions

[58] *Sborn. Deistv. Dogov.*, I–II, 1928, p. 30.
[59] *Ibid.*, III, 1927, p. 10.

failed to yield the coveted treaty. The establishment of Manchukuo and the comparatively recent bloodshed around Lake Hasan seem to justify Soviet fears that the Pact of Paris, fragile as it is, is the only guaranty for peace along their Far-Eastern frontiers.

Rejoicing over diplomatic successes in the west and perturbed by failures and potential hostilities in the east, the U.S.S.R. continued to solidify the integrity of its borders. The bilateral understandings with foreign countries having been achieved, the Soviets found it imperative that the obligations undertaken by these powers individually should also become mutually binding among them. A route to that end was found in the need for a common understanding of the term aggression itself. Not that aggression had not been defined before. The difficulty was that neither the refusal to submit disputes to pacific settlement, nor the ordering of troops into the demilitarized Rhineland zone, both of which acts were understood to constitute aggression according to the Geneva Protocol of 1924 and to the Locarno Agreement, respectively, furnished a formula of aggression satisfactory either to the Western Powers or to the Soviets. Whatever the reasons which prompted the former to search for a definition which proved abortive in one instance and of purely local application in the other, these definitions had no bearing upon the more settled designs of the Soviets. Nor did the previous definition imply a sufficiently wide participation of states to suit the goal of the Kremlin. Never failing to seize an opportunity, and already encouraged by the previous experience in 1929 in regard to the Briand-Kellogg Pact, Litvinov again proved his ingenuity when, in 1933, at the London Economic Conference, he proposed to the states parties to the Moscow Protocol of 1929 to sign a multilateral convention by which the following actions were to constitute aggression: (1) Declaration of war on another state, (2) invasion by armed forces even without declaration of war, (3) an attack by any type of armed forces, even without declaration of war, (4) naval blockade of the coasts and ports, and (5) support to armed units which have been organized on its territory and have invaded the territory of another state.[60] The proposal was accepted, and on July 3, 1933, the Convention was signed by Afghanistan, Estonia, Latvia,

[60] This definition was proposed by M. Politis and adopted by the Committee on Security at the Disarmament Conference on May 24, 1933 (for French and Russian texts, cf., *Dogovory o neitralitite, nenapadenii i o soglastital'noi protsedure* . . ., pp. 172ff.).

Persia, Poland, Roumania, and Turkey. The next day a similar Convention was signed by Soviet Russia, Roumania, Czechoslovakia, Turkey, and Yugoslovia,[61] to which Finland adhered on July 23. In the meantime, Lithuania signed a similar separate Convention with the Soviets on July 5.

Having thus established itself as the dominant power of Eastern Europe and having indicated its shift from doctrinary isolation and ideological neutrality to the policy of *Realpolitik* and of partiality presaging mutual assistance, the Soviet Union became a willing recipient of diplomatic gifts from those who sought its friendship. The consummation of a Treaty of Non-Aggression with Italy, signed on September 2, 1933; [62] the extension for ten years of the pacts of non-aggression and neutrality with Estonia, Latvia, Lithuania, Finland, and Poland; [63] *de jure* recognition by and resumption of diplomatic relations with the United States of America, Roumania, Czechoslovakia, Bulgaria, and Hungary; [64] the comprehensive Eastern Pact and, finally, the admission of the Soviet Union into the League of Nations on September 18, 1934, are not only evidence of Litvinov's triumph, but further proof that Soviet foreign policy henceforth was to be directed toward a united front of the countries favoring international peace against the united front of the nations fomenting aggression. This new issue in Soviet foreign policy brought to an end the third stage of the communist understanding of world peace from a revolutionary standpoint.

While it is impossible to enumerate here all the methods resorted to for a rapprochement between the U.S.S.R. and the capitalist world, it must be pointed out that political treaties were not the only manifestation of Soviet anxiety for security. Economic, consular, juridical, humanitarian, and many other fields were made to serve for closer collaboration and, hence, also as instrumentalities for strengthening the international position of the U.S.S.R. The importance of closer economic relations with the capitalist world was admitted by the Soviets as early as 1921. As it was at the same time

[61] *Sborn. Deistv. Dogov.*, VIII, 1935, pp. 27, 12, and 31, respectively. The signatories to the Convention of July 4, 1933, were Soviet Russia, Roumania, Czechoslovakia, Turkey, and Yugoslavia.

[62] *Ibid.*, p. 8.

[63] Individual Protocols of Prolongations with the first three countries were signed on Apr. 4, 1934, with Finland on Apr. 7, 1934, and with Poland on May 5 of the same year (*ibid.*, pp. 25, 11, 15, 21 and 16, respectively).

[64] *Ibid.*, pp. 4, 5, 6, 19 and 23, respectively.

that the New Economic Policy of Lenin was also inaugurated, the two became integral supplementary parts of one single process. Whatever the results at home, in the field of international economics the Soviet policy was subjected to considerations of economic independence on the one hand, and of the maximum development of international trade, on the other. In terms of national security, this meant that the increase in Soviet foreign trade had to be calculated so as not to bring about economic capitulation to international capitalism. This general principle remained a consideration of permanent standing throughout Soviet history, and found its official revolutionary sanction at the Fifteenth Congress of the Russian Communist Party in December, 1927: "In planning our economic activities in the field of international relations . . . we must base our policy on the idea of a maximum development of our economic relations with foreign countries so far as such relations . . . contribute to the economic strength of the Union. We must make it more independent of the capitalist world and broaden the socialist foundation for further industrial expansion of the Union." [65] This policy of economic expediency, which remains in force even today, in the words of Florinsky, meant that "the former crusaders of world revolution at any cost have exchanged their swords for machine tools, and now rely more on the results of their labor than on direct action to achieve the ultimate victory of the proletariat." [66] Whatever were the other considerations which prompted the Soviets to sponsor the peaceful co-existence of the capitalist and communist worlds, the security of the U.S.S.R. and hence, also, the possibility for fomentation of revolutions in the future were by no means minor factors. This has been admitted by the Soviets themselves, witness the statement found in the editorial of *Izvestiia*, April 23, 1931:

"The Soviet Union is willing to develop its economic relations with the outside world, and to promote the conditions needed for their success. The growth of the economic strength of our socialist country is to be accompanied by furthering its ties with the world markets. It is impossible that this process can be prevented as long as there is a *peaceful* co-existence between the U.S.S.R. and the capitalist encirclement." [67]

[65] *XV S'ezd Vsesoiuznoi Kommunisticheskoi Partii (b). Stenograficheskii Otchet*, p. 1292.
[66] Florinsky, *op. cit.*, p. 216.
[67] Italics in the original.

THEORY ON TRIAL

In attempting to analyze the revolutionary undertaking of the Soviets to secure world peace, it must be pointed out at the beginning that the end of the civil war and of the Allied intervention coincided with the inauguration of the communist program of international revolution by means of international peace. Theoretically, the war-cry of the communists, "To the masses," meant a laborious process of preparing the proletarian masses for eventual revolutionary action. Concretely, it meant the preservation of actual international peace, which by then had come to be considered the paramount prerequisite for carrying out this preparatory work effectively.

To the Soviets the change in the tactics of the Communist International spelled further retreat from their original revolutionary enthusiasm and ambitions. At the Fourth Congress of the Comintern which met in November, 1922, Radek admitted that "in spite of the fact that the crisis of the world proletariat is by no means over, the characteristic feature is the loss of faith by the proletariat in the possibility of seizing power in the near future." [68] From Lenin's point of view, however, the fact that the Soviets thus found themselves on the defensive, was not sufficient cause for sinking into dark pessimism. Ever practical, he fully realized that a frontal attack by the now firmly established political power of the proletariat in the U.S.S.R. would not be enough because, even in case of victory, there was always the possibility that their enemies had provoked the attack in order to "throw us back for many years." Hence, although chagrined by the delay, he was not less fully aware of the need for further retreat. It was at this same Congress of the Third International that he admitted the necessity of further retreat when he said that it was "essential not merely as a matter of theory but also of practical politics." [69] He understood this retreat as a mere practical expedient which did not mean the abandonment of world revolution, but was merely provisional in character. The practical problem was to find a way to cover this retreat.

To Lenin, it was not difficult to find a solution. Without altering the ultimate end—the abolition of capitalism throughout the

---

[68] *Chetvertyi Vsemirnyi Kongress Kommunisticheskogo Internatsionala*, p. 132.
[69] *Ibid.*, pp. 62–64.

world—he ordered that Trotzky's idea of permanent revolution be discarded and prescribed, in its stead, that henceforth the establishment of socialism in one country be the revolutionary strategy of the Soviets. The feasibility of such a strategy had been foreseen by him long before he was called upon to put this theory to a practical test. In 1915, he wrote:

"The unevenness of its economic and political development is an absolute law of capitalism. From this it follows that the victory of socialism is originally possible in a few or even in one separate capitalist country. The victorious proletariat of this country, having expropriated the capitalists and organized socialist production at home, could rise against the remaining capitalist world, attracting to itself the exploited classes in other countries, organizing their revolts against the capitalists, and, if necessary, using even military force against the exploiting classes and their states." [70]

At the Fifteenth Congress of the Russian Communist Party it was said that "in case of delays in the socialist revolution in other countries, the victory of socialism in one country will, in the historical ending of modern capitalism, result in the final victory; that is, in such a victory as will remove not only the internal but also the international obstacles to complete socialist development, leading thus to the victory of communism." Simultaneously it was stated that the policy of the Communist Party was, "and will remain, the policy of the victory of socialism in our country, and at the same time, the policy of the final victory of socialism in the world at large." [71] Whatever the difference between these two,[72] victory in a single country must connote the dictatorship of the proletariat and the triumph of socialist economy over the capitalist elements within the country. When applied to the immediate needs of the Soviet Union, it meant an exemplary solidification within the U.S.S.R. of the proletarian régime in its entirety. As to the international policies, the above declaration suggests that the victory of socialism in Russia is not considered an aim in itself but merely an instrumentality for the further expansion of communism. To assure the possibility of using this means in the future, an environment had to be created where victory at home could be achieved. In other

[70] Lenin, XVIII, 133.
[71] *XV S'ezd Vsesoiuznoi Kommunisticheskoi Partii (b)*, p. 673. (Cited in Florinsky, *op. cit.*, pp. 165–166.)
[72] For an excellent analysis of the issue, *cf.* Florinsky, *op. cit.*, pp. 125–168.

words, the existence of the U.S.S.R. in its capitalist environment had to be safeguarded.[73]

Theoretical sanction of such a fusion of domestic and foreign policies was found in the Marxian formula of close interdependence of the two. In the words of Lenin "there is no more erroneous or harmful idea than the separation of foreign and domestic policies." [74] At the Twelfth Congress of the Russian Communist Party in 1923, Zinoviev voiced the same opinion when he said: "It is not so easy to draw a mechanical distinction between foreign and domestic policy. . . . This applies both to the Soviet State and to Soviet politics. Our domestic policy is closely and inseparably bound up with our foreign policy." [75] He repeated it a year later at the next congress when he said that "never before has our international policy been so closely bound up with our domestic policy as it is now." [76] That this was not alone his individual opinion is evidenced by the resolutions of these Congresses supporting these postulates.

It is impossible here to enter into a narrative of the particulars as to how this retreat by the building of socialism in one country first was accomplished in the field of domestic affairs. Suffice it to say that according to Lenin, Soviet efforts to this end would have been limited to cultural work, had it not been for the international relations which the Soviets had to carry on in order to fight for the survival of the Soviet Union as a world power.[77] That there was to be a struggle was admitted by Lenin on several occasions. Thus, in one place he wrote: "we live not only in a state, but in a system of states, and the existence of the Soviet Republic side by side with imperialistic states for any great length of time is unthinkable. In the end either one or the other must win." [78] In another place he emphasized the same idea when he said that "so long as the Soviet Republic remains a lonely borderland of the capitalist world, it would be ridiculous to imagine . . . that this or that danger will disappear. For as long as such fundamental antagonisms remain,

---

[73] *Cf.* also discussions held at the VII and VIII Plenary Sessions of the Communist International.

[74] *Leninskii Sbornik*, XXI, 66.

[75] *Dvenadtsatyi S'ezd Rossiiskoi Kommunisticheskoi Partii (b) 17–25go Aprelia, 1923*, p. 617.

[76] *Trinadtsatyi S'ezd Rossiiskoi Kommunisticheskoi Partii (b) 23–31go maia 1924, Stenograficheskii Otchet*, p. 50.

[77] Lenin, XVIII, pt. II, 140ff.

[78] *Ibid.*, XVI, 102.

naturally the dangers will likewise exist. One cannot run away from them." [79] How, under pressure of this constant fear, Soviet diplomacy succeeded in placing the Soviet Union among the Great Powers has been told in the preceding pages. It remains to analyze briefly how this foreign policy fitted in with Marxian ideology.

It has already been pointed out that the Marxian-Leninist interpretation of political events rests on the principle of the class conception of social phenomena, including war and peace. Since war and peace involve foreign relations, are interlocked with domestic policies, and are of historical significance as regards the sequence of political developments, it follows that, methodologically, class interests as the determining factor in the revolutionary process must also shape the concrete efforts of the proletarian Soviets in regard to peace. As the importance of this for the foreign relations of the U.S.S.R. is self-evident, and as the significance of the fusion of foreign and domestic policies has just been pointed out, only the historical evaluation, from the standpoint of class distinction, need be examined at this juncture. The importance of class distinction was admitted by Lenin when he said that "Marxian methodology consists, first of all, of taking into account the *objective* content of a given historical process at a definite given time and in definite, concrete circumstances, so as to understand, first of all, which class is the dominating factor in the furtherance of progress under these concrete circumstances." [80]

Having accepted this as the basis for the international relations of a proletarian state, Lenin was only taking the first step when he voiced his theory of establishing socialism in a single country. His successors had no alternative but to continue the Kremlin's foreign relations on this basis inaugurated by Lenin in 1922, and to maintain that struggle for world peace was to be accepted as a condition under which the armament of the world proletariat for ultimate revolutionary action could best be effected. With such a purpose in view, Soviet foreign policy, while formally envisaging world peace, from the standpoint of Marxian methodology and revolutionary tactics first of all reflected a rapprochement of the Soviet proletariat with the working masses in capitalist and colonial countries. Then it permitted the Kremlin to take advantage of the difficulties encountered by the capitalist states, in the general systematic develop-

[79] Lenin, XVII, 408–409.
[80] *Ibid.*, XVIII, 106.

ment of economic relations with the outside world. It also furthered the simultaneous solidification of Soviet economic strength and independence. Finally, it enhanced the never-ceasing efforts to increase military preparedness against the time when the Soviets would see fit to continue their peace policies by "different [forcible] means." [81]

Among the efforts of the U.S.S.R. for peace in the interests of their own security, the attention paid by Soviet diplomacy to the countries of the East and Near East was not a mere mechanical procedure in the process of protecting Soviet Russia with a cordon of neutral border states. The rapprochement of the Kremlin with the Levant and Far Eastern peoples was nurtured also by significant revolutionary ideology. It will be recalled that the whole structure of Lenin's foreign policy was based on close coöperation and friendship with the oppressed peoples in the colonies and semi-colonial dependencies of the Great Powers. Fully aware of the truism that weak spots are the most vulnerable ones, Lenin did not fail to see that in the capitalist world the relations of the Great Powers with their overseas colonies were by no means happy, and that it was precisely this weakness of which advantage might be taken. Hence, the Soviet concentration of attention on the possibilities afforded by the none-too-satisfied peoples living across their southeastern and eastern borders.

Armed with one of the fundamental principles of Marxism—the self-determination of oppressed nations—Lenin made the program of Soviet international relations with these peoples an integral part of the general strategy pursued by proletarian internationalism. In other words, he took for his starting point the fact that there was an impassable gulf between the oppressed and the oppressor nations, and that after the World War the relations between the capitalist countries and the peoples entertaining revolutionary hopes for liberation became "a struggle of a small group of imperialistic nations with Sovietism and the Soviet States." [82] Immediate renunciation of unequal treaties, persistent assurances of friendship, and, later, the conclusion of treaties envisaging peaceful co-existence between the U.S.S.R. and its eastern neighbors, are formal manifestation of the Soviet understanding of the foreign policy prescribed by Lenin in regard to these countries.

[81] *Supra,* p. 27.
[82] Lenin, XXV, 352.

In the general scheme of Soviet international bargaining, this diplomatic courtship was logical. The fact is that Lenin always counted upon the oppressed nations as the revolutionary reserves in the struggle against capitalist counter-revolution. Whatever the true extent of the moral support given to him by colonial and semi-colonial peoples, Lenin was sure that their development had reached a point where it "cannot but bring about the crisis of capitalism the world over." [83] A firm believer in ultimate armed conflict between the Soviets and the non-communist world, Lenin proved himself no less an optimist in regard to the revolutionary rôle which he predicted would be played by oppressed nations. When in 1923, speaking of the international situation, he said that the victorious powers were commencing to make concessions to their colonial subjects, he did not fail to explain that this was not a magnanimous extravagance which they could well afford at the time, but sheer necessity, since by so doing they "postponed revolution in their colonies and created a semblance of 'social peace'." He elaborated upon this optimism when he added that the outcome of the forthcoming conflict between the U.S.S.R. and the non-communist powers will "in the end depend on the fact that Russia, India, and China contain the gigantic majority of the [world's] population. [Yet] it is precisely this majority which during the last years has been drawn, with extraordinary speed, into the struggle for its liberation. Therefore, from this standpoint, there can be no doubt as to the ultimate outcome of the struggle." [84]

To make possible ultimate victory for the Soviets, Lenin prescribed that "measures be taken to secure the survival of the communist régime, at least until [the materialization of] the war between the counter-revolutionary civilized West and the retarded peoples of the East." The establishment of modern civilization among the latter was to serve as the practical means to this end. In the light of communist strategy this noble aspiration was not motivated by sentiments of a purely humanitarian nature, but was rather the training of potential reserves for ultimately becoming active revolutionary allies. The Soviets may well be credited with diplomatic ingenuity, for it is difficult to deny the soundness of the principle itself. The fact is that any progress made by colonial peoples,

[83] Lenin, XXVII, 415.
[84] *Ibid.*, 415–417.

whether it be enlightenment in things political, or economic well-being, would breed aspirations hardly consistent with the plans of their imperial masters. This, in turn, would force the latter to concentrate their efforts and attention on things colonial. The result to the Soviets of such a distraction would be only too obvious: postponement of aggression against the U.S.S.R., *i.e.,* peace, during which the dictatorial régime of the Russian proletariat would be left at liberty to proceed with building revolutionary barricades at home.

The peace policy of the Soviet Union in regard to the Levantine countries and the empires in the Far East was only one of the phases in the general scheme of taking advantage of the difficulties confronting the capitalist world. It must be pointed out that to a Marxist, the difficulties of real importance were not the minor, incidental frictions, but contradictions due to fundamental economic causes. Again Lenin may be quoted:

> "If we are going to make use of petty, incidental discords we shall become either petty politicians or insignificant diplomats. This will lead nowhere. There are a multitude of diplomats playing this kind of a game, only to make a career within a few months and then to become nonentities again." [85]

As to the fundamental contradictions, they may be divided broadly into three categories, according to Lenin. First, there is collision between the working and work-giving classes, *i.e.,* the basic controversy between communism and capitalism. Second, the controversies between the individual imperialist powers, on the one hand, and the consortia of capitalist states, on the other. Finally, the third category comprises the difficulties between the Great Powers and their colonial and semi-colonial domains. The division of the world into two camps, one of capitalism and one of socialism, which resulted from the establishment of the Soviet régime,[86] is representative of the general antagonism between international capitalism and the international proletariat. According to Lenin, the revolutionary importance of this was illustrated both in the days of Brest-Litovsk and during the civil war and Allied intervention. He attributed the survival of the communist régime to the antagonism between the Allied and German imperialisms, on the one hand, and between the smaller nations and the greater powers, on the other.

[85] Lenin, XXV, 501.
[86] *Supra,* p. 111.

Lenin's explanation of the Soviet victory during the four-year period from 1918 to 1922 is in point. To quote:

"We were able to survive and to defeat the powerful coalition of the Entente Powers which was supported by White armies only because there was no unity among these Powers. Up to this time we have been victorious not only because of the serious conflicts among these imperialistic powers but precisely because these conflicts were not incidental domestic disagreements but deeply rooted fundamental economic struggles of the imperialistic powers among themselves." [87]

In view of the irreconcilability of the capitalist and communist régimes, the first impression is that the ideological antagonism of the non-communist powers toward the U.S.S.R. should have resulted in a conciliatory relationship of these powers *inter se,* and that there was neither time nor justification for conflict in the capitalist camp. The facts, however, point to the contrary, witness not only the continuous political and economic rivalry which raged under the blessing of the Versailles peace, but also the discord in regard to the attitude to be taken toward the Soviets. According to Lenin, in his day there prevailed two tendencies, neither of which was sound in his opinion: "one sponsored the inevitable union of all capitalist powers [against the Soviets], while the other was inciting one capitalist power against another." [88] This situation did not end with Lenin's death; it continues to flourish today. The same is true also in regard to the basic principles underlying these two tendencies. The organic antagonism toward the communist conception of things remains the starting point for capitalist countries in their dealings with the Soviet Union. At the same time, the economic possibilities which the riches in the U.S.S.R. afford continue to lure these powers into a competitive, but by no means always friendly, race for the favors of their ideological foe.

OF FEAR AND HOPE

The crusade against war has been the natural response of Soviet diplomacy to this basic conflict between capitalism and communism. If it be recalled that the dynamics of friction in the imperialistic camp are not subject to precise rules and are non-calculable before-

[87] Lenin, XXVI, 7.
[88] *Ibid.,* XXIII, 6–7.

hand, the Soviet aversion to war presents no mystery, for it is only under conditions of peace that the fluctuations in the attitude of the non-communist world toward the U.S.S.R. can be best evaluated and reacted upon most advantageously. The Soviet rapprochement with Germany at Rapallo, the uneasiness of the Kremlin at the time of Germany's entry into the League of Nations, the anxiety of the Allies caused by Germany's determination to disregard the dictates of Versailles, and the resultant Soviet non-aggression pacts with France and Poland are vivid illustrations of this in the field of politics. That the Soviets also saw the advantages of peace in their economic pursuits is proved by the proceedings at Genoa. "We understand perfectly well," said Lenin, "what lies at the bottom of this conference: we know that it is trade. The bourgeois countries must have trade with Russia. They know that without one or another form of economic intercourse [with us] their disintegration will continue to progress as it has been progressing thus far." [89] To him this preservation of peace was for the purpose of securing not only political independence but economic and revolutionary integrity as well. His belief that international revolutions were to be augmented henceforth primarily by economic efforts [90] was reiterated with almost primitive self-assurance by Stalin in 1929:

"When the U.S.S.R. is riding in automobiles and the peasants sit in tractors—then let the esteemed capitalists, proud of their 'civilization', try to catch up with us! We shall yet see which of the countries will then be classified as advanced and which as retarded!" [91]

When it became evident that the capitalist and communist worlds had come to co-exist, the communist pursuit of peace for the sake of building socialism in the U.S.S.R. not only remained the focal point of the Soviet foreign policy, but was augmented, for now the revolutionary need of extending the breathing spell was given new impetus. At the Fourteenth Party Congress, held in 1926, Stalin admitted that a new factor had come into being which was now determining the international relations of the Soviet Union:

"A certain degree of provisional equilibrium has been established between our country of socialist construction and the countries of the

[89] Lenin, XXV, 502.
[90] *Ibid.,* XXIII, 182.
[91] Stalin, *Voprosy Leninizma,* 9th ed., p. 441.

capitalist world. This equilibrium characterizes the present stage of the 'peaceful co-existence' of the Soviet and capitalist countries. What we considered once to be a short relief from war has now become a long breathing spell." [92]

This temporary balance between the two worlds was not accepted by the Soviets as a guaranty of peace, however. To Stalin, it meant rather an increase in the danger of foreign aggression, because to him this equilibrium did not eliminate the contradictions which continued to prevail in the capitalist countries. In outlining the revolutionary strategy and tactics of Soviet foreign policy, he viewed the co-existence of the U.S.S.R. and the non-communist states not as a stage of normal development but as a condition forced upon the Soviets by circumstances. His analysis brought him to the conclusion that the two components of that equilibrium—the stabilization of the U.S.S.R. and stabilization in post-war Europe—while concurrent in regard to time, were diametrically opposed as to their tendencies. In revolutionary parlance, to him "the stabilization of capitalism cannot be lasting. This stabilization means an accumulation of factors which lead to the defeat of capitalism. The stabilization of the Soviet régime, on the contrary, signals an accumulation of conditions solidifying the dictatorship of the proletariat, augments revolutionary movements in all countries, and leads to the victory of socialism." [93] The nebulous explanation of Marxists that the main characteristic of capitalism consists precisely in the fact that wars are bred by the stabilization of capitalism, meant that concretely, from the Soviet standpoint, these conflicting tendencies were only a prelude to the inevitable war between the Great Powers and the U.S.S.R. Addressing the same Party Congress, Stalin was outspoken in his opinion of European diplomacy. "They talk about pacifism," he said, "they speak about peace among European states. Briand and Chamberlain are embracing each other. Stresemann casts compliments before England. All this is nonsense. From European history we know that every time that treaties [actually] envisaging a new arrangement of forces for new wars have been signed, these treaties have been called treaties of peace. The signing of these treaties has always been accompanied by noisy cries about peace, [although]

[92] XIV S'ezd Vsesoiuznoi Kommunisticheskoi Partii (b), 18–31 Dekabria 1925g. Stenograficheskii Otchet, p. 8.
[93] Stalin, Ob oppositsii, p. 177.

they were signed for the purpose of depicting new elements of the coming war." [94]

Under the circumstances, the establishment of socialism in Soviet Russia was to be pushed at an increased tempo, so as to render harmless these designs of aggression against the U.S.S.R. Peace was a prerequisite also for increasing the military strength of the Soviets. Here it need only be added that Stalin shared his master's belief that "if the proletariat wishes to rule, it must prove it by its military organization." [95] To his mind peace was needed for "arming" toward the coming revolution. Admitting that socialism can and must be established in the U.S.S.R., he added that to be able to do this, the Soviets must first of all exist. Hence, according to him, in addition to relief from war and attempted intervention, there must be a certain minimum in their favor in the international situations. This minimum was to include, besides the basic contradictions in the camp of capitalism, an increase in the strength of the Red Army in the camp of socialism.[96]

At home, this policy of peace resulted in the struggle against revolutionary inertness and notions of narrow nationalism; [97] in foreign relations it found reflection in the Soviet efforts to find a counteracting remedy for the disappointments of Genoa, Locarno, Germany's membership in the League, and the rupture of British-Soviet relations. The results achieved by the U.S.S.R. in this respect have already been pointed out, as has been the temporary relief which they brought.[98]

To the Soviets the economic crisis of 1929 was more than a logical phase in the process of capitalist disintegration. To them it meant also the termination of the post-war stabilization of capitalism and the beginning of the complete bankruptcy of the non-communist world. Labor unrest resulting from unemployment and the consequent revival of revolutionary enthusiasm abroad were interpreted as positive signs of the end of capitalism. In the press, in learned

---

[94] *XIV S'ezd Vsesoiuznoi Kommunisticheskoi Partii (b), 18–31 Dekabria 1925g. Stenograficheskii Otchet*, p. 15.

[95] Lenin, XV, 51.

[96] Stalin, *op. cit.*, pp. 455–456. For the rôle of the Red Army in the communist scheme of things, *cf. infra*, pp. 266ff.

[97] These were resultant of over-indulgence in placing too much confidence in the self-destructiveness of capitalism, on the one hand, and in the consequent revolutionary transformation of Russia into a proletarian *fatherland* on the other.

[98] *Supra*, pp. 113ff.

discussions, in reports to Communist Congresses, as well as in the official and non-official statements of those who had a right to voice their views, the opinion was uniform, and the picture of the situation of the non-communist world presented for mass consumption in the U.S.S.R. was by no means encouraging for those not in sympathy with Soviet ideals. The rivalry of the Great Powers over colonies was reduced to the mere taking of measures for the suppression of discontent among the colonial peoples, *i.e.*, to the mere policy of saving what had been acquired. The redistribution of world markets, which a few years before had been regarded in communist circles as indicative of a new reorientation of the capitalist nations in regard to each other, as illustrated by the growing unfriendliness between Great Britain and the United States,[99] had now taken a definite turn for the worse. The competition of Great Britain and America in the Far East, the struggle for control of the commercial sea lanes in the Mediterranean, the growing friction between the Allies and Germany over the Versailles system, the revolutionary progress in China, were all declared to have become accelerated after the economic collapse in 1929. Coupled with the suppression of labor abroad, all these changes were acclaimed by the Kremlin as undeniable proof of the foresightedness of Stalin, who, at the Fifteenth Congress of the Communist Party in 1928, predicted that "Europe was obviously entering into a period of new revolutionary enthusiasm." [100]

This natural revival of communist optimism was not the only repercussion in the U.S.S.R. of the events of 1929. Pleasant as the new revolutionary perspectives may have been, this crisis brought new worries to the Soviets from the standpoint of peace and security. Proudly considering their own existence as one of the major causes of the capitalist difficulties, the Soviets were consistent enough to sound anew the warning of danger, the only difference being that instead of the almost forgotten old motto "the Revolution is in danger," now the masses were given to understand in a reasoned way that a change in the peaceful co-existence of the communist and capitalist systems was imminent. The forms which this change was to take were forecast by Stalin at the same Congress:

[99] Stalin's report to the XV Party Congress (*XV S'ezd Vsesoiusnoi Kommunisticheskoi Partii (b), Stenograficheskii Otchet*, p. 41).
[100] *Ibid.*, p. 46.

"Whereas two years ago we could speak and had to speak of a period of certain equilibrium and 'peaceful' coexistence between the U.S.S.R. and the capitalist countries, now we have every reason to declare that this period of 'peaceful' coexistence is disappearing and giving way to a period of imperialistic aggression and preparation for new interventions against the U.S.S.R." [101]

It was pointed out at the Sixteenth Congress of the Communist Party that the basic reason for this change was that the center of gravity had now shifted from conflicts between one great power and the consortia of other nations to differences between individual great powers and that, while the difficulties between the workers and the capitalists continued, as did also the conflicts between the colonies and their masters, a new aspect of the conflict was becoming more and more prominent, namely the problem of revision of the Versailles system.[102] The people of Russia were told, furthermore, that the insolubility of the contradictions in the capitalist world, now augmented by the economic crisis, would lead the non-communist powers to a state of despair from which they would try to emerge by resorting to reactionary measures in things domestic and to imperialistic wars in the field of foreign policy.[103] For the Soviet Union this meant that "every time these contradictions take a turn for the worse, the bourgeoisie begins to look at the U.S.S.R. with the secret hope of settling this or that contradiction in the capitalist camp, or maybe even all of them, at the expense of the U.S.S.R., the country of Soviets and the citadel of revolution, which, by its very existence, revolutionizes the working class and the colonies, prevents new wars and a new redivision of the world, and does not tolerate any [foreign] mastery over its enormous domestic markets, now so desired by the capitalists, particularly in view of the economic crisis." [104]

At the Seventeenth Congress of the Russian Communist Party, Stalin, summarizing the world events for the years 1930 to 1933, reiterated the communist revolutionary hopes and the Soviet fear of aggression when he said that these years had brought about a further augmentation of the contradictions in the capitalist camp.[105] The resignation of Japan from the League of Nations, its aggression

[101] *XV S'ezd. . . .* , p. 47.
[102] Stalin, *Voprosy Leninizma*, 9 ed., pp. 494ff.
[103] *Ibid.*, p. 498.
[104] *Ibid.*, p. 499.
[105] *XVII S'ezd Vsesoiuznoi Kommunisticheskoi Partii, 26 Ianvaria–10 Fevralia 1934g. Stenograficheskii Otchet*, pp. 8ff.

in China and its occupation of Manchukuo, as well as the withdrawal of Germany from Geneva [106] to him meant increase of armaments by the Great Powers, including the United States. The establishment of National-Socialism in Germany and German withdrawal from Geneva indicated the Germanic notions of revenge and revisionism. The "defeat" of Fascism in Spain was regarded as an indication of the instability of dictatorships which are not proletarian. More firmly than ever convinced that war was the only possible outcome of the situation, Stalin concentrated his efforts upon proving that of the four possible types of wars—against another of the Great Powers, against some weak country affording good markets, against some "lower" race, and against the U.S.S.R.—the one against the Soviets was the most logical and the most probable. His appeal for peace and the incidental admission of the need for it can be deduced from the praise which he paid to Soviet diplomacy for restoring an amicable understanding with Poland, gaining recognition by the United States, and achieving the non-aggression and neutrality treaties, as well as in his general remark that "while the capitalist countries prepare themselves feverishly for new wars, the U.S.S.R. continues its systematic and persistent struggle for peace." [107]

It is immaterial whether this fear was genuine or was voiced with the definite purpose of using it as a revolutionary stimulant at home, like the Five-Year Plans and the sporting appeals for competitive rivalry in the form of the Stakhanov movement,—the fact is that this danger was portrayed as real and imminent. What prompted the Soviets to continue their emphasis on peace is of no particular significance either, whether it was communist adherence to the rules of tactical consistency prescribed by revolutionary strategy, or realization of Soviet unpreparedness for effective action. World peace became more essential to the U.S.S.R. than ever before and, to cement the fragile structure of Soviet security, Litvinov was ordered to proceed with the completion of a barrier around the Soviet Union. As already described, the efforts which had been inaugurated by his predecessor, Chicherin, in 1921, and continued in the treaties of 1925–1928, were now crowned by the agreements of non-aggression and neutrality signed between 1929 and 1933.[108]

[106] October 14, 1933.
[107] *Ibid.*, p. 8.
[108] *Supra*, pp. 113 and 119ff.

That this policy of peace was a policy of postponing war, *i.e.*, a mere struggle to extend the breathing spell during which the Soviets could strengthen themselves politically, economically, industrially and militarily [109] in their revolutionary advance, is also apparent from the sanction which the Soviet diplomacy received from the Headquarters of the World Revolution—the Communist International.

It was in 1928 that at the Sixth Congress of the Communist International the post-war development of the capitalist world was subjected to a revolutionary analysis from the standpoint of the immediate needs of the Kremlin. The importance attached to this analysis is evidenced by the fact that it was placed on the agenda of the Congress as a problem introductory to all the others that were to be dealt with. It was found that the post-war capitalist world had gone through two periods. The first one lasted from 1918 to 1923; this was defined as a period of acute crisis for the capitalist system, during which direct revolutionary actions of the proletariat against capitalism were in progress. The second period commenced after the defeat of the German Revolution in 1923, and was characterized by the partial stabilization of capitalism and the ebbing of the revolutionary wave. This was the period of equilibrium between the two worlds. At the time of the meeting of the Congress in question, the capitalist countries were entering a third, new, period when capitalist stabilization had begun to shake and the general crisis was being intensified. To quote the resolution adopted at this Congress on this point:

"The third period, in which the contradictions between the growth of the productive forces and the contraction of markets become particularly accentuated, is inevitably giving rise to a fresh series of imperialist wars among the imperialist states themselves, wars of the imperialist states against the U.S.S.R, wars of national liberation against imperialism and imperialist intervention, and to gigantic class battles." [110]

Among the various problems discussed was the rôle of the U.S. S.R. as a factor in world revolution and the importance of peace thereto. It was again emphasized in the usual revolutionary phraseology that the Soviet Union was inevitably becoming the cradle of international revolution and hence a dominating factor in the history

[109] *Cf.* Stalin, *Voprosy Leninizma,* 9th ed., p. 14.
[110] *Kommunisticheskii Internatsional v Dokumentakh, 1919–1932,* pp. 709ff.

of the world. To fulfill its destiny, the Soviets must survive as the world's revolutionary power plant to supply both energy and a living example. As a precursor of the world union of socialist republics, the Soviet Union is charged with the important duty of fighting for its existence. The obligation of the U.S.S.R. to safeguard the interests of the world proletariat imposes upon its government the duty to maintain an international *status quo* in which the Soviets may grow strong enough to inspire the workers in other countries with enthusiasm and admiration for the proletarian achievements in the former Russian Empire. To this end, the Soviet Union had to launch a program of vast economic socialist reconstruction, and having thus become preoccupied with the development of an exemplary proletarian state, it needed peace "as one needs air." [111]

The description of the task which fell upon Soviet diplomacy and the latter's success therein needs no repetition. Nor is it necessary to elaborate upon the fact that the Soviet fear of foreign aggression remained traditional. That the germs of this fear were born not only in the difficulties encountered by the capitalist world but in the very existence of the Soviets, however, is of interest to note. As disclosed through the proceedings of this Congress, they were to be sought in the difference between the policies of the capitalist countries and those of the U.S.S.R.:

"In the capitalist countries the proletariat fights against the capitalist states, in the U.S.S.R. the proletariat defends its government, it defends the proletarian state. In the capitalist countries we are for revolution; in the U.S.S.R. we are for evolution, for internal peace, for the peaceful development of socialism. In the capitalist countries we are for the destruction of the capitalist system; in the U.S.S.R. we are working for the transformation of a class society into a socialist society, and eventually into a communist society. In the capitalist countries we are strongly opposed to any coöperation among the classes; in the U.S.S.R., on the contrary, we are for class coöperation." [112]

This communist sentiment in regard to Soviet peace policies was faithfully repeated at each of the four Plenary Sessions of the Party held from 1929 to 1933. The ever-increasing alarm was evident in assertions that the border nations were busying themselves with increasing their armaments, and that conflicts with the U.S.S.R. were

[111] *Shestoi Vsemirnyi Kongress Kommunisticheskogo Internatsionala. Stenografischeskii Otchet*, II, p. 24.

[112] *Ibid.*, V, 4 (cited in Florinsky, *op. cit.*, pp. 195–196).

being provoked through raiding Soviet offices abroad; that the capitalist countries were becoming more and more despondent in their hope for governmental changes in the Soviet Union and for assuring an "economic peace" among themselves; and, finally, that the Great Powers had come to a realization of their own inability to cope with the difficulty of keeping their colonies in subjugation.[113] At the Thirteenth Plenary Session of the Party Executive Committee it was definitely stated that the Soviet Union was facing a world in which the economic difficulties had reached a stage where the crisis had become not only economic but revolutionary. In the field of international relations this meant the beginning of an era of new wars and revolutions. To the Soviets the most convincing outward sign of this new era was the undeniable decline of the League of Nations, which now, after the disappearance of Germany and Japan from the list of its members, was no longer in a position to regulate peaceful relations even between Great Britain and France. Then, too, the efforts at disarmament had the anomalous result of forcing the nations into a race for armaments, and the London Economic Conference, instead of bringing relief, had only intensified the tariff war. Finally, the none-too-discreet international maneuvering of London, the openly admitted aspirations of Tokio, the transparent threat of Berlin, and the only too obvious despair of Paris were interpreted as certain indications of capitalist preparation for a new aggression against the U.S.S.R.[114]

Whatever the actual reason for this hysteria, whether genuine unregimented emotionalism of revolutionary enthusiasts, or a suave, premeditated campaigning of cool-headed Soviet politicians, it can hardly serve as a dependable criterion for an impartial appraisal of facts. Hence, it is only logical that neither Soviet pessimism nor capitalist denial of the charges preferred against them by Moscow can be taken at their face value.

It is only too true that the position of the U.S.S.R. was not an easy one. Ideologically isolated from the rest of the world, the Soviet Union found itself also in political solitude. Having no Soviet neigh-

---

[113] Tenth Plenary Session, July 3–19, 1929 (*Kommunisticheskii Internatsional v Dokumentakh, 1919–1932*, pp. 876ff.). *Cf.* also the thesis advanced at the Session of the Enlarged Presidium of the Comintern, held Feb. 8–28, 1930, and at the XI and XII Plenary Sessions held on Mar. 25 to Apr. 13, 1931, and Aug. 27 to Sept. 15, 1932 (*ibid.*, pp. 915, 952, and 973, respectively).

[114] *XIII Plenum IKKI. Stenograficheskii Otchet*, pp. 12ff.

bors to which it could turn for help in case of need,[115] the U.S.S.R. was well justified in being particularly interested in safeguarding whatever it had gained through the Bolshevik Revolution. If it be recalled that the Soviets always considered themselves as the vanguard of world revolution, there was nothing condemnable in the Kremlin's desire and efforts to solidify and further these gains. Nor should it be surprising that peace was considered by the Soviets as the paramount prerequisite for the effectuation of their immediate needs and ultimate plans. In fact, the ingenuity of Soviet diplomacy in finding a way for the peaceful co-existence between Moscow and the capitalist countries during the years 1921 to 1934 is by no means inferior to the records of diplomats in other capitals.

At the same time, it is true that the position of the Great Powers was not less difficult. When the Versailles rearrangement commenced to show its weakness, there was nothing out of the ordinary in their desire to salvage whatever they could from the peace edifice which was on the point of collapse. There was likewise nothing unnatural in that this resulted in political, national, and economic friction. Still less surprising should it seem that this discord contributed greatly to the lack of uniformity, skillfully perpetuated by Moscow, in their relations with the Soviet Union. In fact, much as they may have regretted the errors of 1918–1920, the non-communist diplomats who labored for peace during these years may well be credited with the realization of the value of peace with the U.S.S.R., whose rôle in the international set-up they could not fail to see.

Under the circumstances, it may well be true that, irrespective of the true nature of their mutual feelings toward each other and regardless of their actual ultimate designs, both of these worlds— capitalism and communism—were utterly unprepared for an armed conflict. The Great Powers could not afford a war against the Soviets, nor was the U.S.S.R. yet in a position to expand its open revolutionary aggression beyond the boundaries of the Proletarian Fatherland. Reciprocal accusations of antagonism, violent as they may have been at times, do not furnish sufficient ground for a denial of this. Neither the communist propaganda abroad nor the capitalist intrigues in the U.S.S.R. can alter the historical fact that an equilibrium was established between Moscow and foreign powers, and that this equilibrium was both voluntary and necessary. As

[115] Stalin, *Voprosy Leninizma,* 11th ed., p. 79.

such, it made each of the opposing camps accept peace as a welcome
relief on the one hand, and a mandatory restraint on the other.

Revolutionary Panorama: Peace through Embrasures

Prior to summarizing the Soviet conception of peace, the attitude
of the U.S.S.R. toward the wars of this period must be mentioned.
During 1921–1933, the Soviets had managed to keep from being
involved in wars with foreign powers. Therefore, their attitude
toward war must be judged from the reaction which the wars waged
outside the Soviet Union had on the Kremlin. To avoid confusion,
at this juncture it may be pointed out that the term "war" may
connote a variety of social phenomena, depending either upon the
degree of discrimination used in applying the word, or upon the
philosophical conception attached thereto for a definite purpose. Thus,
for a Marxist, events in the Ruhr may well appear to contain the
germ of a national war or rebellion against the enslavement imposed
by the Treaty of Versailles. An analogous viewpoint may be taken
by communists in regard to the turmoil in China which is to them
primarily a revolutionary war for national liberation. On the other
hand, the Greco-Turkish War of 1920–1922 was a war between two
different nations, for purposes obviously different from revolutionary
aims, and conducted in a fashion to which the rules of international
law were well applicable.

An analysis of the issue in the Ruhr would entail a study of all
the revolutionary difficulties which arose in various countries from
1922 to 1933, and since from the standpoint of international relations
they are nothing but domestic revolutions, their study must be
omitted here even if they are extremely interesting in view of the
Marxian interpretation of their revolutionary implications as regards
war.[116] The Soviet attitude toward the revolutions and war in China
is discussed elsewhere in connection with the Japanese aggression in
Asia. This leaves only the Greco-Turkish war to be analyzed here,
as it was the only international, *de jure* war in the strictest sense of
the term which occurred during this period.

At the beginning of this conflict Turkey suffered grave reverses.
The Greek divisions seized Smyrna and occupied Anatolia. The diffi-

[116] Lenin's views on the issue are found in v. XIII of his writings.

culty of the situation of the Ottoman Empire was aggravated still further by the simultaneous co-existence of two parallel governments at home: one under the protection of the British expeditionary forces in Constantinople, and the other in Anatolia, headed by Kemal Pasha. The former was an obedient servant of Great Britain, ready to follow London's directions.[117] The Anatolian régime of Kemal, on the contrary, was unmistakably nationalistic and definitely ambitious to throw off the dictates of the Great Powers imposed upon Turkey at Sèvres.

In his search for help, Kemal had the choice of two roads to follow. One was to take advantage of the rivalry between Great Britain and France over the spoils in Asia Minor, and come to an understanding with one of them. The other was to turn northward, and, by sparing no effort in presenting to the Kremlin the miseries of his oppressed and backward country, to solicit the sympathy of the U.S.S.R. Shrewd as he was, Kemal took steps in both directions. As a result of the mutual advantages which a rapprochement with France afforded, his relations with that country improved comparatively soon, whereas the relations between Ankara and Moscow not only developed at a much slower tempo, but were, at the same time, much more cautious.

It will be recalled that one of the unwritten rules of proletarian tactics has always been that permanent alliances with non-communist states should be avoided, as such commitments may force the Soviets into wars for other than defensive purposes, or may involve them in conflicts arising out of problems utterly alien to the communist cause and spirit. There should be little surprise, therefore, that Kemal's original offer of an alliance was rejected by the authorities in the Kremlin, who in reply suggested the mere non-committal establishment of diplomatic relations in its stead.[118] At the same time, however, although objecting to a regular alliance, the Soviets saw the advantage of collaboration with Turkey in its struggle against the Allies. The result was that the U.S.S.R. expressed its readiness to help Kemal Pasha in fact, if not by virtue of formal signed promises. Military supplies and technical advisers commenced to arrive in Turkey, although negotiations for a treaty still remained fruitless. As a matter of fact, the issue over Batum for a

[117] It was this Government which signed the Treaty of Sèvres, Aug. 10, 1920.
[118] Note of June 2, 1920 (Kliuchnikov i Sabanin, *op. cit.*, III, p. 26).

while became so tense that there was danger of an armed conflict between Moscow and Ankara which, in the meanwhile, became *de facto* confrères in the field against Greece. Finally, however, the need of peace prevailed and the already mentioned treaty was signed on March 16, 1921, by which Batum was to stay in Russia, while Kars and Ardagan were ceded to Ankara.[119]

As has been said, on March 18, 1921, the Soviets signed their Peace Treaty with Poland and the U.S.S.R. entered into the third period of its struggle for peace. Therefore, actually, the Soviet attitude toward the Greco-Turkish war should be analyzed from this point on. The events in Asia Minor continued to keep Ankara dependent upon Moscow. In the summer of 1921, the Greek Army pressed forward into Anatolia, and it was only through Soviet military help that in the fall their advance was brought to a standstill, which extended to the next spring. During these months Turkey's friendship with Moscow, on the one hand, and with France, on the other, grew warmer in direct proportion to the military help received. In the summer of 1922, Kemal started his counter-advance. Smyrna was recaptured in September. The Greek army was in full retreat. On September 1, 1922, King Constantine abdicated. On October 11, at Mudania, the armistice was signed. On November 1, 1922, the Ottoman Empire became a republic under the dictatorial authority of Kemal Pasha, later known as Kemal Attaturk.

The fact that for almost a year and a half the Soviets extended material military help to Turkey is in itself suggestive of the communist attitude toward this war. It is from the language of certain of the provisions of the Soviet-Turkish Treaty of 1921, however, that any shadow of doubt must disappear. Thus, in the preamble, the Contracting Parties took cognizance of the "solidarity between them in the struggle with imperialism," while in Article 4 they admitted the mutuality of interests between the "nationalist liberation movement of the peoples in the East and the struggle of the workers of Russia for a new social system."

From what has been said about Marx's and Lenin's classification of wars,[120] the very terms "struggle with imperialism" and "national liberation movement" prompt the conclusion that to the Soviets this was an Ottoman war for national liberation, while in

---

[119] *Sborn. Deistv. Dogov.*, II, 1921, pp. 72ff.
[120] *Supra*, pp. 28ff.

regard to Greece and its Allied sponsors it was an imperialistic war "par excellence." As a revolutionary war for national liberation, in the opinion of the Soviet writers, this war freed the Turkish people also from "barbaric absolutism and created the conditions prerequisite for the independent existence of Turkey, which thus far has been a semi-colonial possession of the European imperialist powers." [121]

The feeling of revolutionary fellowship toward Kemal Pasha which at this time was nurtured by the Kremlin, and the not less righteous indignation from a revolutionary standpoint toward the imperialist Allies sponsoring the aggression against him, may serve as a partial explanation of the "surprise" expressed by the Soviet Delegation at the Genoa Conference on May 2, 1922, that "in spite of the proposal of Russia that Turkey should be invited to the Conference of Genoa, she was excluded from it." [122] The fact, however that no mention was made by Chicherin of Greece, which was also excluded, substantiates the idea that it was considered by the Kremlin as having definitely fallen into the imperialist camp. As an imperialist power, therefore, Greece could wage no war other than an imperialistic one.

In appraising Soviet efforts for world peace it must be borne in mind that an evaluation of the formal records alone does not suffice. Like any other undertaking which has for its purpose the further development of society, the peace policy of the U.S.S.R. has two aspects: a concrete manifestation and an intrinsic meaning. To pass judgment on the former, one must obviously be cognizant of the conditions which prevailed previously, be informed of the events which took place during the period being analyzed, and see the results and the differences between conditions antecedent and after.

The Treaty of Peace with Poland, signed in 1921, has already been described, and mention has been made of the fact that it terminated the armed hostilities in which Soviet Russia had been engaged since 1917. Whatever one's feelings toward the Soviets, it cannot be denied that the uncertainty as to the future of the régime which

---

[121] N. Vasil'ev, "Novoe vo vneshnei politike Turtsii," *Mirovoe Khoziaistvo i Mirovaia Politika,* 1939, No. 6, p. 40. *Cf.* also telegram sent by IX All-Russian Congress of Soviets to Kemal Pasha on Jan. 6, 1922 (*Izvestiia,* Jan. 6, 1922).

[122] *The Soviet Union and Peace,* p. 97. *Cf.* also proceedings of the IV Congress of the Communist International (*Kommunisticheskii Internatsional v Dokumentakh, 1919–1932,* pp. 259ff.).

was bought at so exorbitant a price made the Kremlin's outlook on things at home and abroad grim, if not verging upon despair. Nor is there longer any doubt that from these difficulties the Soviets emerged triumphant both in the field of domestic rearrangement and in regard to their international security. From the brief record of their diplomatic successes given in the foregoing pages one may derive an even more jubilant conclusion and say that the Soviet success in its dealings with the capitalist world was not limited to the mere survival of the Dictatorship of the Proletariat, but resulted in gaining for the U.S.S.R. the prestige of a great power—a distinction rightly enjoyed by its imperial predecessor, carelessly undermined by the government of Kerensky, and willingly exchanged for the peace signed at Brest-Litovsk. Today, the persistent glorification of the Soviet peace policy and the never-ceasing emphasis upon its consistency, proclaimed daily in the U.S.S.R. during this period, no longer appear as sheer campaigning calculated to secure political credits abroad. From 1921 to 1933, the Soviets were sincere: they wanted peace.

But so also did the other powers and, like the Soviets, they were also sincere in this longing. True, it may well be that the collective peace efforts of the non-communist world, whether through the agency of the League of Nations, or by resort to such mutual pledges as the Briand-Kellog Pact, were motivated by such desires as that for the preservation of the international *status quo* dictated at Versailles. Also, one may probably find a certain degree of justification for the Soviet's sarcastic ridicule of Hitler's appeals for "European Peace," or of General Araki's assurances that the Japanese are "apostles of peace." [123] Finally, it must be admitted that the formal pacifism of the Great Powers was not always consistent when put to practical test.

It is, however, a matter of conjecture whether these shortcomings, individually or collectively, should justify the summary condemnation of the states of the capitalist world as being hypocritical in using appeals for peace merely as a cloak beneath which to conceal their preparations for new wars. Whatever truth there may be in such an accusation, to accept it *sine grano* would appear to some just as unwarranted as it would appear naive to others to subscribe

[123] *XIII Plenum IKKI. Stenograficheskii Otchet*, p. 15.

unreservedly to the Soviet claims that only their policy of peace is consistent, honest, and wise.

It is likewise a matter of personal opinion whether the unqualified accusation of the Soviet Union of propagating world revolution is sufficient ground for subjecting the U.S.S.R. to political and moral ostracism, as a nation which only resorts to appeals for peace as a subterfuge for the purpose of achieving its revolutionary ends. Whatever the justification for such non-communist distrust of things Marxian, insistence upon Marxian infallibility would be just as presumptuous as it would be preposterous to ascribe angelic purity to the capitalists' pursuit of peace.

Simple logic requires that the charges of indulging in Machiavellianism, which the communist and non-communist worlds have mutually preferred against each other with such vigor and persistency that they have become a permanent characteristic of their dealings with one another, must be either false or true. In case these mutual accusations are false, then there can be no difference in the qualitative value of the peace policies of the U.S.S.R. and of the non-communist Powers inasmuch as their search for peace, equally devoid of Machiavellian methods of diplomacy, could have been prompted only by motives equally sincere and common to both. However, the events which were to follow proved that the pessimism in this regard which was shared by the communists in the U.S.S.R. and their adversaries outside was not ill-founded: the accusations mutually exchanged between the U.S.S.R. and the capitalist world were true.

This being the case, it may at first appear that in this instance, too, the Soviet and the non-communist peace policies are of equal value, since both are unworthy of trust. The fact is, however, that for the present study the superficial parity is a minor issue. The fact of primary importance is that peace was made to serve some purpose, and that it is precisely in the difference in purposes that the difference between non-communist and Soviet peace policies is to be sought. Neither the derogatory adjectives used by the Soviets nor the none-too-complimentary description of Moscow's pacifism by non-Marxian statesmen can change the cardinal idea of these policies. Whatever the true nature of the "bourgeois" peace, it differs from the peace pursued by the Kremlin. Indeed, whether imperialistic or unselfish, hypocritical or sincere, expedient or spontaneous, the peace policy of the capitalist nations is primarily a policy of non-Marxian political ideology. On the other hand, whether egoistic or altruistic, deceitful or honest, mandatory or voluntary, the Soviet policy is first of all a Bolshevist policy of the revolutionary international proletariat.

Commissioned to serve the needs of world revolution, the proletarian peace-makers were confronted with the double task of keeping the U.S.S.R. out of war and of preventing, for the time being, the inception of war in the capitalist camp west of its political border from the Baltic Sea to the mouth of the Danube. While there is no doubt that the international political situation, coupled with economic difficulties, influenced the outward manifestation of their endeavors to avoid complications with foreign powers, there is no need to emphasize again that this meant, first of all, survival of the proletarian régime, and that the price which the Soviets paid for this was the final jettisoning of Trotzky's idea of continuous revolution. It is, however, in the explanation given to the masses as to why peace in western Europe was necessary to the Soviets that the true Marxian significance and the communist understanding of world peace are to be sought. What, indeed, was the need of the diplomatic fusion of the revolutionary peace policy of the U.S.S.R. with the "chauvinistic" pacifism of the capitalist camp, and how much value could be placed in the treaties of non-aggression if it was known that they would be declared "scraps of paper" after preparations for aggression against the country of the dictatorial proletariat had been completed?

Verging on the maniacal in their fear of capitalist aggression, the Soviets reasoned quite appropriately that their amicable understandings with foreign powers would result at least in the postponement of war against the U.S.S.R., if not in the absolute prevention thereof. Its international agreements with non-communist countries handicapped them in shaping their military understandings and rapprochements *inter se*. The war-preventing potency of the serum thus injected into the political veins of Europe by the Soviets through their treaty arrangements was increased, furthermore, by the possibilities which these arrangements afforded for self-advertisement on the one hand, and revolutionary propaganda on the other. The Soviet Union realized that being a champion of peace meant not only expansion of political credits abroad, but also the luxury of independent opinion. As to propaganda, the ever-repeated assurances of peaceful intentions were in themselves one of the most powerful means to enlist the admiration of the proletarian masses abroad, while the treaties and other official documents could, in case of need, be used admirably by these masses as undeniable evidence against the trustworthiness of their own respective non-proletarian governments.

Hence the peace policy of the Soviets during this period envisaged, first of all, the prevention of war against the U.S.S.R. This, in turn, afforded security to the Soviets for the establishment of socialism in one country, as an alluring example of the communist future. As the period of erecting such a revolutionary edifice was considered by the communists as a necessary stage in the process of blending mankind into a homogeneous community of classless and stateless men, international peace was to the Soviets a *modus vivendi* under which the cause of world revolution could be advantageously furthered.

In other words, while this peace to Moscow as the seat of the Soviets meant a *de facto* abstention from war, to Moscow as the headquarters of the Third International, the world peace meant a temporary abandonment of concrete revolutionary aggression. The struggle between world capitalism and the international proletariat settled down to trench warfare between the two.

CHAPTER V

RESTLESS RECONNAISSANCE: IN SEARCH OF
FRIENDS, 1933–1939

RESTLESS RECONNAISSANCE: IN SEARCH OF FRIENDS, 1933-1939

ENTER HITLER

As has been shown, the Soviet peace policy was born amid the short-lived yet exalted initial communist vision of Marxian world peace via *Blitzrevolution*. It was nursed in the anguish of uncertainty and desire for the physical termination of the Allied intervention and of the civil war during the years from 1918 to 1922. Finally, it matured into the definite communist program of entrenchment during the pre-League years, a period which may also be characterized as one of revolutionary modelling.

The rise of Hitler to power in 1933, and his adoption of National-Socialism as the basis for the policies to be followed by the former German Empire were of far-reaching significance for the Soviet peace program. Not only the theoretical credo of Hitler as expounded in *Mein Kampf*, but also the repercussions which his becoming the *Führer* had in the capitals of Western Europe, forced the Soviets again to reorient their foreign policies and to attach a new meaning to their struggle for peace. It was under the impact of this change in Germany that the third period of the Soviet struggle for the preservation of world peace in the non-communist meaning of the term, was ushered in, only to last until September 3, 1939, when the World War of a quarter of a century ago resulted in its own logical aftermath—the present war. What the peace policy of the Kremlin would have been had political change not overtaken Germany is a matter of conjecture. What the new problems were is a matter of record.

The events which have taken place in the world, and particularly in Europe since 1933, have not only followed one another with accelerated rapidity but have been of unprecedented potential magnitude and importance. Memories of the years from 1914 to 1918 being still very much alive, the anxiety of the reading world matched that of the statesmen. The result of this was that in spite of the short space of only seven years, there are already several works available for those who are interested both in the chronological and in the substantive presentation of European history during this period, including that of the Soviets.[1] Moreover, it is only too true that since the inception of the Third Reich, Germany has become the nerve center of Europe, controlling the diplomatic pulse of other nations. Hence, it is mainly in the light of her behavior and in the reactions of the "victorious" Great Powers thereto that the Soviet foreign policies of this period find their justification. Finally, it has been promised that the present study will include an attempt to analyze the Soviet-German Pact of Non-Aggression of August 23, 1939, which shook the world and unleashed the conflicting forces in the present turmoil. This obviously calls for not only an examination of the formal diplomatic events, but also for an evaluation of the Marxian approach thereto. For these reasons, the present study perforce must be limited to a mere summary portrayal of Nazi ideology, a skeleton outline of the political events which took place in Western Europe, a brief description of the German-Soviet relations during this period, and a general analysis of the Kremlin's reactions toward these events in the light of the Marxian notions of war and peace.

The appearance of National-Socialism cannot be attributed to any particular outward cause. It is rather the result of complex reactions to the changes which had befallen Germany. Aside from revolt against the Versailles system and the economic deadlock, these reactions were based on a three-fold disillusion: the disappearance of the regimentation inherent in the Germanic notion of social order, the realization of the Marxian fallacy, and an awakening of apprehension because of the fragility of the capitalist world.

The peace dictated at Versailles was an unprecedented shock to Germany's pride. The greatest discomfort, however, was caused not so much by demotion to a second-rate standing as by the collapse of the imperial régime which to the German masses had been the embodiment of the stability of order, the perfection of the mechanics of discipline, and the manifestation of the essentiality of authority.

---

[1] *Cf.* Vera Micheles Dean, *Europe in Retreat* (New York, 1939); Frederick L. Schuman, *Europe on the Eve. The Crisis of Diplomacy 1933–1939* (New York, 1939); and Arnold Wolfers, *Britain and France between Two Wars* (New York, 1940).

The fall of Hohenzollern Germany was a psychological disillusion for which the privileges of democratic self-authority, proclaimed at Weimar, were a poor remedy.

Inflation brought Germany to economic despair. With it came also the change in the evaluation not only of things material but abstract. The disappearance of respect for money, which had become valueless, gave rise to an analysis of doctrines which maintained that economic relationship is the basis of human society. The natural result was that whatever belief was left in the materialistic values preached by Marxian socialism, was bound to become obsolete. Primarily an economic philosophy, Marxism is essentially a doctrine of relativity. Devoid of the precision so dear to the German mind, it became a poor ideal for the German masses, who during the days of inflation learned only too well the true working of relativity in practice. In this bitter experience, belief in individual security disappeared. With it vanished also the faith in a new Marxian world which promised individual well-being through the collective security of a classless society. To the psychological vacuum of the non-imperial régime was added the emptiness of the Marxian mirage.

The world crisis of 1929 was the last link in the chain of Germany's disillusions. Embittered though it was against the victorious capitalistic countries, Germany well realized that the Marxian world was far from materialization. Germany was likewise fully aware of the fact that although many advantages could be derived from association with the Soviets, the latter were bound to remain in political isolation for years to come. Hence the conviction that, in the end, the rehabilitation of Germany, if it was to be permanent, must be based upon coöperation with the more stable capitalist world. The economic collapse of the world brought this illusion, too, to a sad end. The whole structure of the capitalist world no longer appeared a dependable foundation for the reconstruction of *Deutschland*.

It was of this triple disillusion that National-Socialism was born. The new movement, neither spontaneous nor non-revolutionary in its dynamics, not strictly domestic and yet not international in its scope, represented a reaction combining revenge, despair, and opportunism. As such, it saw a practical solution for Germany in the establishment of a German *Volksgemeinschaft* in the *Völkergesell-*

schaft of the world, the abstract sanction for which was furnished by the ephemeral notion of the righteousness of the idea.

Expounded in Hitler's *Mein Kampf* and in his numerous speeches before the Reichstag, interpreted in the voluminous writings of his spiritual disciples, and put to practical test by his lieutenants in the field, the aims and dogmas of National-Socialism leave no doubt as to the repercussions of grave concern which they were bound to have in the non-Nazi world.

It will suffice to recall that the fundamental Nazi principle of international order emanates from the notion of national self-sufficiency based on racial contentedness.[2] According to this principle every community should be comprised of persons of the same race, as it is only under such conditions that imperialism can be eliminated from international politics and world peace firmly established. It is a matter of personal opinion whether world peace is conceivable under such a theory, or whether it is endangered by the very obvious complications germane to the concurrence of Germany's claim to respect the existence of other nations and its opposition to the assimilation of peoples of different racial composition.[3] It is important to note here that Hitler's diplomatic objectives are all-absorbent as to the German race, and militant as to the international relations of the Third Reich. Since its mission is to embrace all Germans, the Third Reich has "not only to rally and to preserve the most valuable original racial elements, but to lead them onwards, slowly but surely, to a position of dominance."[4] Proclaimed to be inherently superior to all other races and hence denied the right to remain stationary, the German *Volk* is to expand. This necessitates taking measures for providing the "world people" with *Lebensraum* in the literal sense of the term.[5]

In the perspective of such a necessity, considerations of the natural political and economic interdependence of the various parts of the world had to be rectified to serve the cause of practical politics.

[2] *Nationale Saturierheit und rassisches Selbstgenügsamkeit* (H. H. Dietze, "Europa als Einheit," *Zeitschrift für Völkerrecht*, 1936, p. 304).

[3] Bumiller, "Die Nationalsozialistische Rechtsidee und das Problem des Völkerrechts," *Deutsches Recht*, 1934, p. 205.

[4] Hitler, *Mein Kampf*, p. 439.

[5] G. Feder, *Das Staats- und Wirtschaftsprogram der Nationalsozialistischen D.A.P.*, p. 13. The *Lebensraum*, in Nazi terminology, is not the mere space sufficient for subsistence, but a domain sufficiently comprehensive to provide Germany with "absolute" freedom of action.

Under the circumstances, Germany had but two choices, in a sense not unsimilar to the problem with which the Soviets were confronted some years ago: either complete surrender and renunciation of all hope of becoming *Grossdeutschland,* or an uncompromising struggle to attain the end set forth by Hitler. Probably it is in the hysteria of the uncompromising appeal which he voiced in this connection that the explanation of his influence upon the German *Volk* is to be found: "Germany will become a World Power, or it will not be at all. To be a World Power, however, it needs a territory which in the present age would give it the necessary importance, and its citizens the means of life." [6]

Never failing in his esteem for power as the source of right and as the basic and essential element in political struggle, and ever disrespectful toward the democracies precisely for the reason that they are inclined to practice concessions in diplomacy, Hitler was fully aware of the fact that "suppressed countries are not won back to the bosom of the common Reich by protests, but by the stroke of a mighty sword." [7] In view of such a vigorous conviction, little value can be attached to his assurances that "the German Government wishes to come to a friendly understanding with regard to all difficult questions with other nations." [8] Nor is there much encouragement for peace in his vision of Greater Germany: "when the boundaries of the Reich include even the last German . . . there arises from the need of its own people the moral right to acquire foreign soil. The plow then gives place to the sword." [9]

A direct challenge to world peace, however, was voiced by Hitler in his ridicule of pacifism and humanity, which he considers conceivable and even "quite good," but only "after the supreme race has conquered and subdued the world in such a measure as to make itself exclusive master . . ." The cynical résumé of the foregoing— "first fight, and then, perhaps—pacifism"—is of a clarity which admits no misunderstanding.[10]

Similarly arrogant is his belief that this supreme race is German:

[6] Hitler, *op. cit.,* p. 742.
[7] *Ibid.,* p. 708.
[8] Speech before the Reichstag, May 17, 1933. *Die Reden Hitlers als Reichskanzler,* p. 61.
[9] Hitler, *op. cit.,* p. 1.
[10] *Ibid.,* p. 334.

"if the German people had possessed that safe herd instinct based on blood
. . . the German Reich would probably today be mistress of the globe . . .
Then perhaps we could have attained what today so many misled pacifists
hope to get by whining and blubbering: Peace . . . upheld not by the
olive branches of lacrimose hired female mourners, but established by
the victorious sword of a master nation which leads the world to serve a
higher culture." [11]

Entertaining no illusions as to the peaceful mission of the League
of Nations and accepting armed violence as the only means for
settling international disputes, National-Socialism is no less explicit
as to the direction of the Germanic *Drang*. As of old, eastward it
must be, even if Hitler's troops have been ordered to march westward
for the present:

"We start anew where we terminated six centuries ago. We reverse the
perpetual migration of Germans to the South and to the West of Europe
and fix our gaze on the land in the East . . . If we speak of new lands, we
are bound to think first of Russia and her border states." [12]

To safeguard the rear for his ultimate expansion eastward,
friendly relations had to be cultivated with Italy and Great Britain,
while the old accounts with France were to be settled with finality.
What this meant, has been unmistakably indicated by Hitler:

"We must take up an active policy and throw ourselves into a final and
decisive fight with France, with the greatest of German aims at stake. Only
then will the perpetual and fruitless struggle between us and France be
brought to a conclusion, the condition, however, being that the annihilation of France be looked upon solely as a means of making the expansion of
our people finally possible." [13]

In view of the present war it is too early to tell whether
Germany's plans for friendship with Great Britain have changed, or
whether after the destruction of France, Hitler will seek new understandings with London which would enable him to carry out his
aspirations in the East. There can be no doubt, however, that
Hitler's program of aggrandizement hardly fitted in with the plans
of other powers, let alone their aspirations for peace. True, the
capitals in Western Europe probably would not have minded seeing
Germany satisfied at the expense of the Soviet Union—a country

[11] Hitler, *Mein Kampf*, p. 437.
[12] *Ibid.*, p. 742.
[13] *Ibid.*, pp. 766–7.

unpleasantly overshadowing others not only by its size but also by the revolutionary aspirations cultivated within its borders. Not at the price demanded by Hitler, however. On the other hand, the Soviets may have had no objection to seeing the colonial powers weakened by Germany, so as to incite revolutions in their overseas possessions, particularly in view of the fact that Hitler contemplated substituting a territorial policy for the colonial one. The only obstacle here was that for fomenting these revolutions in the colonies, the price—the territories in the East to be absorbed by Greater Germany—was to be paid largely by the U.S.S.R. As to the smaller countries in Central Europe, they had no choice but to wait, in the hope that the powers which had brought them into independent existence would not let them die by violence.

Nor was there much encouragement that some peaceful rearrangement might be reached by arguing with Hitler on the basis of international ethics and law. Admitting no difference between the two,[14] the totalitarian National-Socialist State is content to use as a criterion for its behavior the simplest of all formulas—"either right or wrong."[15] It is only too obvious that the intrinsically flexible conceptions of right and wrong become a very rigid dogma for the *Realpolitik* of the Third Reich: their very flexibility is always made to justify the aspirations of the German *Volk* for world domination —Hitler can do no wrong!

As to international law proper, according to National-Socialism it rests on the three inherent and inalienable basic rights of states— the right of self-preservation, the right of equality, and the right to sovereignty.[16] Any violation of these rights, be it by force or by rules of positive law, constitutes an infringement upon national state rights and cannot be considered legally valid. There is room for a question as to whether this principle has also a reciprocal effect upon Germany in case it violates the rights of some other state to self-preservation, equality, and sovereignty, and the consistency of Nazi insistence upon the right of equality and the notion of inequality, upon which the whole framework of Hitler's theory rests, may well

[14] H. Kraus, "Das Zwischenstaatliche Weltbild des Nationalsozialismus," *Juristische Wochenschrift*, 1933, p. 2421.

[15] Carl Schmidt, *Nationalsozialismus und Völkerrecht*, p. 17.

[16] Dietze, *op. cit.*, p. 307. For a brief analysis of the National-Socialist conception of international law, see Preuss, "National Socialist Conceptions of International Law," *Am. Pol. Science Review*, August, 1935.

be challenged. Yet the important point for the moment in the field of concrete international policies is that this meant the scrapping of the Versailles Treaty, and the launching of power politics to cut an outlet from the economic deadlock.

Confronted with such threatening designs of Germany, the Western powers, particularly England, France, and Italy, had but one course: if the privileges and advantages which they enjoyed after the Versailles peace were to be retained intact, the materialization of Hitler's ambitions had to be prevented at any cost. To effect this, a rapid rearrangement of policies became essential.

Wanted in Europe: Blueprints of Peace

One of the very first results of the new situation was that Great Britain and France were once again brought together in spite of the fact that Great Britain saw no reason why normal relations could not prevail between the British Crown and the German Republic, while France continued to regard the Reich as its traditional enemy. As is now well known, this rapprochement resulted in an understanding reached in 1935 between London and Paris that in the future the two governments would consult each other regarding the European situation.

In the meanwhile, Mussolini advanced his plan for checking the danger which the change in Germany foreshadowed. Neither desirous to see Hitler's power grow at the expense of changing the *status quo* in the Balkans, nor willing to abandon Italy's ambition to equal Great Britain, France and Germany in greatness, he proposed that these four countries enter into a pact for the purpose of reconstructing Europe by concerted efforts. As a practical means to such an end, he suggested that the Peace Treaties be revised, in conformity with the provisions of the League Covenant, in cases which might cause difficulties, and that the results of the Disarmament Conference, at that time in session,[17] should be accepted as the first step toward the restoration of Germany's right to parity.

This proposal had immediate repercussions in the countries left out. Poland and the smaller European states in the Balkans found good reason to become alarmed, as there was no guaranty that

---

[17] The plan was submitted by Mussolini in March, 1933, *i.e.*, only two months after Hitler became the Führer.

Mussolini's scheme would not result in composite dictatorial domination of these four powers over the Danubian countries. While uniform in purpose, the outward manifestation of their opposition to Mussolini's proposal took two distinct forms: Poland launched a policy of independent bargaining, while Czechoslovakia, Yugoslavia and Roumania, further to counteract the possibility of France's coming to terms with Germany, formed their own regional "bloc." It may be noted that in both cases the outlook was far from promising. Poland, a potential political battleground between Nazism and Communism, found itself faced with the difficulty of choosing between Berlin and Moscow. In the Little Entente, on the other hand, coördination was hampered by the fact that Roumania and Yugoslavia were economically dependent much more upon Germany than upon Czechoslovakia, with the result that their orientation toward the Reich could not be altered at once.

On January 26, 1934, Poland concluded with Hitler a non-aggression pact to last for ten years, thus casting its preference in favor of Germany, and by 1936 it had become even more estranged from France after the latter rejected Warsaw's invitation to form a common front against the Third Reich. The Balkan "trio" was soon joined by Turkey and Greece, which in 1933 signed a non-aggression pact ending their own post-war difficulties. The newly formed "quintet" became united under the motto "Balkans for the Balkans." The original notion of mere collaboration among the original three was transformed into a mutual understanding of the five, guaranteeing their political *status quo*.[18]

In the cross-currents of conflicting interests, this arrangement in the Balkans, while fitting in with the plans of Great Britain and France, could not be looked upon with favor in Rome. Whatever the dangers of Hitler's designs in southeastern Europe, to Mussolini this collaboration of the Balkan States appeared as an unforeseen menace—this time of Pan-Slavic unity. To counteract this, and to hinder the Third Reich in its contemplated absorption of Austria,

[18] The pact signed between Turkey, Greece, and Yugoslavia on Feb. 9, 1934, provided that these countries mutually agreed "to assure . . . the maintenance of the present territorial boundaries in the Balkans" (*L.N.T.S.*, CLIII, 155). Bulgaria, for obvious reasons, refused to sign this pact, although in September of the same year, she agreed to adjust her boundary differences with Yugoslavia, while on July 31, 1938, the Balkan Entente concluded a pact with Bulgaria at Salonika, abrogating military clauses of the Treaty of Neuilly and the Convention of Lausanne. In return, Bulgaria signed a non-aggression pact with her four Balkan neighbors (*L.N.T.S.*, CXCVI, 372).

Rome hastened to prevent such an *Anschluss* by proposing to collaborate with Austria and Hungary. Sponsored by France, which was likewise interested in checking Hitler in his drive south-eastward, Mussolini succeeded in bringing about the so-called Roman Protocols of 1934, by which numerous economic advantages were given to Austria and Hungary as the price for their opposition to the Reich.[19] The relief, however, was of short duration, for the Italo-Austro-Hungarian block met with the disfavor of the States of the Little Entente, which not only feared that Italy's championship of Hungary's demands for revision might threaten the territorial security of all the states concerned, but also deemed it necessary to show their solidarity with Yugoslavia, perpetually concerned over her none-too-friendly relations with Italy. As is well known, Italy soon became involved in the conquest of Ethiopia, and shifted her stand to the Rome-Berlin axis.

In the meanwhile, France watched with keen interest the effect of Hitler's policies upon the U.S.S.R. It was impossible for Paris to fail to see the true meaning of the Soviet non-aggression pacts described in the preceding pages.[20] Hence, thoroughly cognizant of the danger which the Third Reich presented, and obviously displeased with the congeniality between Berlin and Warsaw, France could not abandon her interest in things East-European. More desirous to enlist new allies than ever before, and yet reluctant to commit herself to pledges of unlimited mutual assistance with the Soviets, France found a compromise in a joint Franco-Soviet proposal that a pact, now usually termed the Eastern Locarno Pact, be signed by the Soviet Union, Germany, Poland, Czechoslovakia, Finland, and the three Baltic States—Estonia, Latvia and Lithuania. As is well known, this would-be treaty of territorial guaranties and mutual assistance against aggression was never signed.[21]

In view of this fiasco,[22] and pressed with the need for allies along the eastern boundaries of Germany in case of eventualities, France now decided to seek direct understandings with the Soviets. Already

---

[19] For texts, *cf.* Wheeler-Bennett, *op. cit.*, 1934, pp. 296–298.

[20] *Supra*, pp. 159ff.

[21] Germany feared that this was a scheme to encircle Germany, while Poland did not wish to have her understanding with Germany (Treaty of Non-Aggression, 1934) impaired.

[22] *Cf. Correspondence showing the course of certain Diplomatic Discussions directed towards Securing an European Settlement, June, 1934, to March, 1936,* Misc. No. 3 (1936), Comd. 5143.

a member of the League of Nations, and more than conscious of Hitler's determination to carry out his plans (now still further proved by Germany's resignation from Geneva), the U.S.S.R. was a willing listener. On May 2, 1935, a pact between France and the Soviet Union was signed providing for mutual assistance.[23] It was followed by a similar pact between the Soviets and Czechoslovakia, of May 16, 1935, the only difference between the two being that the latter had an annex containing provisions that the pact was to be binding for the Soviets only if France came to the assistance of the victim of aggression.[24]

The objections which Hitler voiced to these pacts are easy to understand. While his references to the alleged violation of the Locarno Treaty and of the provisions of Article XVI of the League Covenant are little convincing, his practical considerations were much more real: the newly consummated friendship between the Soviets, France and Czechoslovakia was a serious handicap to Germany's aggression in either direction, be it west or east. New ways had to be sought, and Great Britain became the next object of Hitler's scheming. While diplomatic correspondence regarding these pacts was accumulating in the foreign offices of Berlin and Paris, Germany tried to lure Great Britain away from her commitments to France, other than the bond of the League of Nations. The proposal of a Western Pact limiting air armaments, long desired by the British Government, was suggested by Berlin to effect this alienation. In this Germany succeeded only in part. Instead of the air armament pact, Great Britain, never reluctant to act to its own advantage, concluded a naval treaty with Germany in June, 1935, by which the latter was allowed to increase its navy to a size not to exceed that of one-third of the British.

Italy, in the meanwhile, became involved in the Ethiopian war, and it was France's turn to face another dilemma. On the one hand, the integrity of the League of Nations had to be preserved. This meant the application of sanctions against the country violating its Covenant. On the other hand, the encroachment of Germany upon Austria was not consistent with France's plans. This meant that a continuance of Rome's opposition to Hitler on this issue, so vital to Paris, was to be bought irrespective of the price, whether it be

[23] *Sobr. Zak. i Rasp. S.S.S.R.*, 1936, II, par. 72.
[24] *Ibid.*, 1935, II, par. 130.

through leniency of the League or by direct offers of colonial possessions in Africa. The difficulty of the situation was still further
augmented by the stand taken by Great Britain: it demanded that
Italy be subjected to the full force of the League's authority to apply
sanctions against a violator country. To France, the real reason for
this British attitude was an open secret: London feared Italy's
aggrandizement in the Mediterranean, as this would endanger England's trade routes to India and jeopardize her control of Egypt.

Whatever shortcomings may be attributed to German diplomacy,
it cannot be accused of being dormant. Indeed, while Italy was
preoccupied in Ethiopia and England and France were trying to iron
out the difficulties which had arisen between them in this connection,
Hitler ordered his troops to march into the Rhineland, which they
did on March 7, 1936. The action was well timed. Reluctant to
precipitate a conflict with Germany while deeply involved in the
Mediterranean crisis, Great Britain and France had to content themselves with perfunctory protests, although it must be pointed out that
Germany's remilitarization of the Rhine gave rise to closer coöperation between the British and the French General Staffs. Stimulated
by Hitler's *Anschluss* of Austria,[25] this rapprochement developed into
a political and military alliance, which gradually manifested itself
in the compulsory military service in Great Britain, the joint journey
of the British and French military missions to Moscow, and the
present war.

Needless to say, this worried Germany not in the least. What did
disturb Hitler, however, was the problem of finding a way to break
the ties which united Italy and France in their opposition to his
contemplated *Anschluss* with Austria. As it happens not infrequently
in a state of general confusion, certain things stand out more clearly
than they would have under ordinary circumstances. So, in the maze
of diplomatic complications in which Europe was at that time involved, Hitler saw that time was on his side. Confronted with the
almost unanimous opposition of members of the League of Nations,
and disillusioned in France's wavering during the war in Ethiopia,
Italy had to seek for new allies. In his drive for economic self-
sufficiency, having by this time incorporated Ethiopia in the
Kingdom of Italy, Mussolini decided to renounce all further collaboration with Western democracies and to seek a rapprochement with

[25] March 13, 1938.

the only logical country remaining—totalitarian Germany. Rome's previous fears of an Austro-German union were laid aside. For its part, Germany proved to have no objection, for Hitler knew that the reward would be well worth the effort. As further events proved, his expectations were not overestimated. There appeared on the stage of European politics a new factor—the Rome-Berlin axis, which in 1937 was further cemented by Italy's joining the German-Japanese pact of November 25, 1936, against communism.[26]

The importance which this turn of events had for Germany is obvious. Perpendicular to the axis of Paris-Moscow, the Rome-Berlin axis not only cut in two the life-line of France's opposition to Germany's expansion to the Southeast, but served also as a formidable weapon in Hitler's scheme to turn Italy's attention away from Central Europe. The Spanish civil war was ingeniously made to serve Germany's cause. Skillfully taking advantage of Mussolini's absorption in the Mediterranean problems, Hitler rushed to the aid of General Franco and through the latter made it clear that in return for military support, Italy could obtain strategic footholds in Spain and Morocco that would further threaten the trade communications of Great Britain, and France's route to its source of man-power in northern Africa. In its joy over the possibility of becoming a Mediterranean empire, Italy found itself fighting in Iberia. So did the Soviets.

Whatever the ideological motives of this war against communism,[27] there is no doubt that it was a great success for Hitler, for Germany's support of the Franco régime proved advantageous in more ways than one. It forced both Great Britain and France into the dilemma of piloting safely between the two factions of public opinion—pro-Fascist and pro-Loyalist—each of which found good reason to criticize the government for not taking one side or another. Preoccupied with things domestic, and cautiously following the policy of "peace at any price," neither London nor Paris was in a position to prevent Germany from carrying out Hitler's plans in Central Europe. Then, by having forced—some may prefer to say lured—Italy into actual intervention in Spain, Hitler created a situation where the direct action of Rome was met with the wavering

[26] *Documents on International Affairs* (ed. by Wheeler-Bennett and Heald, 1936), pp. 297–299.
[27] On the Soviet attitude, *cf. infra*, pp. 202ff.

passiveness of the two great western democracies. Obviously, this hardly served as a stimulus for the continuation of good-will between Rome on the one hand, and London and Paris, on the other. The final fact of crowning importance, however, is that by having involved Italy more than ever before in the revived ancient idea of *Mare Nostrum*, Hitler had diverted Mussolini from Central Europe. The field was clear.

The year 1937 was a year of anxiety for the western democracies. Hitler's success in dealing with Italy was augmented by the latter's joining the German-Japanese Pact of 1936, which had been concluded for the purpose of fighting communism. That this ideological formula was merely a camouflage was only too obvious to Great Britain and France. In London and Paris it clearly meant that to the dangers of armed conflict with Germany along the Rhine and with Italy in the Mediterranean and Northern Africa had been added the possibility of war conflagration in the Far East. While Germany basked temporarily in the comfortable enjoyment of diplomatic success, British and French diplomacy was compelled to busy itself with finding an honorable yet bloodless way out of the situation saturated with obvious fear and concealed anger, naive confidence and justified distrust, increasing military preparations and vanishing hope for peace.

In January, a "gentlemen's" agreement was reached between London and Rome, according to which Italy consented to safeguard the territorial integrity of Spain and to maintain the *status quo* in the Mediterranean. In the spring, negotiations were opened with Tokio looking toward the division of China into spheres of influence. Manchuria and Northern China were offered to Japan in return for the preservation of the interests of London and Paris in the south. In the fall, Lord Halifax journeyed to Berlin with a mission the true purpose of which is still to be made known.

None of these attempts to avert disaster bore fruit, however. Italy continued to cherish Mussolini's aspirations. Japan did not stop its military advances into the interior of Asia. Germany's enthusiasm for Hitler's ideas of *Lebensraum* grew apace. If these efforts had any effect, they were rather harmful to London and Paris. The hope of Great Britain and France to utilize the conflicting interests of the Berlin-Rome-Tokio triumvirate failed not for the reason that such conflicts did not exist but because the approaches to

Italy, Japan and Germany severally were made in a rather spasmodic and discordant fashion. The result was that London's overtures made the weakness of London and Paris even more evident and instead of intimidating these three powers individually, they strengthened this aggressive "block" as a whole, because the confidence of these countries in their superiority over the democracies of Western Europe grew in direct proportion to the pleadings.

Apparently, this was the impression which Hitler gathered. Encouraged by such new symptoms, and assured of Italy's "understanding" of the actual state of affairs, he no longer saw any obstacle to carrying his plans into effect. Schuschnigg, the Austrian Chancellor, was invited to visit the *Führer* at Berchtesgaden on February 12, 1938, which he did, firmly resolved to oppose any legalization of the Nazi movement in Austria. Commendable and patriotic though his "insubordination" was, it proved of no avail. On March 12, the German troops marched into Austria whose government, deserted by Paris, London and Rome, had no alternative but to yield to force. The *Anschluss,* which received "legal" sanction through a prearranged plebiscite one month later, was not only Germany's vindication of the humiliation suffered after Versailles but another stepping stone in the execution of the political program outlined by Hitler.

The incorporation of Austria into the Third Reich sealed the fate of Czechoslovakia too. Great Britain and France realized only too well their own inability to resist Hitler by force of arms. True, their military alliance was even more close than prior to the war of twenty-five years ago. This fact, however, was not adequate to remedy the situation. There was still a difference between the two countries as to their general sentiment in regard to Germany: in Great Britain there were two factions, one preferring Fascism to Communism and thinking that Germany was unduly "strafed" at Versailles, and the other fearing the renaissance of Germany and its ultimate hegemony, whereas in France distrust of Germany was complete. The factor which now controlled the march of events was of much greater potency than the feeble attempts of Great Britain and France to preserve peace. It was the determination of Hitler to set aside the tiring procedure of diplomatic negotiations and to unleash the dictatorial methods of power politics in their full fury.

Where this determination led him in his march south-eastward, and where it brought Chamberlain in his endeavors to prevent war is a matter of history. The place was Munich. The time, September, 1938. Shown no mercy at Versailles in 1919, the Germany of Hitler was not inclined to be sentimental at Munich twenty years later. The polished phraseology of the official records of what ensued on that memorable date speak of peace and amicable understanding. The facts, however, betray their real meaning. Only partially prepared militarily, and hence, with their power of persuasion reduced to nil, Great Britain and France capitulated before the dictates of the *Führer*. On September 21, 1938, the official communiqué of the Prague Government announced that under "extraordinary pressure" it was forced to surrender to Germany's demands. When on September 29, 1938, without even the courtesy of referring to the Czechoslovakian Government, an Agreement was signed between Great Britain, France, Italy, and Germany, regarding the cession of Sudetenland,[28] Hitler had every reason to congratulate himself once again: the Republic of Czechoslovakia became virtually a dependency of the Reich, and it was only a matter of time before Prague would become the capital of a German province. With its dismemberment, the *Lebensraum* was increased and one of the obstacles in the path to the Balkans was eliminated. British and French statesmen were forced to occupy themselves with the problem of their own preservation. "Munich"—a crushing bombshell to trusting diplomats in 1938—became the modern synonym for Bethmann-Hollweg's "Scrap of Paper" of 1914.

The diplomatic sequel to this momentous development was ominous indeed. Profiting by the appeasement policy of the democratic powers, of which the surrender of Munich was the apogee, Germany continued her "peaceful" war of fear. In March, 1939, the remnants of Czechoslovakia—Slovakia and Bohemia— were assigned to their respective stations in the political trenches of the "Hitler-Ribbentrop line." At the command of Hitler, Memel and its territory marched away from Lithuania and filed in with the other possessions of Germany. Upon the receipt of Carpatho-Ukrainia, Hungary became a virtual vassal of Berlin. On March 23, Roumania deemed it expedient to sign a commercial agreement with the Reich, and thus became an economic dependency of the Germanic lord. Early in April, Italy, not without "Godspeed" from

---

[28] *Parliamentary Papers. Cmd. 5848; Misc. No. 8 (1938); also, Treaty Series, No. 30 (1939). Cmd. 6047.*

Hitler, annexed Albania. On April 28, 1939, speaking before the Reichstag, Hitler announced the nullification of two treaties which, at the time of their conclusion, had been considered of the utmost importance: the Naval Treaty with Great Britain of June 18, 1935, and the Treaty of Non-Aggression with Poland, so welcome when signed on January 26, 1934.[29] A communiqué issued at Milan on May 7, 1939,[30] announced that in their stead a political and military accord to be known as the Milan Pact had been signed between Germany and Italy.

Projected against these events, the diplomatic efforts of Great Britain and France were no longer the acts of self-confident great powers. True, on March 31, 1939, Prime Minister Chamberlain announced in the House of Commons Great Britain's assurance that Poland would be given assistance in case of need. Then on April 6, this unilateral assurance was replaced by a provisional mutual aid pact which, while pending elaboration of a formal treaty of alliance, brought into being a *de facto* triple alliance between Great Britain, France and Poland.[31] That the obligations in regard to Poland were undertaken by Great Britain with reservations, however, is evident from the very expression that the aid was to be rendered only in case Poland had to fight to defend its "independence." In view of the fact that the difficulties between Germany and Poland were at the time focused on Danzig rather than on Germany's desire to have Poland disappear as an independent State, the implications to be derived from the wording of this British-Polish agreement could hardly be encouraging either to Poland or to the democracies in general as to the real value of Britain's commitments. Nor did the statement made by Chamberlain in the House of Commons on April 13, 1939, to the effect that His Majesty's Government undertook to guarantee the integrity of the borders of Roumania and Greece deserve any more confidence.[32] Whatever the actual value of these assurances, it was becoming more and more evident that under the circumstances, the democratic idea of collective security was gradually giving way to

[29] Notes to that effect were forwarded to Great Britain on April 27, 1939, and to Poland simultaneously with the speech, *i.e.*, on April 28 (*Documents concerning German-Polish Relations and the Outbreak of Hostilities between Great Britain and Germany on September 3, 1939,* Miscellaneous No. 9 (1939). Cmd. 6106, pp. 51 and 24, respectively.)

[30] New York *Times*, May 8, 1939.

[31] *Documents concerning German-Polish Relations* . . . Cmd. *6106,* pp. 36–37.

[32] London *Times*, April 14, 1939, p. 6.

bilateral bargaining—a method basically unsafe for the preservation of world peace, yet undoubtedly convenient from the standpoint of the elasticity which it affords for localizing the unpleasantness of diplomatic waverings in case one's own safety is to be considered.

Nor was there much encouragement in the efforts made by France. After the dismemberment of Czechoslovakia it was generally realized that Danzig and the Polish Corridor were to become the next objectives of Hitler. His assurances that Germany's territorial aspirations would not go beyond the Sudetenland, and his admission on September 26, 1938, that "Poland had the right to access to the sea" were poor guaranties. The fate of Memel and the ultimate dismemberment of Czechoslovakia disqualified him from being any longer worthy of trust; his magnanimous consent to Poland's having an access to the sea did not mean that Danzig was to remain under the control of the League of Nations or that the Polish Corridor was to stay Polish. In fairness to Hitler, however, it must be said that nowhere in his speeches had he ever renounced Germany's right to that strip of territory.

France, having once accepted the policy of following the course charted by Great Britain, did not deviate from this policy even after Munich. As is well known London did little to stop Hitler from marching into the Polish Corridor. Nor did France: the ties which bound together Paris and Warsaw were indeed worn thin. The Franco-Polish alliance of February 19, 1921,[33] and the Guaranty Pact of October 16, 1925,[34] had remained formally intact and unaffected by the long years that had since passed. That the original vigor of their provisions had undergone an acid test, however, and that it was not unaffected is quite obvious. To mention nothing else, Pilsudski's flirtation with Germany, which eventuated in the Non-Aggression Pact of 1934, Polish disappointment at being left out of the Munich negotiations, and, finally, Warsaw's lack of discrimination, manifested in the greedy annexation of Teschen during the dissection of Czechoslovakia, would be sufficient to undermine the friendship between France and Poland. However, the feelings between the two capitals were mutual. In Paris, the premature self-confidence of Poland was considered inconsistent with its need of France's pressure upon Germany from the west. In Warsaw, the reason for the French courtship of Poland was clear: before 1933 it had

[33] *L.N.T.S.*, XVIII, 13.
[34] *Ibid.*, LIV, 353.

been the preservation of the *status quo* established at Versailles; after the appearance of the Nazis, it was the laconic "Stop Hitler." The fact that no adequate cementing of the relations between France and Poland had been undertaken was an omen not unpleasant to Hitler.

Indeed, it was becoming more and more clear to him that the anti-totalitarian chain was not only incomplete, but that the existing links were fragile and insecure. Of the four potential enemies [35] engaged in establishing a concentric *cordon politique* around Germany, recent bipartite understandings as to their obligations toward each other in case of emergency existed only between Great Britain and France, France and Poland, Poland and Great Britain, and France and the U.S.S.R. Thus, barring action by the League of Nations, England and Poland could become Soviet allies in the field only through the clearing-house of the Quai d'Orsay, and of the existing alignments, only the London-Paris alliance could be accepted at its full face value. As has just been said, there was no direct understanding between Great Britain and the U.S.S.R.; the effectiveness of the pacts between France and Poland left much to be desired; British assurances to Poland were limited to the case of threats against the latter's independence, while the Soviet-French Pact of 1935 provided for resort to the agencies of the League of Nations, a procedure no longer effective under the circumstances.

True, on August 25, 1939, an Agreement of Mutual Assistance had been signed by Great Britain and Poland which amounted to a military alliance, and, on September 4, 1939, a military accord had been reached between Paris and Poland.[36] These, however, proved not only belated, but essentially superficial, the latter even verging upon the ironical, for, on September 3, 1939, the thunderous echo of the *Blitzkrieg* along the Vistula reached the steel and concrete shores of the Rhine. Peace was relieved of its last hours of agony by the advent of war.

Friendship at Crossroads

So much for the general developments in Europe since 1933. For a better understanding of the Soviet reactions to all this, a brief survey

[35] In pursuit of isolation and neutrality championed by King Leopold in his speech to the Cabinet, on October 14, 1936, Belgium ceased to be France's ally on April 24, 1937.

[36] *Documents concerning German-Polish Relations* . . ., p. 37, also *Treaty Series No. 58 (1939). Cmd. 6144.*

of the relations between Germany and the U.S.S.R. from the days of
Brest-Litovsk is necessary. In diplomatic documents, verbal statements of communist leaders, and the writings of Soviet scholars, the
range of communist sentiment toward Germany varied from open
protests and revolutionary reproaches to exalted praise and platonic
admiration. There is no doubt, however, that the cultivation and
preservation of Germany's friendship has been of great advantage to
the Kremlin. This was particularly so in the formative years of the
Soviet régime. In spite of the revolutionary upheaval in Russia and
of Germany's surrender at Versailles, both countries remained potentially great powers, and geographically, Germany was the Soviet's
nearest neighbor in that category in the west. Then, too, the fact that
Germany was one of the most industrially developed countries in the
world was likewise of no small importance to Soviet Russia, a country
primarily still agricultural, in spite of Soviet claims to the contrary.
Finally, the importance of Germany's good-will toward the Soviets
had its purely revolutionary aspects, although Molotov's assurance that in their relations with Germany the Soviets "have *always*
been of the opinion that a strong Germany is the necessary prerequisite for durable peace in Europe," [37] is certainly open to question.

The opinions of political scientists may vary as to whether the
theory was applicable to Germany and the Soviet Union that there is
a natural tendency of mutual rapprochement among powers of the
same caliber, be they great or small, victorious or defeated. Economists may have their reasons for disagreeing as to the actual effect of
industrial Germany upon the progress of industrialization in the
U.S.S.R. There is no denying the fact, however, that revolutionary
expediency made all other considerations secondary in importance.
In their struggle for peace, the Soviets received their first encouragement from Germany. Humiliating as it was, the peace of Brest-Litovsk
was more acceptable to Lenin than the danger of Allied intervention
because to him "the war of England, America and Japan against Russia
could not cause even one-hundredth of the damage and suffering that
would be brought about by [Russia's] war against Germany, Austria
and Turkey." [38]

When Germany fell a victim to its own revolution, communist ill-

[37] Report to the Supreme Council of the U.S.S.R., October 31, 1939 (*Izvestiia*,
November 1, 1939). (Italics by author.)
[38] Lenin, XXI, 224.

feeling toward the imperial dictators of Brest-Litovsk was forgotten and the brotherly sympathy of the Russian proletariat for the German people was elevated to a cult of revolutionary affection. The Versailles Treaty, for which the Soviets could not be held responsible, only accelerated the mutual infatuation of the two countries. The unpleasant episode of the nullification of the Brest-Litovsk Treaty by the Soviets was readily forgiven by Berlin in view of the Kremlin's lavish denouncement of the Treaty of Versailles, which was branded by Moscow as a "hundred times more humiliating and rapacious than our Brest Peace." [39] Early in 1923, appealing to the workers of the world in connection with the occupation of the Ruhr basin by French detachments, the Central Executive Committee of the U.S.S.R. voiced its opinion on the Versailles Treaty in the following words:

"Five years ago the imperialistic war was ended by the disgraceful and senseless Treaty of Versailles . . . Workers' and Peasants' Russia at the time categorically protested against the terrible insaneness of that Treaty and warned of the grave consequences which its execution would bring to Europe and to the whole world." [40]

It is a matter of individual opinion whether this desire for cordial relations with Germany was motivated by specific considerations or was merely a particular phase of the general scheme of the Soviets in their peace policy to pay particular attention to the states which had been losers in the World War. The Soviets assert that the latter was the case; witness Stalin's emphasis on the need of "rapprochement with the countries defeated in the World War, the countries which have been most hurt and robbed, and which, consequently, are in opposition to the dominating concert of the Great Powers." [41]

The economic pressure to which Germany and the Soviets were equally subjected in 1922 laid the foundation for the Soviet-German

[39] Lenin, XXIII, 315. It will be recalled that Germany was forced to renounce this treaty also in virtue of the Versailles Treaty (Arts. 116, 259, 292, and 433). At the Extraordinary Session of the League of Nations, April 17, 1935, in discussing Germany's violation of the Versailles Treaty, Litvinov said that he was speaking in the "name of a country which not only was not responsible for this treaty but had never concealed its negative attitude thereto *in toto* and to the disarmament of Germany, in particular" (*Izvestiia*, April 18, 1935).

[40] Kliuchnikov i Sabanin, *op. cit.*, III, pt. I, pp. 227–228.

[41] Report to the XIV Congress of the Communist Party (*XIV S'ezd Vsesoiuznoi Kommunisticheskoi Partii Bol'shevikov (b), 18–31 Dekabria 1925g. Stenograficheskii Otchet*, p. 27). *Cf.* also his Report to the XV Congress of the Party (*XV S'ezd . . . Stenograficheskii Otchet*, p. 49).

friendship incorporated in the Treaty of Rapallo.[42] Besides being a natural reaction of the two countries who found themselves on the defensive against the dictatorial attempts of the Great Powers to force Germany and the Soviets into economic subjugation, this treaty was not only formal testimony of the political friendship and economic interdependence of these two powers, but was a blow at the whole Versailles system as well, for from April 16, 1922, Germany and Soviet Russia were no longer handicapped by the political isolation in which they found themselves hitherto.

It would not be in conformity with the facts to say that the path of the friendship thus consummated was smooth and free from disillusions. Indeed, it is no longer a secret that after the fiasco at Genoa, the Allies busied themselves with finding some way not only to break this union between Berlin and Moscow, but if possible, to enlist Germany in the anti-Soviet bloc of the non-communist powers of Western Europe. The results of these efforts are well known, as is also the significance of the Locarno Treaties of 1925. The Soviet reaction to the post-war "truce" between France and Germany on the basis of the Versailles dictates, and to the appearance in Germany of two factions one with pro- and one with anti-Soviet leanings, is found in Stalin's report to the Fourteenth Congress of the Soviet Union Communist Party, held in 1925. "As to Locarno," said he, "it is nothing but a continuation of the Versailles Treaty and can have but one purpose, namely, preservation of the *status quo* . . . according to which Germany is [to remain] the defeated country and the Entente Powers the victors. . . . The British conservatives wish to preserve the *status quo* against Germany and at the same time expect to use that country against the Soviet Union." [43]

Disappointing as this understanding between Paris and Berlin may have been to Moscow, confidence in the continuance of close relationship between Germany and the Soviets was not diminished, for in the words of Stalin, to think that Germany would consent to these designs of England and France "would mean to believe in miracles." [44] That this optimism was not without good ground was proved shortly. When in 1926 Germany joined the League of Nations —a fact itself suggestive of further alienation of Berlin from the Soviets—the friendship between the two countries instead of being

---

[42] *Supra*, p. 115.
[43] *XIV S'ezd . . . Stenograficheskii Otchet*, pp. 14–15.
[44] *Ibid.*, p. 14.

weakened, found another manifestation, this time in the provisions of the Treaty of Berlin, signed on April 24, 1926,[45] according to which the good-will solemnly promised at Rapallo was to remain the basis for future coöperation. This Treaty of 1926 was extended in 1931, although Germany's ratification of the Protocol did not take place until 1933, *i.e.*, after Hitler had become ruler of the Third Reich.[46]

The rise of Hitler to power in 1933 and the adoption of National-Socialism in Germany was of far-reaching significance for Soviet-German friendship. As a revolt against the Versailles system, the new régime should have been welcomed by Moscow. From this standpoint, the Soviet assertions that the U.S.S.R. wanted to continue its friendship with Berlin may stand analysis. There is nothing unnatural in Molotov's belief that " the development of commercial relations with other countries, irrespective of the provisional forms of political authority therein, does not conflict with Soviet policies." [47] The same applies likewise to his assurance that while "it is well known that during the last six years, *i.e.*, since the authority [in Germany] was taken over by the National-Socialists, the political relations between Germany and the U.S.S.R. have been strained . . . it is also well known that, in spite of the difference in ideologies and in political systems, the Soviet Government was anxious to maintain normal political relations with Germany." [48] Nor is there anything out of the ordinary in Stalin's denial that the change in the political régime in Germany should be an obstacle to further improvement between the two countries:

"Some German politicians say that the U.S.S.R. is now oriented toward France and Poland, and that from an antagonist of the Versailles Treaty it has become its protagonist, and that this change is due to the establishment of the Fascist régime in Germany. This is wrong. Certainly, we are far from being admirers of the Fascist régime in Germany. The importance, however, lies not in Fascism, if for no other reason than the simple fact that Fascism in Italy, for instance, did not prevent us from establishing most cordial relations with that country. Nor does it lie in the alleged change in our attitude toward Versailles. It is not for us who have experienced the shame of Brest-Litovsk to glorify the Treaty of Versailles. We disagree in only one thing [namely] that the world should be involved in another war because of that Treaty. The same must be said also in regard to the alleged

---

[45] *Supra*, p. 120.
[46] *Sborn. Deistv. Dogov.*, VIII, 1935, p. 7.
[47] Report to the Second Session of the Central Executive Committee of the U.S.S.R., January, 1936 (V. M. Molotov, *Stat'i i Rechi, 1935–1936*, p. 172).
[48] Report to the IV Session of the Supreme Council of the U.S.S.R.

reorientation of the U.S.S.R. We have not oriented ourselves toward Germany. We will not orient ourselves toward Poland or toward France. We are oriented as we were before, as we are now, and as we always will be, only toward the U.S.S.R. And if the interests of the Soviet Union demand that we approach one country or another which is not interested in violating the peace, we shall do so without hesitation." [49]

Warning is hardly necessary, however, that these utterances of amity toward Germany were by no means *annuncia ex pietate.* Certainly Hitler's *Mein Kampf* had been carefully studied in the Kremlin. That Hitler's references to "the East" and their practical implications were no mystery to Stalin, was disclosed at the trials and purges, from 1936 to 1938, when the élite of the old revolutionary guard, both in civilian garb and military uniform, were executed,[50] after being "found guilty" of conspiracy with "the Fascist forces of Germany and Japan in fomenting war against the Soviet Union . . . and planning the dismemberment of the U.S.S.R., according to which the Ukraine was to be given to the Germans and the Maritime Province to the Japanese." [51]

It was likewise obvious to the Soviets that Hitler's designs in the east were not limited to physical *Lebensraum* alone, but included an ideological campaign against the principles endorsed by Marxism. In the Kremlin, Hitler's theory of associating the Third International with Semitism was well known, as was also his belief that the Third Reich was the "next great objective of Bolshevism," as "the international Jew does not regard Germany as an ally, but as a state to undergo a similar fate." [52] Nor were the Soviets unaware of the fact that the *Parteitag* staged in Nuremberg in September, 1936, was dedicated to the denunciation of Bolshevism; that Goebbel's cry "Bolshevism must be annihilated" was in full accord with Rosenberg's warning that communism was using Jews to "awaken the underworld in all nations to march against European culture and against the holy traditions of all peoples," and that Hitler's denunciation of Russia as "Bolshevist Jews" was to him sufficient reason for not permitting "ruined states on his doorstep." [53]

[49] *XVII S'ezd Vsesoiuznoi Kommunisticheskoi Partii (b), 26 ianvaria–10 fevralia 1934g. Stenograficheskii Otchet,* p. 14.
[50] *Cf.,* Paul Scheffer, "From Lenin to Stalin," *Foreign Affairs,* April, 1938, pp. 445ff.
[51] Stalin, *O nedostatkakh partiinoi raboty i merakh likvidatsii trotskistskikh i inykh dvurushnikov,* p. 13.
[52] Hitler, *Mein Kampf,* II, p. 750.
[53] Schuman, *op. cit.,* p. 241.

In attempting to analyze Soviet foreign policy after 1933, it must be borne in mind that the transformation of the Germany of Weimar into Hitler's Third Reich did not change the fundamental assertion of the Soviets that sooner or later the U.S.S.R. would become the object of capitalist aggression. This fear of the Kremlin has become a communist credo of permanent standing. The only effect of the change of the régime in Germany on the Soviet Union was that the possibility of such aggression might now be expected from two capitalist camps instead of one: the old anti-communist bloc of the democratic Great Powers and the new totalitarian triple alliance of German Nazism, Italian Fascism, and Japanese Jingoism. Consequently, the general problem of maintaining peace for the sake of survival, was reduced for the Soviets to the dilemma of properly evaluating the potential dangers presented to the Soviet Union by each of these camps, and then deciding which side to take to counteract the designs of those trusted the least.

That the issue was not only a vital but a complicated one, is obvious. Indeed, it will be recalled that the "peace" which the world had been trying to preserve during the last few years, to the communist was actually not peace. To them it was another imperialistic world war, already in progress, even if the old custom of formal declarations of war was no longer observed and the battlefields were to be found not in the familiar concentrated areas of Western Europe, but in such widely separated places as Spain, Ethiopia and China. In his report to the Eighteenth Congress of the Communist Party of the U.S.S.R., Stalin remarked that the main characteristic of the new imperialistic war was that it had not yet become a universal war, and that while the aggressor states were waging it by encroaching upon the interests of the non-aggressor states, the latter—particularly England, France, and the United States—are retreating by making one concession after another: "Thus," said he, "before our very eyes the world is again being redistributed into spheres of influence at the expense of the non-aggressor states, which not only do not put up any resistance, but in some instances even sponsor this." "Incredible as it may appear," he added, "it is a fact." [54]

That the Soviets preferred to coöperate with the democratic

[54] Stalin, *Otchetnyi doklad na XVIII S'ezde partii o rabote TsK VKP (b)*, p. 12. Also: *Istoriia VKP (b)*. To this pessimistic outlook may be added his realistic skepticism that "Nowadays wars are not declared. They simply start." (Interview with Roy Howard, in Wheeler-Bennett, *op. cit.*, p. 465).

powers has already been shown. That they had good reason to do so is likewise not difficult to understand, as Nazism was considered a real danger not only to the integrity of the Soviet Union but also to the well-being of the world proletariat. To illustrate the feelings which prevailed in the U.S.S.R. on these issues, Arzhanov may be quoted:

"Fascism,[55] as a régime of criminal gangsters and as a state system of political banditry, is showing its true face also in international dealings abroad. Having destroyed legal order within its own country and established therein a régime of lawlessness and inequality, Fascism is resorting to this principle in its foreign relations, too. With demogogic cynicism and shamelessness the Fascist 'leaders' sometimes say that they are interested in the peaceful settlement of international problems. However, it is well known that their deeds speak to the contrary. Fascist Germany has rudely and unilaterally violated the old Treaties of Peace—Versailles and Locarno. It also resigned from the League of Nations. It furiously opposes the principles of collective security. The treaties concluded by the Third Reich (with Japan and Italy) are pacts of military aggression. Finally, [it launched] the monstrous and rapacious assault upon Spain. This cannot but unveil the cynical lies of the Fascists speaking of 'law' and 'justice.' 'Law' here means actually the arbitrary rule of highway bandits and crying violation of the very most elementary principles of international law. Fascist utterances about the 'peaceful' intentions of the Third Reich are rendered worthless by the openly chauvinistic propaganda against other peoples and by direct appeals of Fascism to organize a crusade against the U.S.S.R. . . ."[56]

Compared with this militant denial of Nazism, the considerations of the well-being of the world proletariat, as voiced by Varga, appear not only more reserved but more in point as regards the revolutionary aims of the U.S.S.R.:

"At present the aggressive bloc consists solely of the Fascist countries, where there is no democracy, no legalized labor movement, no liberties whatsoever, where the population is utterly suppressed and has not the slightest degree of influence upon state policy, where the 'leaders' employed by the capitalist oligarchies . . . personally decide upon the problems of

---

[55] In Soviet literature the term "Fascism" is used as a general denomination of the totalitarian régime, be it Nazism, Fascism, or Japanese militarism.

[56] M. Arzhanov, "Shpionazh, diversii, interventsiia kak sistema vneshnikh otnoshenii fashistskoi diktatury (Na primere Germanii), "*Mir. Khoz. i Mir. Politika,* 1938, No. 1, pp. 181–182). *Cf.* also Dmitrov's contention that inasmuch as workers and their communist vanguard are the most persistent champions of peace, they must "vigorously oppose any policy of rapprochement with the Fascist aggressors and denounce capitulations of the appeasement policy which deceive people by their false pacifist preachings." (*Edinyi front mezhdunarodnogo proletariata i narodov protiv fashizma,* p. 15).

war and peace. In the non-aggressive countries power is in the hands of the bourgeois democracy, the labor movement is legal, and the working masses have a certain influence on the destinies of their countries.

"We entertain no illusions in regard to the bourgeois democracies. We know that they are nothing but one of the expressions of the bourgeois dictatorship. Yet, in comparison with absolute lawlessness, oppression, enslavement, and the hell which is suffered by the proletariat under Fascism, the bourgeois democracy has not a few advantages. Marxists have always considered the bourgeois democracy as a great advance as compared with feudalism and absolutism." [57]

Customary as it often is for communist authorities to conceal their true meaning in purposely eloquent phraseology, the above lengthy statements should not be regarded as mere revolutionary rodomontades. They may be accepted not only as an authentic *summa summarum* of the persistent Soviet condemnation of Nazism, but also as a pathetic valedictory of the régime which had found it necessary to replace the old Soviet proletarian distrust for capitalist democracies with new friendly affections of the Soviet "democratic" Dictatorship of the Proletariat.

Limitations of space prevent a detailed enumeration of the political charges, dogmatic criticism, and ethical accusations preferred by the Soviets against Hitler and the Third Reich. An analysis of the actual workings of democratic principles in the U.S.S.R. is not the purpose of the present study. Therefore, the foregoing must be accepted merely as suggestive of the fact that from 1933 to 1939 the Soviets once again had changed the course of their peace policy, this time formally aligning their own destinies with those of the democratic Great Powers. The concrete manifestation of this is found in the international dealings of the Kremlin with individual states, in Soviet participation in the work of the League of Nations, and in the communist efforts to create a united labor front of peace against the united capitalist front of war.

The position in which the Soviets found themselves after the appearance of Hitler at the head of the Third Reich would hardly give rise to envy. True, Litvinov had succeeded in making of the neighboring states a buffer belt for the U.S.S.R. with whom pacts of non-aggression were concluded.[58] The recognition which was accorded

---

[57] E. Varga, "25–letie imperialisticheskoi voiny" (*Mir. Khoz. i Mir. Politika,* 1939, No. 7–8, pp. 9–10).

[58] *Supra,* pp. 113ff.

the Soviet Government by Bulgaria, Hungary, Roumania and Czecho-slovakia in 1934 enhanced the possibility of furthering the cause of peace, inasmuch as these countries were also interested in preventing war—for them an obvious danger of annihilation. Finally, the friction which arose between Nazi Germany and its western neighbors was to a certain degree a welcome relief in so far as it reduced the possibility of immediate attack on the Soviet Union either by the Third Reich or by the democratic non-communist Powers of Western Europe. There was no guaranty, however, that the friendship of the countries bound to the Soviets through the pacts of amity and non-aggression was sincere, and there was room for doubt whether the good-will of the countries that had recently recognized the Soviets was genuine enough to afford expectation of close coöperation as to war and peace. Finally, the possibility was not excluded that Western Europe and the Third Reich might come to some understanding, which, for the sake of peace in Western Europe, would result in their common aggression against the Soviets, probably not in the form of a joint crusade, but by giving Hitler a free hand in carrying out his designs in regard to Russia.

It was only too evident to the Soviets that there was not much that the Kremlin could add to its understandings with the limitrophe states in the Baltic and the Levant countries to the southeast. Nor could the resumption of diplomatic relations with the Balkan and Central European countries be considered sufficient ground for exerting immediate pressure to bring them into the sphere of Soviet influence. Neither willing nor ready to become involved in open warfare, the Soviets had only one way out—to prevent a rapprochement between London and Paris, on the one hand, and Berlin, on the other. By this means not only the dreaded war at home might be postponed, but the conflagration in Europe might also possibly be avoided for the time being, which fact in itself would have been no small political credit and advertisement for the Soviets.

Theoretically, this could be achieved in one of two ways: either side with Germany or take sides with the democracies. In the first instance, the integrity of the Soviet Union would have been bought at the price of sponsoring Hitler's hegemony over Western and Central Europe. The understanding with England and France meant opposition to Hitler's philosophy, *ex principio*. As has been said, the last consideration prevailed. Coupled with the realization that an actual attack was far more feasible from the direction of Germany, Poland or Japan—the three equally uncompromising ideological foes—it forced the U.S.S.R. to cast its lot with the democratic capitalist powers.

SOVIET DETOUR TO GENEVA

The political and diplomatic events which took place in Western Europe from 1933 to 1939, have already been briefly described.[59] The general impression of the picture is that with the rise of the Nazis, Germany's withdrawal from the League, the collapse of the disarmament conference, and the conclusion of the German-Polish agreement, France and England became seriously alarmed and redoubled their efforts to find new allies for encircling Germany, and that the Soviet Union was a willing recipient of their offers to that end.

In fairness to the Western Powers it must be pointed out, however, that the Soviets were concerned to an equal degree. To defend themselves against the feared possibility of being encircled by a Paris-London-Berlin-Tokio alignment, the Soviets were relieved to see the estrangement between Paris and Berlin, and only too glad to grasp the opportunity of widening this gulf by siding definitely with the democratic powers. The Kremlin not only joined the League of Nations, but together with France, took the initiative in negotiating the Eastern Locarno Pact. When it became clear that Hitler's objection to this combination had brought the French and Soviet effort to nil, the U.S.S.R. began to press France with propositions of an alliance of the pre-war type. Met with Laval's cautious policy of avoiding extremes, the Kremlin finally consented to a compromise, and on May 2, 1935, the Treaty of Mutual Assistance was signed between Moscow and Paris. It was to last for five years.[60]

It starts with a promise that in case of any threat or danger of attack from some other European state, France and the Soviet Union will immediately consult each other in regard to the enforcement of territorial guaranties on the basis of Article 10 of the League Covenant.[61] Article 2 of the Treaty commits the Contracting Parties to come to each other's immediate assistance in case of unprovoked

[59] *Supra*, pp. 166ff.
[60] *Sobr. Zak. i Rasp. S.S.S.R.*, 1936, II, par. 72.
[61] Article 1.

attack by any European power, this assistance being of the kind contemplated in Article 16 of the Covenant. Article 3 provides that the
same shall apply in case of attack by any other European member
of the League in violation of the articles of the Covenant prescribing
arbitral, judicial or conciliatory settlement.[62] While the last two
articles brought the working of this treaty within the scope of the
jurisdiction accorded the League of Nations, Article 1 of the Protocol
of Signature attached to it provided that neutrality must be maintained by Paris and Moscow in cases when "either of the Contracting
Parties should be subject to attack by one or several other European
Powers not included in the above mentioned tri-lateral agreement."

Two weeks later a similar treaty was signed by the U.S.S.R. and
Czechoslovakia,[63] the only difference being that according to Article 2
of the Protocol of Signature, the obligations undertaken in this treaty
were to be effective between the Contracting Parties "only in so far
as, under the conditions provided in the present treaty, aid is accorded
by France to the party who is the victim of attack."

These treaties were clearly based on strict adherence to the Covenant of the League of Nations, and, as such, manifested actual Soviet
concurrence with the democratic powers as regards the idea of collective security. Indicative at the same time of Soviet cognizance of
other treaties which have been concluded within the framework of
the League, these treaties evidenced the change in Soviet foreign policy which from now on recognized the importance of regional understandings for the preservation of peace and accepted the edifice of
balance of powers as its ideal. Finally, as the inaugural manifestation
of the new Soviet policy of alliances with great democracies, these
treaties, even if they were not military alliances in the strictest sense
of the term but rather defensive understandings, could not help but
create a formidable obstacle to the Western European tendencies
toward appeasement, a notion objectionable to the Soviets.

The same end was also pursued by Soviet diplomacy in Moscow's
relations with Great Britain, whose traditional course of international
behavior has ever been piloting safely between war and peace. True,
the Soviets did not succeed in making London join the anti-Nazi
front to the extent of direct treaty commitments, as in the case of

---

[62] This is to hold also in the event of an attack by a non-member European state,
which obviously meant Germany, which by that time, as said, ceased to be a member
of the League of Nations (part 2 of Art. 3).

[63] *Sobr. Zak. i Rasp. S.S.S.R.*, 1935, II, Nos. 14–15, par. 130.

France and Czechoslovakia. Their efforts proved not entirely without results, however. The British-Soviet Trade Agreement, signed on February 16, 1934, was an inducement, indeed, for closer understanding and a better relationship between the two countries, which in the past had had the unpleasant experience of having their diplomatic relations interrupted for more than two years.[64]

The Montreux Convention of July 20, 1936, was likewise a welcome solution, as it ended the friction between London and Moscow in regard to the Straits.[65] British efforts to keep the Soviet naval forces out of the Mediterranean and the Soviet counter-effort to keep British forces out of the Black Sea now found a compromise: the Straits were opened to Soviet vessels of any size and to the light surface vessels of Great Britain. A victory for the Soviets, this convention was also a convenient instrument for bringing London to a closer understanding with Turkey, which was a Soviet ally, and hence, also, with the Kremlin itself. The extension to Moscow of British credits amounting to ten million pounds sterling, agreed upon on July 28, 1936, and the Agreement of July 17, 1937,[66] between the two countries, providing for the Limitation of Naval Armament and the Exchange of Information concerning Naval Construction, may be cited as further illustrations of Soviet efforts and success in resurrecting the pre-war *Entente cordiale*.

Amid this activity, the old arrangements with the border states were not forgotten. The Treaties of Non-Aggression with the Baltic States, Finland and Poland, were extended or renewed. The Treaty of Friendship and Neutrality with Turkey of 1925 was prolonged on November 7, 1935,[67] and the Neutrality and Non-Aggression Pact signed with Afghanistan on April 24, 1931, was extended on March 29, 1936.[68]

Nor did the Soviets abandon the idea of completing their own defensive encirclement with friendly understandings with countries not yet included in the *cordon politique* serving to neutralize the danger of totalitarian aggression.

On March 12, 1936, at Ulan-Bator the Soviet Union and the Mon-

[64] *Sborn. Deistv. Dogov.*, VIII, 1935, No. 302.
[65] *Izvestiia*, July 20, 1936, No. 167.
[66] *Izvestiia*, Aug. 1, 1936, No. 177 and *Treaty Series No. 17 (1938), Soviet Union. Cmd. 5679.* London, respectively. *Cf.* also Protocol of July 6, 1938, modifying the Naval Agreement of 1937 *(Treaty Series No. 39 (1939). Cmd. 6074).*
[67] *L.N.T.S.*, CLXXIX, 131.
[68] *Ibid.*, CLXXVII, 467.

golian People's Republic signed a Protocol amounting to a mutual assistance pact, according to which "the gentlemen's agreement which had existed between them since November 27, 1934," became a binding obligation to come to each other's assistance in case of threat, or actual attack, against one of the Contracting Parties by a third power.[69] The protest which was lodged by China on April 7, 1934,[70] did not prove an obstacle to the signing of a Treaty of Non-Aggression by the U.S.S.R. and China on August 21, 1937, when Japanese aggression in Asia had revealed its true purpose and extent.[71]

In the endeavors of the Kremlin to counterbalance the Berlin-Rome-Tokio axis, the absence of similar agreements with Germany, Italy and Japan is easy to understand. In regard to Germany, the Soviets had no doubt that Hitler's struggle against the Versailles Treaty was merely a front to conceal his real ambition not only of returning to Germany's domination lands and colonies which had belonged to her before the World War, but of annexing to the Third Reich lands and colonies of other countries. The Soviets put it thus:

"As to the annexation of Austria, this act can hardly be assimilated with the struggle against the Versailles Treaty, or with the protection of the national interests of Germany, which is desirous to regain territories lost in the first imperialistic war. Austria was not a part of Germany either before or after the war. The annexation of Austria by violence is sheer imperialistic rudeness. It undoubtedly unveils Germany's designs to become the dominant power in Western Europe." [72]

Nor could there be two meanings as to Hitler's preaching about national self-determination. The mission undertaken by Hitler to unite all German-speaking peoples in *Grossdeutschland* was to the Soviets nothing but demagogic sophistry, for to them the Marxian doctrine of nationalism, namely that language is not the sole characteristic of a nation, and that self-determination is first of all an expression of free will, was applicable universally. Unrestricted in logic and forgetful of its own practice, the Kremlin interpreted the subjugation of the Czechs and the Slovaks to the Third Reich as an

[69] *Sobr. Zak. i. Rasp. S.S.R.R.*, 1936, II, pp. 482–488. *Cf.* also the interview granted by Stalin to Mr. Roy Howard on Mar. 4, 1936, *i.e.*, even before the signing of this Treaty, in which he admitted that the Japanese attack against Mongolia would be met by Soviet resistance (Heald and Wheeler-Bennett, *Documents on International Affairs,* 1936, pp. 464–465).

[70] *La Documentation Internationale,* May–June, 1936.

[71] *L.N.T.S.*, CLXXXI, 101.

[72] *Istoriia VKP (b)*, pp. 307–318.

obvious proof that these notions of Hitler regarding national issues were hypocritical, to say the least. Hitler's invitation to the non-communist world at large to join him in his crusade against communism was viewed by the rulers of the U.S.S.R. with the same "ethical" con-demnation. To the Soviets, Hitler's anti-communist hysteria was merely a cloak for his attempt to find some common understanding with the capitalistic powers, and a way to assure these powers that Germany was least of all interested in their domestic affairs. It is obvious that if National-Socialism was to be viewed as "war, barbarism and physical destruction" and if "every one who values the interests of humanity must unite in a single front against the barbaric instigators of war," the effort of the Soviets to find a common language with Germany was contradictory to the outward purpose of the agreements concluded with other non-totalitarian states.[73]

The Soviet relationship with Italy, from the very day of the recognition accorded in 1924, had been free from unpleasant disturbances, either political or economic. Far from each other, Rome and Moscow had preferred to overlook the difference between their respective political philosophies and to conduct their international relations on a rather materialistic basis, concentrating on the benefits to be derived from trade. The concurrent realization that peace was essential for the continuance of this not unprofitable coöperation resulted in the already mentioned Non-Aggression Pact signed in 1933 by the Soviets and Italy.[74] The aspirations of Italy in Africa, the Rome-Berlin axis, its extension to Japan, and the joint support of General Franco in Spain by Mussolini and Hitler spelled the end of this idyllic understanding between the Union of the Soviet Republics and the Kingdom of Italy. The doctrines of Fascism were placed in the same category as the principles of National-Socialism. Italy became a close second to Germany as a conspirator undermining world peace. As such, it was removed from the Soviet list of peace-loving countries and numbered among the foremost enemies of the U.S.S.R. While the Treaty of 1933 remained legally in force, its practical value was reduced to nil.

While the relations between the Soviet Union and Japan are discussed elsewhere, at this point a few words must be said in regard to the attitude taken by the Soviets toward Poland. When, speaking at the

[73] *Izvestiia,* Aug. 1, 1936, No. 177.
[74] *Sborn. Deistv. Dogov.,* VIII, 1935, p. 8.

Fourth Session of the Central Executive Committee, on December 29, 1933, Litvinov said that the Treaty of Non-Aggression signed by these two countries in 1932 [75] enhanced the mutual trust and understanding between them, he had good reason for optimism.[76] Poland, at that time very much concerned over the rise of National-Socialism, was only too desirous to assure its own security, even if that involved overlooking old suspicions in regard to her Soviet neighbor in the east. The change in the relations between Berlin and Warsaw in 1934 [77] also changed the "trust and mutual understanding" heralded less than a month earlier by Litvinov. True, a few months later, on June 5, 1934, the Pact of 1932 was extended, but it had already lost its original lure. Vehemently distrustful of the new ruler of Germany, Stalin retired to the policy of suspicion in regard to Poland. In the interview given to Mr. Roy Howard in 1936, he summarized Soviet sentiments toward Poland in a rather pointed remark: "I do not know what specific frontiers Germany could use for her purposes [in case she attacked Russia], but I think that those willing to 'lend' her a frontier can be found." [78]

Whatever the anxiety which characterized the relations of the Kremlin with the "aggressor" bloc, and notwithstanding the illusions created by the outwardly cordial understanding with the democratic Great Powers, the fabric of the Soviet security system was sadly confused and dangerously fragile. True, assurances of goodwill, and invitations to continue the efforts toward peace issued from the foreign offices of Berlin, Rome, Tokio and Moscow, as usual. Treaties envisaging economic and cultural coöperation between the Soviets and the Axis Powers were even signed now and then.[79] That there was much admiration wasted between the Soviets and the totalitarian powers, however, would be "too good to be true." At the same time, the whole framework of the Soviet non-aggression system offered no assurance that it was sufficient to constitute an impregnable consolidation of the non-totalitarian powers into a bloc strong enough actually to balance the scales of war and peace. True, in his speech to the League of Nations on September 21, 1938, Litvinov said that the

[75] *Supra*, p. 125.

[76] M. M. Litvinov, *Vneshniaia politika S.S.S.R. Rechi i zaiavleniia 1927–1935*, p. 65.

[77] On Jan. 26, 1934, a Treaty of Non-Aggression was signed between Poland and Germany (*supra*, p. 167).

[78] Heald and Wheeler-Bennett, *op. cit.*, p. 465.

[79] *Cf.* Appendix.

Soviet Government had given a clear response both to the Czechoslovakian and French inquiries about the Soviet attitude in case of an
attack on Czechoslovakia: "The U.S.S.R. was ready to stand by its
obligations under the pacts of mutual assistance." [80] The optimistic
outlook prompted by such an attitude toward the treaty obligations
loses much of its appeal, however, if it be recalled that commitments
made under duress are little conducive to acceptance at their face
value. The truth of the fact is that the Soviet treaties of non-aggression
and mutual assistance were born of necessity, and not of sudden confidence that the antagonism between the bourgeois democracies of the
capitalist world and the democratic dictatorship of the Soviet proletariat had ceased to be the basis of the relationship between the two
worlds. In the field of concrete politics, neither the appeasement policy of Great Britain and France toward Germany, nor their
compromises with Italy in the Mediterranean basin, nor, finally, their
virtual surrender to Japan in the Far East, appeared to Moscow as
consistent with the notion of sincere opposition to totalitarian aggression. Whether this was interpreted by the Kremlin as a sign of
Machiavellianism or as an indication of weakness, is immaterial. The
fact is that the Soviets were fully aware of the inadequacy of the international set-up for the preservation of peace and deemed it necessary
to augment their own individual efforts for peace by collective action
through revitalization of the League of Nations.

The Soviet Union became a member of the League of Nations on
September 18, 1934. True, for almost a decade and a half the Soviet
distrust for Geneva was a fact of common knowledge, and there may
have been good reason for it, at least from the Soviet standpoint.
Indeed, on July 12, 1922, Litvinov, at The Hague, pointed out that
there were two worlds—a Soviet world and a non-Soviet world and
that with this division there existed bias and hatred. "Only an angel
could be unbiased in judging Russian affairs," he added.[81] This may
well be an exaggeration, as were similar accusations issuing *ad
nauseam* from the Soviet Union. In fairness to the Soviets, however,
certain facts, not altogether favorable to the League, should not be
overlooked. Thus, the statesmen at Geneva showed little interest in
the Soviet-Polish war, although the very first session of the League

[80] *Verbatim Record of the Nineteenth Ordinary Session of the League of Nations,
Seventh Plenary Meeting, Sept. 21, 1938*, pp. 12–13.
[81] Conference at The Hague. June 26 to July 20, 1920. *Minutes and Documents,*
p. 126.

took place precisely during this conflict, and Poland was a member of the League. Nor was there much enthusiasm in discussing the military aid which France was giving to Poland. The efforts which the League finally made in suggesting various lines of demarcation between the two countries were hardly such as to invite Soviet confidence in the League's impartiality. Nor was the refusal of the League to hasten purely humanitarian help during the famine from 1921 to 1922, in spite of persistent appeals by Nansen, accepted by the Kremlin as an encouraging sign. The result was that even the Soviet-British Trade Agreement of 1921 and the consequent attempts of the Great Powers to get the Soviets interested in the work of the League failed to produce the desired effect: the conviction of statesmen in the Soviet Union was that the League of Nations was an instrument in the hands of a few great powers for the imperialistic oppression of other peoples, and that as long as the Soviets remained loyal to the principles of Marxism, they could not coöperate with the powers who were definitely opposed to these principles. It was believed that instead of joining the League, the Soviets should stay out of it, as only by remaining aloof could the Soviet Union hinder the imperialistic designs of Geneva.

All these considerations, however, gave way to graver considerations resulting from the change which befell Germany in 1933. In fairness to the League Powers, it must be said that having once replaced their original antagonism toward the Soviets with a realization of the benefits to be derived from Moscow's participation in the work of the League, they were consistent in their readiness to see the U.S.S.R. join them at Geneva. From this standpoint the Soviet assertions are correct that the capitalist world finally came to recognize the Soviet Union as one of the Great Powers. That Moscow itself now desired to be invited to Geneva is likewise obvious; witness Stalin's viewpoint in the matter: "In spite of the resignation of Germany and Japan from the League of Nations, or, may be, precisely for this very reason, the League may become an obstacle that might prevent or at least postpone war. If this be the case, *i.e.*, if the League may be an obstacle in the path of war and if it prove able to enhance the cause of peace, then we are not against the League." [82]

Under the circumstances, joining the League was now not only considered mandatory from the standpoint of the *Realpolitik* launched

[82] *Pravda*, 1934, No. 4.

by Stalin, but was made to appear consistent with Marxian ideology as well. A suggestion of the latter is seen in the speech of Litvinov on the day of the Soviet's entry into the League: "The idea in itself of an association of nations contains nothing theoretically inacceptable to Soviet state ideology. . . . The Soviet State has never excluded the possibility of some form or another of association with states having a different political social system, provided that there is no mutual hostility and if it is for the attainment of common ends." [83]

That political expediency finally forced the Soviets to accept the invitation to join the League was impliedly admitted by Stalin at the Seventeenth Congress of the Communist Party when he said that "if the interests of the Soviet Union demand that we approach one country or another which is not interested in violating peace, we shall do so without hesitation." Hitler was a symbol of war, and the purpose of the League of Nations was to preserve peace.

Even more in point was Litvinov's statement made in continuation of his remarks just quoted:

"We are now [1934] confronted with the task of averting war by more effective means. . . . There is need of more effective guaranties of security than declarations. We must establish a rule that any state is entitled to demand from its neighbors, near or remote, guaranties for its security, and that such a demand is not to be considered as an expression of mistrust." [84]

On September 5, 1935, he said before the Council of the League of Nations that the state which he represented "entered the League but a year ago, with the sole purpose and with the sole promise to collaborate in every possible way with other nations in the maintenance of indivisible peace." [85]

That peace was the paramount, if not the only, remuneration expected by the Soviets for their coöperation within the League, became evident from his speech at Geneva three years later. On September 21, 1938, vigorously criticizing the behavior of the League during the previous years, he said that the principle of collective security and joint struggle against attacks on the territorial integrity and political independence of League members evidently had been eliminated from the agenda of the League, and wondered whether the

[83] M. M. Litvinov, *Vneshniaia Politika S.S.S.R.*, p. 83.
[84] *XVII S'ezd Vsesoiuznoi Kommunisticheskoi Partii. Stenografischeskii Otchet,* p. 14.
[85] M. M. Litvinov, *op. cit.*, p. 84 and *League of Nations Official Journal,* July to December, 1935, p. 1142, respectively.

work of the League was to be limited to "decisions regarding traffic, assistance to refugees, establishment of an international system of signalling at grade crossings, and to the results of the statistical and other researches of our various commissions?" Obviously disturbed by Nazi aggression, he rather impatiently asked: "What have all these questions, important as they are in themselves, in common with the maintenance of peace, with that main object for which the League was set up?" [86]

In view of the emphasis thus laid by the Soviets upon the problems of war and peace, the details of the U.S.S.R. participation in the work of the League of Nations connected with "minor" issues may well be omitted.[87] The present study may therefore be limited to an analysis of the Soviet attitude toward instances in which the League had failed to prevent the outbreak of wars, and of the Soviet efforts in the League to bring these wars to an end.

The record of the League's failures in preventing war is disheartening. The war between Paraguay and Bolivia, the conquest of Ethiopia by Italy, the civil war and intervention in Spain, and the Japanese aggression in China had come to pass during the short space of time which had elapsed since the entrance of the U.S.S.R. into the League. Of these, the armed and bloody dispute over Chaco-Boreal, in South America, was the least significant as to evidence of Soviet efforts at peace. Fought in far-away lands, the Soviets justly considered it a local conflict and were not directly concerned with it. Having "no bias, favorable or unfavorable, toward either of the parties," the Soviet Government nevertheless took the stand that localization of the conflict "obviously would not be the case with every war," and that the application of economic sanctions was of fundamental importance *ex principio*.[88] In a communiqué addressed to the Secretary-General of the League in March, 1935, the Soviets informed the League that they

---

[86] *League of Nations Official Journal*, Spec. Suppl. No. 183, p. 77.

[87] The same applies to the basic policy of the Soviets to coöperate with the League in its efforts bearing upon the preservation of peace. *Cf.* for instance, Litvinov's denunciation of terrorism as a danger to peace voiced in the League of Nations on Dec. 8, 1934, in connection with the assassination of King Alexander of Yugoslavia (*Pravda*, Dec. 7, 1934); his speech in the League Council on Jan. 17, 1935, in which the solution of the Saar problem was acclaimed as a further step toward world peace (*Pravda*, Jan. 19, 1935); his assurance given to the League Council on Jan. 15, 1935, that impartial as the Soviet Union was in the Shatt-el-Arab dispute between Irak and Persia, it was interested in the peaceful settlement thereof for the sake of preventing war (*Pravda*, Jan. 16, 1935).

[88] *League of Nations Official Journal*. Spec. Suppl. No. 134, pp. 32–33, also, *Pravda*, Nov. 22, 1934.

had taken the necessary measures to raise the embargo as regarded Bolivia and, at the same time, to strengthen it as regarded Paraguay.[89] This was the limit of Soviet commitments as to practical measures for shortening the war.

During the Italo-Ethiopian war the Soviets were much more active.[90] In comparison with other powers, Moscow seemed to be taking up the issue as a matter of principle rather than for any materialistic purpose. The anxiety of France and England over the expansionist designs of Mussolini, combined with the particularly precarious position of France resulting from Mussolini's promise to keep Hitler out of Austria and France's rôle at Geneva compelling Paris to support a pro-League policy of curbing Rome, owing to the British refusal of commitments with regard to Central Europe, meant the sacrifice of the Franco-Italian entente, and permitted Hitler to take advantage of the situation. It is not too much to state that originally some members of the League preferred to appear conveniently disinterested in the issue, others definitely opposed Italy's aggression, while still others retired to the opportunist policy of *sub rosa* appeasement.

The distance separating Ethiopia from Russia was great enough for the Soviets to insist that, as in the case of the war between Paraguay and Bolivia, this aggression of Italy did not actually jeopardize the immediate interests of the U.S.S.R., and that they had opposed it solely on the grounds of general Marxian aversion to any imperialistic violence. To quote Molotov:

[89] *League of Nations Official Journal*, Mar., 1935, p. 449.

[90] Ethiopia was admitted to the League of Nations in 1923, and aside from Liberia was the only African territory not under one of the European flags. In December, 1934, the Ual incident took place, during which several Italians were killed. The compensation demanded by Mussolini was refused by the Negus, who invoked the Treaty of 1928 and submitted the dispute to the League. Now Italy refused. Defying the League, Mussolini started sending troops to Africa. Meanwhile the League Council took no action on the issue, while the members of the League refused to accept munition orders from Italy. Finally, the Council announced that the problem would be taken up at Geneva. A meeting at Paris was suggested by England, France and Italy, with the hope that League action might become unnecessary. The would-be arrangement envisaged a settlement which practically amounted to a peaceful absorption of Ethiopia by Italy. The plan failed. Upon the initiative of London, the League stiffened its attitude toward Mussolini and intervened in September. In spite of this, the shipment of Italian troops to Africa continued. Early in October, 1935, the Council declared that Italy had committed an act of war in violation of the Covenant. Sanctions ensued, and almost simultaneously also the Hoare-Laval plan of settling the controversy was advanced: now only about half of Ethiopia was offered to Italy. By May, 1936, Mussolini took it all by force of arms. The League accepted the end of Ethiopia's independence as a *fait accompli*.

"In the Italo-Abyssinian war, only the U.S.S.R. took an attitude different in principle, alien to any notion of imperialism and devoid of any intention of colonial conquest. Only the Soviet Union declared openly that it took for its starting point the principle of equality and independence of Abyssinia which, à propos, is a member of the League of Nations, and that it cannot support any actions of the League or of any individual capitalist country intending to destroy this independence and equality." [91]

However true this statement, it must be said that the Soviets were by no means open champions of justice at all stages of this conflict. It will be recalled that the U.S.S.R. became allied with France in May, 1935, and that France's position in the issue was not an easy one. The result was that self-interest compelled the Soviets to adopt a policy of waiting: it was over seven months from December 5, 1934, the date of the first serious engagement between Italian and Ethiopian troops at Ual-Ual, before the Soviets voiced their condemnation of the whole affair in the League of Nations. [92]

When once the die had been cast, however, Soviet condemnation of Italian aggression knew no bounds. At the League Council Meeting of September 5, 1935, Litvinov challenged the arguments of Baron Aloisi that Ethiopia, by violating its treaties with Italy, and by preserving within its boundaries the practice of slavery, had placed itself outside the pale of the League Covenant. Without hesitation he denounced the validity of the first of these contentions, saying that the admission of Aloisi's thesis would amount to acceptance by the League of his invitation to the members of the Council "to repudiate in their turn their international obligations, to disregard the Covenant of the League of Nations, on which, in no small degree, depends the whole edifice of international peace and the security of nations." Referring to slavery and other evidences of Ethiopian savagery submitted by the representative of Italy, Litvinov continued his attack by stating his conviction that in the League Covenant there was nothing that entitled the Council to "discriminate between the members of the League as to their internal régime, the color of their skin, their racial distinction or stage of civilization, nor, accordingly, to deprive some of them of privileges which they enjoy by virtue of their membership in the League and, in the first place, of their inalienable right

---

[91] Speech at the Second Meeting of the Seventh Session of the Central Executive Committee of the U.S.S.R. (*Izvestiia*, Jan. 11, 1936).

[92] For a concise history of the Italo-Ethiopian conflict, *cf.* Schuman, *op. cit.*, ch. "Caesar Africanus," pp. 152–201.

to integrity and independence." Having, evidently, not forgotten, even in the heat of argument, his revolutionary duty both in regard to oppressed peoples and to the communist need for peace, Litvinov ventured to include in his criticism of Italian aggression the suggestive remark that "for the development of backward peoples, for influencing their internal life, for raising them to a higher civilization, other means than military may be found." [93]

At the Plenary Session of the League on September 14, 1935, he offered an explanation of the stand taken by the Soviets on the issue. "As you know," said he, "the Soviet Government is, in principle, opposed to the system of colonies, to the policy of spheres of influence and of mandates, to anything pertaining to imperialistic aims." [94] This blending of the general Marxian outlook on the colonial problem with the dictates of Soviet expediency necessitating the preservation of peace resulted not only in Soviet abstract admiration for the League of Nations as an instrument to stalemate the warlike designs of aggressor states, but also in the Kremlin's efforts to make it a workable and effective institution, worthy of the purpose for which it was established.[95] Soviet insistence on the League's application of vigorous sanctions against Italy was the issue in point.

At a Meeting of the League Council on September 5, 1935, Litvinov expressed confidence that the principle of the indivisibility of peace was gaining more and more recognition, and warned that each war was only the result of a previous war and the cause of the next one. Nine days later he referred to these considerations as the real reason why the League should fulfill its purpose to the greatest degree possible. This defense of the League Covenant became the primary concern of the Soviets, and to that end the U.S.S.R. was to be "second to none in the legal discharge of assumed international obligations, more especially in the noble task of securing for all nations the blessing of peace, which mankind never valued or appreciated so much as it does now after the relatively recent ordeals." [96] This meant Soviet loyalty to Article 16 of the Covenant, whose provisions called for sanctions. The Soviets insisted on their application to the fullest extent.

When Austria and Albania, at that time not yet absorbed by Ger-

[93] *League of Nations Official Journal,* July to December, 1935, p. 1142.
[94] *Ibid.,* Spec. Suppl. No. 138, p. 73.
[95] *League of Nations Official Journal,* July to December, 1935, p. 1142.
[96] *Ibid.,* Special Supplement, No. 138, p. 73.

many and Italy, respectively, and Hungary refused to take part in sanctions, and when the representatives of Switzerland, Uruguay, Iran and Peru came forth with wavering reservations and suggestions, Litvinov took the opportunity to launch a severe criticism of such an attitude, and once again to reiterate Soviet insistence on taking the full measures prescribed in the above Article. Said he:

"Mild as the present sanctions were, they had not been accepted with the unanimity for which the Committee had been entitled to hope; and that was a matter of regret. . . . His own country, as he had stated on many occasions, had no quarrel with Italy and no special interest in the present case. By agreeing to economic sanctions the Soviet Union was exposing itself to losses, Italy having been one of her best customers. . . . It was prepared, nevertheless, to submit to these losses. . . . It did so for reasons of solidarity and because of its desire to maintain peace and to fulfill all the obligations it had accepted under the Covenant. But these obligations held good only for so long as they were maintained and fulfilled by other members of the League. Peace could not be based on voluntary contributions: it must be based on specific obligations undertaken by all nations. That was the true spirit of the League." [97]

At home, condemnation of Mussolini's aggression in Africa found expression in four Soviet Decrees of the Council of Peoples' Commissars, two of September 14, and two of November 14, 1935. One of the former prohibited the export of war materials to Italy, while the other provided for the application of financial sanctions to Italy. The Decrees of November 14 limited the importation of goods from Italy to gold, printed matter and musical publications, and extended the embargo on exports to certain additional articles useful for war purposes.[98]

As supplementary to these measures may be mentioned the speech of Molotov at the Second Meeting of the Seventh Session of the Central Executive Committee, and numerous tirades found in the Soviet press. Molotov said that "regardless of all the shortcomings of the League as an organization of capitalist countries, it has retarded, to a certain degree, the instigators of war and aggression. The League may and should be criticized for not always taking sufficient measures, for instance in connection with the Italo-Abyssinian war. . . . It must also be admitted that the League did nothing to prevent this war.

[97] Speech of Oct. 19, 1935, before the Coördination Committee of Eighteen (*League of Nations Official Journal,* Spec. Suppl. No. 145, pp. 27–28).
[98] For English text, *cf. ibid.,* Spec. Suppl. No. 150, pp. 298–300.

However, the fact cannot be overlooked that in this instance the League was hindering not those who were for peace, but those who wanted to help the aggressor. It is from this standpoint that the participation of the U.S.S.R. in the League must be evaluated, this being particularly so in regard to the economic sanctions against Italy, which was recognized as the aggressor." [99]

Even a cursory review of the communist press reveals that the sympathies of the U.S.S.R. were wholly on the side of Haile Selassie, whereas the attitude of Great Britain and France was considered to be by no means of crystal purity and magnanimity.[100] Mussolini's aggression in Africa was definitely branded as a "phase in the ominous program of Italian Fascism contemplating the redistribution of colonies and aggrandizement to fit its imperial designs. . . . The Soviet Union has nothing to do with the redivision of the world. Its attitude toward Italy's attack on Abyssinia is based on two principles. The Soviet Union is against colonial exploitation, and against everything that unleashes the forces of world war. It is for these reasons that the Soviet Union is for the bettering of coöperation among the powers which are ready to safeguard peace and to oppose war." [101]

The same antagonism may be observed toward Germany and even Japan. The Third Reich was accused of taking advantage of Italian aggression by bringing to the forefront the problem of the redistribution of colonies in general. The Empire of the Rising Sun was charged with forgetting the Trade Agreement signed in 1932 by Ethiopia and Japan, and with the approval of Italy's designs, for which Tokio expected similar understanding of its own ambitions in China.[102]

Uniform as was the attitude taken toward Italy by Soviet statesmen, lawmakers, and press at home, and persistent as were the efforts of Soviet diplomats at Geneva, the inevitable could not be prevented. On May 9, 1936, Negus Haile Selassie left Addis-Ababa, and a Royal Decree signed in Rome transformed Abyssinia into an Italian colony. Marshal Badoglio became its first Governor-General and Viceroy, Victor Emmanuel, King of Italy, its Emperor. The anti-aggression peace-makers left Geneva for their homes: the communists returned to Moscow, to console themselves with their loyalty to the Marxian

[99] *Izvestiia,* Jan. 11, 1936.
[100] *Bol'shevik,* No. 19, and *Pravda,* Dec. 20, 1935, No. 349.
[101] *Izvestiia,* Oct. 5, 1935, No. 233.
[102] *Ibid.,* Oct. 18, 1935, No. 244.

principle of peace, while the non-communists withdrew to Paris and London, with the hope that their behavior had not further undermined the never-too-assured friendship of the Kremlin. Hitler was grateful: the League of Nations had admitted the power of defiance, Italy was deeply absorbed in her new enterprise, and the democratic powers had fled into helpless retirement. The road was practically open for his march southeastward, except that some device had to be discovered by which the attention of his western neighbors and of Italy could be further diverted from that part of Europe. Iberia was chosen to serve the purpose.

The literature on the recent events in Spain is already extensive.[103] Civil, from the standpoint of international law, and international, through the instrumentality of intervention, the war in Spain was a complex issue indeed. The Soviet Union and a section of the French Popular Front denounced the rebellion of Franco's Phalangists as a carefully contemplated drive of Fascism against Communism. They believed that fascist idealism was merely a pretext, and that Berlin and Rome were concerned not so much with the danger of communism taking hold in Spain, as with the possibility of securing strategic advantages and sources of raw materials, and of encircling France with a ring of totalitarian states, thus weakening her influence in Europe. Franco's announcement of his twenty-six-point program of social and economic reform, the establishment of a single party modelled after the Italian Fascists and German Nazis, and the formation of the National Council patterned on Mussolini's Grand Council, were pointed out as ominous signs of the true intentions of the Rome-Berlin axis.

In return, Germany and Italy accused the Soviets and their French sympathizers of fomenting and spreading communism in Spain. Their contention was that the Spanish conflict was a concrete warning of the danger which might engulf Europe unless drastic measures were taken against the Red peril. The consolidation of the various socialist factions, with the exception of the anarchists, under the government of Negrin, who replaced the left-wing socialist, Largo Caballero, was interpreted merely as a sign of complete communist domination over the other parties.

[103] For a brief, comprehensive narrative of international politics bearing upon this war, cf. Schuman, op. cit., (ch. VII: Campaign in Iberia) ; for an analysis of legal issues and an abundance of documents, see Norman L. Padelford, *International Law and Diplomacy in Spanish Civil Strife* (N. Y., 1939).

The drama which was unfolding on the plateaus of Iberia presented Great Britain and France with a difficult dilemma. The vigor of the mutual accusations left little doubt in London and Paris that they were facing the prospect of Fascist and Communist intervention in Iberia. At the same time, national sentiments offered no clear-cut suggestion as to the course to be taken either by Downing Street or by the Quai d'Orsay. In England the conservatives were more antagonistic to the dictatorship of Stalin than to the totalitarian authority of Hitler and Mussolini, while general public opinion considered both these régimes hostile to democracy and, hence, poor bargains. In France the situation was no better. Ideologically, the Rightists welcomed the task undertaken by Franco's Rebels. The communists criticized Premier Blum for not helping the Loyalists in Spain and not suppressing the reactionaries at home. At the same time, France feared both the Rome-Berlin control over Spain and the precipitation of a *casus belli* by opening its southern frontier for the passage of military assistance to the Madrid Government. The result was that in order to pacify both rivals, London and Paris chose the middle course. Moscow was consoled by their refusal to accord *de jure* recognition to General Franco, while the appeasement of Hitler and Mussolini was accomplished by preventing the entrance of troops and the shipment of munitions from France into the territory occupied by the Loyalists. Having chosen the policy of non-intervention, Great Britain and France, later to be joined by twenty-seven other states, whose representatives composed the London Non-Intervention Committee, became onlookers, "blind" not only to the well-known fact that foreign arms and men were reaching both factions, but also to the open secret that Germany and Italy supplied them for the Phalangists, and Moscow for the Loyalists.

Although the civil disturbances in Spain commenced almost at the same time that the Soviet Union became a member of the League, the real interest of the Kremlin in the Spanish civil war was not aroused until July, 1936. Preoccupied with the more vital issues of mutual-assistance pacts, happenings in China, the position taken by Poland, the Ethiopian affair, and the hopeful unrest of the Popular Front in France, the Soviet press limited itself to mere accounts of fighting incidents. It was not until the issue acquired the aspect of an international struggle between Fascism and Communism that the Fascist intervention in Spain was publicly denounced, communist solidarity

with the Spanish Loyalists openly expressed,[104] and the actual participation of the Soviet Government in the efforts to settle the difficulty
initiated.

Upon the receipt of an invitation from Britain and France to join
with other nations and partake in the organization of a Non-Intervention Committee, the Soviets expressed their willingness to uphold
the principle, but their consent was half-hearted. On the one hand,
the cause of the Loyalists was dear to the revolutionary ambitions of
Moscow, and as their government was the one that had been recognized *de jure,* there was no sound legal ground for the U.S.S.R. to
refuse help. On the other hand, General Franco had declared himself
an open foe of communism, and the fulfillment of their obligations by
Hitler and Mussolini was no longer certain. However, the practical
need of safeguarding the common democratic front against the totalitarian bloc called for preserving friendly relations with Great Britain
and France. Hence, on August 23, 1936, the Soviets, "deploring the
tragic events for which Spain is the theater," announced that the Government of the U.S.S.R. had resolved "to abstain rigorously from all
interference, direct or indirect, in the internal affairs of that country."
Pending the proclamation of similar declarations by the Italian, German and Portuguese Governments, the Soviets raised the embargo
on all war materials for Spain.[105]

It soon became evident, however, that this concerted effort to
localize the issue was mere diplomatic fiction. War supplies were
pouring into Spain, and the Soviet press was full of indignation.[106]
Litvinov's attempts to force the League of Nations into action for
the purpose of checking the danger of a conflagration of war proved
vain.[107] Geneva remained silent.[108] Finally, on October 7, 1936, the
Soviets warned the Chairman of the Non-Intervention Committee
that if the violations of the Non-Intervention Agreement were not

[104] A great mass meeting was held on Aug. 3, 1936, in Moscow (*Pravda,* Aug. 5,
1936).

[105] For English text, *cf.* Padelford, *op. cit.,* pp. 228–229.

[106] *Cf. Pravda,* Sept. 12, 22, 27, and Oct. 1, 1936.

[107] Speaking before the Assembly, Sept. 25, 1936, Litvinov urged that the non-
intervention measures were essential to the preservation of European peace (*League of
Nations Official Journal,* Spec. Suppl. No. 155, p. 64.)

[108] It was only in Jan., 1937, that the Council's resolution affirming the obligation
of states to refrain from intervening in the internal affairs of other states, and recom-
mending that the non-intervention be made as stringent as possible (*League of Nations
Official Journal,* Jan., 1937, pp. 18–19). On the documents concerning relation of the
League of Nations to the Spanish civil war, see Padelford, *op. cit.,* Appendix XI, pp. 617–
628.

immediately ended, they would consider themselves free from the obligations imposed by the agreement.

No improvement was forthcoming, and the communist press grew more and more indignant.[109] Finally, on October 23, 1936, the Non-Intervention Committee was informed that the Soviet Government was disillusioned in the failure of certain powers to live up to their promises, and being desirous not to hold itself longer responsible for the present position, "obviously unfair to the legal Spanish Government and population," was compelled to "declare that pursuant to its declaration of October 7th, it cannot consider itself bound by the Non-Intervention Agreement to any greater extent than the remaining participants in this Agreement." [110] Men, food, and arms at once began to leave Soviet ports on the Black Sea for Spanish ports on the Mediterranean.

Fighting in Spain continued. So did the intervention, the "non-neutral" shipping and the incidents on the high seas and in territorial waters.[111] The British and French proposals of October 10, 1936, to establish an effective control over Spanish ports, and suggestions for mediation or a plebiscite in Spain were echoed in the Soviet Union by Litvinov's acceptance of these ideas *ex principio*, though the press ridiculed the idea, pointing out that good intentions alone would not suffice; to be effective they would have to be supported by deeds. When international control had completely broken down due to the sinking of vessels suspected of war trade, the chaos became intolerable and the alarm general. The indignation of the Soviets was equalled by the anxiety of London and Paris.

On September 5, 1937, a conference was called by France and Britain at Nyon. While neither General Franco's nor Negrin's Government was given the privilege of being present, invitations were sent to the Governments of Albania, Bulgaria, Egypt, Germany,

[109] Public opinion in the Soviet Union was aroused to a degree where the Government was commanded to rectify the situation and either to stop the intervention of Fascists or to insist on permitting the Loyalists to buy arms (*Pravda,* Oct. 11, 1935, to Oct. 14, 1935). In the editorial of *Pravda,* Oct. 15, 1936, the following appeared: "The Government of the U.S.S.R. under no circumstances will tolerate the perversion of the Non-Intervention Agreement into a tool for aiding the Spanish rebels. The people of the U.S.S.R. are fully on the side of the legal Spanish Government which is defending the rights and the freedom of the Spanish people."
[110] *Pravda,* October 24, 1936.
[111] For the list, see Padelford, *op. cit.,* Appendix XV, pp. 663–674. On the general Soviet attitude, *cf.* Litvinov's speech at the Eighth All-Union Congress of Soviets (*Mir. Khoz. i Mir. Politika,* 1937, No. 1, pp. 164ff.).

Greece, Italy, Roumania, the Soviet Union, Turkey, and Yugoslavia. Of the intervening powers contending in Spain, only the Soviets accepted. Their foes—Germany and Italy—took no part in the proceedings.[112] On September 14, the Nyon Agreement on the anti-submarine patrol of warships and airplanes to stop the lawless interference with shipping in the Mediterranean was signed.[113] As a formal testimony of the prevailing anti-war sentiment, this Agreement may rightly be considered a victory for the policy of collective security, credit for which must go in no small degree to the Soviets. As a practical guarantee, however, it soon lost its value. Indeed, already in October, 1937, Great Britain and France approached Italy with a suggestion that the withdrawal of volunteers be considered, in return for which General Franco would be accorded belligerent rights. Mussolini's reply was the shipment of more troops and airplanes, and the proposal that the price should be paid before the withdrawal of Italian troops began. To this London and Paris acquiesced by the compromise that a count of the total number of foreigners in Spain be taken. This suited Mussolini but was not satisfactory to the Soviets. In their opinion this hypocrisy not only jeopardized the whole purpose of the collective efforts made theretofore, but gave the Soviets good ground to suspect that Great Britain and France had acted in bad faith. Unable to afford a complete break with the two democracies, however, the U.S.S.R. informed the Non-Intervention Committee that it was willing to grant belligerent rights to Franco, but only under condition that the evacuation of the interventionists from Spain be complete.[114] As is well known, this scheme came to nothing. The struggle continued. So did foreign intervention. And so also did the inability of the non-aggressors to bring peace to Spain.

Whatever the real reasons for the Kremlin's interest in the survival of the non-totalitarian régime in Spain, neither the diplomatic

[112] The Soviet Government suggested that the issue should be brought before the League of Nations. To prevent the embarrassment of Germany and Italy in going to Geneva, however, Nyon was suggested as a more convenient rendezvous. According to Litvinov, the Spanish question was withdrawn from the League "in order to secure the coöperation of the principal authors of the Spanish tragedy, who cannot bear the spirit of Geneva" (*League of Nations Official Journal*, Spec. Suppl. No. 169, p. 79). The consideration in the end proved needless: the Soviet charges of sinkings preferred against Italy resulted in the withdrawal of the Rome-Berlin axis from the conference.

[113] On the Nyon Conference, cf. Padelford, *op. cit.*, pp. 25–52. Text of the Agreement, *ibid.*, pp. 608–609.

[114] *Ibid.*, pp. 114–133ff.

efforts of the Soviets,[115] nor national laws and enactments,[116] nor the sentiments of proletarian sympathy and good will [117] could prevent forces beyond their control from solving the Spanish strife in a non-communist way. The war in Iberia ended with victorious General Franco becoming the dictatorial ruler of Spain. It was only through this transformaton of formerly Royal and lately Socialist Spain into the present Phalangist State that semblance of peace descended over Europe. The exhausted League of Nations was laid to rest in peace at Geneva. The submarines in the Mediterranean left their undersea war stations and came up to enjoy peace on the surface. The diplomats in London, Paris, and Moscow sighed with relief that war had been removed from their burden of diplomatic worries. Only one thing was lacking to complete the bliss of tranquility—confidence in world peace. The events which were to follow proved beyond doubt that this lack of confidence was well justified: today only the League of Nations is no longer disturbed.

The Soviet interest in the Far East is of long standing, having

[115] The Czechoslovakian crisis and the rapid events in Europe, as well as preoccupation in Far-Eastern affairs, meant that the Soviets could give but little attention to Spain. To Moscow it became evident that Great Britain and France had virtually given up their resistance to intervention and whatever voice was raised in the U.S.S.R. was more for self-satisfaction than to influence the issue in one way or another (*cf. Izvestiia,* June 27, 1938, and July 11, 1938). That not much hope was left in the U.S.S.R. for the Loyalist victory was evidenced by the readiness of the Soviet Government to grant recognition of belligerency to both sides, even on condition of "partial" withdrawal of interventionists (*cf. Izvestiia,* Oct. 16, 1938). It was too late: General Franco was in the last stages of his march to complete victory. (*Cf.*, also, Padelford, *op. cit.,* pp. 137ff., and Appendix XI, pp. 617–625).

[116] Pursuant to the Declaration of Aug. 23, 1936 (*supra,* p. 204), the Peoples' Commissar for Foreign Trade issued on Aug. 28, 1936, an order prohibiting exportation of war materials to Spain; on Feb. 20, 1937, the Council of Peoples' Commissars decreed that the entrance and recruiting of volunteers into Spain was illegal (Padelford, *op cit.,* pp. 300 and 364. He also mentions an Administrative Order regarding Soviet vessels and the observation and control system, *ibid.,* p. 509).

[117] A general summary of the proletarian sentiments was given at the Eighteenth Congress of the Soviet Communist Party (March, 1939) by Manuilsky. Having explained that Loyalist resistance was due to the fact that the Communist Party of Spain cemented various socialist factions into one formidable force and that the Spanish people were receiving support from the international proletariat and, first of all, from Stalin, he said that the proletarian struggle in Spain "brought about the admiration of millions of workers and revengeful hatred in the capitalist world." "By this example," he concluded, "the Spanish people invited all other people to struggle against the fascist instigators of war and incited the solidification of forces for peace and freedom in all capitalist countries. Around Republican Spain was created a sentiment of wide mass solidarity . . . It takes various forms, ranging from collections of money to mass meetings and demonstrations, and from the formation of committees of Spanish defense to political walk-outs and the formation of volunteer units." (*Mir. Khoz. i Mir. Politika,* 1939, No. 4, p. 57).

been inherited from the preceding régimes. The U.S.S.R. continued its vigilant watch over the Red Empire's interests in the lands washed by the western waters of the Pacific. As the events which took place on the Far-Eastern scene must be projected against the turmoil of war-torn China, the Soviet policy must be examined in regard to Moscow's relations with China, on the one hand, and with Japan, on the other. The connecting links between the two were the problem of the Eastern Chinese Railway and the fate of Manchuria.

Of the two aspects which characterize the Soviet relationship with China—diplomatic and revolutionary—the former occupies a much less conspicuous place in the records of the U.S.S.R. While the official resumption of diplomatic relations took place only in 1924, the Soviet interest in things Chinese found its first concrete manifestation already in 1921 when the R.S.F.S.R. and Outer Mongolia, a part of China as it was, signed an Agreement regarding establishment of friendly relations between the two countries.[118] On May 31, 1924, a Treaty on General Principles for the settlement of general problems was signed between the U.S.S.R. and China, according to which Mongolia was recognized to be "an integral part of the Republic of China." [119] This, however, did not prevent the Soviets from influencing this Chinese province to an extent that in November of the same year a constitution was drafted by the Russian advisers at Ulan-Bator which proclaimed Mongolia "an independent People's Republic in which all power belongs to the laboring people." [120] Finding itself in no position to defend its interests in Outer Mongolia, China was forced to appear no longer aggressor in the new *de facto* protectorate of the Soviet Union. The Soviet advance into Mongolia was reinforced by a "gentlemen's agreement which had existed since 1934," later formulated in a Protocol of Mutual Assistance, signed on March 12, 1936,[121] which provided for automatic military obligations. As foretold by Stalin in a statement made a few days previously during the interview with Mr.

---

[118] Nov. 5, 1921 (*ibid.*, p. 471). Also, Exchange of Notes, Aug. 8, 1924. For treaties concluded between the U.S.S.R. and China, see Appendix and *cf.* Taracouzio, *op. cit.*, Appendix XXIV, p. 453; on Soviet-Chinese relations, Litvinov, *op. cit.*, pp. 31, 33, 112, 271–272. For the history of Mongolian independence, *cf.* G. M. Friters, "The Prelude to Outer Mongolian Independence" and "The Development of Outer Mongolian Independence" (*Pacific Affairs*, X (1937) pp. 168ff. and 321ff., respectively).

[119] Art. 5 (*Sborn. Deistv. Dogov.*, I–II, 1925, p. 31).

[120] Art. 1. For text of the Constitution, see V. N. Durdenevskii i E. F. Lundshuveit, *Konstitutsii Vostoka*, pp. 157–162.

[121] *Sobr. Zak. i Rasp. S.S.S.R.*, 1936, II, par. 213.

Roy Howard,[122] it drew a protest from Nanking. The Soviets magnanimously replied that Moscow continued to recognize Chinese sovereignty over Outer Mongolia. Whatever the logical or legal interpretation of such a relationship between the Kremlin and the Mongolian People's Republic, it resulted in China's abandonment of political control over a province which apparently still belonged to it *de jure,* and in the reduction of commercial relations between the two to nil.[123]

In spite of this early aggression in Mongolia, the Soviet Union managed to remain on a friendly footing with China. Needless to say, this was made possible through the revolutionary prestige which the Soviets enjoyed there up to 1927, and particularly from 1925 on. It was only after Chiang Kai-shek broke with the Kuomintang in 1927 and turned against the Chinese Communist armies,[124] that this cordiality was dealt a severe blow. Diplomatic relations were then severed. When, however, in 1931 and 1932 the Japanese armies started to reveal the true designs of the Mikado's Empire on the mainland of Asia, Nanking realized the change in the situation.[125] A non-aggression pact was promptly offered to Moscow, but was declined as premature. In its stead, in 1932, formal diplomatic relations were reëstablished.[126] It was only in 1937 that appreciation of the common danger of Japan to the U.S.S.R. and China culminated in a Pact of Non-Aggression, according to which they undertook to refrain "from any aggression against each other" and from "taking any action or entering into any agreement which may be used by the aggressor or ag-

---

[122] On Mar. 4, 1936, Stalin said that if Japan ventures to attack the Mongolian People's Republic, seeking to destroy its independence, the U.S.S.R. will have to come to its assistance. "We will assist the Mongolian People's Republic in the same way as we helped in 1921" (Heald and Wheeler-Bennett, *Documents on International Affairs,* 1936, pp. 464–465).

[123] The Soviet peaceful penetration into Sinkiang through the increase in trade (especially after the construction of the Turkestan-Siberian Railway in 1930) and by inducing a revolutionary orientation toward the U.S.S.R. had practically the same result, the only difference being that no diplomatic documents exist to that effect.

[124] This struggle came to an end only in 1936 by the *coup d'état* of General Chang Hsuch-liang.

[125] For this phase of Japanese aggression in China, *cf.* W. W. Willoughby, *The Sino-Japanese Controversy and the League of Nations* (Baltimore, 1935); Albert E. Hindmarsh, *The Basis of Japanese Foreign Policy* (Cambridge, 1936); Henry L. Stimson, *The Far Eastern Crisis. Recollections and Observations* (New York, 1936); *Official Journal of the League of Nations* (for 1931 and 1932) and Special Supplements Nos. 101–102 and 111–113; Manley O. Hudson, *The Verdict of the League: China and Japan* (World Peace Foundation, 1933, pp. 22–63).

[126] Exchange of Notes was made at Geneva on Dec. 12, 1932.

gressors to the disadvantage of the Party subjected to aggression." [127]

Much more happy were the relations between the U.S.S.R. and China in regard to mutual revolutionary understandings and aspirations. The renunciation of all the unequal treaties of Imperial Russia, and the willingness to assist China in her domestic problems and foreign relations resulted in the virtual alliance of the Russian Communist Party with the Nationalist Party of Canton. When the Kuomintang, led by Dr. Sun Yat-sen, failed to obtain sadly needed help from abroad, the Soviets became its last hope. More than eager to cultivate this possible field of communist expansion, the Soviets were only too willing to oblige. In rendering their help, the Soviets were greatly aided by the Chinese Communist Party, which had been admitted into the Kuomintang by Sun Yat-sen in 1924, in expectation that through this fusion the Marxian ideas of the communists would disintegrate and become absorbed into the nationalistic sentiments of the Nationalists. Although this did not materialize, the Soviets, while continuously furthering their own cause, rendered great help to the Nationalist cause. Competent military advisers were made available, among them Bluecher, who travelled to China as General Galens, and later became one of the few Soviet marshals to escape the fate of Tukhachevsky, executed in the army purge of a few summers ago. The organization of the Kuomintang into a strong party, and the stabilization of its political control over China, was the work of Michael Borodin, later discovered to have used his diplomatic office as the center of communist propaganda—a revelation by no means complimentary to the Soviets.

The truth of the matter is that Chiang Kai-shek accepted Soviet interference in China merely as an opportunity to promote his own authority and was never very happy about the influence exerted by the communists and the U.S.S.R. It was an open secret to him that if the national aspirations of the Kuomintang were not to be transformed into the international program of Marxism which would jeopardize his own power, the relations between Nanking and Moscow had to be changed. The Soviet advisers were forced to return to Moscow. The latter retaliated by severing diplomatic relations, which, for the time being, worried Chiang not in the least.[128] This official rupture between

---

[127] Signed on Aug. 21, 1937 (*L.N.T.S.*, CLXXXI, 102).

[128] *Kitaiskaia Revoliutsiia i Kommunisticheskii Internatsional. Sbornik Statei i Materialov*, Moskva, 1929.

Nanking and Moscow did not disturb the Russian communists either. The bond of unity already established between the V.K.P.[129] and the Chinese Communist Party not only survived this diplomatic set-back, but was furthered and invariably glorified on every convenient occasion, witness the proceedings of the Soviet Communist Congresses, the Congresses of the Third International, remarks made by statesmen time and again, and various writings too numerous to be listed here. The resumption of diplomatic relations in 1932 and the Non-Aggression Pact of 1937 are further official proof.

Amid these political and doctrinal maladjustments, the problem of the Chinese Eastern Railway, which, during the civil war from January, 1919, to October, 1922, had been under Inter-Allied supervision, was an issue of no small significance. The conflicting financial interests of the various foreign investors, the want of a generally recognized Russian Government, and the disorganized joint control over the conduct of its business, made the whole problem a source of constant friction. It was only on May 31, 1924, that an understanding between the Soviets and China in regard to the administration of this important overland artery of trade and commerce was reached, when an Agreement regarding the railway was signed by the Soviet and Peking Governments.[130] As a purely commercial enterprise, this railroad was to be managed henceforth by an even number of Russian and Chinese directors, the jurisdiction of the Chinese authorities extending to the administration of matters "bearing upon the rights of the Chinese National and Local Governments." [131] One of the most important of its provisions, which, for the most part, dealt with the mechanics of administration, was the mutual pledge neither to "permit, within their respective territories, the existence and/or activities of any organizations or groups whose aim is to struggle by acts of violence against the Governments of either Contracting Party," nor to "engage in propaganda directed against the political and social systems of either Contracting Party." [132]

The protests lodged against this new arrangement by the Japa-

[129] The initial letters for "Vsesoiuznaia Kommunisticheskaia Partia (Bol'shevikov)," which in translation means "All-Union Communist Party of Bolsheviks."

[130] *Sborn. Deistv. Dogov.*, I–II, 1925, p. 327. Since Manchuria, then ruled by Marshal Chang Tso-lin, did not recognize Peking, the Soviet Union made a separate supplementary agreement with the "Governments of the three Autonomous Eastern Provinces of the Chinese Republic" (*ibid.*, V, 1930, p. 118).

[131] Preamble, *ibid.*, p. 327.

[132] Art. 6 (*L.N.T.S.*, XXXVII, 175).

nese, American, and French interests resulted in a constant struggle between the Soviet and the Chinese Governments over the actual control of the railway from 1924 to 1929.[133] The dominating position originally gained by the Soviets in this entanglement soon yielded to the Chinese authorities, who, in 1926 not only succeeded in seizing the railway, but took over the administration of the Russian section of the city of Harbin. Communist propaganda was declared to be the reason for such a turn of events. From a legal standpoint the Chinese Government had a good case, as this propaganda consti- tuted a gross violation of the pledge given in the above-quoted inter- national agreement of 1924. In point of fact, this action was a great set-back to Soviet revolutionary ambition. On May 27, 1929, the Chinese police engineered a raid on the Soviet consulate in Harbin, which not only resulted in substantiation of Chinese suspicions con- cerning Soviet revolutionary activities, but unearthed the full extent of communist propaganda. A lively exchange of charges and counter- charges followed. Concentration of armed forces was ordered on both sides of the border. The little that remained of formal inter- course between the two countries was terminated completely.

Dangerous as the situation was, the desire for peace prevailed, and soon informal negotiations to settle the difficulty were begun by the Soviets. On December 22, 1929, at Harbin, a Protocol was signed by Simanovsky, delegated to negotiate on behalf of the So- viets, and Tsai Yun-sheng, representing the Manchurian Govern- ment, which reëstablished the situation that had existed prior to the seizure of the railway by the Chinese authorities. The Nanking Government approved this Protocol on February 8, 1930,[134] accept- ing it, however, not as a *bona fide* restoration of the original legal *status quo,* but merely as a temporary *modus vivendi* in the dispute over the railway. The further negotiations which were arranged to take place in Moscow early in 1930 did not begin until October and lasted for almost a year. They disclosed that the Chinese Gov- ernment was desirous of purchasing the railway. The Soviets were reluctant to relinquish their interest in the investment. An agreement was not to be reached: in 1931 the Japanese started their aggression in Manchuria, and the whole issue had to give way to the problem of authority to discuss the deal with the Soviets.

[133] *Cf.* Willoughby, *op. cit.,* I, ch. XV.
[134] On the Sino-Soviet difficulties, *cf.* Litvinov's report to the Central Executive Committee of the U.S.S.R., Dec. 4, 1929 (Litvinov, *op. cit.,* pp. 27–33).

Soviet-Japanese relations in Manchuria have been saturated most of the time with a mixture of hidden fear, artificial friendliness, and simultaneous preparations for war. Much as the Soviets were opposed to the old aggressive policies of Imperial Russia, they decided not to remember that these policies had been indignantly denounced by the proletarian dictators immediately after taking over authority, and found the idea of sharing influence in Manchuria with Japan no longer objectionable. Indeed, when Japan began the intensive building of railroads in Manchuria, it became evident to Moscow that Tokio's interests on the mainland of Asia were not limited solely to economic advantages. To safeguard itself against unpleasant eventualities, the Soviet Government in 1926 proposed that the two Governments should revive their former spheres of influence. Japan entertained no such desire. The seizure of the Chinese Eastern Railway presented Japan with a dilemma. Apprehensive of the Soviet communist activities in Manchuria, on the one hand, and by no means willing to condone the expropriation of the railroad by China, on the other, as this would jeopardize Japan's own designs in that province, Tokio resorted to the policy of avoiding commitments one way or the other. The Briand-Kellogg Pact afforded a convenient way to carry this policy out. The Japanese Government promptly called attention of the Soviet and Chinese Governments to their obligations under this Pact. It worried Tokio not in the least that having done so, it later refused to join the other signatories of the Pact who were willing actually to invoke it.[135] Of real importance was the preservation for the time being of good relations with the Soviets and the prevention of China's strengthening her hold over Manchuria. Success was complete. In 1932 Manchuria became the puppet state of Manchukuo, and Japan the virtual master of the Soviet-owned Chinese Eastern Railway.[136]

The situation thus created became intolerable to all parties concerned. Tokio realized full well that expropriation of the line would not be tolerated by Moscow, a foe much more formidable than China. In Moscow it was quite properly admitted that the Japanese control over Manchuria placed the railway virtually within the orbit

[135] The Far Eastern Problem. Official Texts and Summary of the Lytton Report (*International Conciliation*, January, 1933, No. 286).

[136] For the Soviet denouncement of Japanese occupation and the Kremlin's implications drawn therefrom, *cf.* Litvinov's speech at the Fourth Session of the Central Executive Committee, Dec. 29, 1933 (M. M. Litvinov, *Vneshniaia Politika S.S.S.R., Rechi i Zaiavleniia. 1927–1935*, pp. 71–75).

of the Japanese Empire. The sale of the line was the only logical solution.

Aware of the negotiations which actually began between Tokio and Moscow in June, 1933, China protested that under the Sino-Soviet and the Mukden agreements of 1924, the approval of the Chinese Government was necessary to the transfer of title. It missed its aim. To accommodate themselves, both Japan and the Soviets were in silent agreement that international morals need not always coincide with the dictates of international law. The Japanese Government maintained that Manchukuo was a sovereign entity no longer bound to Nanking. The Soviets preferred to overlook the fact that the subjugation of Manchuria by Japan was an act of capitalistic aggression, and for practical purposes contended that the imperial régime in Manchukuo was a *de facto* successor to the rights of China, including those to the Chinese Eastern Railway.[137] On March 14, 1935, the arrangements for the sale were completed, and the transaction itself was formulated in an Agreement to that effect signed on March 23, 1935.[138] With the simultaneous change of its name to the North Manchurian Railway, the last traces of Chinese grounds for a claim in the future were obliterated.

Contrary to hopes that this settlement would create an "atmosphere for the peaceful and mutually amicable solution of all future problems that may arise between the Soviets and Japan," and notwithstanding the belief that it would "be welcomed by all friends of peace both in Japan and in the U.S.S.R.," [139] the Agreement of 1935 did not eliminate the tension between Tokio and Moscow. Having admitted in the course of these negotiations that Japan had become the factual master of Manchuria, the Soviets realized that the position of Manchukuo was not unsimilar to the status imposed by the Kremlin upon Outer Mongolia. In regard to war and peace this meant a definite turn for the worse, for instead of being separated from each other by two buffer provinces, Japan and the U.S.S.R. now found themselves facing each other along thousands of miles of ill-defined boundary.

Their basic distrust of each other now provoked a series of border skirmishes, and called for even greater vigilance. The con-

---

[137] *Chinese Year Book, 1935–1936*, pp. 368–369. Also, *Izvestiia*, May 12, 1933.

[138] *Sobr. Zak. i Rasp. S.S.S.R.*, 1935, II, p. 129ff.

[139] From Litvinov's reply to the Japanese newspaper correspondents (*Izvestiia*, Mar. 15, 1935).

centration of larger armies on each side of the boundary became essential, and the prospects of peace grew less and less certain. To avoid a major armed conflict, diplomatic action was invoked. Cautious not to enter into direct negotiation on the issues, which included controversies along the boundary separating the Republic of Outer Mongolia from the "Empire" of Manchukuo, Moscow and Tokio forced Ulan-Bator and Hsinking, respectively, to take formal steps toward opening of negotiations for the settlement of the annoying friction.

A conference was convened at Manchuli in June, 1935, at which it was proposed that diplomatic relations be established between these two "independent" states. Interrupted in July, but resumed in October, the negotiations came to an impasse: Manchukuo's contention that diplomatic relations were essential for terminating the border incidents met with the refusal of the Outer Mongolian delegation to acquiesce in such a theory. The conference was adjourned for a year. Meanwhile, Moscow and Tokio agreed that two commissions should be appointed, one to define the frontier and the other to settle the disputes. Before these had been appointed, Japan and Germany joined in the Anti-Communist Pact of 1936. This doomed to failure all the plans for effecting a rapprochement between Mongolia and Manchukuo. The incidents continued. So did the anxiety of Moscow and Tokio. It was only on September 16, 1939, *i.e.*, after the Soviets had cast their lot with Germany, that an agreement was reached between the two governments which silenced the armed conflicts and provided for the organization of another boundary committee.

In spite of the formal peace, the relations of the Soviet Union with the Empire of the Rising Sun never have been altogether happy. The continued assurance of mutual amity between the two countries is a rather meager camouflage. Indeed, the Agreement of July 15, 1920,[140] regarding an armistice between the Far Eastern Republic (DVR) and Japan did not terminate Japanese interference in Russian affairs. The intervention continued, in the form of support given to Merkulov's Anti-Bolshevik Government of the Maritime Province. Nor did the fall of this government and the withdrawal of the last Japanese units from Vladivostok in October, 1922,

[140] Kliuchnikov i Sabanin, *op. cit.*, III, 38. On the Soviet-Japanese relations before 1934, see Litvinov's speech at the Fourth Session of the Central Executive Committee, Dec. 29, 1933 (Litvinov, *op. cit.*, pp. 71–75).

replace the mutual distrust with whole-hearted cordiality. Tokio's and Moscow's pledges of friendship in matters of commerce and trade were robbed of their true value on the one hand by the Japanese aversion to communism sponsored by the U.S.S.R., and, on the other hand, by the Soviet concern over the contemplated dismemberment of China by Japan. It was not until January 20, 1925, that a treaty was concluded between the Soviet Union and Japan by which diplomatic relations between the two countries were established and a legal basis for the present relationship laid.[141]

In return for *de jure* recognition and Japan's promise to withdraw its troops from Northern Sakhalin, the Soviets consented to limit their propaganda to official and semi-official acts, offered extensive economic privileges in the form of concessions for fisheries and for the exploitation of oil, timber, and minerals, and recognized the validity of the Portsmouth Treaty of 1905 granting Japan a special position in Southern Manchuria. To what extent the promises in regard to propaganda have been fulfilled is a matter of controversy. The difficulties encountered in connection with the fishery concessions are well known.[142] The greatest discomfort for the Soviets, however, was caused by the advantage taken by Japan of its special status in Southern Manchuria, which was recognized by the Soviets.

The apprehension felt in Moscow when Japanese aggression in Manchuria was launched is not difficult to understand, for it was not to the interest of the Kremlin to see an unfriendly influence spread along the Soviet borders from Chosen to Manchuli. Whatever the true reasons for the Soviet determination not to be drawn into war with Japan, in these difficulties, the U.S.S.R. must be given full credit for being extraordinarily desirous of peace. Yet the conciliatory spirit which dominated Soviet statesmen did not lead them into the folly of neglecting military preparations for eventualities. Indeed, it soon became known that reinforcements of Red troops had been rushed to the Far East and that the development of the basic industries east of the Urals was progressing at an accelerated

---

[141] *Sborn. Deistv. Dogov.*, III, 1927, pp. 10ff.

[142] A convention regulating Japanese fishery rights in Soviet waters was signed on Jan. 23, 1928 (*ibid.*, V, 1930, p. 89). Revised several times, the arrangements still remain in operation. In 1936 a renewal of the Agreement for eight years was contemplated, but the Nazi-Japanese anti-communist pact angered the Soviets. Only yearly extensions resulted.

tempo. In addition to this, the concentration of efforts to double-track the Trans-Siberian Railway and the survey of the ground for a new line from Taishet to Khabarovsk, as well as the Kremlin's artificial promotion of colonization east of Lake Baikal, were unmistakable signs of Soviet anxiety over the developments in Asia.

These domestic measures found their counterpart in the Soviet endeavors to secure a non-aggression pact with Japan. The approaches made in this connection by Litvinov to Yoshizawa in 1931 have already been mentioned.[143] The proposition was twice brought forth toward the end of 1932. In reply to this, the Japanese Government expressed surprise and stated that any thoughts of aggression against the U.S.S.R. were utterly alien to Japanese policy. The Soviet-Japanese Treaty of 1925 and the common commitments embodied in the adherence of Moscow and Tokio to the Briand-Kellogg Pact were considered sufficient to maintain peace in the Far East.[144] The whole situation remained in flux.

The establishment of Manchukuo naturally did not improve matters. Nor did the German-Japanese Pact of November 25, 1936. To the Soviets, the enthronement of Henry Pu-yi at Hsinking as the Emperor of Manchukuo rendered the political borders of the U.S.S.R. more than ever exposed to the concrete danger of invasion. The understanding between Tokio and Berlin inaugurated a concerted totalitarian campaign against the theoretical foundation of the U.S.S.R. On the other hand, the Soviet-Mongolian Protocol of 1936 and the Soviet Treaty of Non-Aggression with China signed in 1937, were regarded in Tokio as an unfriendly Soviet encroachment upon Japanese designs in Asia and as an unwarranted support of the anti-Japanese sentiments among the Chinese. The coveted non-aggression treaty with Japan has thus far remained one of the unfulfilled dreams of the Soviets. For the present it is immaterial whether such a pact would ease the tension or not. Under the present circumstances, war continues to threaten peace, and peace has lost its true meaning.[145]

The coöperation of the Soviets within the League of Nations in

[143] *Supra,* p. 126.
[144] *Japan Year Book,* 1934, pp. 191–192.
[145] The armed incident which took place in 1937 over Bolshoi and Sennukha islands in the Amur River, and the not unwarlike clash around Lake Hasan in 1938, when artillery and tanks were brought into action, are illustrative of the actual state of peace between the U.S.S.R. and Japan. (*Cf. Mir. Khoz. i Mir. Pol.,* 1938, No. 9, pp. 208–212, and Molotov's speech before the Moscow Soviet, Nov. 6, 1938, on the occasion of the twenty-first anniversary of the Soviet régime, *ibid.,* No. 11, pp. VII–VIII).

connection with Japanese aggression in China, after 1934 was of necessity limited. It will be recalled that Japan resigned from the League in 1933. Therefore, the Soviet attitude can be gathered only from the reactions of the Soviet delegates at Geneva to the Chinese appeals to the League. The most important of these appeals was that made on behalf of the Chinese Government by Dr. Wellington Koo on September 16, 1937, after the new on-rush of the Japanese armies into the interior of China.[146] There should be no surprise that Litvinov denounced the Japanese policy in Asia. Indeed, only five days later, reviewing the work of the League for the previous year, he said that "on the continent of Asia, without declaring war, without a shadow of cause or justification, one state attacks another." [147] Speaking on the situation in China, on October 5, 1937, he expressed his satisfaction that the Far East Advisory Committee of the League "found in the action of the Japanese Government all the elements that constitute aggression," and, after having voiced his wish that " the League of Nations should itself take certain steps to give China not only moral but also some substantial assistance," concluded his appeal with the hope that, "if it becomes necessary, the League of Nations will do its full duty towards China." [148] Distracted by the developments in Europe, neither the Soviets nor the League were insistent enough to check the Japanese advance. The futile appeals of Litvinov at Geneva were accompanied by no more effective sympathy for the Chinese people, expressed at various times and through various means in the U.S.S.R. The Treaty of Non-Aggression with China, signed in 1937, and the later Treaty of Commerce, signed in 1939, were inadequate to vitalize the League of Nations to a sufficient degree to enable it to silence Japanese guns in the Far East.

Extra-Curriculum: Kremlin's United Labor Peace Front

In its campaign for the preservation of world peace, the Soviet Union did not limit its efforts to separate dealings with individual states and to its collective efforts through the League of Nations. The political solidarity between the Nazi Reich, Fascist Italy, and militant Japan not only presented a danger for the international

[146] *League of Nations Official Journal,* Spec. Suppl. No. 177.
[147] Speech on Sept. 21, 1937, *ibid.,* Spec. Suppl. No. 169, p. 79.
[148] *Ibid.,* Spec. Suppl. No. 177, p. 31.

status quo from the standpoint of the geographical boundaries of states great and small. The Rome-Berlin-Tokio axis, comprising three powers bound together by political doctrines uncompromisingly opposed to the ideas sponsored by Marx, became a formidable ideological foe of the Kremlin. To counteract both dangers, the collective organization of peace had become the keynote of Soviet policy following the ascendancy of National-Socialism in Germany. Avowedly based on the solidarity of all those interested in world peace, whether capitalists or proletarians, Soviet efforts through diplomatic channels alone could not guarantee the safety of the U.S.S.R., or the preservation of world peace. Hence the formal endeavors of the Soviet Government had to be reinforced by the world proletariat itself.

Emphasis upon a united front among the rank and file of the Communist Party itself, as well as among the workers of the world, irrespective of their formal party affiliations, became the focal concern of the Soviet peace policy in the field of revolutionary peace strategy. It was only natural that the Third International should become the guiding spirit of this united labor front. As early as 1927, at the Eighth Plenary Session of the Executive Committee of the Communist International it was resolved that

"In the struggle against war, Bolsheviks must transfer the center of gravity to the masses and place it in the struggle of classes." [149]

Dogmatically, there is nothing new in this resolution. It was Marx himself who in 1864 pointed out these tactics:

"If the liberation of the workers calls for brotherly unity and coöperation of the toilers, how can they carry out this noble duty when foreign policies, in their pursuit of criminal ends, play upon national sentiments and when predatory wars waste the blood and the wealth of the people?" [150]

It is true that the Soviet Government has always emphatically denied any relation with the Third International, in spite of the convenient and suggestive coincidence of its ranking officials having been invariably officials of the Comintern.[151] It is significant that the establishment of a united labor front became mandatory and that this massing of revolutionary reserves was to be effected by ironing

[149] *Rezoliutsii VIII Plenuma Ispolkoma Kominterna*, pp. 78–85.
[150] Marx, *Izbrannye Proizvedeniia*, II, p. 341.
[151] Paul Scheffer, "From Lenin to Stalin," *Foreign Affairs*, April, 1938, pp. 445–453; also Batsell, *Soviet Rule in Russia*, pp. 717–719.

out the differences in the Party itself, by observing uniformity of action in every country, and by uniting all workers in the common cause of peace.

The difficulties within the Party have been repeatedly admitted at various times by the communists themselves. It was at the Seventh Congress of the Communist International, however, that Bolshevik self-criticism struck hardest at the sectarian distortions which had been hindering the work of the Party. Particular stress was laid upon the organizational failure to take into account the specific features of communist movements in various countries. To correct all this, uniformity of action was no longer to be judged by the old stereotype formulas of the mechanical application of the experience of the communist movement in one country to that of communist parties in all other countries. The internationalization of Bolshevik experience on the basis of decentralization was the new remedy for the old ills concerning party tactics in regard to revolutions. Concretely, it called for greater independence of lower party organizations from the higher hierarchical units as to the adaptability of the party work to local conditions. In the field of foreign relations, the old Marxian dictum on the rôle of the proletariat in the international relations of a state was catapulted to new heights of practical necessity. The proletariat was instructed to concentrate upon "taking possession of the secrets of international policies, vigilance over the diplomacy of their governments, and in case of necessity, sabotage of their acts by all means at their disposal," and reminded that the "struggle for this kind of foreign policy constitutes an integral part of the general struggle for the liberation of the toiling masses." [152] That this became precisely the *modus operandi* of the proletarian united front later was admitted by Dmitrov:

"While under no conditions admitting any shifting to the bourgeois position, the proletariat must actively interfere with the foreign policies and the policies of national defense by submitting their own programs and demands." [153]

The official proletarian sanction of the consolidation of the workers in a united front against "Fascist barbarism and the horrors of

[152] Manuilsky, *op. cit.*, pp. 75ff., 25ff., and Marx, *op. cit.*, p. 342. Also report by Kuusinen submitted at the Thirteenth Plenary Session of the Communist International (*XIII Plenum IKKI, Stenograficheskii Otchet*, pp. 13ff.).

[153] Dmitrov, "Edinyi front v Bor'be za Mir," *Kommunisticheskii Internatsional*, 1936, No. 9, p. 6.

imperialist wars" [154] is found in the proceedings of the Seventh World Congress of the Communist International held in Moscow in September, 1935, and in the resolutions which it adopted. A justification for the need of a united front was implied in the solemn declarations that this Congress was to manifest the proletarian struggle against the bitterest enemy of the working class—Fascism, and hence also against imperialist wars. As a Congress which signified the "complete triumph of unity between the proletariat of the country of victorious socialism, the Soviet Union, and the proletariat of the capitalist countries which is still fighting for its liberation," [155] this Congress became also the fountain of spiritual enthusiasm and the source of tactical instructions for the proletarian struggle for peace and the defense of the U.S.S.R.

Speaking at the meeting of the Soviet Communist Party on September 14, 1935, Manuilsky said that the Seventh Congress which "expressed the burning anti-fascist hatred of the masses," turned "its fire mainly against Fascism." [156] In the sphere of international relations, this meant that the peace policy of the Soviets, while sponsoring proletarian internationalism in its struggle against the national and racial dissension of Nazism and of other "isms," envisaged more than the mere safety of the U.S.S.R. Expecting at least to retard the conflagration of war, this Congress took upon itself the duty of safeguarding the revolutionary gains thus far accumulated, for which purpose new auxiliaries had to be pressed into service.

The approval by the Seventh Congress of the decision adopted in 1928 by the Sixth Congress in regard to the struggle against imperialist wars,[157] strictly speaking, introduced nothing new as to the communist desire for international peace. Peace remained, as of old, their immediate objective. What it did introduce, however, was a change in proletarian class tactics. As a supplement to the diplomatic "united front of peace against the united front of war," the new tactics of uniting communists with non-communist international working classes called for two new basic tasks: the unified organization of toilers on a world-wide scale, and political unity of action.

[154] Dmitrov's speech on Aug. 20, 1935, at the Seventh Congress of the Communist International (*Seventh World Congress of the Communist International. Resolutions*, p. 8).

[155] *Ibid.*, p. 5.

[156] D. Z. Manuilsky, *The Work of the Seventh Congress of the Communist International*, p. 18.

[157] *Kommunisticheskii Internatsional v Dokumentakh, 1919–1932*, pp. 793ff.

With the passing years the communist belief has been steadily growing that there is a great difference between the vanguard activities of Bela Kun in Hungary in 1919, or Rosa Luxemburg and Karl Liebknecht in Germany at about the same time, and the progress of organization made within the party during the years that since had come to pass. It must be kept in mind, however, that, simultaneously, the gulf between the schools of the Second and the Third Internationals, pointed out in Lenin's criticism of the former,[158] has been constantly growing wider. If it be recalled, furthermore, that the controversy between Stalin and Trotzky was by no means a happy experience for the Communist Party, the magnitude of the task of uniting the workers of the world into a common labor front acquires the proportions of a large and difficult undertaking. The difficulties of the problem, however, did not shatter the confidence of Moscow that it could be solved.

As a party of the proletarian revolution and of the struggle for the proletarian dictatorship, the communists believed that there were two good reasons for their self-confidence in the righteousness of the new plan and in the feasibility thereof. First, it was accepted as a fact that the communist parties of various countries, having received their "baptism of fire in big class battles" and having "passed the test of underground work," were now in a position to understand better the dictates of revolutionary expediency. Second, the communists have come to a realizaton of the fact that unless the forces of the working class are united in both the economic and the political spheres, the victory of the proletariat cannot be achieved. In the words of Manuilsky, the split in the working class movement is of great advantage to the bourgeoisie, as it enables the latter to prevent the victory of the proletariat. "In fighting for the proletarian dictatorship," said he, "communists are preparing for the achievement of complete proletarian unity; only under the dictatorship of the proletariat will the influence of the bourgeoisie upon the proletariat be destroyed and all possibility of splitting the working class disappear. That is why communists are the genuine vehicles for the unity of the working class movement." [159] In practice, united leadership is an essential condition for success in the struggle, and this struggle must not signify unity merely between leading labor bodies.

[158] Lenin, "Krakh II Internatsionala" (*Works, XIII*).
[159] D. Z. Manuilsky, *op. cit.*, pp. 45–46.

The slogan must be mass struggle, which means that the unification of various workers' factions in a common proletarian front is a "task not only of bolshevizing the Communist Parties, but of bolshevizing the working class." [160] This process of "bolshevization" obviously cannot abandon the communist aims and to this end the new united party must unreservedly serve the interests of the proletarian revolution. Consequently, the creation of a new party is possible only on condition that there be "complete independence from the bourgeoisie and a complete severance of the bloc between Social-Democracy and the bourgeoisie," and, that "unity of action be first brought about." [161]

This unity of action was, as has been said, the other main task of the new tactics. It envisaged united-front tactics in a new manner which meant joint action with the Socialist-Democratic Parties, reformist trade unions, and other organizations of the toilers against the class enemies of the proletariat. According to Dmitrov,

"in the face of Fascist danger, Communists may, while reserving for themselves freedom of political agitation and criticism, participate in election campaigns on a common platform and with a common ticket of the anti-Fascist front, depending on the growth and the success of the united front movement, also depending upon the electoral system in operation. . . . Considering that unity of action is an urgent necessity and the surest way to bring about the political unity of the proletariat, the Seventh Congress of the Communist International declares that . . . they are ready to begin immediate negotiations with the corresponding parties of the Second International for establishment of the unity of action of the working class against the offensive of capital, against Fascism and [against] the threat of imperialist war. . . . The establishment of the united front of the working class is the decisive link in the preparation of toilers for the forthcoming great battles of the second round of proletarian revolution." [162]

In practice this was to mean that the Social-Democrat workers were to come over to the position of the class struggle and, while collaboration with the bourgeoisie must cease, efforts must be made that the united front of workers take over the government control and fight capitalism and not the class. Strikingly resembling the communist tactics prescribed for the proletariat in regard to war,[163] the action

---

[160] Manuilsky, *op. cit.*, p. 50.
[161] *Seventh World Congress of the Communist International. Resolutions, p.* 37.
[162] *Ibid.*, pp. 29 and 38.
[163] *Cf.* the Resolutions of the Seventh Congress on the Report of M. Ereoli on the tasks of the Communist International in Connection with the Preparations of the Imperialists for a New World War (*ibid.*, pp. 40ff.).

of the united front in domestic politics is also not unlike the above-mentioned rule prescribed by Marx for taking over the control of foreign policies.

Whatever the actual reasons for the new stand taken by the communists at this Congress, be it fear of totalitarian dictatorships or confidence in their own victory in the U.S.S.R., the moral justification for it must have been found in the thesis which was advanced by Lenin at the Second Congress held in the Fall of 1920: "The proletariat may be a truly revolutionary and truly socialist class only on the condition that it act as a vanguard of all toiling and exploited masses, and as a leader in their struggle for the overthrow of the exploiters. . . ." [164]

At the Eighteenth Congress of the Soviet Communist Party, held in Moscow in 1939, it was reported that the effect of the new communist policy abroad was gratifying indeed. It was said that in the United States anti-fascist sentiments were forcing into retreat the reactionary preachings of Father Coughlin. In France, labor succeeded in preventing the "Croix de Feu" of Colonel de la Rocque from becoming the ruling authority. In Great Britain the movement of Mosley was pushed into oblivion. In Spain the consolidation of various socialist factions into a single Loyalist group was expected to result in the ultimate defeat of Franco. In China the struggle against the Japanese invasion was supposedly strengthened by the rapidly growing solidarity of the workers in various provinces.[165] Not only countries in the western hemisphere but also India and other colonies were said to be on the way toward realizing the real danger of Fascism.[166] True, the Popular Front in France considerably influenced the stand taken by Paris in the Spanish crisis. It is also undeniable that the joining of various Socialist groups under the banners of Loyalists prolonged the civil war in Spain. It may also be correct that the numerous appeals of the communists to the workers of the world during the Italo-Ethiopian war,[167] may have had a certain effect on the revolutionary fusion of the socialists and the Marxists.

[164] *Kommunisticheskii Internatsional v Dokumentakh, 1919–1932*, pp. 90–92.

[165] *Cf.* the Appeal of the Central Committee of the Chinese Communist Party of Dec. 25, 1937 (*Mir. Khoz. i Mir. Politika*, 1938, No. 6, p. 181).

[166] "Doklad delegatsii VKP(b) v IKKI na XVIII S'ezde VKP (b)" (*ibid.*, 1939, No. 4, pp. 54ff.). For correspondence of the Executive Committee with the Socialist Workers' International on the coördination of action, *cf., ibid.*, 1937, No. 7, pp. 147ff.

[167] *Cf. Humanité*, Oct. 8, 1935, No. 13444; Oct. 9, 1935, No. 13445; and Nov. 6, 1935, No. 13473.

The total effect of all this, however, could hardly be anything but an unpleasant disillusion to Moscow.[168] Germany's advance to the southeast continued until Austria and Czechoslovakia lost their independence. Mussolini did not stop fighting in Africa until Ethiopia was conquered. In Spain the civil war ended only with the complete victory of General Franco. These practical fiascoes did not mean to the Kremlin, however, that their cause was lost.

Manifold and just as may be the charges preferred against the Soviets by their antagonists, an impartial observer must admit that in their pursuit of the revolutionary world peace, the Soviets are painfully persistent and commendably stoic. The failures which had been making the growing fears of other statesmen poor guaranties against war, were accepted by the Soviets as an impetus for improving their own future "peace" efforts. Cynical as in the light of the Kremlin's recent aggression it indeed is, the Soviet contention has not changed that whatever the outward manifestations of Moscow's foreign relations under changing circumstances, they have not deviated from the often repeated formula voiced by Stalin that the U.S.S.R. is for peace and friendly coöperation with all countries that make no attempt at jeopardizing Soviet interests, and with all neighboring countries that do not, directly or indirectly, encroach upon the integrity of Soviet territory. This challenging attitude of the Soviet Union is still considered by the Kremlin to rest on good reasons. According to Stalin these are: the realization of its own strength, the enjoyment of moral and political unity, as well as of the friendship among the socialist community of the various peoples inhabiting the U.S.S.R., and confidence in the reasoning power of the countries opposed to war. The aim of the Communist Party itself, according to Stalin, must be the promotion of peace and extreme vigilance that the Soviet Union be not drawn into armed conflicts by instigators of war who are "accustomed to have some one else pull their chestnuts out of the fire."

It must be said that Stalin did not fail to point out that the Soviet desire for peace was accompanied by a fearless readiness on the part of the U.S.S.R. to fight in case of need and by a dutiful willingness to protect those who have fallen victims of aggression. Neither did he omit to mention that the Red Army and Navy and

[168] Fogarashi, "Bor'ba za mir—bor'ba za edinyi front" (*Mir. Khoz. i Mir. Politika*, 1936, No. 7, pp. 13–26).

the moral support of the proletariat in other countries lend a great deal of encouragement to the Soviets in the stand they have taken in the issue of war and peace. Finally, he admitted that in connection with all this, the duties of the Communist Party included also the strengthening of the proletarian armed forces and the solidification of friendly ties among workers all over the world.[169]

The three-fold policy pursued by the Soviets since the rise of Hitler to safeguard international peace, by resorting to individual treaty arrangements, by sponsoring concerted efforts through the offices of the League of Nations, and by launching a campaign to unite labor into a common proletarian anti-war front, made the halo of Christian love of peace shine brightly over the vari-colored cupolas of once-crowded churches in the now atheistic Kremlin. Leaving out of account the obviously different opinion of the totalitarian governments, and the natural admiration of non-Russian communists abroad as poor criteria, the general reaction has been to acclaim the Soviets as welcome crusaders against war. Amid the rush of disturbing events, individual theories to the contrary carried no weight. Statesmen and diplomats abroad preferred to conceal their real sentiments, and, like their confrères in Germany, Italy, Japan and the U.S.S.R., to follow the dictates of expediency. This meant that, formally, political credits were liberally extended and mutually exchanged. That this was done without adequate collateral, however, is now recognized. The present war and the Soviet rôle in it are evidence of this.

ON THE MARXIAN GRANDSTAND: PARADE OF WARS AND PEACE

To conclude this review of Soviet foreign relations since the establishment of the Third Reich, the Soviet revolutionary evaluation of the armed conflicts which have taken place since 1933 and an analysis of international peace from the Marxian standpoint remain to be undertaken. It is not an exaggeration to say that with the possible exception of the war between Paraguay and Bolivia, neither Italy's campaign in Ethiopia, nor the bloodshed in Spain, nor, finally, Japanese penetration into China have yet been defined with finality

---

[169] Speech at the XVIII Party Congress, March 10, 1939 (*Izvestiia*, March 11, 1939, No. 57).

in terms clearly understood in international law. It is common knowledge that during these conflicts modern war weapons have been used and actually put to rigid, practical tests on the proving grounds of Ethiopia, Iberia, and China. It is also a fact that the regulations covering the status of prisoners of war were sometimes magnanimously observed, and that the diplomatic records bearing upon these wars reveal no small concern of the states over lifting "blockades," maintaining "neutrality," or recognizing "belligerency." Finally, from Addis-Ababa, Madrid, and Nanking appeals were reaching Geneva, requesting the League of Nations to recognize their respective bloody struggles as wars in the fullest sense of the term. Even today authorities on the subject appear reluctant to commit themselves. "Armed conflict" is still waiting to be incorporated among the precepts of international law as a definite legal concept which, while short of *de jure* war so far as formal declaration goes, would nevertheless be recognized as connoting a status not altogether free from legal consequence, as to both the rights and the obligations pertaining to *de jure* war. For whatever reason, in referring to the events in Africa, Spain, and the Far East, there is a tendency to resort to a variety of non-committal, nebulous terms describing the actual order of things rather than connoting the legal substance thereof.

The Marxist has no difficulty in this respect. It will be recalled that the non-communist classification of wars does not apply to the revolutionary estimate of international armed conflicts.[170] Litvinov's references to legal aspects, made by him in the League of Nations, must be viewed as tactical moves in pursuit of definite diplomatic ends rather than as evidence of his academic interest in this particular principle of international law. Nor was it considered essential longer to adhere to basic principles relative to war. In May, 1919, the Soviets protested that "Vilna, the capital of the brother republics of Lithuania and White Russia, had been attacked by Polish troops without any justification and without any previous declaration of war." [171] When, in turn, in the winter of 1939, likewise without justification and without a previous declaration of war, the Soviet Union took from Finland the city of Viipuri and the sur-

---

[170] *Supra,* pp. 28ff.
[171] *Krasnaia Kniga,* p. 56. On the earlier Soviet theories on war, *cf.* Taracouzio, *op. cit.,* ch. IX, pp. 311ff.

rounding portion of Southern Karelia, the Kremlin proved that this disregard of the international law of war had become its own practice. Stalin's remark that "nowadays wars are not declared" but "simply start," [172] was more than ridicule of the capitalist world for its fallacious loyalty to the rules of international law. It was more than a mere summary condemnation of the theories of "totalitarian war," according to which the modern tactical requirements of suddenness and surprise have rendered the traditional diplomatic prerequisites of ultimatums and declarations not only superficial and unnecessary but strategically dangerous. It was a proposition advanced to justify the Soviet's own actions in the future. It was also another reminder that wars are, first of all, continuations of peace policies only by different, *i.e.*, forcible, means. It is, therefore, in this light that the Soviet attitude toward the four wars in question is to be analyzed.

Little documentary evidence as there is in regard to the Soviet outlook on the war between Paraguay and Bolivia, the issue appears clear. Inasmuch as neither of these countries has adopted the Dictatorship of the Proletariat as a suitable form of government, and since each of them enjoys a non-communist social order, as well as complete independence and recognition by the civilized world, both must be classified as capitalist states. As such, they are automatically disqualified to be regarded as backward or semi-colonial, which in fact they are not. (In passing, it may be remarked that this is fortunate, for were they such, the Marxian classification of their war would have been rather a difficult problem, for the communist list of wars does not include any war between two backward or semi-colonial countries.) As a war, waged between two capitalist countries, it was an imperialistic war *par excellence*. The approximate equality in military strength of the two antagonists precludes the possibility of raising the query as to whether or not considerations of equality influence the communist appraisal of wars. In the Soviet estimate the Bolivian-Paraguayan war stands apart from the military operations in Ethiopia, Spain, and China.

The Italo-Ethiopian war invites different considerations. Aside from the difference in the international standing of the two, the degree of Ethiopia's cultural, social, and economic development, and the relationship of Italy's aggression in Africa to Rome's expansion-

---

[172] *Cf.* his talk with Mr. Roy Howard (Heald and Wheeler-Bennett, *op. cit.*, p. 465).

ist program in general, are important factors which prompt the Soviets to approach the whole issue from a specific revolutionary standpoint. It was the belief of the U.S.S.R. that had Ethiopia been a strong country, Italy would not have ventured to undertake the campaign in Africa. It was only because of Ethiopia's weakness and retardedness that Rome ordered its legions to march into its territory.[173]

Much as this little country had been strengthened by the transformation of its feudal system to that of a state with a centralized government, and despite its membership in the League of Nations, in the eyes of the world it was still a political entity where much remained to be done to bring it up to the standard of modern civilization. Whatever the latter presupposes, to the Soviets the domain of Negus Haile Selassie was a country which yet had not reached the stage where capitalism was possible. Backward, from the revolutionary standpoint, it was an object of the imperialistic rivalry of capitalist countries contemplating the rearrangement and expansion of their colonial domains. In this marathon of capitalist aggression, Italy's early start in Ethiopia was, to the communists, nothing but an imperialist war in which the roar of guns was symbolic of the thunder of approaching conflict among capitalist countries themselves, as well as between the non-communist and communist worlds.

If it be recalled that the Soviet Union has repeatedly voiced its objection to a new redivision of the world, the Kremlin's sympathies for Ethiopia should not be surprising. Denouncing the redivision of overseas possessions and the exploitation of colonial peoples *ex principio*,[174] in practice the Soviets viewed the struggle of Abyssinia as the revolutionary war of a backward, semi-colonial people to achieve national liberation. As such, it was of interest to the international proletariat. As a champion of the latter, the Soviet Union could not consent to the proposals made in the League of Nations to settle the conflict by subjecting Ethiopia to the control of a capitalist country, even though this was to be effected in the guise of a mandate. On January 10, 1936, Molotov said that the "Italo-Abyssinian war is a typical imperialist war for colonial possessions" and added that in their attitude toward Ethiopia the Soviets have demonstrated Moscow's loyalty to the principle of "independence and national

[173] *Pravda,* Sept. 5, 1935.
[174] *Izvestiia,* Oct. 5, 1935.

equality of all peoples.[175] It was in full accord with the appeal issued
three months earlier by the Executive Committee of the Third International that the imperialist struggle for the possession of Abyssinia be stopped immediately. "Proletarians of the world, unite!
Not a single train, not a single ship to help the Italian war in
Abyssinia! . . . Hands off the Abyssinian people! . . . Long live
the Soviet peace policy! . . ." [176] were the concluding words of the
proletarian approval given to the Soviet revolutionary tactics.

The proportions, duration, and effect of the conflict in Spain
made it outwardly a war. The choice of adjectives fitting its description is extensive. Varied also are the individual tests. From the
standpoint of international law, it may have been a civil war; for
practical purposes, an international war; to the Soviets, however, it
was but another manifestation of the militant antagonism which prevails between the totalitarian and communist régimes. Expressed in
class struggle at home and in intervention from abroad, this war was
also a further proof of the irreconcilability of the capitalist and Marxian worlds, admittedly enjoying "peaceful" co-existence. The collection of funds in the Soviet Union for Spanish Loyalists, shipments of
food consigned to Valencia and Barcelona, the war activity of the Soviet fliers, tanks, and general staff advisers in the anti-Franco forces, as
well as the efforts of Soviet diplomats at Geneva and elsewhere, were
by no means moves sponsored by humanitarian motives only to save
the toiling masses of Spain from starvation or to prevent their gradual strangulation by assuring them a speedy victory over General
Franco. True, they evidenced the "sympathy with which one of the
most democratic and free countries" watched "the heroic and agoniz-
ing struggle of the [Spanish] people . . . against Fascist barbarism
and enslavement," [177] but they were saturated also with sentiments
of a purely revolutionary character.

Speaking at the Eighth All-Russian Congress of the Communist
Party, Litvinov discarded the idea that the Soviets had any intention
to establish communism in Spain, by saying that such "fairy tales
are for small children and big fools," and that they are circulated for
the purpose of concealing the true reasons for Soviet interest in Span-

---

[175] Speech at the Second Session of the Eighth Meeting of the Central Executive
Committee of the U.S.S.R. (*Izvestiia*, Jan. 11, 1936).

[176] *Humanité*, Oct. 10, 1935.

[177] Litvinov's speech at the Eighth All-Union Congress of Soviets (*Mir. Khoz. i Mir.
Politika*, 1937, No. 1, p. 166).

ish events. What really caused anxiety to the U.S.S.R., according to him, was the fact that it was confronted "with an attempt to establish Fascism in Spain by force" and that "if this attempt proves successful, there would be no guaranty that it would not be repeated in some other country, only on a much larger scale." [178]

If Stalin's assurance that "export of revolution is nonsense" be assumed to be genuine, and if it is correct that "each country, if it so desires, will make its own revolution," [179] then there is no denying that to the Soviets a proletarian victory in Spain was of paramount importance. It is almost superfluous to say that since the very term "revolution" is a flexible one, revolutions themselves differ. Depending upon the angle from which the Spanish struggle is analyzed, Franco's rebellion may well be called a revolution. The Soviets did not come to his assistance. Their interests lie with proletarian revolutions. The Loyalist's cause was the revolutionary cause. Soviet official references to the Loyalist struggle as a struggle for democracy does not alter this fact, particularly if it be recalled that, when emanating from Moscow, the term "democracy" is not barred from connoting a régime of proletarian dictatorship. A class struggle of the working masses against the reactionary forces of capitalism, the civil war in Spain was also a revolutionary war for the ultimate supremacy of the proletariat.

It was a revolutionary war not only as a local problem but as an international issue. Aside from being a direct challenge to the spread of communism in Western Europe, the intervention of Hitler and Mussolini in Spain was considered the initial phase in the anti-communist crusade against the Union of Socialist Soviet Republics. In this view, the trenches occupied by the Loyalists were virtually political barricades to save the Soviet Union.[180]

Dolores Ibarruri admitted at the Plenary Session of the Central Committee of the Communist Party in June, 1937, that the consolidation of socialists and communists in Spain into a united front against General Franco was based on the idea that the Marxian theory be accepted as its guiding spirit and that this front was to fight not only for the supremacy of proletarian authority in Spain,

---

[178] *Mir. Khoz. i Mir. Politika*, 1937, No. 1, p. 166.

[179] Interview with Roy Howard (in Wheeler-Bennett, *op. cit.*, p. 466).

[180] *Cf.* Art. 16 of the Spanish Program drawn up on Aug. 17, 1937, for the concerted action of the Socialists and Communists (*Mir. Khoz. i Mir. Politika*, 1937, Nos. 10–11, p. 264).

but also for the protection of the Soviet Union.[181] Speaking on behalf of the International Brigade of Volunteers which was withdrawn from the ranks of the Loyalists in October, 1938, Marti said in his farewell: "We are leaving! But we are not departing to rest. We are going to struggle! . . . We shall not rest. We are only changing the front!"[182] It is unimportant what his destination was. Nor is it essential whether he and his followers lived up to their promise. The significance of the above remarks lies in the proof which they afford that the war in Spain was also a revolutionary war of the international proletariat for the protection of the Soviet communist fatherland, far away though it was.

All these considerations may be freely applied to the war in China, too, except that here the issue is not a clear-cut struggle between the two political factions, but a complicated conflict between three mutually antagonistic forces: the Imperialism of Japan, the Nationalism of the Kuomintang, and the Marxism of Chinese communists. The war in the Far East has thus become a triangular affair: Japan is waging war against the two Chinese factions; the Kuomintang, against Japan and the communists; and the latter, against Japan and the Nationalists. As in the case of Spain, the Soviet Union is officially a mere onlooker, and, as then, its sympathies are naturally with those who fight in the cause of labor. Hence, also, the differences in the communist appraisal of each of the phases of the struggle in China.

The Soviets have always looked upon Japan as one of the great countries, capitalistic in its social structure and imperialistic in its political design. By Tokio's rapprochement with Berlin and Rome it assumed all the qualities usually inherent in the totalitarian régimes.[183] Hence, the Soviets could see in the Japanese penetration into Asia, nothing but an imperialist aggression, and in the war of China against the Mikado's armies a national-revolutionary war. The fact that this armed resistance is being carried out independently by two mutually antagonistic factions—the Kuomintang Army of Chiang Kai-shek and the Red Army of Chinese Communists— does not alter the nature of China's struggle against Japanese imperialism. This superficially friendly union of two political factions

[182] *Kommunisticheskii Internatsional,* 1937, No. 7, p. 64.
[182] *Humanité,* Oct. 28, 1938.
[183] Today, a formal military alliance between them would be only logical.

against foreign invasion is an illustration of the second group of wars envisaged by Lenin, namely those waged for national liberation from imperialism,[184] during which either the proletariat itself wages such a war or supports other factions. The first impression is that in fighting Japan, the Chinese proletariat is performing both these revolutionary duties. How consistent this is, however, with the actual state of affairs as to the Kuomintang is to be briefly pointed out.

As an anti-Soviet movement, envisaging the freedom of China from both communism and foreign control, the Kuomintang may rightly appear to Marxists as an agent of capitalist imperialism, and the war between Chiang Kai-shek and Japan an imperialistic war between two capitalist systems. If it be recalled, however, that, according to Lenin, every revolutionary war for national liberation is directed against imperialism, and objectively is an integral part of proletarian world revolution,[185] the position of the Kuomintang must appear to Moscow paradoxical, to say the least: in his struggle for national liberation, Chiang Kai-shek finds his armies fighting imperialism, which he himself, in communist opinion, represents, and at the same time supporting the proletarian world revolution, to which he is unreservedly opposed.

Under the circumstances, the position of the proletarian faction itself becomes dualistic. True, there is no question as to its relationship with Japan. Here the dilemma is clear: from the revolutionary standpoint the Chinese people must either be transformed into a firmly enslaved colony of imperialists, or bring about revolutionary release from their yoke. Concretely, however, this means that Chiang Kai-shek and his Kuomintang Party must also be overthrown. In fact, this was admitted at the Thirteenth Plenary Session of the Communist International, when it was reported that liberation from imperialism calls also for an anti-imperialist struggle in Kuomintang China, and that this struggle is to be directed "not only against the Japanese and other imperialists, but also against the Kuomintang as agents of imperialism." [186] Hence, logically, in their revolutionary war with Japan for national liberation, the Chinese toiling masses must solicit the coöperation of their Chinese

[184] *Cf.* Lenin, XIII, 439–440.
[185] *Supra,* pp. 39ff.
[186] *XIII Plenum IKKI. Stenografisheskii Otchet,* p. 17.

imperialist antagonists, the idea being, however, that the communist movement is to prevail as the political core of a united China.[187]

In 1928, at the Ninth Plenary Session of the Executive Committee of the Communist International, an appeal was issued to the workers of the world to "perform their international proletarian duty of solidarity by helping the heroic proletariat of China." [188] At the Seventh Congress of the Communist International held in 1935, the question was put rather plainly: "either to resist the offensive of Japanese aggression—and then there is life; or to renounce resistance against the external enemy—and that is death." [189] This familiar formula for hysteria, which was voiced long ago by Lenin in regard to the Soviets, mentioned by Hitler in regard to Germany, and experienced later in Spain, meant the need of a united national front. At the Eighteenth Congress of the Soviet Communist Party it was admitted that in their struggle against Japan, the Chinese people "have terminated their civil strife and are forging their national unity," and that the "war in China has become the greatest war of a semi-colonial country for its national liberation ever known in history." [190]

Whatever the actual results thus far of the understanding between the Kuomintang and the Chinese communists and irrespective of their hopes for the future,[191] to Marxists the outwardly paradoxical blending of theoretical abstractions with revolutionary expediency is not an unsound strategy. If this war in China, revolutionary as it is to a Marxist, is nothing but a phase in the proletarian struggle for world revolution, and if the concentration of communist forces is not strong enough to deal a decisive offensive on all fronts at once, it should be fought with patience. This credo of revolutionary believers in the ultimate communist commonwealth means that under certain circumstances piecemeal victories are the only safe way to effect a final victory. It also means that resort to patience is not necessarily limited to the trenches alone. Retreats in the field

[187] Manuilsky, op. cit., pp. 59–61.

[188] Kommunisticheskii Internatsional v Dokumentakh, 1919–1932, p. 767. Cf. also discussions on the Chinese situation held at the Sixth, Seventh, and Eighth Plenary Sessions (ibid., pp. 619–624, 668–680, and 717–729, respectively).

[189] Wang Ming, The Revolutionary Movement in the Colonial Countries, p. 15.

[190] Report of Manuilsky (Mir. Khoz. i Mir. Politika, 1939, No. 4, pp. 57–58).

[191] The communist belief is that the ever-growing national sentiment, the territorial extent and the unlimited reserves of man power, as well as the determination of the Chinese people to free themselves from foreign control, preclude any possibility that the Japanese stay in China is permanent (Istoriia VKP(b). Kratkii kurs, p. 318).

must sometimes be accompanied by a concession of theories, and the trickery of General Staffs, supplemented by the Machiavellianism of statesmen. Hitler, the Führer of German anti-Marxism, as he originally declared himself, found it profitable to follow the tactics preached by his foe, the communists. The non-communist and non-totalitarian world may find it profitable to take notice of this.

Taken collectively, to the Soviets these wars that spanned the world—wars in South America, Spain, Africa, and the Far East—were two-fold phenomena. To the U.S.S.R. as a member of the League of Nations, they were armed conflicts disturbing the formal international peace still needed by Moscow. To the Soviet Union as the proletarian fatherland, they were premature eruptions, not to be found in the Marxian blueprints of world peace.

In view of such a dual understanding of the wars which had come to pass since the rise of Hitler, peace to the Soviets must likewise have more than one meaning. The impression that the Soviets have remained loyal to their appeals for peace and persistent in their efforts to preserve it is not an illusion. Indeed the necessity of enduring the co-existence of the communist and non-communist worlds was still very real to them. Then, their bi-lateral security treaties, their denunciation of aggression in the League of Nations, and their resort to the united labor front against war were permeated with a genuine desire to prevent war and to stop bloodshed. Finally, their belief that the progress made in the social reconstruction of society in the U.S.S.R. is an important factor for keeping peace intact is not a glamorous self-glorification, but a justified warning that the socialized U.S.S.R. of today is no longer the weak R.S.F.S.R. of Brest-Litovsk days.

At the same time, however, the continued submissiveness to this co-existence, the accelerated manifestation of their championship of peace by joining the League, and the intensified strengthening of the Red armed forces at home create the impression that the Soviet banners of international good-will have been kept fluttering not by the natural currents of amity for the non-communist world, but by the threatening elements of artificially propelled duress. From this standpoint, the fourth period of the Soviet peace policy does not differ essentially from the previous ones. It is only by a shift of purpose that the change has taken place. During the years that passed from the Treaty of Riga to the rise of National-Socialism in

Germany, the survival of the proletarian régime and a breathing spell for the building of a model socialistic order in the U.S.S.R. were the primary causes for the Kremlin's need of international peace. By 1933, the first of these concerns was no longer disturbing to communist statesmen, as the Soviet Union was rightly considered a firmly established Great Power. The worries of survival were forgotten, and from that time on, international peace lost its significance for the Soviets in this regard. As to the transformation of the former imperial order of things into a socialist community, in 1933 the Soviets were merely in the first stage of their scheduled plannings for bringing about this change. To complete the task, time was still essential, and for this, international peace continued to be essential for Soviet success even during this fourth period. The mere assurance of existence did not reduce Soviet anxiety for preserving international peace, however, as new worries were in store for Soviet diplomats. Confronted with the threatening program of National-Socialism, on the one hand, and the rapid growth of contradictions in Western Europe, on the other, the Soviets were fully aware that the political clouds were being dangerously over-charged with conflicting aspirations and that it was only a matter of time before the storm would arrive. At the same time, in spite of the fact that socialism was soon declared victorious in the U.S.S.R., the mere encirclement of the Soviet Union by a cordon of neutral states no longer appeared a sufficient guaranty of safety. Security called for more substantial political alignments. The individual and often spontaneous understandings of previous years had to be replaced by something more fundamental and dependable. The problem of the balance of power became a cardinal issue. Its possibilities had to be outlined and the advantages of various combinations carefully estimated. All this called for time, as did also the mechanics of final formalities. To make full use of their bargaining power during this formative stage and to assure the fullest advantages in the end, the Soviets, not without good reason, considered international peace of paramount importance.

There is a difference also in the Soviet outlook on revolutionary world peace during this period as compared with previous years. It will be recalled that at the beginning of the third period of the Soviet struggle for peace, the Communist International was in its infancy. The Party membership in foreign countries was small. The very program of the Party was provisional.[192] The organization was weak and the friction within the Party unsettled. All this had considerably changed by 1933. The Third International has become a formidable world Communist Party. United in ultimate purpose, it has become larger in size, better experienced in discipline, more mature in outlook, and shrewder in tactics. The progress made thus far, however, did not blind Party leaders to the fact that the power of Soviet example alone was not enough to warrant action. Much still remains to be done before the organization of the liberal bourgeoisie into an independent revolutionary force opposed to the capitalist national-reformist bourgeoisie is advanced to the stage where the next revolutionary step could be taken. In the field of international relations this meant the consolidation of revolutionary forces. Rapprochement of communists with other labor parties was the first necessity. To iron out old differences for the common cause was the new order of the day. The rise of Hitler and the growing uneasiness in the capitalist world gave accelerated tempo to this consolidation.

The extent of this essential task made the Soviets realize that much as the communists had increased in strength, mere propagandist repudiation of capitalism and criticism of the passive attitude taken by non-communist revolutionary forces would lead nowhere.

Hence, it was now ruled that in order to utilize the growth of the working class to the utmost, communists must intervene actively in the present mass movements and raise this movement to the level of the cause pursued by the proletariat. To this end, increasing efforts were to be made for the restoration, political and military, of unity of labor, under the slogan of struggle against the capitalist onrush of Fascism which, to the communists, meant war. Practical as it had now learned to be, Moscow knew that until this unity was achieved, *i.e.*, until the Kremlin had complete control over all the factions of labor throughout the world, or at least throughout Europe, it would be folly to permit international peace to end. To jeopardize this peace meant to undermine the whole scheme of revolutionary tactics. The time had not yet come, and peace had to be safeguarded at all costs and by all means. The international tran-

[192] The final program was adopted on Sept. 1, 1928, at the Sixth World Congress of the Communist International.

quility of this period remained a mere instrumentality for achieving ultimate communist world peace. Revolutionary world peace itself did not change its substance. Nor could it change. Only its relationship to the Soviet pursuit of peace was altered. A glance through the revolutionary telescope of Marxian astronomers would reveal that in the Milky Way of human notions of peace only one star— communist world revolution—has changed its position. Another look would suffice to disclose that it has been thrust into meteoric motion and that its line of direction is toward the Earth. In terms of the international relations of the U.S.S.R., this means that communist world peace since 1933 has no longer been the goal "once removed" of the preceding period. Nor is the war between capitalism and communism any longer strictly a trench war.

Military preparations and concentration of troops in the noncommunist world were met with revolutionary preparations and concentration of proletarian reserves behind the communist lines. The problem reduced itself to a question of initiative. On the inverted triangular front of Democracy, Nazism, and Communism, the barbed wire of treaty arrangements was considered no serious obstacle. As in all warfare, when the basic preparations for an attack have been completed, only the patrol reconnaisance remains to be performed. On August 23, 1939, the communist patrol went into action. In no-man's-land Stalin met the Führer, and, in spite of considering "National-Socialism and racism to be the deadly enemies of all working people and of civilization itself," [193] withdrew from the field, magnanimously promising to remain a "neutral." The guns in Western Europe went off. The world was taken by surprise. It should not have been. The Soviets were merely continuing their peace-time revolutionary policy of peace, only by forcible means—war. On August 23, 1939, the communist policy of peace entered its fourth phase: attack.

[193] Litvinov's speech in the League of Nations, Sept. 28, 1936 (*League of Nations Official Journal*, Spec. Suppl., No. 155, p. 64).

CHAPTER VI

ADVENTUROUS AFTERMATH: AUGUST 23, 1939

ADVENTUROUS AFTERMATH: AUGUST 23, 1939

BLISSFUL SLUMBER

To the world at large, the German-Soviet Non-Aggression Pact of August 23, 1939, was a bewildering shock. To the foreign offices of other countries and to students of international affairs it was probably a genuine surprise. To Moscow, however, it was a certainly not unforeseen possibility.

Hitler's foreign policies may have appeared to the non-professional observer as a revenge for the humiliation of Versailles. Germany's psychological disillusion in its own democracy, in the doctrinary visions of Marxism, and in the evident weaknesses of the capitalist world may well have been overlooked. Due credit may not have been given to the fact that the immediate cause of Berlin's restlessness was to be sought first of all in Germany's economic deadlock. Amid the innumerable speculations in regard to the foreign policies of the Third Reich, the greatest significance was attached to Hitler's abstract notion of German aversion to two forces which to him appeared identical both in substance and extent —semitism and communism. The persecution of non-Aryans, which for some reason or other was limited to the Jewish race, and the suppression of communism which meant rigid regimentation of labor, were accepted as the main outward manifestations respectively of these two aversions.

On the other hand, Stalin's foreign policies might appear to an outsider as only the commendable and non-wavering insistence of the Kremlin upon the preservation of international peace at any cost whatsoever. The fundamental doctrinal difference between Marxism and capitalism, proletarian delight at the difficulties of the non-communist world, and the revolutionary determination of the Third International did not necessarily disturb the pleasant mirage created by the official assurances of Soviet statesmen and diplomats. Reports contradictory to the alleged Soviet state of affairs were frequently dismissed as biased derogation of communist achievements and as unpleasant shadows in the bright skies of political tranquility. Nevertheless, projected against these enigmatic yet cherished illusions, the general impression was that Stalin's love for peace was likewise saturated with communist aversion to two forces which to him appeared equally counter-revolutionary—national chauvinism and capitalism. The struggle for liberation of oppressed nationalities and the ruthless extermination of private wealth were the outstanding features of communism and those which had left the most lasting imprint upon the masses abroad.

Any attempt either to analyze the true meaning of Hitler's credo and to evaluate its real influence on the formulation of Germany's international demands, or to study the revolutionary substance of Marxism and to estimate its rôle in shaping the Soviets' international aspirations, was forced into the background by the summary superficial feeling that the Third Reich and the Soviet Union, in spite of their peace litanies, were respectively the world's bulwark against the Red peril and the core of the world front against Fascism.

This generalization was characteristic also of the judgment of those who devoted their time to the study of international affairs either professionally or otherwise. Here the conclusions were not only more analytical, bearing the evidence of familiarity with the available documentary proofs, but were often so convincing as to invite predictions as to the future. It is precisely because of this latter tendency that an explanation of the surprise caused by the Nazi-Soviet Pact of 1939 is needed here.

Indeed, in a maze of conflicting practical interests, it is not easy, even for those directly concerned, to chart a precise course of the policies to be followed, particularly if this has to be done under pressure of time, hampered by lack of confidence, and when the goal itself is none too clear. When permeated with theoretical abstractions, the confusion grows in direct proportion to the efforts to adjust the concrete needs to the dictates of the dogmas. Such a background in itself justifies a lack of uniformity in professional opinion to which individual sentiments and preferences contribute in no small degree.

Under the circumstances, therefore, it was only natural that the diplomatic turmoil in Europe which preceded the present war, should appear as a chaotic attempt of the Great Powers to counteract the decision of Hitler to break away from the limitations established at

Versailles. However, amid the various moves to that end, including freely uttered assurances of mutual help and understanding, concerted action at Geneva against actual resort to arms, and often none too scrupulously observed international promises—there were two sets of facts which left no doubt as to the general trend of events. In the field of concrete diplomacy, these were the consolidation of the totalitarian powers into the Rome-Berlin-Tokio Axis, on the one hand, and the determination of Great Britain, France and the U.S.S.R. to oppose their aggression by forming a united democratic bloc, on the other. In the domain of abstract feelings, these were the generally admitted reciprocal antagonisms between Democracy, National-Socialism, and Communism, and the no less commonly known "longing" of these three irreconcilable forces for peace.

The solution of this political problem seemed obvious: if peace efforts should fail, Hitler would have to wage his war against the formidable democratic coalition of London, Paris and Moscow. The Nazi-Soviet pact proved the erroneousness of this answer. The cause of the surprise is not difficult to trace: as in mathematics, a quantity multiplied by an unknown coefficient results in an unknown product, so in things Bolshevist, an assurance multiplied by an unknown intent is reduced to an enigma. Ironically enough, the non-communist hypothetical acceptance of Soviet intentions in this European problem as a known quantity, substantiates Lenin's saying that "there is no abstract truth, for the truth is always concrete." [1] It is precisely in overlooking the concrete facts that the calculations of the world as to Europe's future proved wrong. These concrete facts may be divided into two categories. To one belong the events which, in the pandemonium of war preparations, could readily be either unnoticed or miscalculated. To the other belong the gross misunderstanding of Marxism and of Soviet manipulations with its doctrines.

As to the facts of the first category, the Soviet entrance into the League of Nations was acclaimed as a change in the Kremlin's outlook on the non-communist world and as a genuine move to support the struggle against war. True as this was, the fact was overlooked that this was not a change in substance but in tactics, and the element of permanency was conditioned by the dictates of expediency. The same applies to the Soviet non-aggression pacts. In other words,

[1] Lenin, XXVI, 135.

in the enjoyment of finding a new ally, the western democracies were willing to disregard the fact that Soviet rapprochement was made under political and revolutionary duress.

Then, too, little attention was paid at the time to the fact that Soviet foreign policies always reflect domestic pursuits, from which they cannot be separated, since according to Lenin "there is no more erroneous nor more harmful idea than [that] of separation of foreign and domestic policies." [2] The victory of Bolshevist socialism is the paramount purpose pursued by the Soviets within the boundaries of the U.S.S.R. Hence, as an integral part of communist foreign relations, the vision of a similar victory in other countries must likewise dominate the Kremlin's dealings with the outside world, in spite of official denials. The interest which the Soviets took in Spain and the enthusiasm with which the formation of the Popular Front in France was received in the Soviet press prove that Soviet coöperation in the interests of peace was not limited to official treaties and activity at Geneva. It was also expressed in a fashion not alien to the international revolutionary pursuits of Moscow.

Furthermore, in an atmosphere saturated with fears and uncertainties, considerable leniency was shown to the liberties which the Soviets took in regard to their solemn declarations. Not that other countries are angelically pure in this respect. At the Eighteenth Congress of the All-Union Communist Party, on March 10, 1939, Stalin solemnly declared that one of the principles upon which the Soviet foreign policy rested was the proletarian support of nations that "have fallen victims of aggression and are fighting for their independence." On March 15, 1939, the German troops marched into Prague. Moscow's reaction was to do nothing. Stalin's words uttered only five days before evidently meant nothing, likewise. Speaking before the Union Council on August 31, 1939, Molotov said: "We have treaties of non-aggression with Poland and other countries whose semi-Fascist régimes are well known." [3] A few weeks later, Soviet Russia took half of Poland. Finally, it will be recalled that at the Seventeenth All-Union Party Congress, held in 1934, Stalin had said that in the Nazi-Soviet relations, the Kremlin was concerned not so much with the Hitler régime as with the struggle within the Reich between advocates of coöperation with

[2] Lenin, in *Leninskii Sbornik*, XXI, 66.
[3] *Izvestiia*, March 11, 1939, No. 57.

Soviet Russia and the opponents of that policy.[4] At the Eighteenth Congress he emphasized the lack of any real reason for war between Germany and the Soviets, and accused enemies of the communist régime of provoking a war between Berlin and Moscow.[5] Suggestive as this placidity toward the Third Reich was, the possibility of any coöperation between the two countries was considered out of the question by the rest of the world. Even such exchange of "courtesies" as the particular attention paid by Hitler to the Soviet Ambassador at the New Year's reception of 1939, and the Soviet's recall of Litvinov from abroad, did not alter the soothing belief in the good faith of the Kremlin. Moscow's desire for peace seemed to be an urge strong enough to keep the Soviet Union in the democratic camp.

In the atmosphere of almost fatalistic submission to the inevitability of war, this oversight is not incomprehensible. Even more understandable is the neglect to appraise Soviet foreign policies in the revolutionary light of the Marxian credo. While belated regrets seldom mend the harm done, had the aim of the Soviets been scrutinized more carefully and regarded more as a matter-of-fact problem, there would have been no doubt that the pact signed by Ribbentrop and Molotov on August 23, 1939, was only a logical step for the Soviets to take. An explanation of this statement will at the same time constitute a summary of the Soviet application in practice of the Marxian dogmas on war and peace.

ALIBIS AND MIRAGES

The indignation of many and the bewilderment of not a few caused by this *coup diplomatique* is summarized by the impression that since the signing of that treaty there is nothing left of the traditional Soviet policy. Outwardly good reasons for such an opinion are to be found in the change of the Soviet attitude toward the anti-Nazi powers, in the apparent conciliation between National-Socialist Germany and Communist Russia, and in the termination of the Soviet policy of non-aggression.

[4] *XVII S'ezd Vsesoiuznoi Kommunisticheskoi Partii* (b) 26 ianvaria–10 fevralia 1934g. *Stenograficheskii Otchet*, pp. 13–14. *Cf.* also Molotov's speech at the 2d session of the Central Executive Committee in 1936, when he said that development of economic relations with foreign countries, irrespective of their structure or program, is in conformity with the sound policy (Molotov, *Stat'i i rechi, 1935–1936*, p. 172).

[5] *Izvestiia*, March 11, 1939, No. 57.

It was only natural that when forced to explain their newly consummated understanding with Germany, Soviet statesmen took the
easiest way out: shifted the blame to someone else. The would-be
Soviet allies in the anti-Nazi camp were the logical victims. The League
of Nations, which not so long ago had been considered the last bulwark
against war, was now denounced as an outstanding instrument for
provoking war, and the sole purpose of Soviet membership therein
was now explained by the Kremlin's desire to reduce the danger of
war sponsored by Geneva.[6] The democratic virtues of Great Britain
and France earlier admitted by the Soviets lost their charm.[7] Statesmen in London and Paris were now branded as dictatorial conspira-
tors acting in bad faith. Stalin's distrust of the British is well known.
As long ago as 1927 he said: "The British bourgeoisie do not like to
fight with their own hands. They always preferred to wage war by
using others. Sometimes, they actually succeeded in finding fools
who were ready to pull chestnuts out of the fire for them."[8] For
obvious reasons, this view had never been mentioned again since
the rise of Hitler, but it was now resurrected and brought to the
forefront as one of the justifications of the change in the Soviet policy, and acclaimed as another proof of Stalin's genius. The Franco-
Soviet Treaty of Non-Aggression of 1935, enthusiastically glorified
not so long ago, was now described as an instrument which France
had signed as an insurance policy against her failure in negotiations
with Germany to attack the Soviets. The appeasement policy of
Chamberlain and Daladier which had culminated at Munich was
denounced as a malicious betrayal of the idea of collective security.
Consequently, it was now asserted that in their negotiations with the
Kremlin, the governments in London and Paris were engineering not
a peace front but a war front, and wanted to have the Soviet Union
to carry the burden, while England and France themselves could retire
to the policy of neutral profiteering. Concretely, to the Soviets this
meant that the former would-be allies wanted to provoke the Soviets
to a war with Germany, during which Nazism and communism, foes
equally distasteful to the Western European democracies, would
mutually wear themselves to a point of complete exhaustion and fall
prey to the democratic supremacy of Great Britain and France.

[6] *Izvestiia*, Dec. 17, 1939, No. 290. It must be noted that on Dec. 14, 1939, the League
Council expelled the U.S.S.R. from the League of Nations.

[7] *Supra*, pp. 187ff.

[8] Stalin, *Ob oppositsii*, p. 611.

Great Britain and France, which in March, 1939, were described by Stalin as "non-aggressor states" suffering from the aggression of Germany, had become, a few months later, according to Molotov, warmongers. Said he: "It is well known that during the last few months such conceptions as 'aggression' and 'aggressor' have been given new, concrete substance. . . . Now, if we speak of the great powers, Germany is a state longing for peace and quick termination of war, while England and France, that only yesterday were against oppression, are now for the continuation of war, and against peace." [9] Either sincerely convinced or merely pretending that these countries were afraid of placing themselves on an equal footing with the U.S.S.R., as this would result in strengthening the position of the Kremlin and the influence of communism, Soviet statesmen spared no effort in insisting that the main purpose of the rapprochement of London and Paris with the Kremlin was to use the Soviets merely as tools for their own interests.[10] Proudly crediting themselves with loyalty to Stalin's precept that Soviet policy should always be oriented toward the U.S.S.R. only, and that it was not the intention of the Kremlin to be provoked into conflicts by the "instigators of war who are accustomed to have someone else pull the chestnuts out of the fire for them," [11] the proletarian dictators let their obedient subjects know that the vital interests of the Soviets now dictated friendship with Germany, and that the Pact of 1939 was the way to safeguard these interests.

The illusion that the Soviets had abandoned their traditional policy of antagonism to Fascism was also created by the outwardly sudden change in the relationship between Berlin and Moscow. It is not the purpose of this study to analyze the motives which prompted National-Socialism to discard its hatred for the teachings of Marx. That the Kremlin permits no theoretical abstractions to stand in the way of the practical ends pursued by the Soviets, however, is a well-known fact. This was reiterated by Molotov shortly after the signing of the Pact, when he emphasized the fact that

[9] *Izvestiia*, March 11, 1939, No. 57, and Molotov, *O vneshnei politike Sovetskogo Soiuza*, p. 4.

[10] Molotov's speech, Aug. 31, 1939 (*Izvestiia*, Sept. 1, 1939, No. 202) and Lenin, "Sovetsko-Germanskiia otnosheniia," *Mir. Khoz. i Mir. Politika*, 1939, No. 10, p. 38. *Cf.* also the already mentioned speech of Stalin at the Eighteenth Congress of the All-Union Communist Party.

[11] Stalin, *Voprosy Leninizma* (11 ed.), p. 436, and *Izvestiia*, Sept. 1, 1939, No. 202; also an editorial in *ibid.*, Aug. 24, 1939, No. 196.

"ideological differences as well as differences in the political systems of the two countries cannot and must not prevent the establishment of friendly political relations between the two countries." [12] The actual purpose of the Soviet coup will be shown later. The official explanation is to be found in Molotov's commentary accompanying the Government's presentation of the treaty to the Supreme Council of the U.S.S.R. for ratification, on August 31, 1939. To quote:

> "It was only yesterday that the policy of the German Fascists was unfriendly toward the U.S.S.R. Yes, it was only yesterday that in the field of foreign relations we were enemies. Today, however, the situation has changed and we have ceased to be enemies."

His utterances that this treaty might be accepted as a "turning point in the history of Europe, and even not of Europe alone," and that it was "in the interests of the toiling masses of the Soviet Union" (even if he did not explain that these interests included also the revolutionary aims of the communists), did not alter the uniqueness of his explanation. It was both unprecedentedly simple and arrogantly challenging.

It is immaterial whether or not the perfection of international diplomacy consists in "transforming yesterday's enemies into good neighbors." The important point is the hypocrisy of the Soviet spokesman when he said that the peace thus established between the Third Reich and the country of the Soviets served to promote international peace.[13] This could be true only on the assumption that Moscow's plan was to postpone the war by making it impossible for Great Britain and France to back Poland, thus compelling Poland to surrender Danzig and the Corridor. In other words, this would have meant a repetition of Munich, with the difference that instead of London's surrender of Czechoslovakia to Hitler, here Moscow would have been handing over to him the city of Danzig and the Polish Corridor.

The last reason for the general impression that there is nothing left of the traditional Soviet aspirations for peace is the apparent termination of the Soviet policy of non-aggression. Whatever the accusations preferred by the U.S.S.R. against Great Britain and France, regardless of the Soviet claim that the Nazi-Soviet Pact brought peace to Eastern Europe, and in spite of the continued assur-

---

[12] *Izvestiia*, Sept. 1, 1939, No. 202; also an editorial in *ibid.*, Aug. 24, 1939, No. 196.
[13] *Ibid.*, Sept. 1, 1939, No. 202.

ances of the Kremlin that its intentions are peaceful, the facts speak to the contrary. The fourth partition of Poland, the virtual conquest of Estonia, Latvia, and Lithuania, and the war in Finland are the events in point.

On September 1, 1939 Hitler's divisions crossed the Polish frontier from the north, west, and south. Seventeen days later the "neutral" divisions of Stalin did the same thing from the east. Less than two weeks thereafter, the German and Russian armies met jubilantly in the heart of Poland. They were no longer the enemies of a quarter of a century ago but friends who came to share in the spoils of their conspiracy. On September 28, three days before Warsaw fell, Herr Ribbentrop and Comrade Molotov signed a Treaty of Friendship and Boundaries between the Third Reich and the U.S.S.R.[14] Poland, the "Quasimodo of Versailles," again ceased to exist and the territory of the Union of Soviet Socialist Republics "was increased by 196,000 square kilometers, and its population by 13,000 people." [15] After the down payment made on August 23, 1939, the balance of the total price of this gain, paid by the Soviets in the field, was ridiculously low. "The grand total of the losses which our Red Army suffered in Western White-Russia and the Western Ukraine," said Molotov, "comprise 737 killed and 1,782 wounded." [16]

The Kremlin's argument in support of the Soviet march into Poland was that Poland could no longer be considered an independent state, and that therefore Soviet neutrality did not apply here; that the move was forced upon the U.S.S.R. by considerations of safety; and, finally, that the Soviets could not leave "their abandoned brothers of Western Ukrainia and Western White-Russia to the caprices of fate." [17] If these assertions be accepted as sincere, not much can be said for Soviet ability to judge the facts. If they are intentional misrepresentation of the facts, they, obviously, have no validity. In either event, the Soviet argument is labored and superficial and, as such, carries no conviction.

---

[14] *Izvestiia*, Sept. 29, 1939, No. 226.

[15] Lemin, "Torzhestvo Stalinskoi Politiki Mira" (*Mir. Khoz. i Mir. Politika*, 1939, No. 11, p. 82).

[16] Report to the Supreme Council, Oct. 31, 1939 (*Izvestiia*, Nov. 1, 1939, No. 253).

[17] *Ibid*. The same idea was conveyed also in the Soviet Note to the Polish Ambassador in Moscow, Sept. 17, 1939 (*Mir. Khoz. i Mir. Politika*, 1939, No. 9, p. 15). Simultaneously with this note, the foreign ambassadors accredited to Moscow were informed that in regard to their respective countries the Soviet Union remained neutral (*ibid.*, p. 15).

Indeed, though the continued existence of the Polish Republic may be open to argument and there may be a question as to the applicability of Soviet neutrality to Poland, the aggressive nature of the Soviet participation in the dissection of Poland is quite apparent. It will be recalled that at the Eighteenth Congress of the All-Union Communist Party it was Stalin himself who, in denouncing the appeasement policy of Chamberlain and Daladier, said that a "policy of non-interference means the sponsoring of oppression and the unleashing of war." [18] Obviously, this was not meant as a reproach that Great Britain and France had not sent their armies to occupy and annex Czechoslovakia, but rather a suggestion that they should have come to its defense. Six months later, Moscow interpreted this dictum of Stalin in precisely the opposite way. Instead of putting into practice the precepts of Stalin, and going to Poland's assistance, the Soviets insisted that to interfere would mean to provoke world war, and, therefore, annexed half of Poland in the name of peace.

The arguments emphasizing the need to safeguard the integrity of the U.S.S.R. and the altruistic duty of the Kremlin to look out for the forsaken peoples living in the annexed portion of Poland are no more convincing. The hypocrisy of the proletarian statesmen in this connection is evident at once from the following facts: a large country though it was, and one with a large military establishment, Poland proved utterly unable to resist the German onrush. Certainly, the eastern provinces alone could have presented no danger to the Soviets, particularly after the defeats suffered by the Polish army during the German *Blitzkrieg*. And, the Red Army had been consistently glorified by the Soviet dictators as the greatest in the world—undefeatable, loyal, and brave! Nor is the argument convincing that the Soviets were protecting themselves against danger from Germany. They gladly accepted a common frontier with the Third Reich in spite of the fact that a buffer state, weak though it might be, would have been better protection.

Opinions may vary about Soviet annexation of Eastern Poland on the score of the duty of the Kremlin to look after the forsaken peoples living there: the apologists of the Soviet cause will accept without hesitation Molotov's report that the masses in eastern Poland welcomed their liberation and the new victory of the Soviets with "indescribable enthusiasm," and that nine-tenths of the population

[18] *Izvestiia*, Mar. 11, 1939, No. 57.

took part in their first opportunity to exercise "universal, direct and equal electoral rights," showing their eager anticipation of joining the U.S.S.R.[19] Those less enthusiastic about things Bolshevist will skeptically point out that the instructive experience of the peoples in the Baltic provinces in 1918–1919, when the Soviets invaded these countries with the same altruistic motives, was not calculated to enhance optimistic enthusiasm in the masses anywhere, let alone the peoples in Poland who, for two decades had been Soviet neighbors and had had opportunity to learn about the life in the proletarian fatherland at close range. Whatever the arguments to the contrary, the fact is that no time was lost by the Kremlin in incorporating the newly acquired lands into the U.S.S.R.,[20] and imposing upon them the régime of proletarian dictatorship, thus making the Soviet advance into Poland a double aggression: imperialistic from the standpoint of a Greater U.S.S.R. and revolutionary in the sense of Marxian world peace.

The Kremlin's penetration into the Baltic states was likewise aggressive. It will be recalled that the relationship between these states and the U.S.S.R. rested basically on the Treaties of Peace of 1920 which terminated the wars of these former Baltic provinces for their independence from the Soviets,[21] and on the Non-Aggression Pacts of 1926 and 1932.[22] What took place in these countries after the Soviet-Nazi Pact of 1939 is a matter of record: on September 28, 1939, the U.S.S.R. signed a Treaty of Mutual Assistance with Estonia. A similar treaty was signed with Latvia on October 5, 1939. Lithuania followed suit on October 10, 1939.[23] Purporting to assure mutual safety, these treaties provide that the Contracting Parties are to "render mutually any kind of assistance, including military, in case of direct attack or threat of attack by any of the Great European Powers," and are "not to enter into any agreements

[19] *Izvestiia*, Mar. 11, 1939, No. 57.

[20] Western White-Russia and Western Ukraine (Galicia) were incorporated in the White-Russian S.S.R. and the Ukrainian S.S.R., respectively, by the Decree of the Supreme Council on Nov. 1, 1939 (*Izvestiia*, Nov. 4, 1939, No. 256).

[21] *Supra*, pp. 84ff.

[22] *Supra*, pp. 120ff.

[23] *Izvestiia*, Sept. 29, 1939, No. 226; Oct. 6, 1939, No. 232; and Oct. 11, 1939, No. 236. Supplementary to the first two of these treaties were the Treaties of Commerce signed on the same respective dates, while the Treaty of Mutual Assistance with Lithuania provided also for the transfer of the much-disputed city of Vilna to Lithuania —a magnanimity on the part of the Soviets used by the Kremlin as proof of the communist good will.

or coalitions directed against one of the Contracting Parties." [24] In return for a promise to supply them with war materials, the Soviet Union was given the right to establish military, naval and air bases in Estonia, Latvia, and Lithuania [25]—an ominous prelude to the ultimate absorption of these states by their "protectors."

Indeed, it is questionable whether the establishment of the Red armed outposts in Estonia, Latvia, and Lithuania secured these countries the protection of their independence and their social order.[26] On the other hand, there is no doubt that through these treaties, "the Soviet Union has become a great naval power on the Baltic Sea" and "the strategic position of the U.S.S.R. has improved drastically." [27] Simultaneously with the arrival of the Soviet armed forces in these Baltic states, the residents of German extraction were recalled by Hitler to their "echt Vaterland," and had to leave their Estonian, Latvian, and Lithuanian homes, which their ancestors had occupied for six centuries. It is immaterial for the present purpose whether this abandonment of the Baltic provinces by Hitler, contrary as it was to his eastward *Drang für Lebensraum*,[28] was part of the bargain with Stalin, silently incorporated in the Soviet-Nazi Pact of 1939, or whether he was made the victim of shrewd *Realpolitik* on the part of Stalin. The importance of this new Soviet stand in the Baltic is that this championship of peace by the Kremlin was not a peaceful move but an act of sheer aggression. Estonia, Latvia and Lithuania realized the significance of the friendly proposals made to them by Stalin. They were also fully aware of the difference between their own strength and that of the U.S.S.R. The result was surrender— the least bitter bargain of the two ominously bad choices. Had they resisted, the Soviets would have insisted upon "safeguarding" peace, even if it had had to be done at the point of the sword. Evidence of this was later furnished by the Soviet attack on Finland, which resisted the "friendly" offerings of Moscow.

The Soviet war against Finland is the culminating evidence of the Kremlin's change from a policy of non-aggression to one of aggression. True, the U.S.S.R. did not consider itself at war. (Such

[24] Arts. I and IV, respectively, in treaties with Estonia and Latvia, and Arts. II and VI in the Treaty with Lithuania.

[25] Art. 2 and 3, respectively.

[26] Molotov's speech, Oct. 31, 1939 (*Izvestiia*, Nov. 1, 1939, No. 253).

[27] Lemin, *op. cit.* (*Mir. Khoz. i Mir. Politika,* 1939, No. 11, p. 82).

[28] *Supra*, p. 164.

was the substance of the Soviet reply to the invitation of the League of Nations to stop the war and discuss the Finnish-Soviet controversy at Geneva).[29] In fact, on December 2, 1939, the U.S.S.R. had signed a treaty with the "Democratic Republic of Finland," headed by Mr. Kuusinen, a resident of Moscow.[30] It is obvious, however, that this practice of dealing with governments [31] fictitiously established *ad hoc* could not change the nature of the bloody struggle along the Mannerheim Line. Nor was it effective in convincing the outside world that the "formidable onrush of the Red Army" was merely the Soviet reply to the "abominable provocation of the Finnish instigators of the war." [32]

Molotov admitted that the U.S.S.R. had strategic needs in Finland, but denounced the rumors that the Soviet Union had asked for the city of Viipuri and the northern shores of Lake Ladoga. He also denied that the Soviets had aspirations for the Aaland Islands and designs along the Swedish and Norwegian borders. He admitted, however, that Moscow wanted a mutual-assistance pact patterned after those concluded with the Baltic States. He also reiterated that for the sake of protecting Leningrad from attack by sea and by land, the Soviets wished to have the Finnish-Soviet boundary on the Karelian Isthmus moved northward for a "few tens of kilometers," and desired that the Hanko, Rybachii and Srednii peninsulas be leased to the Soviets as sites for Red naval bases. In exchange, the Soviets offered a considerable part of Soviet Karelia, the protection of Finnish integrity, and a promise of increase in trade.[33]

As to the proposed exchange of territories, it is of no importance whether Viipuri was or was not included in the three thousand nine hundred and seventy square kilometers of the Karelian Isthmus, to be exchanged for the seventy thousand square kilometers of Soviet Karelia.[34] The strategic importance of the bargain for the Soviets is revealed when it is recalled that in 1890, Bismarck did not hesitate to give Great Britain the vast expanse of Zanzibar in Eastern Africa in exchange for the tiny island of Heligoland in the North Sea.

In regard to the Soviet designs on the Aaland Islands and

[29] *Izvestiia*, Dec. 14, 1939, No. 287.

[30] Text in *Izvestiia*, Dec. 3, 1939, No. 279.

[31] *Cf. supra*, p. 100.

[32] Lemin, *op. cit.* (*Mir. Khoz. i Mir. Politika*, 1939, No. 11, p. 83).

[33] *Izvestiia.*

[34] Art. I of the treaty signed by Molotov and Kuusinen on Dec. 2, 1939 (*Izvestiia,* Dec. 3, 1939, No. 279).

northern Sweden and Norway, neither official assurances nor individual speculations have any weight.

As in the case of Estonia, Latvia and Lithuania, Soviet desire for peace and the protection of Finland took the form of imperialistic and revolutionary aggression, the only difference being that war was waged by the Soviets to fulfill this peaceful mission. There is no guaranty that this aggression will not be continued by the Kremlin in other parts of Europe.

As to the general belief that after August 23, 1939, there was nothing left of the traditional Soviet peace policy, it should be pointed out that it is still very much a part of the communist program and dictates the shape of present-day events. Whatever the apparent value of the grounds given for this belief, the fact is that Soviet policy has not deviated from its tradition. Only the outward manifestation has changed. Its substance—world revolution—is the same. It is for this reason that the Treaty of Non-Aggression with Germany was to the Soviets a not unforeseen occurrence.

Mars, Marx and Moscow

Indeed, since the rise of Hitler, to those familiar with the international politics of a quarter of a century ago, when nations were neither so desperate as to accept war as a "fatal destiny," nor so brazen as defiantly to insist that the prevention of war necessitates preparedness for it by the massing of troops in the zones of potential battlefields, there could be no mystery as to the ultimate end of the concentration of national efforts on things military. Yet, notwithstanding this, and in spite of the fact that after Versailles the war-torn nations formally opposed any kind of armed conflict, they continued to speed headlong toward another crisis which culminated in the present war, the outcome of which may readily exceed in suffering that which befell the world after the Sarajevo assassination in 1914. It may appear untimely at this hour to discuss the validity of the political, economic and legal arguments advanced to accept war as a normal historical phenomenon, or to estimate the value of the numerous concerted efforts of the nations to prevent bloodshed, including those made by the Soviets. From the standpoint of the revolutionary approach to the problems of war and peace, however, it is neither too late nor yet premature to call attention to one essential difference between 1914 and today, a difference which, on account of its subtlety, has evidently been utterly disregarded amid the pandemonium of unregimented emotions, yet which is precisely the reason why the rapprochement with Germany was not unforeseen by the Kremlin.

Twenty-five and some odd summers ago the world had plenty of external political divergencies. Yet at the same time it was a harmonious family of nations from the standpoint of its social-economic structure. In 1917, this system of "capitalist" states was broken up by the establishment in one of them of a régime based upon the Marxian conception of social order. The transformation of Imperial Russia into a union of communist states and the accompanying appearance of the "pacifist" yet ever revolutionary Third International, with its headquarters in Moscow, is the difference in point. In 1914, Emperor Nicholas II sincerely wanted international peace. In 1939, the longing of Dictator Stalin for such peace may well be questioned. In 1914, the dangers associated with war were limited to the alterations of the political boundaries of states. In 1939, the communist hope was that a new conflagration would result in undermining the stability of the entire social-economic composition of non-communist nations, precisely the order which the non-Soviet states are eager to protect.

In this connection, there is no point in entering into the well-known controversy anent the true nature of the relationship between the Government of the U.S.S.R. and the Third International. The Soviet Government, as said, has always emphatically denied any relationship between the two, in spite of the convenient and suggestive coincidence that its ranking officials are invariably found to be officials of the Comintern as well. It must be recalled, however, that no denial has ever come from the Kremlin that Lenin's interpretation of Marxian theories continues to serve as an infallible guide for Soviet policies. His postulates bearing upon war and the proletarian tactics during war have already been given and need not be repeated.[35] For a better understanding of the significance of the difference between 1914 and 1939, one additional little-known fact must be mentioned.

When the World War started, few realized its basic significance to Lenin. Yet as early as January, 1913, he had written to Maxim

[35] *Supra,* pp. 32ff.

Gorky: "A war between Austria and Russia would be a very useful thing for revolution (in all Eastern Europe), but there is not much chance that Franz Josef and Nikki [36] would give us this pleasure." [37] Later, during the War, when he said that it had opened an era of socialist revolutions, although he himself was not yet sure whether the revolution would take place during this War, after it, or during the one which would follow—the world laughed at his prophecy. The change which befell the Russian Empire and the post-war history of the world, as well as the present war—are all proof that he was doubly right: the predicted era was ushered in by the World War and this war of 1914–1918 was not the last.

Today Lenin is dead, but his heritage lives on, and his rejoicing over the events of 1914 is no longer difficult to understand. His widely acclaimed official theory of war, which has become the pride of every conscientious communist, that one must struggle against the very root of wars—capitalism—and that inasmuch as capitalism has not yet been exterminated, the struggle must be conducted not against wars in general, but against reactionary wars,[38] is misleading to non-communists. The fact is that the communist objection to reactionary wars applies only to wars involving the Soviets. Indicative of the usual opportunist policy of the communists, this little known *de facto* limitation of the communist objection to aggressive wars is an explanation and at the same time a vindication of the Soviet betrayal of the democracies of Western Europe.

It is true that, formally, the Soviet Government has always been the most extreme advocate of peace, and its coöperation with the League of Nations in matters of armed aggression may have increased its prestige as a champion of peace. As the Soviets deny any relationship between themselves and the Third International, Litvinov, in the expedition of his missions abroad, must formally have represented Stalin, the Dictator of the U.S.S.R., and not Stalin, an official of the Comintern. In other words, from the point of view of official diplomacy, the present war was not wanted by the Soviets. General opinion accepts this without question. The point, however, is that as a revolutionary expedient this "formally" unwanted war was wanted nevertheless. As a war waged outside of the U.S.S.R.

[36] Emperor Nicholas II of Russia.
[37] Lenin, XVI, 378.
[38] *Supra*, pp. 25ff.

it was wanted both in Moscow, the seat of the Third International, enjoying the hospitality of the Soviets, and in Moscow, the capital of the Soviet Union, warmly extending this hospitality.

Firm in its aims, and bound neither by solemn promises of peace nor by any international agreements, the Third International has no reason to object to wars in which the Soviets take no part, as it has nothing to lose. Quite the contrary; from a new conflict it anticipates great advances for its cause, irrespective of the formal results. Indeed, it matters little who is the victor. The point is that someone will be the loser. Then, too, it must be remembered that the privations which the masses—both military and non-combatant —suffer during war have always been and always will be a great stimulus to popular discontent, affording fertile ground for open resentment against those who caused the misery. Finally, one must bear in mind that although all this was true in regard to the World War, there is a significant difference between 1914 and today: while twenty-five years ago revolutionary ambitions were left to individual initiative, today they are directed by a formidable organization whose lieutenants are standing by the world over, waiting for orders. The argument that national pride will be a sufficient safeguard against the sentiments induced among the exhausted masses by revolutionary propaganda is unreal. By unleashing the hounds of war, the nations set in motion forces which place no value on national pride. In Russia the assassination of the Imperial family followed close upon patriotic manifestations. Today it may take an even shorter time to change the ancient salute with outstretched arm into the outstretched communist symbol of far-reaching class hatred.

The war was also wanted by the Soviet Union. Allegedly most "democratic" in form and substance, officially most persistent in its championship of peace, and certainly most uncompromising in its denouncement of dictatorial oppression of peoples abroad, Moscow had good reason to wish to see another European conflagration. Loyal to Stalin, the Kremlin remembered what a "useful thing" for revolution was the war between Austria and Russia in 1914 and what "pleasure" it gave Lenin. In 1939, Germany, Poland, Great Britain, France and the other countries of Western Europe were as much capitalist states as were Austria and Russia twenty-five years ago. The revolutionary *usefulness* of a conflict between them and communist *pleasure* in seeing it take place may be even greater today. In 1913, Lenin's desire for revolution was limited to Eastern Europe; today, there is no basis for judging exactly the immediate limits of the communists' revolutionary desires, now that Lenin's remote dream has become an actuality as to one-sixth of the globe.

Speaking at the Eighteenth All-Union Party Congress, Stalin criticized the "appeasement" policy and denounced non-interference as one of the best ways to provoke war. "In the policy of non-interference," said he, "is an obvious tendency and desire not to hinder the aggressors in their sinister deeds; not to prevent, for instance, Japan from becoming involved in war with China, or even better, with the Soviet Union; not to prevent, let us say, Germany from becoming drowned in European affairs and engage in war with the Soviet Union; [in other words, it tends] to let all the parties at war become stuck in the mire of war; to sponsor them quietly; and to give them the chance to weaken and exhaust each other, so that later, when they are sufficiently weakened, they [themselves] could come to the forefront with fresh forces and dictate—of course 'in the interests of peace'—their own conditions to the exhausted parties at war." [39]

The logical soundness of such a strategy requires no proof. Its practical advantages have been realized more than once. Hence, if there was any novelty in this revelation of Stalin, it was in the fact that he also was fully aware of the benefits afforded by such a strategy. The implication in his remarks that the Soviets intended to abstain from following such tactics is immaterial. The fact is that Stalin, realistic as always, could not fail to see that the U.S.S.R. was not excluded from resorting to precisely such a policy, particularly if revolutionary reasons were taken into consideration. Under the circumstances, as far as he was concerned, the problem of instigating a war was reduced to the matter of determining the proper time, and to finding the proper victims.

The details of what happened in Moscow in August, 1939, are not yet known. The facts recorded thus far are few. Nevertheless, they are ominous. It was evident that after the dissection of Czechoslovakia, Poland was next on Hitler's agenda of aggression. It was also apparent that Great Britain and France had reached the limit of their surrender to Hitler's demands, and that any further aggression of the Third Reich would be met with armed resistance

[39] *Izvestiia*, Mar. 11, 1939, No. 57.

by England and France. The effect which the presence of British and French military missions in Moscow may have had, and the advantage which the Soviets may have taken of this fact, remains unknown. But there is no doubt that in the minds of the Soviet dictators, the time was opportune, the foreign armies were ready, and only a little encouragement was needed. On August 23, 1939, the Soviet-Nazi Pact was signed. A few days later, peace came to an end. The Soviets had what they wanted: war in Western Europe and peace in the U.S.S.R.

Whatever the Soviet assertions to the contrary, this war has been thus far both "a useful thing" and a "pleasure." The annexation of half of Poland was a gratifying territorial gain and the Red military control imposed upon the Baltic states and Finland is definitely a great improvement from the standpoint of war strategy. Some may think that this expansion indicates Soviet reversion to the pre-revolutionary notions of Greater Russia. Others may believe that this was the Soviet way of manifesting revenge for having been utterly disregarded and forgotten during the Versailles reallotment of Central European territory. Others, again, may see sheer opportunism as the main factor of this aggrandizement.

To a revolutionary, however, the significance of the usefulness of the present war to the Soviets lies much deeper. The results of the German-Soviet Pact of 1939 thus far include virtual elimination of the belt of buffer states, and extension of the boundaries of the Red Empire to those of the Great Powers in Western Europe.[40] The present war must indeed be a pleasure to every communist, and to Stalin in particular. It not only affords Moscow another breathing spell— this time to consolidate its gains thus far in foreign lands—but promises even further revolutionary expansion, when this "imperialistic" war is transformed into civil wars in the various warring countries.[41] Stalin must find great satisfaction in this war for other reasons also. At the Sixth World Congress of the Communist International, it was stated that the purpose of the Soviet policy of peace was "to guard international revolution and to protect the constructive work of socialism, which revolutionizes the world by its very

[40] The question of non-communist independence of the Baltic States and Finland affords little optimism for these countries. Nor is the outlook of the Balkan States for their own future bright enough to blind them to the danger presented equally by the West and the East.

[41] Lenin, XIII, 79–80.

existence and growth." [42]   The Brest-Litovsk Treaty was signed in 1918 to give the Soviets an opportunity to launch this socialism, and the years which followed were years of building an exemplary communist society in the U.S.S.R.   In 1935, at the Seventh World Congress of the Communist Party, it was declared that the "victory of socialism in the U.S.S.R. has been achieved."   In the words of Manuilsky, "The possibility of building up socialism in a single country, brilliantly foreseen by Lenin and Stalin, has become a reality, palpable and tangible, for millions of peoples throughout the world."   According to him, this victory of socialism in the U.S.S.R. is of world-wide importance, as it is causing a profound change in the minds of the toilers of the whole world by its revolutionizing effect.   By "instilling into them confidence in their own strength and a conviction of the necessity and practical possibility of the overthrow of capitalism," this victory "has become a great political, economic and cultural force, which influences world policy. It has become the center of attraction and the rallying point for all peoples, countries, and even governments which are interested in the preservation of international peace.   It has become the stronghold of the toilers of all countries against the menace of war.   It has become a mighty weapon for consolidating the toilers of the whole earth against world reaction." [43]

In sharp contrast to this illusion are the facts.   True, considerable socialist progress has been made in Russia since 1917.   To say, however, that the example of the U.S.S.R. has filled the toiling masses elsewhere with exalted revolutionary enthusiasm is a misstatement.   The belief that the proletariat has become strong enough to influence world policies is also erroneous.   The Soviet Union had to find a way to relieve itself of its embarrassment on this account, and revolutionary action seemed the only remedy.   Concretely this meant that a situation had to be created where revolutions could be furthered, for under the circumstances only through revolutions abroad can Marxian logic and the policy of the Soviets be justified.

It is true that Lenin had opposed the theory of what he called "exporting" revolutions, when he said:

"Maybe some authors [of such theory] think that the interests of world revolution call for pushing it ahead, and that the best medium for

---

[42] *Kommunisticheskii Internatsional v. Dokumentakh, 1919–1932,* p. 810.

[43] *Seventh World Congress of the Communist International. Resolutions,* pp. 53–56.

this would be a war and not peace, as the latter may give the masses an impression of the 'legalization' of imperialism. Such a 'theory' would run diametrically contrary to Marxism, which has always denounced 'furthering' revolutions which develop in accordance with the growth of the class conflicts generating these revolutions. . . ." [44]

This argument can hardly stand analysis, however. Indeed, this objection of Lenin applied only to the furthering of revolutions at the expense of Russia's safety. He also said that while "the interests of international revolution require that the Soviets after having overthrown the bourgeoisie in a given country must *help* this revolution, the *form* of this assistance must be chosen according to their own resources and power." In the present conflict, the U.S.S.R., "neutral" as it officially is, seems to have no grounds to fear that its safety might be jeopardized. The revolutionary duty to help world revolution makes it mandatory for the Soviets to do more than to serve as a mere passive example. Freedom to choose the form which this concrete furtherance of revolution may assume, does not preclude war fought outside the U.S.S.R. It will be recalled, furthermore, that at the Sixth World Congress of the Communist International it was admitted that the Soviet policy of peace is an international policy "constituting the basis for taking advantage of the conflicts between capitalist states." [45] War—a conflict *par excellence*—may also be an excellent means for securing revolutionary world peace in the Marxian sense of the term. As such, a war may be viewed not only as desirable but as well-nigh obligatory, provided that the Soviet Union, as a state, is not involved in it. As to the present war, if the Soviets are to retain the glory of a true Marxian institution, they themselves not only must stay out of it (thus far—barring the Finnish campaign—they have succeeded admirably) but must promote it until it results in the mass opposition to the bloodshed and misery: revolution.

Words and Deeds

However misleading and void of morality the Soviet assurances of their desire for peace may have been, in view of such a revolutionary attitude toward the present war, they did not contradict Marxian logic. This fact is evidenced in the communist abstract

[44] Lenin, XXII, 300.
[45] *Kommunisticheskii International v Dokumentakh, 1919–1932*, p. 810.

notions of war and peace, in the concurrent interests of the Soviet Union and the Third International, in concrete Soviet diplomacy, and in the insistence of the Kremlin upon complete disarmament.

The Marxian notions of war and peace already have been analyzed.[46] Here it need only be recalled that the Soviet appeals for international peace did not envisage this peace as an end in itself, but served merely to make this peace a provisional instrumentality for furthering the Kremlin's march toward the communist revolutionary world peace in the World Union of Soviet Republics. When the time came that this "means"—international peace—no longer adequately fitted the circumstances, it had to be replaced— quite possibly temporarily only—by "other (namely, *forcible*) means": war.[47] To indulge in indignant denunciation of the Nazi-Soviet Pact of 1939 is of no avail, since Soviet dislike of non-communist Machiavellianism has given way to the view that it is a proper and perfectly normal revolutionary *modus operandi*. To the Soviets, this Pact and incitement to the present war were a practical manifestation of Marxian dialectics in the realm of international politics.

As to the ties between the Government of the U.S.S.R. and the Communist International, three simple facts need be recalled here: the Soviet Government is a proletarian authority exercising the will of the All-Union Communist Party; the latter is the dominating member of the Communist International; and the program of the Communist International envisages world revolution. It is useless to go beyond this interrelationship among the three and try to elucidate the methods by which the U.S.S.R. fulfills its proletarian revolutionary obligations on a world-wide scale. The issue is still controversial. All that can be said at present, therefore, is that sympathizers of the communist cause will insist that there is no relation whatsoever between the two, and that the aims of the Communist International have nothing to do with the Soviet attitude towards war and peace. Antagonists of the Soviets will claim that the Soviet Government is nothing but an agent of the Communist International, and that the international policies of the Soviets in regard to war and peace are to be explained precisely by the ties which bind together the U.S.S.R. and the Comintern.

[46] *Supra*, pp. 19ff.
[47] *Supra*, p. 27.

In the realm of concrete Soviet diplomacy, the whole issue of the Kremlin's military and non-aggression understandings with other countries may be summarized in a general evaluation of the foreign relations of the U.S.S.R. Prior to so doing, the communist attitude as to the possibility of such understandings between a country of proletarian dictatorship and non-communist bourgeois states must be pointed out. Foreseeing the necessity for Soviet coöperation with other countries in things military in the future, Lenin took this problem under consideration very soon after the establishment of the Soviet régime in Russia. Lenin's realism prompted an affirmative answer as to the possibility of such understandings. His revolutionary analysis, however, prescribed different considerations for different situations. Concretely, he took for his starting point the fact that from a revolutionary standpoint the non-communist states with which such understandings were possible were divided into two groups. To one belonged those states which are weak whether economically or as to the realization of their national aspirations. To the other belong the imperialist nations.

The coöperation of the Soviets with oppressed non-communist countries is not only possible but mandatory. At the Eighth Congress of the Soviets in 1920, Lenin pointed this out:

"For [our] politics the imperialist oppression of peoples who did not have the luck to be numbered among the victors, is of the greatest importance, because such an imperialistic world policy generates rapprochement, union and friendship of all suppressed peoples." [48]

It is true that in this he referred primarily to the situation as it prevailed at that time, and to the Soviet relations with Turkey and Germany in particular. It will be recalled that shortly after that Congress, the Soviet Union signed a Treaty of Friendship and Amity with Turkey and supported the former Ottoman Empire in its struggle against the dictates of the Allies. The Treaty of Rapallo and the other agreements with Germany which soon followed, witnessed the sympathetic attitude of the Soviets toward this bourgeois yet at the time nationally oppressed country.[49] From the revolutionary standpoint, the Soviets viewed Turkey as a country which at the time stood on the threshold of agrarian revolutions. Germany to them

[48] Lenin, XVII, 407.
[49] For list of treaties with these countries, cf. Taracouzio, op. cit., Appendix XXIV, pp. 462–464 and 476–477.

was a country already overtaken by democratic revolution and in a stage preparatory to the establishment of the proletarian régime. Irrespective of this difference in regard both to their class structure and to their revolutionary rôle, Turkey and Germany were nationally oppressed bourgeois countries, as far as Lenin was concerned, and as such received Soviet encouragement in the form of the aforementioned treaties. The Soviet Treaties of Friendship with Persia and Afghanistan [50] are other illustrations of this revolutionary magnanimity of the Kremlin.

Today, the system established at Versailles has disappeared. So also has the early post-war distress of Germany and Turkey. The Third Reich has become an imperialist power oppressing other peoples. Turkey has matured into a Republic by no means sympathetic to the ideas sponsored by her neighbor to the north, and has grown to a point where Ankara no longer hesitates to act accordingly. Yet, notwithstanding these changes, the basic idea of Lenin still remains in force, that a Soviet state has not only the right but is bound to have friendly agreements with nationally oppressed and economically exploited nations.

Soviet rapprochements with imperialist powers are likewise not only permissible but obligatory. There is a great difference, however, in the underlying principle. While a political alliance of the Soviets with oppressed peoples is a direct revolutionary union, understandings with imperialist powers are based on the idea of taking advantage of the discords between the capitalist powers themselves. As such, these understandings rate as indirect revolutionary tactics. Theoretical justification of this is found in Lenin's analysis of the uneven fluctuations in the economic and political development of capitalism. Concrete manifestation of communist flexibility in the field of international promises was set forth by him in his letter of August 20, 1918, to the American workers:

"When the vultures of German imperialism in February, 1918, led their armies against disarmed and demobilized Russia . . . I did not hesitate to enter into the well-known agreement with the French monarchists. French Captain Sadoul—in words a Bolshevik sympathizer, and in fact a loyal servant of French imperialism—introduced to me a certain French captain, named De Lubersac. 'I am a monarchist,' said De Lubersac, 'and my only aim is the defeat of Germany.'—'Cela va sans dire,' was my reply. This did

[50] Taracouzio, op. cit., pp. 472–473 and 450, respectively.

not prevent me from coming to an understanding with De Lubersac in regard to the services offered to us by French officers who were specialists on mine-warfare. . . . This was an instance of 'agreement' which must be approved by every conscientious worker, an agreement reached in the interest of socialism. We shook hands with the French monarchists knowing perfectly well that each of us would have willingly hanged the other 'partner.' Our interests for the time being coincided. [To stop the] advancing German plunderers, we, in the interests of the Russian and international socialist revolution, made use of the similarly plundering conflicting interests of other imperialists." [51]

He explained the apparent anomaly of his dealings with a political foe by saying that in so doing he was serving the interests of the workers of Russia as he was merely "fulfilling the most justified and imperative duty of the proletariat in any kind of war: maneuvering until the proletarian revolution should be ripe." In admitting this, Lenin was honest enough to add that "at no time would he hesitate one second to enter into a similar 'agreement' with the German imperialists, in case an attack of British and French troops on Russia should dictate such an act."

As one of Lenin's doctrines which guide Soviet diplomacy, this statement of his illustrates clearly that for the Soviets their compromises and alliances with non-communist states can be only provisional understandings by which they are bound to nothing. In other words, in the political strategy of the U.S.S.R. there is always the silent reservation that the expediency of revolutionary evaluation of the concrete facts which condition the provisional concurrence of interests, is of much greater importance than the sanctity of formal international promises. This was proved beyond a doubt at the time of the signing of the Pact with Germany in 1939, as was also the fact that the instructions of Lenin on proletarian diplomacy in general are by no means inept when applied to considerations of war and peace. According to Lenin such tactics "will further the cause of socialist revolution, hasten its approach, weaken the international bourgeoisie, [and] strengthen the position of working classes." [52]

Translated into terms of practical diplomacy, such tactics spell Machiavellianism. It would be unfair to single out the Soviets, however, as the only country resorting to such methods. Tradition cred-

[51] Lenin, XV, 377–378.
[52] *Ibid.*, p. 378.

its Sir Henry Wotton with defining an ambassador as "an honest man, sent to lie abroad for the good of his country." [53] In spite of the growing tendency of the non-totalitarian world to expedite the business of diplomatic bargaining by frankness, unfortunately some may still find good reason to accept the expression "lie" in its usual sense connoting dishonesty, rather than in its old sense signifying mere residence. That the diplomacy of National-Socialism was stripped of honesty by Hitler long before the present war commenced, is admitted by many. As to the Soviets, no one can deny that their pacts of non-aggression and other military understandings were nothing but a repetition of Lenin's own overtures with De Lubersac, only on a much wider scale. In the light of the aforesaid, the Soviets' rejoicing over the war and their past insistence on disarmament are likewise consistent with Marxian logic.

PARADOX OF TWO KREMLINS: DISARMAMENT

The Soviet disarmament proposals, presented originally by Litvinov at the Fourth Session of the Preparatory Commission of the League on November 30, 1927,[54] are well known. The Soviet program was both simple and revolutionary. It called for complete disarmament, which was to be realized by (1) the disbandment of all armed land, air and naval forces, (2) the destruction of all arms, warships, military airships, fortresses and factories for military production, (3) the abolition of compulsory military service, (4) the suppression of appropriations for war purposes, (5) the abolition of military and naval administrative branches of Government. Prohibition of military propaganda and instruction were to accompany these measures. As a substitute for national armed forces, the Soviets proposed that a police service be maintained, the personnel of which "shall be employed by voluntary contracts of service, shall be authorized in the territory of each of the contracting states for the purpose of customs and revenue, police supervision, internal police and the protection of State private property." [55]

While this proposal was being scrutinized by the various Governments, the Soviets prepared a yet more elaborate, draft convention

---

[53] Walton, *Life of Wotton*, p. 155 (cited in Wilson, *op. cit.*, 9th ed., p. 167).

[54] For the Soviet declarations, *cf. The Soviet Union and Peace*, pp. 112–244.

[55] *League Documents*, C.667, M.225, 1927, IX.

of sixty-three articles, which Litvinov presented at the next Session, that of March 15, 1928. It is a matter of record that, identical though these proposals were in aim with the object of Article VIII of the League Covenant, they came to nothing. They not only ran counter to the general principles of the triple formula of disarmament, security and arbitration, which underlay the previous disarmament work of the League of Nations, but encountered the well-grounded suspicion of the non-communist powers as to the sincerity of the Soviets.

When it became obvious that these original Soviet proposals were not acceptable, Litvinov, evidently prepared for failure, drew from his pocket another draft convention, this time proposing "partial and gradual disarmament." According to this new proposal, the world was to be divided into four groups according to the size of their existing armaments. Proportionally, the strongest powers were to reduce their armaments by fifty per cent, those somewhat less strong, by thirty-three per cent, and the weakest by twenty-five per cent. The fourth category consisted, according to the Soviet formula, of states already disarmed as a result of the Peace Treaties. This new draft provided also for the abolition of air warfare, poison gas, various types of guns, etc. Finally, it suggested the institution of a permanent international control commission composed of representatives of the legislature and workers' organizations.[56]

Needless to say, this attempt of Litvinov met with failure, too, as did later efforts of the Soviets in this direction.[57] To the non-communist peace-makers at Geneva, peace without strong standing armies appeared an anachronism. To the Soviets, this attitude was another illustration of the difficulties encountered by Marxism in the course of its extension throughout the world. Their tactics had failed. While practical considerations were obviously the main reasons for the rejection by the non-communist powers of the Soviet disarmament proposals, their objections are also well justified from the standpoint of the inconsistency between the Soviet policy of disarmament and Marx's view of the rôle of the army whether in the wars which he prophesied or as a constituent element of the communist state, on the one hand, and the basic Soviet policy of military preparation for coming wars, on the other.

[56] *League Documents,* C.165, M.50, 1928, IX.
[57] *Cf. supra,* pp. 116ff.

As to the communist prophecy of wars, it was Marx who said that as long as there were class distinctions and class antagonism, the last word of social science would be war, or death. [58] Lenin restated this as follows:

"The suppressed class which does not intend to learn how to use arms, or to have them, fully deserves to be treated as slaves. We cannot indeed forget, without becoming bourgeois pacifists or opportunists, that we live in class society and that there is no other way of escaping from it but through class struggle and the overthrow of the ruling class. . . . Our watchword must be armament of the proletariat for the purpose of defeating, suppressing, and disarming the bourgeoisie." [59]

Trotzky's testimony as to the use of arms must certainly be admitted as true, in spite of his disagreement with Stalin: "The revolutionary class which has won power by force of arms, must, and, indeed, will, suppress with arms any attempt to take its power away from it. Where it finds an enemy army, there it will counter with an army of its own." [60] The thesis advanced at the Sixth World Congress of the Communist International reiterates Lenin's pessimism in regard to international peace:

"In our era of imperialistic wars and world revolution, revolutionary civil wars of the proletarian dictatorship against the bourgeoisie, wars of the proletariat against bourgeois states and capitalism, as well as national-revolutionary wars of oppressed peoples against imperialism are unavoidable, as Lenin has shown." [61]

The assertions of Soviet protagonists that these statements have no bearing upon the problem of disarmament are not convincing, for Lenin's theory of arousing the proletariat does not imply rule by an armed mob, but suggests proletarian control by a proletarian standing army. This is substantiated by the Marxian theory of the state and of the Dictatorship of the Proletariat. Indeed, the essential characteristics of the state, according to Engels, are quite different from the generally accepted features of unity, permanency, etc. According to Lenin the state is "a machine of suppression of one class by another." [62] As an organization having for its purpose "forcibly keeping the exploited classes in a condition of suppres-

[58] Marx, *Literaturnoe nasledstro*, III, p. 250.
[59] Lenin, XIII, 452.
[60] Trotzky, *Osnovnye voprosy revoliutsii*, p. 69.
[61] *Kommunisticheskii Internatsional v Dokumentakh, 1919–1932*, p. 797.
[62] Lenin, *Gosudarstvo i Revoliutsiia*, p. 179.

sion," [63] the state, to a communist, must embody public power of coercion, "because a self-organized army of the people has become impossible since the division of society into classes." [64] In other words, the fact that, "the state presupposes a public power of coercion separate from the aggregate body of its members," [65] means that the army is essentially an instrument of the ruling class. As such, to a Marxist it is one of the main characteristics of the state. This was recognized by Marx who said that, among the tools of suppression, the government of a state needed the army.[66] In perfect conformity with this is the communist view of the army as expressed in the Program of the Soviet Communist Party:

"In an era of disintegration of imperialism . . . it is impossible to retain the old army, or to build a new one on the so-called national or super-class basis. The Red Army, an instrument in the hands of the proletarian dictatorship, must necessarily be openly a class army, *i.e.*, it must be composed exclusively of the proletariat and the peasantry, which is closely related therewith. Only with the abolitions of classes will the class army become a universal socialist militia." [67]

Aside from being an essential component of the communist state, armed forces are important to a Marxist also from the standpoint of his interpretation of the Dictatorship of the Proletariat. The historical materialism expounded by Marx resolves itself into a class-struggle conception of history, leading to a class-domination theory of the state. By this theory the state itself is reduced to a social status where the ruling class subordinates to its authority the destinies of the other classes composing the human element of the state. This applies in equal degree to capitalist states and to the communist form of a social body politic. The only difference between this communist concept of the state and the non-communist formula is that, in the capitalist world, non-proletarian domination within a state presupposes the permanent co-existence of separate sovereign political entities, whereas proletarian class domination in a state envisages the absorption of these entities in a single classless and

[63] Engels, *Socialism, Utopian and Scientific*, p. 208.
[64] Engels, *Origin of the Family*, p. 206.
[65] Engels, *op. cit.*, p. 142.
[66] Marx, *Class Struggle in France*, p. 158.
[67] Ovlovskii i Malkis, *Sovetskoe Voenno-Ugolovnoe Pravo*, p. 32. *Cf.*, however, Engels, who in his letter to Marx of Jan. 16, 1868, said that even a communist society can afford a system of socialist militia only to a certain extent. (*K. Marx i F. Engels*, XXIV, 14.)

state-less commonwealth. Thus the outward form of the class domination in non-communist states may vary from autocratic rule to liberal self-government, but in a Marxian state, the proletarian class domination admits of no variety; there is only the Dictatorship of the Proletariat.

Being only a transition form of the state on the road to self-annihilation, this Dictatorship, as formulated by Stalin, is "a new kind of Dictatorship against the bourgeoisie." [68] According to Lenin,

"The scientific conception of a dictatorship is nothing but an authority unrestricted by laws and absolutely unlimited by any rules, resting directly upon violence." [69]

With such theoretical sanction, the Dictatorship of the Proletariat must, in practice, express itself in "the fiercest and most merciless war of the new class against its more powerful enemy—the bourgeoisie," [70] and the state authority which it represents must rest "directly upon violence." This violence, according to Lenin, "in the twentieth century, as throughout civilization in general, rests not merely upon fists and clubs, but upon the *army*." [71]

That the army is also important to the Soviets in their dealings with the outside world has been evidenced in such a variety of ways and so repeatedly that it is impossible to go into details here. A few random illustrations may be taken from the innumerable Soviet records. Typical of the consideration given their armed forces by the Soviets is one of the resolutions passed by the Third Congress of Soviets on March 16, 1925, which delegated to the Government of the U.S.S.R. "the proper care of the Red Army and Air forces, always keeping in mind that the fundamental guaranty against an attack upon the State of Workers lies in the actual strength of the armed forces of the Union." [72] Akin to this in spirit, and illustrative of the tenor of the regularly repeated statements of Voroshilov, are the Orders of the Day for the Red Forces of May 1, 1932:

"The policy of peace does not mean the renunciation of defense. On the contrary, the country of Soviets shall permit no one to invade its territory, to devastate socialist undertakings, and to trample the fields of the

---

[68] Stalin, *Leninism*, p. 115.
[69] Lenin, VII, pt. I, p. 121.
[70] *Ibid., Levyi Kommunism*, p. 6.
[71] *Ibid.*, XIII, 450 (italics by author).
[72] Art. 4.

collectivized farms. The guarantee of this is the constantly growing strength of the Red Army. . . . Comrades, improve your military and political training and solidify the revolutionary iron discipline of the Red Army. With still greater insistence, try to master the technique of actual fighting! Let us adhere closer to the general policy of the [Communist] Party and to its Central Committee." [73]

One of the slogans advanced on the occasion of the fifteenth anniversary of the Bolshevist revolution was "Long live the bulwark of the Soviet peace policy—the Red Army of the Soviet Union." [74] In 1920, at the Ninth Congress of the Russian Communist Party, Lenin said that the Soviet efforts at peace "must be accompanied by the utmost military preparedness and absolute prevention of disarming the Red Army." [75] Thirteen years later, speaking on December 29, 1933, at the Fourth Session of the Central Executive Committee of the U.S.S.R., *i.e.*, shortly after the signing of the above-mentioned treaties of non-aggression, Litvinov echoed the dictum of Lenin: "While agreeing to coöperate with other states," said he, "we cannot forget that we are dealing with capitalist states. . . . Being thus forced to be on the defensive, we shall continue as of old and even more to strengthen and improve the basis of our safety—our Red Army, Red Fleet and Red Air Force." [76] At the Sixth World Congress of the Communist Party the need for strengthening the Red Army was implied in a statement to the effect that "the Bolshevist Revolution has proved to every honest communist the absolute necessity of the armament of the proletariat," and that the duty of the proletariat in the Soviet Union, "as that of a warrior for socialism consists of making all the necessary preparations for such a war,—political, economic, and military; of strengthening the Red Army, the power weapon of the proletariat, and of training the working masses at large in military science. Imperialistic states show an outrageous conflict between their policy of colossal armaments and their 'olive-oiled' [*sic*] phrases concerning peace. The Soviet State knows no such conflict between preparation for defense in revolutionary wars and the consistency of its peace policy." [77] At the Eighteenth All-Union Party Congress, on

[73] *Izvestiia,* May 1, 1932.
[74] *Ibid.,* Nov. 7, 1932.
[75] Lenin, XXV, 102.
[76] *Izvestiia,* Dec. 30, 1933.
[77] Cl. 60 and 32 (*Kommunisticheskii Internatsional v Dokumentakh, 1919–1932,* pp. 825, and 811, respectively).

March 13, 1939, Voroshilov pointed out with much emphasis the Soviet need for a strong army:

"One thing is clear to us . . ., namely, that at all times and under any conditions we must have a strong and undefeatable Workers and Peasants Red Army and a similarly strong and undefeatable Red Fleet. We know now, more than ever before, that only true military preparedness of the Red Army and of the Red Fleet can serve as a dependable guaranty against war adventures directed against the Soviets, and that only in this way, that is, by still further strengthening our military power, can we protect ourselves against dirty Fascist attempts to . . . violate the territorial integrity of the Soviet State." [78]

As a counterpart to such a general policy toward the army, the Soviet administration of the Red armed forces is only further proof of the importance attached thereto by the Kremlin. It must suffice here to point out that the reinstitution of the rank of officers which had been abolished in December, 1917, and the introduction of numerous revolutionary medals and decorations, now so lavishly bestowed upon the Red warriors even in time of peace, were not only a well calculated effort of the Soviets to lure into their army the citizenry of the U.S.S.R. but also an attempt to standardize the outward *esprit* of the armed forces in a fashion patterned after armies abroad. The infusion of the rank and file with revolutionary doctrinism and the subjection of the Red armed forces to strict disciplinary regulations contributed greatly to the transformation of the originally disorganized Red Guard into a formidable Soviet force so organized as to make it easy for those in power to impose upon "millions of men a *single* will." [79] Finally, the progress made by the Soviets in the mechanical, technical and economic phases of the military preparation of the U.S.S.R. and the tactical reorganization of the army on the basis of a standing All-Union army, instead of territorial arrangement, as it has been until recently, are by no means wasted efforts.[80] They all serve to prove that to the emancipated proletariat the strengthening of its own army is a primary concern.[81]

Opinion may differ as to the real source of authority in the Soviet

[78] *Izvestiia*, Mar. 15, 1939.

[79] Lenin, XVIII, 276.

[80] *Cf.* Voroshilov's report to the XVIII All-Union Congress (*Izvestiia*, Mar. 15, 1939).

[81] K. Marx i F. Engels, VIII, 461.

Union. The foes of communism may insist that it is the Third International. The Kremlin vigorously denounces any formal relationship with it. Opinion may also differ as to the actual reason for Soviet ambition to have a strong army. Some may say that the encirclement of the U.S.S.R. by the capitalist world is the true reason. Others may think that it would be utterly unnatural for a state, irrespective of its form, to exist without an army. There is no ground for diversity of opinion, however, when the problem is analyzed from a revolutionary standpoint.

An essential component of a proletarian state pursuing revolutionary ends, the Red Army is an essential part of the U.S.S.R., for it is a revolutionary force in more than one way. Functionally, its revolutionary rôle is three-fold. Its first duty is to safeguard the exercise of the revolutionary authority of the Dictatorship of the Proletariat. Its second task is to protect the integrity of the proletarian fatherland in the event of war. Its third purpose, according to Stalin, is to "solidify the dictatorship of the proletariat in one country and to be made use of as a starting point for the overthrow of imperialism in all countries." [82]

In other words, the Red Army is a revolutionary force not only in regard to the geographical boundaries of the U.S.S.R. It is a revolutionary force from the standpoint of world revolution, as well as a means of solidifying revolutionary expansion beyond the confines of the Soviet Union and as an international proletarian organization. The former has been proved by the record of Soviet fliers and tanks in Spain, by the Soviet march into Poland, by the establishment of Red naval and air bases in the Baltic States, and by the war with Finland. That the Red Army is an international organization calls for no elaborate proof. As a communist force it must be international in spirit. As an army "composed of the most conscientious and organized elements of the working masses," [83] it cannot but be international in purpose, witness the slogans advanced on the tenth anniversary of the Soviet régime: "The Red Army is the armed force of the World Revolution! . . . conscientious workers of the whole world consider the Red Army as an army of their own and as a fighting unit of World Revolution! The Red Army is the van-

[82] Stalin, *Ob osnovakh Leninizma*, p. 47. *Cf.* also the Soviet decree of Feb. 23, 1918, in which it was said that the Red Army "shall serve as support for the forthcoming revolutions in Europe." (Cited in *Entsiklopediia Gosudarstva i Prava*, I, 191.

[83] *Sobr. Uzak. i Rasp. R.S.F.S.R., 1918*, par. 245.

guard of the World Revolution!" [84] Stalin's remark may be quoted as conclusive:

"The [Communist] Party is proud of the fact that the Red Army has succeeded . . . in becoming the greatest revolutionary fighting force, to the dismay of the enemies of workers and to the joy of all oppressed and enslaved [peoples]!" [85]

Projected against all this, the Soviet overtures at Geneva in regard to disarmament appear naïvely insincere, to say the least. True, disarmament appears to be an ideal of socialism. The fact is, however, that this ideal can be reached only in a socialist classless and stateless world where there will no longer be either need or possibility of war. Furthermore, this ideal socialist community is not expected to materialize by a process of peaceful evolution. For a Marxist, the communist commonwealth of mankind can become a reality only after a period of the dictatorial authority of the proletariat. The meaning of this dictatorship has already been pointed out. It has likewise been said that this dictatorship is based on the violent suppression of non-proletarian elements by force. And, it will be recalled that to a communist this force is represented by the army.

It is only too obvious that the force of an army depends upon its arms and equipment, and that the Soviet army is no exception to this. Consequently, when the term "disarmament" is applied to the Soviet conception of a communist state and its revolutionary rôle, the contradiction becomes self-evident. Indeed, disarmament involves an act by which the Red Army would be robbed of the essential source of its revolutionary force. With the disappearance of the latter, the concept of the dictatorship *per se* is reduced to nil. This, in turn, connotes the premature disappearance of the communist state. Obviously, when proposing complete disarmament at Geneva, the Soviets were hardly suggesting a suicidal act. The truth of the matter was that while in terms of communist tactics "the replacement of the slogan 'armament of the proletariat' by that of 'disarmament' could serve at the time only as a revolutionary slogan," [86] in the light of Soviet revolutionary expediency, Litvinov's

[84] A. Kadishev, *Chto dolzhen znat' molodoi krasnoarmeets*, pp. 30 and 36.

[85] Stalin, *O trekh osobennostiakh Krasnoi Armii*, p. 3.

[86] Cl. 60 of the thesis advanced in 1928 at the Sixth World Congress of the Communist International (*Kommunisticheskii Internatsional v Dokumentakh, 1919–1932*, p. 825).

program of disarmament was another illustration of the Kremlin's deceit in its international bargaining. As such, the Soviet policy of championing world disarmament, though outwardly inconsistent with the revolutionary need of an army, was not in discord with the Marxian credo that the end justifies the means.

Aside from all this, the fact that the Soviet-Nazi Pact of 1939 was not an unforeseen possibility for the Soviets, and that the present war is not in conflict with the communist aims of the proletarian dictators of the U.S.S.R., is substantiated also by the communist admission of the revolutionary purpose of both peace and war. Thus, one of the resolutions adopted at the Sixth World Congress of the Communist International read:

"The international policy of the Union of Socialist Soviet Republics, corresponding both to the interests of the proletariat in power in the Union of Socialist Soviet Republics and to the interest of the international proletariat, and uniting most intimately every ally of the proletariat in the [idea of] proletarian dictatorship, and, finally, constituting the basis for taking advantage of the conflicts between capitalistic states,—is *a policy of peace.* Its purpose is to guard international revolution and to protect the constructive work of socialism, which revolutionizes the world by its very existence and growth; it consists in the maximum postponement of the armed conflict with imperialism. . . . The peace policy of a proletarian state in no way signifies that the Soviets have come to terms with capitalism, as is claimed by social-democrats and their Trotzkyist followers for the purpose of discrediting the Soviets in the eyes of the international proletariat. This [policy of peace] is Lenin's policy of the Dictatorship of the Proletariat. It is merely another—in this situation a more advantageous—form of the struggle against capitalism, which has been consistently followed by the U.S.S.R. since the October Revolution." [87]

As to war, in the words of Lenin, it "in itself does not change the direction in which the policies were developing before the war; it only accelerates this development." [88]

By superimposing this conception of war upon the communist version of the Soviet peace policy, one can readily produce an alibi for the Soviet rapprochement with Germany. Indeed, on the one hand the Soviet peace must be a revolutionary peace: it envisages the protection of the proletarian interests both within and outside the U.S.S.R., invites taking advantage of conflicts between the capitalist states, and affords continuance of the proletarian struggle

[87] *Kommunisticheskii Internatsional v Dokumentakh, 1919–1932,* pp. 810–811.
[88] Lenin, XIX, 52.

against capitalism. On the other hand, the war which ensued and which at the time of this writing is still in progress, did not terminate the Soviet policy of peace. Nor has the present war changed the direction of the Soviet peace policy, for in the situation which prevailed in the fall of 1939, it was merely considered a "more advantageous form" of the struggle against capitalism. As a different form of the struggle for revolutionary world peace, war replaced the Soviet policy of international peace which had to be discarded as no longer fitting the circumstances.

Soviet "Neutrality"

A few words must be said about the Soviet attitude toward so-called neutrality, as the prospect of remaining neutral in the anticipated major armed conflict in the capitalist camp was one of the important aspects of the Soviet policy of peace and war. As a legal concept, neutrality has been interpreted in a variety of ways. At one extreme, it has been referred to as "the situation which exists between states which take no part in the war and the belligerents"; [89] at the other extreme, it has been considered a mandatory limitation of the sovereign rights of a state not participating in war to adopt, during the course of a war, new measures or to alter measures which it has previously adopted, "for the purpose of better safeguarding its rights and interests as a neutral or better fulfilling its duties as a neutral." [90]

As a practical issue, neutrality has suffered no less numerous distortions. Hugo Grotius suggested that neutral states should conclude Treaties of Neutrality with the parties at war.[91] Machiavelli denounced neutrality altogether, for to him outright participation in a war was not only more honest but more profitable as well.[92] His-

---

[89] *The Three Friends,* 166 U. S. 1, 52.

[90] Quoted from Art. 13 of the draft convention prepared by the Harvard Research in International Law (*A.J.I.L.,* XXXIII (1939), p. 316). For the controversy which arose among the American scholars on the issue, *cf.* Eagleton, "The Duty of Impartiality on the Part of a Neutral" (*ibid.,* XXXIV (1940), pp. 99–104).

[91] "It would be very commodious . . . if such a League could be made with both parties engaged in war" (*De jure Belli ac Pacis,* III, C.XVII, iii; from English translation by William Evarts, London, MDCLXXII).

[92] ". . . If two of your potent neighbors be at war, they are either of such condition that you are to be afraid of the victor or not; in either of which cases it will be always for your benefit to discover yourself freely, and make a fair war. For in the first case, if you do not declare, you shall be a prey to him who overcomes, and it will

tory shows that Grotius's vision of neutrality has been practiced but in the form of pre-war treaty understandings based on anticipation of coming events which has not always proved correct. Machiavelli's notion of the dishonesty and ultimate unprofitableness of neutrality has given way to considerations of the advantages of peace based on the material returns to be derived from neutral profiteering. Due to modern progress, neutrality is today no longer essentially straightforward voluntary *de jure* abstention from a war. It has become indirect compulsory *de facto* participation by means other than arms.[93] To the Soviets, today's regrettable disregard for the rules of international law, lack of belief in the pledged word, and the not less unfortunate subjection of international relations to calculations dictated either by fear or by desire of aggression, have rendered treaties of neutrality—essentially an element of peace—potent stimulants to war. To quote Litvinov:

"A particular characteristic of neutrality in the contemporary imperialist system is the fact that neutrality is subjected to the ends pursued by the aggression. As a rule, a treaty of neutrality is nothing but one of the elements in the preparation for war, one of the elements in making an aggression 'harmless.' "[94]

Although this denunciation of the modern world was directed against capitalist countries, it would be prejudice to say that this does not also apply to the Soviets. The Soviets argue that their treaties of neutrality and non-aggression are different, being directed as they are specifically against aggressive wars. Moreover, their provisions make no distinction between war and intervention, but refer to any form of action by arms, and neutrality clauses contained therein are made to supplement a general denunciation of aggression. These contentions are not convincing, however, witness the German-Soviet Pact of 1939 which unleashed the present war.

---

be a pleasure and satisfaction to him that is conquered to see you his fellow-sufferer; nor will anybody either defend you or receive you, and the reason is because the conqueror will never understand them to be his friends who would not assist him in his distress; and he that is worsted will not receive you because you neglected to share his fortune with your arms in your hands. . . . And those princes who are ill-advised to avoid some present danger by following the neutral way are most commonly ruined." (Machiavelli, *The Prince*, XXI.)

[93] *Cf.* President Roosevelt's speech of Oct. 5, 1937: ". . . There is a solidarity and interdependence about the modern world, both technically and morally, which makes it impossible for any nation completely to isolate itself from the economic and political upheavals in the rest of the world. . . ." (N. Y. *Times*, Oct. 6, 1937.)

[94] Litvinov, *Vneshniaia Politika S.S.S.R.*, p. 136.

That the Soviets did not attach much value even to their own treaty obligations is proved by their treaty with Poland. Here the Soviets, in pledging neutrality in case of aggression by a third power, defined aggression very broadly as "any acts of violence . . . even if such acts are committed without a declaration of war and avoid all warlike manifestations as far as possible." [95] How the Kremlin interpreted neutrality as to Poland, when the latter was made the victim of Hitler's aggression in 1939, is too well known to need further comment.

Nor is there much doubt as to Soviet appreciation of the fact that their neutral profiteering is not limited to economic benefits alone. A convincing proof of this is to be found in the absorption of Eastern Poland by the U.S.S.R. Then, too, the military penetration of the Soviets into the Baltic countries was by no means a purely economic move on the part of the Kremlin, nor was the Soviet war against Finland an aggression undertaken solely for economic purposes. The fact is that the Soviets also find in neutrality a convenient opportunity to expand their communist domain.

Conveniently unhampered by other nations preoccupied with war, the Soviets are at liberty to give a very flexible interpretation to neutrality. The degree of their adherence to its principles is not controlled by the rules of international law, but depends upon the dictates of Marxian expediency. To establish the limits of the Soviet discretion in the application of these dictates is an impossible task. It will be recalled that the Soviet Union has not subscribed to any definite rules on neutrality, a fact extremely convenient from the standpoint of permitting the Soviets always to "appeal to the conception of war, the duty of proletarian coöperation, and the general social and political situation as the decisive factors in shaping its attitude." [96] Under the circumstances, all that can be said now is that the vigilant "neutrality" of the communist realm during a major conflict in the capitalist world is neither inconsistent with the Soviet peace policy of the past nor contradictory to the Kremlin's outlook for the revolutionary world peace of the future.

The possibility of such an agreement as the Soviet-Nazi Pact of 1939 was not unforeseen by the Kremlin, and the present war was a

[95] Art. 1 of the Treaty of Non-Aggression with Poland of July 25, 1932 (*Sborn. Deistv. Dogov.*, VII, 1933, p. 13).

[96] Taracouzio, *op. cit.*, p. 339.

not unwelcome turmoil. A summary reproach to the Soviets is hardly justified, however. Indeed, unethical and distasteful as was the sudden abandonment by the Soviets of their peace collaboration with the Allies, the change was not actually inconsistent with the aims pursued by the communists. Nor was it contradictory to the means prescribed by Marx and Lenin for achieving these aims. Indeed, while to the non-communists, every post-war peace is anticipated to result in a static social *status quo,* to the communists this peace in the capitalist world is not destined to be permanent. In the past the Soviets have enjoyed the growing friction in the capitalist camp under the blessings of peace. Today, listening to the thunder of war, they rejoice over a more violent form of this friction. Tomorrow they may again prefer peace, to celebrate the next stage of the same friction—proletarian revolutions abroad. As long as the forces in control of the international revolutionary movement survive and as long as the principles of Marxism are not given up by these forces, international peace and wars among capitalist countries are of equal significance to the communists and always subject to the dictates of revolutionary expediency. So it has been thus far, and so it will be in the future.

CONCLUSION

THE WAR OF WORLDS

THE WAR OF WORLDS

IDEOLOGIES IN ARMS

To conclude this study, the communist attitude toward the present war in Western Europe and the Soviet stand therein must be pointed out. In revolutionary parlance, this war is being waged by capitalist powers entertaining no communist illusions and professing no interest in the liberation of oppressed colonial peoples. As such, it is to Marxists an imperialist war, *par excellence*. From the standpoint of the rôle played in it by the Soviets, however, this war is merely the inaugural imperialist phase of a struggle to which the Soviets have become a party, and which is to communists not only an imperialist war but a revolutionary war in which the Soviets are struggling for self-preservation and the communists for world domination. A brief analysis of the present turmoil will make this clearer.

In the war raging in Western Europe at the time of this writing, the U.S.S.R. is officially neutral, as are the other countries still untouched by the war. This does not mean, however, that it plays no part in it. That legal concepts of neutrality are no longer applied in practice and that the Soviets as well as other neutrals are actually assisting the warring nations in one way or another is a minor issue. The important fact is that the Soviet Union, like the rest of the world, has actually entered a war which is being waged on a much larger scale than the physical struggle in Western Europe. True, in Great Britain and France this struggle may rightly be called a war against Germany. In the Third Reich it may well be fought as a war against France and England. The Soviets, for their part, may maintain with no less justification that this war is nothing but a logical phase in the conflict which, from the communist standpoint, was bound to engulf the capitalist world.

It would be erroneous, however, to localize the present war geographically, that is, to limit it to states in Western Europe, and to restrict it to an armed conflict within the capitalist world only. The present war between Germany and the Allies is no longer an isolated issue, but the initial stage of a totalitarian war among three mutually antagonistic social forces, each of which has its own plans for the international organization of human society. The Soviets represent one of these forces at war. The other two are represented by the Allies and by the Totalitarian States of non-communist variety. If it be borne in mind that of the latter, only the Third Reich entertains world-wide aspirations, and if it be observed that of the powers united in the Berlin-Rome-Tokio axis, Germany appears to be the strongest, it becomes clear that this war of the three régimes for world supremacy is in reality an uncompromising struggle between Democracy, National-Socialism, and Communism. The fact that the war between the Allies and the Third Reich is merely an integral part of a triangular contest of modern ideologies renders the present formal neutrality of the U.S.S.R. mere tactical revolutionary abstention from actual armed participation in the struggle. That this abstention is provisional is suggested by the incompatibility of the non-Totalitarian, National-Socialist, and Communist philosophies. Indeed, their fundamental notions regarding man's spiritual aspirations, their ideas of the relationship between man and the state, and their conceptions of war and peace, do not suggest that a compromise is capable of settling the controversy without resort to arms, or invite the hope that this struggle will be of short duration.

In the World War of 1914–1918, the democratic credo "In God we trust," which consoled those who fought that war to end wars, the Germanic, "Gott mit uns," inscribed on the buckles of military belts and on the front plates of spiked helmets, and the Russian triple formula, "For Faith, Tsar, and Country," were indeed significant. They were not only emblematic of the fact that God was the common God of all the Christian warring armies, but were also characteristic of the universality of man's spiritual vision of Deity. Today, this is no longer true.

Of the three rival forces now at war, only Democracy has preserved the notion of Christian universalism. There is no longer any basis for a claim that the present war is fought in the name of God. On the contrary, an inquisitive mind may justly ponder upon the mutual effect of the Christian principle of brotherly love and unselfishness, on the one hand, and the natural right of self-preservation, on the other, as applied to international relations. Christian teachings no longer seem applicable to all conditions. In connection with the changes which befell spiritual notions in Germany and Russia, it must be remembered that today's Christian paradox is a paradox of application and not one of the principle itself, which continues to envisage the universality of God.

True, the changes which the establishment of the Third Reich wrought in Germany included a change in the Christian fundamentals of faith. Yet it would be erroneous to say that Christianity is categorically denounced by National-Socialism. Indeed, the Nazi program drafted by Hitler specifically proclaims the adherence of National-Socialism to positive religion: "We demand liberty," said he, "for all religious confessions in the State in so far as they do not in any way endanger its existence or do not offend the moral sentiment and the customs of the Germanic race. The Party, as such represents the standpoint of Positive Christianity without binding itself confessionally to a particular faith." [1] To admit, however, that Christianity in the Third Reich retains its character of universality would be incorrect. Rather a hazardous attempt has been made to racialize Christianity so as to make it fit into the Nazi *Weltanschauung*.

In order to be successful, such an undertaking must overcome numerous flagrant contradictions between this *Weltanschauung* and Christianity. Thus, while National-Socialism rests on the racial superiority of the Germanic race in general, and on antagonism toward the Jew in particular—that is to say, on the principle of inequality—Christianity prescribes equality and teaches that "there is neither Greek nor Jew." [2] Then, too, National-Socialism glorifies honor and struggle, and places them, together with heroism and war, at the head of the list of human values, whereas Christianity calls for love and peace. Finally, according to Hitler, Christianity should be confined to the purely spiritual domain of man, and denied the right of influencing his material life. To a non-Nazi Christian, religion is a force which shows its beneficial effect precisely in regulating man's temporal behavior.

In comparison with Hitler's rather non-committal tolerance of divergencies between the various Christian confessions in dogma and cult, the critical attitude within the Party toward Christianity

[1] Article 24.
[2] *Col*. III, 11.

is striking. Thus, Rosenberg does not hesitate to emphasize the non-Aryan elements of Christianity, and, in an attempt to preserve its Germanic purity does not fail to call attention to the fundamental differences between the requirements of Christian tolerance and of Germanic supremacy.[3] The theory of Bergmann is more uncompromising. Viewing Christianity as a religion of egotism resting upon the individual's fear of the last judgment, he declares it ill-befitting Germans, who believe in self-sacrifice in the name of the race, and calls for a return to the faith of the German mystics of the thirteenth century.[4] Hauer made an even more arrogant attempt to prove the incompatibility of Christianity and Germanism. To him, the Christian worship of God takes the form of pagan reverence for the chosen race. God is revealed in the blood of man. Since perfection remains the outstanding characteristic of Deity, and whereas, according to National-Socialism, the German race is not only the most perfect of all races, but is destined to establish among men conditions in which the Christian principles of love and good-will can be made truly workable, there should be little surprise that Hauer declares the German *Volk* to be the most suitable abode for God, and *Grossdeutschland* heaven on earth.[5]

It is a matter of individual preference whether or not to regard these doctrines as anti-Christian. In Hitler's Germany, the aim of National-Socialism is to bring about a super-confessional "Church," where all Germans can worship the German God.

The stand taken by the communist rulers of the Soviet Union on the spiritual aspirations of man are simple and firm. Whatever the constitutional and administrative semblance of Soviet tolerance for the Church,[6] to the communists, God is merely an expression of oppression, and religion is "opium." Uncompromisingly materialistic, the Soviets want "no interference from God or gods in any way or manner,"[7] and prefer to have human well-being based upon Marxian principles of temporal economic equality and freedom rather than upon the Christian ideals of love and moral restriction.

Whereas the first World War was primarily a struggle of arms,

[3] Rosenberg, Alfred, *Der Mythus des XX. Jahrhunderts* (IV ed., Münich, 1932).

[4] Bergmann, Ernst, *Die 25 Thesen der Deutschreligion* (Breslau, 1934).

[5] *Deutsche Gottschau* (Stuttgart, 1934).

[6] *Cf.* Gidulianov, *Otdelenie tserkvi ot gosudarstva v S.S.S.R.* (3rd ed., Moscow, 1928).

[7] Krassikov, *Na tserkovnom fronte*, p. 41.

the present conflict is also a war of three spiritual concepts: the democratic universalism of Christianity, the racial limitation of the Germanic Deity, and the atheism of Marxism.

As to the mutual relations of the individual and the state, there was considerable difference in the personal rights of the various peoples engaged in the war twenty-five years ago. Various, also, were the constitutional provisions which regulated the relationship between these individual's rights and the warring states to which they belonged. Yet there was unity in regard to the fundamental status of man and the basic purpose of the state. Indeed, irrespective of color, race, or creed, man's pursuit of individual happiness was his inalienable right, and irrespective of form, composition, or government, the state was the ultimate expression of man's instinct for communal aggregation. The interrelation between the two resulted in man becoming the source, and the state the protector, of the culture growing out of this relationship. The present war no longer evidences this unity.

Of the three forces now in conflict, only the democracies retain the Christian notions of man's sovereign right to the pursuit of happiness and of the state as an end in itself. To suit the respective philosophies of National-Socialism and Communism, these concepts have been given new meanings in the Third Reich and the Soviet Union respectively.

To Hitler, the creative genius resides not in the individual, but in the blood. The primordial elements generating culture are to be sought not in the democratic interfunctionalism between the individual and the state, but in the composite entity of the race. This primacy of race over other criteria divides the relationship between man and state into two distinct functions: man's sovereign right to pursue individual happiness is subordinated to his duty to labor for the collective happiness of the race, while the state itself is made the curator and protector of the creative race, so that a community of living beings of the same physical and spiritual essence can be preserved in its purity. In contrast to the democratic notions of the individual and the state, to Hitler, man, as a mere component unit of the race, is an entity forced to delegate his sovereignty to the race and to the leader, and the Third Reich, as a *Führerstaat*, is a state founded upon the principle of authority bestowed upon the leader not from below but from above.

The Marxian theory regarding the status of the individual in the community and the communist view of the state differ as much from both the democratic and the National-Socialist idea as these two from each other. The difference between Communism and the non-totalitarian order of things is similar to the difference between National-Socialism and Democracy in the sense that, like the former, Communism denies to man his sovereign democratic right to pursue his individual happiness, and severs the democratic functional relationship between man and state. Although resembling National-Socialism in this respect, Marxism has a fundamentally different conception of human society. To Hitler, the basis of society is the race; to a Marxist, it is the class. Accordingly, while to a Nazi, the individual is absorbed in the race, for whose well-being man sacrifices his individual happiness, to a Communist, it is the class which absorbs the individual and commands him to abandon his own well-being for the sake of the class to which he belongs. The intrinsic difference between the Marxian concept of the state and that of National-Socialism is that for the latter, the state is a governing authority of a single leader superposed upon the race and necessary for the preservation of the latter's purity, while, for a Marxist, it is the communal authority of a class superimposed upon society and necessary for the regulation of economic class conflicts. The external difference is likewise significant: the Third Reich is a unified state and, as such, implies abandonment of the conception of the state as a federation of autonomous units. The Union of Socialist Soviet Republics is a state resting upon the principle of national self-determination, and, as such, envisages precisely a federation of such states. It must be pointed out in addition that while National-Socialism envisages the state as a positive factor leading to a permanent domination of the chosen race, the state for a Marxist is a negative phenomenon, destined to wither away with the ultimate disappearance of classes.

The spiritual and secular irreconcilability of these three social forces now contesting for domination, are also reflected in their mutual disagreement in regard to war and peace.

However great the variety of opinion as to the nature and purpose of war,[8] it must be admitted that war today can no longer be viewed as an armed conflict taking place at geographically limited

[8] *Supra,* pp. 19ff.

"fronts," and limited by legal restrictions as to the methods of warfare. Nor is its aim a victory limited in extent or time. The totalitarian war of today involves countries in their entirety, both population and land, allows complete freedom in choosing the means, and has for its purpose the total and permanent destruction of the foe. These common features of modern war are applicable to the three-cornered war of Non-Totalitarian, National-Socialist and Marxian ideologies, but their effect is quite different in each of these rival camps.

War for each of these philosophies involves all the people and all the land. Yet, in the Non-Totalitarian camp it affects man as a sovereign individual and involves land as a geographical entity, the symbol of national unity. For a National-Socialist war is a social phenomenon involving man as an exponent of race, and may extend beyond the state, wherever species of this race are to be found. To a Marxist, war is a struggle of classes enveloping the whole world, for humanity and classes are inseparable.

There is also a difference between the three antagonists in regard to methods of warfare. Today, in the physical conduct of war not only the rules pertaining to the legality or illegality of the methods, but the most basic principles of humanitarianism are no longer held binding. The Soviets proved this during their war with Finland. The Allies and Germany are daily furnishing new evidences of it at the time of this writing. Then, too, it is obvious that resort to "fifth column" activities is no longer considered an immoral means of aiding victory. In their struggle against capitalism, the Soviets have been resorting to this principle ever since November, 1917. The Third Reich proved its effectiveness in Austria, Czechoslovakia, and Norway. There is no good reason to think that the Allies are blind to the possibilities afforded by this auxiliary weapon. If there is a difference between the three political forces now at war from the standpoint of the subversive methods resorted to, it is to be sought not in the principle itself but in the degree of organized preparedness for such novel warfare.

In this respect the democracies are the weakest of the three. Whether it is because of their unfortunate tradition of relying on isolated defense measures in each separate emergency, or is due to the fact that in a crisis the workings of democracy become cumbersome, transforming its peace-time strength into war-time weakness, the fact is that democracies are not organized as a united social force on a world-wide scale. This results not only in the absence of concerted ambition, and of the policy of enforcing democratic régimes upon countries in which no basic individual liberties exist, but also in a dangerous lack of coördination in times of common crisis, when the enjoyment of liberty is endangered in the already existing democracies themselves. Hence, whatever the scope of Allied subversive activity in Germany and the U.S.S.R., the assumption is not unwarranted that these efforts do not represent a strongly united action of sovereign democracies internationally organized for the destruction of National-Socialism and Communism, but are merely the localized and traditionally provisional measures of self-defense.

Since the very notion of the supremacy of a single race excludes the coördination of several independent entities, which is theoretically feasible for democracies, National-Socialism is not internationally organized either. The difference here, however, is that while in the Non-Totalitarian camp this organized unity is needed and lack of it is a definite disadvantage, for National-Socialism it is superfluous, and the lack of it is an advantage, for a single will is not subject to the danger of being divided into factions likely to cause indecision. Compared with non-totalitarian dormancy and lack of coördination, National-Socialism affords a much better concentration of organization both in regard to unity of purpose and uniformity of action.

Communism is in a still more advantageous position. Its international organization as well as its ultimate aim are well known. Rigorously controlled from Moscow by the Third International, it has vanguards organized in every country—its local Communist Parties.

Not only are the methods of warfare not uniform, but the purpose of the struggle differs in this war of worlds. Granting that this purpose is the total and permanent destruction of the foe alike for Democracy, National-Socialism, and Marxism, the difference here is not subjective but objective, not in the act of destruction itself, but in the object to be destroyed. If the equality of men both before God and in the exercise of their natural rights is the basis of the non-totalitarian social philosophy, then democracies must be fighting not a physical foe but an abstract principle. In the Third Reich this foe is the National-Socialist claim to racial supremacy, denying the natural privileges of non-Germanic peoples; in the U.S.S.R., it is economic equality, to be achieved at the price of relinquishment of the innate human right to individual happiness and freedom to decide upon the communal structure. In fighting these, the non-totalitarian states are at war not with Germany and the Germans or with Russia and the Russians in the physical sense of the term: their aim is primarily the destruction of the régimes which are trying forcibly to deny man his inalienable rights.

The enemy which Hitler is fighting to destroy is not essentially an abstract notion. As the supremacy and purity of the Germanic race are the ultimate aims of National-Socialism, it is the physical man that becomes the focal point in the issue. As a concrete entity and the representative of a definite type of blood, to Hitler, man has but two choices: either to enjoy his racial superiority, or to submit himself to the domination of another strain. In the latter case, the surrender may take place either freely or under pressure. The degree of force used will depend upon the capacity to resist of those to be conquered. Since, however, resistance in itself suggests lack of finality of the surrender, in a totalitarian war the primary aim of National-Socialism is the physical destruction of those whose permanent surrender to the racial supremacy of the Germans is considered improbable.

The foe of the communists, on the other hand, is both abstract and physical. Visionary, yet materialistic, communists fight and intend to destroy not only the idea of capitalism and exploitation, but capitalists and exploiters themselves. Universal and cosmopolitan, communism lays no restrictions upon the place and makes no distinction as to the race. Convinced, like National-Socialists, of their own righteousness, and determined, like Hitler, to stand fast by its own principles, the Third International, like the Third Reich, reserves for itself liberty of choosing the methods, and claims the privilege of being patient as to the time.

In the field of formal international relations, these divergencies in regard to war engender other mutual disagreements among these three forces, for instance a difference in outlook upon the interrelation of war and foreign policy. Cynical though it is, Clausewitz's theory that war is a continuation of peace policies by different means [9] is equally true for Democracy, National-Socialism and

[9] *Supra,* p. 27.

Communism. The difference lies not in the degree to which this truism is accepted by the various states, but in the emphasis upon the factors which characterize war as an international phenomenon. The primacy of peace in the international relations of the non-totalitarian states suggests that for them war is the result of diplomatic failure. In the Third Reich, the primacy of race renders mandatory the expansion of Germanic domination beyond the geographical boundaries of Germany, and gives war, as an aggressive instrumentality for the effectuation of this expansion, predominance, over the evolutionary methods of peace. This means that in National-Socialism, international policy is made subservient to war, and war is considered to be the purpose and not the result of diplomatic endeavors. The effect upon war of the Marxian primacy of class struggle has already been analyzed: it is both the result and the purpose of communist revolutionary diplomacy. In other words, for democracies war is a painful necessary evil. To Hitler it is an uncompromising racial duty. To the Soviets an arbitrary revolutionary facility.

Given such a diversity of mutually incompatible characteristic features, Non-Totalitarianism, National-Socialism, and Communism must also differ from each other in regard to the peace which they envisage, whether it be international peace connoting a condition of tranquility among the states, or world peace, signifying a warless status of mankind as a congregation of human beings.

To believers in the democratic order of things, these two aspects of peace coincide, as they are nothing but two reciprocating elements of a single social phenomenon. As a result of the free consent of separate individuals to form a community of equals, and of the voluntary consent of the sovereign states, thus formed, to peaceful co-existence, international peace from a non-totalitarian standpoint is at the same time world peace. To the non-totalitarian world, resting on universal Christian leniency in the spiritual field, acquiescing in the recognition of the individual's natural rights, subscribing to a voluntary contractual bond between man and the state, and believing in common in the negation of war, world peace is *Pax gentium*—a political arrangement regulated by a benevolent compromise among the elements constituting the community of men and the family of nations.

To National-Socialism, international peace and world peace are likewise synonymous. Yet the forces which bring about the fusion of these two concepts are quite different from those upon which the peace of the democracies rests. To Hitler, peace is not the result of the free consent either of men or of states to peaceful co-existence, but is a condition established and maintained by force of arms. While the non-totalitarian concept of peace today is reminiscent of the ancient Greek efforts during the third and second centuries before Christ, the peace of National-Socialism is a modern version of the tranquility imposed upon the world by the legions of ancient Rome. To the National-Socialist world, resting upon an intolerant preference for a Germanic God, sanctioning the absorption of individual rights in the collective will of race, denying the creative essence of the contractual bond between man and the state, and refusing to accept war as a destructive phenomenon, the ultimate world peace is *Pax germanica*—a blood relationship regulated by the forcible submission of the non-Germanic elements of the community of men and the family of non-Germanic races to the unilateral, uncompromising and autocratic will of the chosen race.

To Marxism, international peace and world peace are not identical. As has been said, to a communist international peace cannot be an end in itself, but is merely a means to an end, while world peace is an end in itself—a materialistic nirvana in which man will live in a community of the human species utterly oblivious to such notions as economic classes, sovereign states, international wars, and international peace. To the Marxian world, resting on an objectively impartial denial of Deity, no longer worried either by the sovereignty of the individual or by his absorption in race or class, relieved of modern concerns over the relationship between man and the state, and having removed war both from the concrete features of life and from the abstract notions of the mind, world peace is *Pax communa*—a communal twilight in perpetual motion and regulated neither from within by benevolent compromise among the different social strata now composing human society, nor from without by the forcible control of one of these factions over the others.

Résumé

It has been said that the war between these three ideologies brooks no compromise. There is indeed nothing in common between the non-totalitarian universality of the Christian God, the National Socialist racialization of the Germanic *Gott*, and the Marxian denial of any Deity whatsoever. Then, too, there is nothing in common between the democratic unity between man and state, the National-Socialist subservience of the relationship between the two to racial functionalism, and the Marxian negation of the problem altogether. There is nothing in common, furthermore, between the democratic acceptance of war as a regretted necessary evil resultant of diplomatic failures, the Nazi elevation of war to a noble duty purporting to guide diplomacy, and the Marxian predominance of the revolutionary criteria over war as an international phenomenon. Finally, there is nothing in common between the democratic regulation of the ultimate world peace by benevolent compromise, the National-Socialist maintenance of this peace by violence, and the Marxian negation thereof as a practical problem.

There is no good ground for thinking that the present war in Western Europe will settle the issue. Pessimism on this score results not only from the above-mentioned divergencies between the non-totalitarian, National-Socialist, and Marxian ideals. It is founded, also, on the features which they have in common. True, of these, the well-being of man has been practiced by Christianity for centuries, was recognized by Marx about one hundred years ago, and was promised by Hitler shortly before he came to power in Germany. This abstract agreement has little practical effect, however, as an aid to compromise or to shortening the conflict, due to the difference in the application of this principle in the Democracies, in the Third Reich, and in the Soviet Union. The other "common" features are antagonistic *per se*.

Indeed, all three contenders believe in the righteousness of their respective causes. Each is convinced of its final victory and none is willing to relinquish the struggle or to surrender. All three are cognizant of the fact that uniformity is the only possible basis of world peace; not one would admit that the disappearance of one of the others would suffice. All three know that two must die, but none will consent to be one of the two. Each one wishes to be the sole survivor and all are aware that if the result is to be final, the struggle will be long and merciless.

Under the circumstances, the Soviets can harldy visualize the present war in Western Europe as the last one. Peace will come again. So will wars. In this historical process the duration and scope of peace may differ, and the time and place of wars may change. As a historical process in itself, however, this succession of peace and war will recur as of old, unavoidable until mankind regulates its life on principles common to all.

The ideals which have guided Democracy in its pursuit of human happiness in the past and which will control its international relations in the future, are known. The National-Socialist outlook on war and peace remains to be clarified both by the originators of Nazism and by the students thereof.

As to Communism, the present study has been an attempt to emphasize the fundamental differences in the concept of war and peace held by the non-communist democracies and the Soviet Union. While to the former, international peace is an end in itself, to the communists it is merely a means serving a much more imposing purpose. As such a means, the Soviet international peace may appear to the non-communist layman as the destructive equivalent of the non-Marxian conception of war. On the other hand, to the communist, it is merely a phenomenon elevating war to a constructive revolutionary concept. Sanctioned by the Third International and executed by the proletarian Union of Soviet Socialist Republics, the omnipotent conclave and the formidable vanguard of world revolution, respectively, the Soviet war and peace policies are nothing but a testimony of the Kremlin's loyal adherence to the Marxian program of revolutionary world peace and to the meticulous maneuvering prescribed by Lenin for the effectuation of this program. In other words, in this study an attempt has been made to show that to the Soviets, international war and peace are not two diametrically opposed and mutually exclusive phenomena, but two equally important means, supplementing each other in the communists' advance toward their final revolutionary goal. It has been pointed out, furthermore, that in this Marxian fusion of war and peace, the Kremlin's choice in any given instance will depend upon its estimate of the revolutionary situation, revolutionary expediency, and revolutionary opportunism. Then, too, it has been shown that to communists revolutionary expediency is of much greater importance than the sanctity of formal international promises, which to them are only provisional understandings by which they are bound to nothing. Finally, it has been pointed out that the communist conception of war and peace subjects them to no restrictions either of time or place. In the past, disappointment in Soviet assurances was experienced by some; at present, new disillusions may be in preparation by the Kremlin for others; for the future, however, there is no reason why the revolutionary war and peace policy of the U.S.S.R. should be a mystery to the rest.

As to the Soviet-Nazi Pact of 1939, it has been said that the shock which it caused has been accepted in the non-communist world as natural and that summary accusation of Soviet diplomacy as being Machiavellian has been advanced as justification for the surprise. In fairness to the Soviets, however, it must be repeated that inconsistency is not one of the shortcomings of the Bolsheviks. Much more surprising is the failure of the non-communist nations to realize the essence of the Marxian understanding of war and peace, to perceive the logical sequence in the Soviet diplomatic peace overtures, and to appreciate the precision in the timing of the tactical changes expedient in the communist march toward ultimate revolutionary world peace.

Since in the final appraisal of the Soviet pursuit of peace and struggle against war, as in any social issue, individual sympathies control one's judgment, the actual value of spontaneous accusations against communism is of minor importance. Of no greater significance is the degree of truth which some are inclined to find in the no less spontaneous praise of this modern social force. To an impartial observer, of paramount importance is the fact that the democratic interpretation of war and peace is drastically different from the corresponding concepts of the U.S.S.R. For the democracies both war and peace, are a *via dolorosa* leading to the edifice of national integrity under the aegis of international *Pax Gentium*; to the Soviets, they are merely legitimate communist maneuvering envisaging a peaceless and warless world in which a reorganized classless and stateless community may enjoy social *Pax Communa*. To a pro-communist, Moscow's ridicule of democratic idealism and the Kremlin's assertion that the Marxian realistic way of accepting, using, and pursuing war and peace is the only one worthwhile, may appear well justified. An advocate of freedom has good reason to say that if the right to reply is to be preserved for the states which cherish this right, there is only one answer to give to this challenge of Moscow: If realism is to be accepted as the only criterion of international relations, then the elusiveness of the Soviet interpretation of war and peace must ever be borne in mind, and the Kremlin's offerings of peace and friendship, appraised accordingly.

BIBLIOGRAPHY

BIBLIOGRAPHY

1. Source Materials

Bol'shaia Sovetskaia Entsiklopediia (The Great Soviet Encyclopedia), vv. 1–41, 43, 56–65, Moskva, 1926-1939.

Brest-Litovskaia Konferentsiia. Zasedanie economicheskoi i pravovoi kommissii (Brest-Litovsk Conference. Meetings of the economic and legal committees), Pod red. B. E. Shteina, Izd. NKID, Moskva, 1923.

Desiat' let sovetskoi diplomatii (Ten years of Soviet diplomacy), Izd. NKID, Moskva, 1927.

Gaagskaia Konferentsiia (The Hague Conference), Izd. NKID, Moskva, 1922.

Godovoi Otchet NKID k VIII S'ezdu Sovetov (The annual report of the NKID to the VIII Congress of Soviets), Izd. NKID, Moskva, 1921.

Ibid., k II S'ezdu Sovetov S.S.S.R. Mezhdunarodnaia Politika v 1923 godu (The annual report of the NKID to the II Congress of Soviets of the U.S.S.R. International Policies in 1923), Izd. NKID, Moskva, 1924.

Ibid., k II S'ezdu Sovetov S.S.S.R. Mezhdunarodnaia Politika v 1924 godu (The annual report of the NKID to the III Congress of Soviets of the U.S.S.R. International Policies in 1924), Izd. NKID, Moskva, 1925.

Istoriia Vsesoiuznoi Kommunisticheskoi Partii (bol'shevikov). Kratkii kurs. Pod red. kom. Tsk VKP(b) (The history of the All-Union Communist Party), Moskva, 1938.

Izvestiia Vserossiiskogo Tsentral'nogo Ispolnitel'nogo Komiteta Sovetov Krest'ianskikh, Rabochikh, Soldatskikh i Kazach'ikh Deputatov (Herald of the All-Russian Central Executive Committee of the Soviets of Peasants', Workers', Soldiers' and Cossacks' Deputies) [Since the formation of the Soviet Union the title reads: "Izvestiia Tsentral'nogo Ispolnitel'nogo Komiteta Soiuza Sovetskikh Sotsialisticheskikh Respublik i Vserossiiskogo, etc."], Moskva, 1917–1940.

Kommunisticheskii Internatsional v Dokumentakh. Resheniia, tezisy i vozzvaniia kongressov Kominterna i plenumov IKKI. 1919–1932. Pod redaktsiei Bela Kuna (Communist International in documents. Resolutions, theses and appeals of the congresses of the Comintern and plenary sessions of IKKI [Executive Committee of the Communist International], Partiinoe Izdatel'stvo, Moskva, 1933.

Kommunisticheskii Internatsional (Comintern).

1 Kongress Kommunisticheskogo Internatsionala (2–19 Marta 1919). Protokoly zasedanii (1st Congress of the Communist International, March 2–19, 1919. Protocols of the meetings), Petrograd, 1921.

2 Kongress Kommunisticheskogo Internatsionala (19 Iulia–7 Avgusta,

1920). Resoliutsii i Ustav. (2d Congress of the Communist International, July 19–August 7, 1920. Resolutions and the By-Laws of the Comintern), Petrograd, 1921.

3 Vsemirnyi Kongress (22 Iunia–12 Iulia, 1921 g.). Stenograficheskie Otchety (3d World Congress, June 22–July 12, 1921, Stenographic reports), Petrograd, 1922.

4 Vsemirnyi Kongress (Noiabria 5–Dekabria 3, 1922 g.). Izbrannye doklady rechi i rezoliutsii (4th World Congress, November 5–December 3, 1922. Selected reports, speeches, and resolutions), Moskva-Petrograd, 1923.

5 Vsemirnyi Kongress (Iunia 17–Iulia 8, 1924). Stenograficheskie Otchety (5th World Congress, June 17–July 8, 1924, Stenographic reports), Moskva, 1924.

6 Vsemirnyi Kongress. Vypuski 1–6. Stenograficheskie Otchety (6th World Congress. Vls. 1–6. Stenographic reports), Moskva, 1929.

7 Vsemirnyi Kongress. D. Z. Manuil'sky, *Itogi* . . . (7th World Congress. D. Z. Manuilsky, *Results* . . .), Moskva, 1935.

Kommunisticheskii Internatsional (Comintern). V Rasshirennyi Plenum IKKI. Stenograficheskie Otchety. Tezisy i Rezoliutsii (V Enlarged Plenary Session of the IKKI [Executive Committee of the Communist International]. Stenographic Reports. Theses and Resolutions), Moskva, 1925.

Ibid., VI–VII Rasshirennye Plenumy (VI–VII Enlarged Plenary Sessions), Moskva, 1926–1927.

VIII Plenum IKKI. Tezisy i Rezoliutsii (VIII Plenary Session of the IKKI. Theses and Resolutions), Moskva-Leningrad, 1927.

Ibid., IX–XIII Plenumy IKKI. Rezoliutsii i Postanovleniia (IX–XIII Plenary Sessions), Moskva-Leningrad, 1928–1939.

Krasnaia Kniga. Sbornik diplomaticheskikh dokumentov o Russko-Pol'skikh otnosheniiakh s 1918 po 1920 g. (The Red Book. A collection of diplomatic documents on Russo-Polish relations 1918–1920), Gosizdat, Moskva, 1920.

Londonskaia Konferentsiia 16 iulia–16 avgusta 1924 g., so vstupitel'noi stat'ei K. Radeka (The London Conference, July 16–August 16, 1924), IKA, Moskva, 1925.

Marksizm i natsional'naia problema. Sbornik pervyi. Stat'i Otto Bauera, K. K. Kautskogo, I. Stalina i S. Semkovskogo (Marxism and the problem of nationalities. Volume I. Essays by Otto Bauer, K. K. Kautsky, J. Stalin and S. Semkovsky), Melitopol', 1924.

Materialy Genuezskoi Konferentsii (The materials of the Genoa Conference), Izd. NKID, Moskva, 1922.

Mezhdunarodnoe polozhenie R.S.F.S.R. v 1922 godu (International position of the R.S.F.S.R. in 1922), Izd. NKID, Moskva, 1923.

Mirnye peregovory v Brest-Litovske. Pod redaktsiei A. A. Ioffe (Peace negotations at Brest-Litovsk), t. I, Izd. NKID, Moskva, 1920.

Mirovaia Politika v 1924 godu. Sbornik statei pod redaktsiei F. Rotshteina

(World policies in 1924. A collection of essays edited by F. Rotstein), IKA, Moskva, 1925.

Pervyi S'ezd Narodov Vostoka. Baku, 1–8 Sentiabria 1920 (The 1st Congress of the Peoples of the East), Petrograd, 1920.

Pravda. Organ Tsentr. Kom. i Mosk. Kom. VKP (b) (*The Truth,* Organ of the Central Committee and of the Moscow Committee of the Communist Party (bolsheviks)), Moskva, 1917–1940.

Puti mirovoi revoliutsii. Sed'moi rasshirennyi plenum IKKI 22 noiabria–16 dekabria 1926. Stenograficheskie otchety (Roads toward the world revolution. Stenographic reports of the VII Plenary Session of the Executive Committee of the Communist International, Nov. 22–Dec. 16, 1926), t. I–II, Gosizdat, Moskva, 1927.

Rezoliutsiia X Plenuma IKKI o politicheskom polozhenii (The resolution of the X Plenary Session of the Executive Committee of the Communist International), Gosizdat, Moskva, 1929.

Rezoliutsii i Ustav Kommunisticheskogo Internatsionala, priniatye vtorym kongressom kommunisticheskogo internatsionala (19– go iulia–7 avgusta 1920 g). (Resolutions and the Statute of the Communist International accepted at the 2d Congress of the Communist International, July 19–August 7, 1920), Petrograd, n.d.

Rossiiskaia Kommunisticheskaia Partiia (b) [*RKP* (b)]

  6 S'ezd, 8–16 Avgusta 1917 g. Protokoly (6th Congress. Protocols), Moskva-Leningrad, 1927.

  7 S'ezd, 6–8 Marta 1918 g. Stenograficheskie Otchety (7th Congress. Stenographic Reports), Moskva-Leningrad, 1913.

  8 S'ezd, 18–23 Marta 1919 g. Rezoliutsii i postanovleniia (8th Congress. Resolutions and decrees), Moskva, 1919.

  9 S'ezd 29 Marta–4 Aprelia 1920 g. Stenograficheskie Otchety. Rezoliutsii i postanovleniia (9th Congress. Stenographic Reports. Resolutions and decrees), Moskva, 1920.

10 S'ezd, 8–16 Marta 1921 g. Stenograficheski Otchety. Rezoliutsii i postanovleniia (10th Congress. Stenographic Reports. Resolutions and decrees), Moskva, 1921.

11 S'ezd, Mart 27–Aprel' 3, 1922. Rezoliutsii i postanovleniia (11th Congress. Resolutions and decrees), Moskva, 1922.

12 S'ezd, 17–25 Aprelia 1923 g. Stenograficheskie Otchety. Rezoliutsii i postanovleniia (12th Congress. Stenographic Reports. Resolutions and decrees), Moskva, 1923.

13 S'ezd, 23–31 Maia 1924 g. Stenograficheskie Otchety s prilozheniem materialov sektsii i kommissii. Rezoliutsii (13th Congress. Stenographic Reports. Resolutions), Moskva, 1924.

Rossiiskaia Kommunisticheskaia Partiia (b) [RKP (b)] [now changed to Vsesoiuznaia Kommunisticheskaia Partiia (VKP (b))].

14 S'ezd, 18–31 Dekabria 1925 g. Stenograficheskie Otchety. Rezoliutsii i postanovleniia (14th Congress. Stenographic Reports. Resolutions and decrees), Moskva-Leningrad, 1926.

15 S'ezd, 2–19 Dekabria 1927. Stenograficheskie Otchety. Rezoliutsii i postanovleniia (15th Congress. Stenographic Reports. Resolutions and decrees), Moskva-Leningrad, 1928.

16 S'ezd, 26 iunia–13 iulia 1930 g. Stenograficheskie Otchety. Rezoliutsii i postanovleniia (16th Congress. Stenographic Reports. Resolutions and decrees), Moskva-Leningrad, 1930.

17 S'ezd, 26 ianvaria–10 fevralia 1934 g. Stenograficheskii Otchet (17th Congress. Stenographic Reports), Moskva, 1934.

Sbornik deistvuiuschchikh dogovorov, soglashenii i konventsii zakliuchennykh R.S.F.S.R. s inostrannymi gosudarstvami (A collection of treaties, agreements, and conventions of the R.S.F.S.R. with foreign states), vyp. I–V, Gosizdat, Peterburg-Moskva, 1921–1923.

Sbornik deistvuiushchikh dogovorov, soglashenii i konventsii zakliuchennykh s inostrannymi gosudarstvami (A collections of treaties, agreements, and conventions in force with foreign states), vyp. I–VIII. Izd. NKID, Moskva, 1924–1935.

Sbornik deistvuiushchikh dogovorov, soglashenii i konventsii vstupivshikh v silu do 1–go ianvaria 1925 goda (A collection of treaties, agreements, and conventions with foreign states which came into force prior to January 1, 1925), Izd. 2, Izd. NKID, Moskva, 1928.

S'ezdy Sovetov R. S. i K. Deputatov. II–XIII Vserossiiskie S'ezdy. 1917–1925. Stenografisheskie Otchety (II–XIII All-Russian Congresses of Soviets. Stenographic Reports), Petrograd-Moskva, 1917–1925.

Ibid., Postanovleniia (Resolutions), Petrograd-Moskva, 1917–1925. I–VIII Vsesoiuznye S'ezdy, 1922–1939. Stenograficheskie Otchety (I–VIII All-Union Congress of Soviets. Stenographic Reports), Petrograd-Moskva, 1922–1939.

S'ezdy Sovetov S.S.S.R. v Postanovleniiakii Rezoliutsiiakh. Pod obshchei redaktsiei Akad. A. Ia. Vyshinskogo (Congresses of Soviets of the U.S.S.R. in resolutions), Moskva, 1939.

Sistematicheskoe Sobranie Vazhneishikh Dekretov 1917–1920 (A systematic collection of most important decrees for 1917–1920), Moskva, 1920.

Sistematicheskoe Sobranie Deistvuiushchikh Zakonov Soiuza Sovetskikh Sotsialisticheskikh Respublik (A systematic collections of the laws of the U.S.S.R. in force), Knigi I–V, Moskva, 1927.

Sistematicheskoe Sobranie Zakonov R.S.F.S.R. deistvuiushchikh na 1–e ianvaria 1928 g. (A systematic collection of laws of the R.S.F.S.R. in force on January 1, 1928), I–III, Moskva, 1928–1930.

Sobranie Kodeksov R.S.F.S.R. (A collection of the Codes of the R.S.F.S.R.), IV izd., Izd. NKIust. R.S.F.S.R., Moskva, 1928.

Sobranie Zakonov i Rasporiazhenii S.S.S.R. (A collection of Laws and Ordinances of the Union of S.S.R.), Moskva, 1923–1933.

Sovetskaia Rossiia i Pol'sha (Soviet Russia and Poland), Izd. NKID, Moskva, 1921.

Sovetskii Soiuz v Bor'be za Mir. Dokumenty i vstupitel'naia stat'ia (The

Soviet Union in the Struggle for Peace. Documents and an introductory chapter), Gosizdat, Moskva, 1929.

Tsentral'nyi Ispolnitel'nyi Komitet S.S.S.R. Sozyv I. Stenograficheskie Otchety i Postanovleniia, 1922–1923 (The Central Executive Committee of the U.S.S.R. Session I. Stenographic Reports and Resolutions, 1922–1923).

Ibid., Sozyv II . . . 1924–1925 (Session II . . . 1924–1925).

Ibid., Sozyv III . . . 1925–1927 (Session III . . . 1925–1927).

Vashingtonskaia Konferentsiia po ogranicheniiu vooruzhenii i tikho-okenaskim i dal'nevostochnym delam 1921–1922 g. (The Washington Disarmament Conference 1921–1922), Izd. NKID, Moskva, 1924.

Vsesoiuznaia Kommunisticheskaia Partiia (b) v rezoliutsiiakh ee s' ezdov i konferentsii [1896–1926] (The All-Union Communist Party resolutions at its congresses and conferences [1896–1926], Gosizdat, Moskva, 1927.

Vsesoiuznaia Kommunisticheskaia Partiia (b) [VKP (b)]. Konferentsii Vsesoiuznoi Kommunisticheskoi Partii (b). XIII–XVII. Stenografi-cheskie Otchety. Rezoliutsii i postanovleniia (Conferences of the All-Union Communist Party (b) XIII–XVII. Stenographic reports. Resolutions and decrees), Moskva-Leningrad, 1924–1932.

2. TREATISES

Andogskii, A. I. Puti razresheniiu tikhookeanskoi problemy (Means of solving the problem of the Pacific), Kharbin, 1926.

Avarin, V. "Nezavisimaia" Manchuriia ("Independent" Manchuria), Leningrad, 1934.

Bammel', Gr. Teoriia i praktika dialekticheskogo materializma v izbrannykh otryvkakh iz proizvedenii V. I. Lenina (Theory and practice of the dialectic materialism in selected essays by Lenin), Moskva, 1924.

Berlin, L. E. Vashingtonskaia konferentsiia po ogranicheniiu vooruzhenii i tikhookeanskim i dal'nevostochnym voprosam (The Washington con-ference on the limitation of armaments and on the problems in the Pacific and Far East), Moskva, 1924.

Berman, Ia. L. Osnovnye voprosy teorii proletarskogo gosudarstva (Funda-mental problems of the theory of the proletarian state), Moskva-Lenin-grad, 1930.

Berman, Ia. L. i Medvedev, A. R. Uchenie o proletarskoi diktature v sovet-skom prave (Theories of the proletarian dictatorship in Soviet law), Vyp. 1, 2–e izd., Moskva, 1929.

Bernshtein, I. N. Ocherk kontsesionnogo prava S.S.S.R. Pod redaktsiei Reikhelia (Essay on the law regarding concessions in the U.S.S.R.), Moskva-Leningrad, 1930.

Borisov, A. Podzhigateli voiny na Vostoke (Promoters of war in the East), Moskva, 1936.

Boshkovich, B. Malaia Antanta. Social'no-Ekonomicheskii-Politicheskii Ocherk (Little Entente), Moskva, 1934.

Bukharin, N. I. Lenin kak Marksist (Lenin as a Marxist), Moskva, 1924.
Bukharstev, Dm. et al. Podgotovka vtorogo tura imperialisticheskikh voin. Sbornik . . . (Preparations for the second series of imperialist wars. A collections of essays . . .), Moskva, 1924.
Drunin, V. P. Pol'sha, Rossiia i S.S.S.R. (Poland, Russia, and the U.S.S.R.), Moskva, 1928.
Fokke, D. G. Na stsenie i za kulisami Brestskoi tragikomedii (Behind the stage of Brest-Litovsk) [v. XX of *Arkhiv Russkoi Revoliutsii*], Berlin, 1930.
Ganetskii, A. Sovetsko-Germanskii torgovyi dogovor (The Soviet-German Treaty of Commerce), Moskva-Leningard, 1926.
Gorn, V. Grazhdanskaia voina na Sievero-Zapadie Rossii (The civil war in Northwestern Russia), Berlin, 1923.
Grimm, E. D. Sbornik dogovorov i drugikh dokumentov po istorii mezhdunarodnykh otnoshenii na D. Vostoke 1842–1925 (A collection of treaties and other documents relative to the history of international relations in the Far East, 1842–1925), Moskva, 1927.
Gurko-Kziazhin, V. A. Arabskii vostok i imperializm (The Arabian Near East and imperialism), Moskva, 1926.
Gurvich, G. S. Printsipy avtonomizma i federalizma v sovetskoi sisteme (Principles of autonomy and federalism in the Soviet system), Moskva, 1924.
Iavorskii, S. Liga Natsii i podgotovka novykh voin (The League of Nations and the fomentation of new wars), Moskva, 1928.
Ivanov, L. Liga Natsii (The League of Nations), Moskva, 1929.
———Anglo-Frantsuzkoe sopernichestvo 1919–1927gg. S predisloviem E. B. Pashukanisa (British-French rivalry in 1919–1927), Moskva, 1928.
Ivin, A. Kitai i Sovetskii Soiuz. S predisl. L. Karahana (China and the Soviet Union), Moskva, 1924.
Kakurin, N. Kak srazhalas' revoliutsiia (How the revolution struggled), tt. I–II, Moskva, 1925.
———i Melikov, V. A. Voina s belopoliakami 1920 g. (War with Poland in 1920), Moskva, 1925.
Kamenev, L. Anglo-Sovetskii dogovor i S.S.S.R. Rech' proiznesennaia 6 Sentiabria 1924 g. na partiinom sobranii v Leningrade (The British-Soviet treaty and the U.S.S.R. A speech delivered on Sept. 6, 1924, at the Party meeting in Leningrad), Leningrad, 1924.
Kliuchnikov, Iu. V. i Sabanin, Andrei. Mezhdunarodnaia politika noveishogo vremeni v dogovorakh, notakh i deklaratsiiakh (Recent international politics in treaties, notes, and declarations), Chasti I–III, Moskva, 1925–1929.
Knorin, V., ed. Kratkaia Istoriia VKP (b) (A short History of the All-Union Communist Party), Moskva, 1934.
Korovin, E. A. Mezhdunarodnye dogovory i akty novogo vremeni (International treaties and acts of modern times), Moskva-Leningrad, 1925.

————Sovremennoe Mezhdunarodnoe Publichnoe Pravo (Contemporary Public International Law), Moskva, 1926.

Lapinskii, P. Garantiinyi dogovor i mezhdunarodnoe polozhenie (Treaty of guaranty and the international situation), Moskva, 1925.

Lazovskii, I. i Bibin, I. Sovetskaia politika za 10 let po natsional'nomu voprosu v R.S.F.S.R. (The Soviet policy for the last ten years on the problem of nationality in the R.S.F.S.R.), Moskva, 1928.

Lenin, V. Gosudarstvo i Revoliutsiia. Uchenie Marksizma o gosudarstve i zadachi proletariata v revoliutsii (The state and revolution. The Marxian theory of the state and the problems of the proletariat in revolution), Izd. 3, Moskva, 1925.

————Imperializm kak noveishii etap kapitalizma (Imperialism as the latest stage of capitalism), Sobr. Soch. XIII.

————Izbrannye stat'i po natsional'nomu voprosu. S predisl. i primech. I. Tovstukhi (Selected essays on the problems of nationality), Izd. 2, Moskva-Leningrad, 1925.

————Kommunisticheskii Internatsional. Stat'i i rechi. Predislovie N. N. Popova. Primechaniia K. P. Novitskogo (The Communist International), Moskva, 1926.

————Konferetsiia zagranichnykh sektsii RSDRP (Conferences of the foreign branches of the Russian Social Democratic Labor Party), Sobr. Soch. XIII.

————O lozunge soedinennykh shtatov Evropy (Concerning the watchword of the United States of Europe), Sobr. Soch. XIII.

————O mezhdunarodnom rabochem dvizhenii (On international labor movement), Sbornik Statei, I–IV, Moskva, 1926.

————O natsional'nom voprose (Concerning the problem of nationality), Izd. 2, Moskva-Leningrad, 1925.

————O programme mira (Concerning the peace), Sobr. Soch. XIII.

————Pis'ma A. G. Shliapnikovu i A. M. Kollontai (Letters to A. G. Shliapnikov and A. M. Kollontai), Pod. red. i s predisl. L. B. Kameneva, Moskva, 1926.

————Polozhenie i zadashi sotsialisticheskogo internatsionala (The status and problems of socialist international), Sobr. Soch. XIII.

————Sochineniia (Works), I–XXX, 3d ed., Moskva, 1935.

————Sotsialisticheskaia revoliutsiia i pravo natsii na samoopredelenie (Socialist revolution and the right of nations to self-determination), Sobr. Soch. XIX.

————Sotsializm i voina (Socialism and war), Sobr. Soch. XIII.

————Tezisy po natsional'nomu i kolonial'nomu voprosam, priniatye na II kongresse Kommuniticheskogo Internatsionala (Principles on national and colonial problems accepted at the II Congress of the Communist International), Sobr. Soch. XIV.

Lemin, I. Ugroza voiny i mirnaia politika S.S.S.R. (The danger of war and peace policy of the U.S.S.R.), Moskva, 1935.

Levidov, M. K istorii soiuznoi interventsii v Rossii (History of the Allied intervention in Russia), Leningrad, 1925.

Lisovskii, P. Abissinskaia avantiura Ital'ianskogo fashizma (Italian adventure in Abyssinia), Moskva, 1936.

Litvinov, M. Vneshriaia Politika S.S.S.R. Rechi i zaiavleniia (Foreign Policy of the U.S.S.R. Speeches and statements). 1927–1935. Moskva, 1935.

Maiskii, I. Vneshniaia politika R.S.F.S.R. 1917–1922 (Foreign policies of the R.S.F.S.R., 1917–1922), Moskva, 1922.

Maksimovskii. Lenin o sovetskom stroitel'stve. Sobranie tsitat i otryvkov (Lenin on the soviets. Collection of essays and extracts), Moskva, 1925.

Margulies, M. S. God Interventsii (One year of intervention), 3 vls., Berlin, 1923.

Marushevskii, V. V. Belye v Arkhangel'ske. Red. P. E. Shchegolev (The "Whites" in Archangel), Leningrad, 1930.

Miliukov, P. Rosiia na perelome (Russia at the crossroads), tt. I–II, Paris, 1927.

Mints, I. i Eideman, R., red. Krakh germanskoi okkupatsii na Ukraine (Po dokumentam okkupantov) The end of the German occupation in the Ukraine), [Moskva], 1936.

Notovich, F. Razoruzhenie Imperialistov, Liga Natsii i S.S.S.R. (The disarmament of imperialists, the League of Nations and the U.S.S.R.), Moskva, 1929.

Orlovskii, S. i Malkis, V. Sovetskoe voenno-ugolovnoe pravo (Soviet military criminal code), Moskva, 1928.

Palienko, N. I. Konfederatsii, federatsii i Soiuz Sovetskikh Sotsialisticheskikh Respublik. Vst. stat'ia M. Vetoshkina (Confederations, federations, and the U.S.S.R.), Khar'kov, 1923.

Pashukanis, E. Ocherki po mezhdunarodnomu pravu (Essays on international law), Moskva, 1935.

Pavlovich, Mikh. (Vel'tman, M. P.) Sovetskaia Rossiia i imperialisticheskaia Iaponiia (Soviet Russia and imperialistic Japan), Moskva, 1924.

————Sovetskaia Rossiia i kapitalisticheskaia Angliia. Ot epokhi tsarizma do pravitel'stva Chemberlena-Boldvina (Soviet Russia and capitalist England. From the era of tsarism to the administrations of Chamberlain and Baldwin), Moskva, 1925.

————Bor'ba za Aziiu i Afriku (The struggle for Asia and Africa), Moskva, 1923.

————Turtsiia v bor'be za nezavisimost' (Turkey in the struggle for independence), Moskva, 1925.

Petrov, E. Sotsial'naia revoliutsiia i mezhdunarodnaia politika v perepiske Marksa i Engel'sa (Social revolution and international politics in the correspondence between Marx and Engels), Leningrad-Moskva, 1925.

Popov, N. N. Natsional'naia politika sovetskoi vlasti (The national policies of the Soviets), Moskva, 1924.

Radek, K. Vneshniaia politika Sovetskoi Rossii (The foreign policies of Soviet Russia), Moskva, 1923.

————Piat' let Kominterna (Five years of the Komintern [Communist International]), Ch. I–II, Moskva, 1926.

Rakovskii, Kh. G. Liga Natsii i S.S.S.R. (U.S.S.R. and the League of Nations), Moskva, 1926.

————Rumyniia i Bessarabia. K semiletiiu anneksii Bessarabii (Roumania and Bessarabia. The seventh anniversary of the annexation of Bessarabia), Moskva, 1925.

Reisner, M. A. Gosudarstvo burzhuazii i R.S.F.S.R. (Bourgeois state and the R.S.F.S.R.), Moskva, 1923.

Riazanov, D. Anglo-Sovetskie otnosheniia v otzenke K. Marksa. Istoriko-kriticheskii etiud (Anglo-Russian relations as viewed by K. Marx. An historical critical essay), Petrograd, 1918.

Roi, M. N. Kitaiskaia revoliutsiia i Kommunisticheskii Internatsional (The Chinese revolution and the Third International), Moskva, 1928.

Sabanin, A. V. Mezhdunarodnaia politika v 1929 godu. Dogovory, deklaratsii i diplomaticheskaia perepiska (International politics in 1929), Moskva, 1931.

Savvin, V. P. Vzaimootnosheniia Tsarskoi Rossii i S.S.S.R. s Kitaem (Relations of Tsarist Russia and the U.S.S.R. with China), Moskva, 1930.

Shchegolev, N. E. Kolchakovshchina (The era of Admiral Kolchak), Leningrad, 1930.

Sergunov, S. Ugroza Chekhoslovakii—ugroza vsemu miru (Threat to Czechoslovakia—threat to all the world), [Moskva], 1938.

Shlikhter, A. G., red. Chernaia Kniga. Sbornik statei i materialov ob interventsii antanty na Ukraine v 1918–1919 gg. (The Black Book. Collection of essays and materials on the Allied Intervention in the Ukraine in 1918–1919), [n.p], 1925.

Shtein, B. E. Brest-Litovskaia Konferentsiia. Zasedaniia pravovoi i ekonomicheskoi kommissii (The Brest-Litovsk Conference. Meetings of the legal and economic committees), Moskva, 1923.

————Gaagskaia konferentsiia (The Hague Conference), Moskva, 1922.

————Genuezskaia konferentsiia (The Genoa Conference), Moskva, 1922.

Shtein, B. S. S.S.S.R. v bor'be za razoruzhenie. Sovetskaia delegatsiia na IV sessii podgotovitel'moi kommissii po razoruzheniiu (The U.S.S.R. in the struggle for disarmament. The Soviet delegation at the IV session of the preparatory committee), Moskva, 1928.

————Torgovaia politika i torgovye dogovory Sovetskoi Rossii 1917–1922 gg. (Commercial policy and commercial treaties of Soviet Russia from 1917 to 1922), Moskva, 1923.

————Vneshniaia torgovaia politika S.S.S.R. (The foreign trade policy of the U.S.S.R.), Moskva, 1925.

Shtein, B. S. i Rappoport, A. Iu. Sovetsko-Germanskii dogovor 12 oktiabria 1925 g. (The Soviet-German Treaty of October 12, 1925), Moskva, 1927.

Sigrist, S. V. Vneshniaia politika S.S.S.R. v mezhdunarodnykh dogovorakh (The foreign policies of the U.S.S.R. in international treaties), Leningard, 1927.

Stalin, J. K mezhdunarodnomu polozheniiu (On the international situation), Moskva, 1924.

————Lenin. New York, 1928.

————Natsional'nye momenty v partiinom i gosudarstvennom stroi-tel'stve (National and party aspects in the administration of the state), Izd. 2–e, Moskva-Leningrad, 1926.

————O Lenine i Leninizme (Lenin and Leninism), Moskva, 1924.

————Voprosy Leninizma (Problems of Leninism), Izd. 9, Moskva, 1932.

————O trekh osobennostiakh Krasnoi Armii (Three characteristics of the Red Army), Moskva, 1938.

————Leninizm i gosudarstvo (Leninism and the State), Moskva, 1925.

————Rovoliutsionnaia rol' prava i gosudarstva (The revolutionary rôle of the law and the State), Izd. 3, Moskva, 1924.

————Revoliutsionnaia rol' sovetskogo prava (The revolutionary rôle of the Soviet law), Moskva, 1931.

————Uchenie o gosudarstve i konstitutsii R.S.F.S.R. (The state and the constitution of the R.S.F.S.R.), Moskva, 1923.

————Stat'i i rechi ot shestnadtsatogo do semnadtsatogo s'ezda VKP (b) (Essays and addresses between XVI and XVII Congresses), Moskva, 1934.

————Marksizm i natsional'nyi vopros (Marxism and the problem of nationalities), Moskva, 1937.

Tanin, M. 10 let vneshnei politiki S.S.S.R., 1917–1927 (Ten years of foreign policy of the U.S.S.R.), Moskva-Leningrad, 1927.

————Mezhdunarodnaia Politika S.S.S.R. 1917–1924 (The international policies of the U.S.S.R. 1917–1924), Moskva, 1925.

Taracouzio, T. A. The Soviet Union and International Law, New York, 1935.

Trotskii, L. Piat' let Kominterna (Five years of the Komintern), Ch. I–II, Moskva, 1926.

————Sochineniia (Works), I–XXI, Moskva, 1925–1927.

————Voina i Revoliutsiia (War and revolution), I–II, Moskva, 1923–1924.

————Ot Oktiabria do Genui. Mezhdunarodnye otnosheniia R.S.F.S.R. Spravochnik (From October Revolution to Genoa. International Relations of the R.S.F.S.R.), Moskva, 1922.

Vaksberg, M. A. Pravovoe polozhenie soiuznykh respublik—chlenov Soiuza S.S.S.R. (The legal status of the union republics—members of the U.S.S.R.), Irkutsk, 1925.

Valerin, R. Ot razryva do vosstanovleniia anglo-sovetskikh otnoshenii. Mezhdunarodnyi obzor za 1924–1929 gg. (From the suspension to the

BIBLIOGRAPHY 311

restoration of Anglo-Soviet relations. An international review of the years 1924–1929), Moskva, 1930.

Varga, E. Mezhdu VI i VII kongressami Kominterna. Ekonomika i politika 1928–1934 gg. (Between the VI and the VII Congresses of the Communist International. Economics and politics in 1928–1934), Moskva, 1935.

Vinogradov, B. Mirovoi proletariat i S.S.S.R. (The world proletariat and the U.S.S.R.), Moskva, 1928.

Zinov'ev, G. Bol'shevizatsiia—stabilizatsiia (Bolshevization—stabilization), Moskva, 1925.

————Mirovaia partiia Leninizma (The world's Lenin party), Moskva, 1925.

————Sochineniia (Works), I–VIII, Moskva-Petrograd, 1923–1926.

————Voina i krizis sotsializma (War and the crisis of socialism), Petrograd, 1920.

————Mezhdunarodnye perspektivy i bol'shevizatsiia kompartii (International perspectives and bolshevization of the communist parties), Moskva, 1925.

Zonneshtral'-Piskorsky, A. A. Mezhdunarodnye torgovye dogovory i soglasheniia 1919–1924 (International commerce treaties and agreements 1919–1924), Moskva, 1925.

3. PERIODICALS

Kommunisticheskii Internatsional (Communist International), Moskva, 1921–1939.

Leninskii Sbornik (Lenin Almanach), I–XXXII, Izd. Inst. Lenina, Leningrad, 1924–1938.

Leniniana (Leniniana), I–V, Izd. Inst. Lenina, Moskva-Leningrad, 1924–1928.

Letopisi Marksizma (Annals of Marxism), Zapiski Instituta Karla Marksa i F. Engel'sa. Pod red. D. Riazanova, I–(VIII), Gosizdat, Moskva, 1926–1928.

Mezhdunarodnaia Zhizn' (International Life), Izd. NKID., Moskva, 1923–1930.

Mezhdunarodnoe Pravo [*Revue Soviètique de Droit International*] (International Law), No. 1–3, Izd. I MGU, Moskva, 1928.

Mirovoe Khoziaistvo i Mirovaia Politika (World Economics and Politics), Moskva, 1926–1940.

Pod Znamenem Marksizma (Under the Banners of Marxism), Moskva, 1921–1940.

Proletarskaia Revoliutsiia (Proletarian Revolution), Moskva, 1921–1931.

Sovetskoe Stroitel'stvo (The Soviet Construction), Moskva, 1919–1937.

Vlast' Sovetov (Power of the Soviets), 1919–1939.

APPENDIX

SUBJECT INDEX OF THE SOVIET TREATIES, AGREEMENTS AND CONVENTIONS IN FORCE[1]

---

[1] A considerable number of these treaties became automatically obsolete as result of the events which took place in Europe while this book was being published.

PART I

AGREEMENTS REGARDING PEACE, ESTABLISHMENT OF
RELATIONS AND OTHER POLITICAL QUESTIONS

Country	Date and Place of Signing	Substance of Treaty or Agreement	Russian Source: Sborn. Deistv. Dogov. Vol.,Yr.;No.,Page
		1. PEACE TREATIES AND TREATIES REGARDING ESTABLISHMENT OF RELATIONS	
Afghanistan	Feb. 28, 1921 Moscow	Treaty of friendship	I, 1924; 3:40
Austria	Dec. 7, 1921 Vienna	Provisional agreement	I, 1924; 2:35
——	Sept. 8, 1923 Vienna	Exchange of notes on the extension of the provisional agreement of Dec. 7, 1921, to the Union of S.S.R.	I, 1924; 1:34
China	May 31, 1924 Peiping	Treaty on general principles for the settlement of general problems	II, 1925; 107:16
——	Sept. 20, 1924 Mukden	Agreement between the government of the U.S.S.R. and the government of the Three Autonomous Eastern Provinces of the Chinese Republic	V, 1930; 214:118
Czecho-slovakia	June 5, 1922 Praha	Provisional agreement [on establishment of trade relations]	I, 1924; 28:188
——	June 6, 1922 Praha	Provisional agreement [idem]	I, 1924; 29:192
Denmark	April 23, 1923 Moscow	Preliminary agreement	I, 1924; 10:63
Estonia	Feb. 2, 1920 Tartu	Treaty of peace	I, 1921; 17:100
——	Nov. 25, 1921 Moscow	Treaty respecting future relations	I, 1924; 31:207

Country	Date and Place of Signing	Substance of Treaty or Agreement	Russian Source: Sborn. Deistv. Dogov. Vol.,Yr.;No.,Page
Estonia	May 27, 1922 Moscow	Supplementary protocol to the treaty of November 25, 1921	I, 1924; 33:212
———	Feb. 17, 1923 Moscow	Supplementary Protocol to the treaty of November 25, 1921	I, 1924; 33:212
Finland	Oct. 14, 1920 Tartu	Treaty of peace	I, 1921; 6:76
Germany	April 16, 1922 Rapallo	Treaty [of Rapallo on General Problems]	I, 1924; 8:158
———	Nov. 5, 1922 Berlin	Agreement regarding the extension of the agreement of April 16, 1922 to the Union Republics	I–II, 1928; 11:17
Iran	Feb. 26, 1921 Moscow	Treaty	I–II, 1928; 30:107
Japan	Jan. 20, 1925 Peiping	Convention regarding the general principles of mutual relations	III, 1927; 130:10
Latvia	Aug. 11, 1920 Riga	Treaty of peace	I, 1924; 13:75
———	Aug. 3, 1921 Moscow	Treaty [political]	I, 1924; 14:86
Lithuania	July 12, 1920 Moscow	Treaty of peace	I, 1922; 13:50
———	Feb. 14, 1921 Moscow	Political treaty	I–II, 1928; 23:68
———	April 5, 1922 Kharkov	Supplementary treaty to the treaty of February 14, 1921	I, 1924; 17:110
Mongolian People's Republic	Nov. 5, 1921 Moscow	Agreement regarding establishment of friendly relations	II, 1921; 47:28

Country	Date and Place of Signing	Substance of Treaty or Agreement	*Russian Source:* Sborn. Deistv. Dogov. Vol.,Yr.;No.,Page
Poland	March 18, 1921 Riga	Treaty of peace	I, 1924; 20:121
Turkey	Oct. 13, 1921 Kars	Treaty of friendship	II, 1921; 52:72
———	Oct. 13, 1921 Kars	Treaty of friendship	I–II, 1928; 33:120
———	Jan. 21, 1922 Ankara	Treaty of friendship	I, 1924; 25:167
Yemen	Nov. 1, 1928 Sanaa	Treaty of friendship and commerce	VI, 1931; 220:6

2. EXCHANGE OF NOTES (TELEGRAMS RELATING TO THE ESTABLISHMENT OF DIPLOMATIC RELATIONS)

Country	Date and Place of Signing	Substance of Treaty or Agreement	Russian Source
Albania	Feb. 25–26, 1924 Moscow-Vienna	Exchange of notes regarding recognition *de jure*	VII, 1935; 279:3
Austria	Sept. 17, 1934 Rome	Exchange of notes regarding recognition *de jure*	I–II, 1925; 101:5
State of the Saudi Arabia	Feb. 16, 1926 (April 17, 1927) Djedda	Exchange of notes regarding recognition *de jure*	IV, 1928; 156:14
Bulgaria	July 23, 1934 Moscow-Sofia	Exchange of notes regarding recognition *de jure*	VIII, 1935; 281:5
China	Aug. 8, 1924 Moscow	Exchange of notes regarding recognition *de jure*	II, 1925; 107:16
Czecho-slovakia	June 9, 1934 Geneva	Exchange of notes regarding recognition *de jure*	VIII, 1935; 293:23

Country	Date and Place of Signing	Substance of Treaty or Agreement	Russian Source: Sborn. Deistv. Dogov. Vol.,Yr.;No.,Page
Denmark	June 18, 1924 London	Exchange of notes regarding recognition *de jure*	II, 1925; 105:12
France	Oct. 28, 1924 Paris-Moscow	Exchange of notes regarding recognition *de jure*	I–II, 1928; 36:143
Great Britain	Feb. 1–8, 1924 Moscow-London	Exchange of notes regarding recognition *de jure*	II, 1925; 102:6
Greece	March 8, 1925 Berlin	Exchange of notes regarding recognition *de jure*	II, 1925; 103:11
Hungary	Feb. 4, 1934 Rome	Exchange of notes regarding recognition *de jure*	VIII, 1935; 282:6
Iceland	June 22–24, 1926 Moscow	Exchange of notes regarding recognition *de jure*	V, 1930; 191:12
Italy	Feb. 7, 1924 Rome-Moscow	Exchange of notes regarding recognition *de jure*	II, 1925; 106:15
Norway	Feb. 15 (Mar. 10), 1924 Oslo	Exchange of notes regarding recognition *de jure*	I–II, 1928; 28:30
Roumania	June 9, 1934 Geneva	Exchange of notes regarding recognition *de jure*	VIII, 1935; 289:19
Sweden	Mar. 15–18, 1924 Stockholm	Exchange of notes regarding recognition *de jure*	II, 1925; 111:27
United States of America	Nov. 16, 1933 Washington	Exchange of notes regarding recognition *de jure*	VIII, 1935; 280:4
Uruguay	Aug. 21–22, 1926 Berlin	Exchange of notes regarding recognition *de jure*	V, 1930; 192:13

Country	Date and Place of Signing	Substance of Treaty or Agreement	Russian Source: Sborn. Deistv. Dogov. Vol.,Yr.;No.,Page

3. TREATIES OF NEUTRALITY, NON-AGGRESSION, PEACEFUL SETTLEMENT OF DISPUTES AND ON CONCILIATION PROCEDURE

Country	Date and Place of Signing	Substance of Treaty or Agreement	Russian Source
Afghanistan	June 24, 1931 Kabul	Pact of neutrality and non-aggression	VII, 1933; 244:3
China	Aug. 21, 1937	Treaty of non-aggression	
Estonia	May 4, 1932 Moscow	Treaty of non-aggression and amicable settlement of disputes	VII, 1933; 257:32
———	June 16, 1932 Moscow	Convention regarding conciliation procedure	VII, 1933; 258:34
———	April 4, 1934 Moscow	Protocol extending the treaty of May 4, 1932	VIII, 1935; 295:25
Finland	Jan. 21, 1932 Helsinki	Treaty of non-aggression and amicable settlement of conflicts	VII, 1933; 253:21
———	April 22, 1932 Helsinki	Convention on conciliation procedure	VII, 1933; 254:24
———	April 7, 1934 Moscow	Protocol extending the treaty of Jan. 21, 1932	VIII, 1935; 291:21
France	Nov. 29, 1932 Paris	Treaty of non-aggression	VII, 1933; 255:27
———	May 2, 1935 Paris	Treaty of mutual assistance	SZiR, SSSR, 1936 II, No. 7, §72 [1]
Germany	April 24, 1926 Berlin	Treaty [of neutrality and non-aggression]	IV, 1928; 157:16
———	Jan. 25, 1929 Moscow	Convention regarding conciliation procedure	V, 1930; 190:10

[1] "SZiR SSSR" are the first letters of Sobranie Zakonov i Rasporiazhenii S.S.S.R. (Collection of Laws and Ordinances of the U.S.S.R.) Reference to this source is made hereafter in instances where the treaty is not found in the official Sborn. Deistv. Dogov. (The Collection of Treaties and Agreements of the U.S.S.R.)

Country	Date and Place of Signing	Substance of Treaty or Agreement	*Russian Source: Sborn. Deistv. Dogov.* Vol.,Yr.;No.,Page
Germany	June 24, 1931 Moscow	Protocol extending the treaty of April 24, 1926, and the convention of January 21, 1929	VIII, 1935; 283:7
Iran	Oct. 21, 1927 Moscow	Treaty of guaranty and neutrality	IV, 1928; 159:23
Italy	Sept. 2, 1933 Rome	Treaty of friendship, non-aggression and neutrality	VIII, 1935; 284:8
Latvia	Feb. 5, 1932 Riga	Treaty of non-aggression	VII, 1933; 246:6
———	June 18, 1932 Riga	Convention regarding conciliation procedure	VII, 1933; 247:8
———	April 4, 1934 Moscow	Protocol extending the treaty of February 5, 1932	VIII, 1935; 285:11
Lithuania	Sept. 28, 1926 Moscow	Treaty of neutrality and non-aggression	IV, 1928; 158:19
———	May 6, 1931 Moscow	Protocol regarding renewal of the treaty of September 28, 1926	VII, 1933;248:11
———	July 5, 1933 London	Convention defining aggression	VIII, 1935; 286:12
———	April 4, 1934 Moscow	Protocol extending the treaty of September 28, 1926	VIII, 1935; 287:15
Mongolia	(Nov. 27, 1934) March 12, 1936 Ulan-Bator	Protocol on mutual assistance	*SZiR SSSR,* 1936 II, No. 23, §213
Poland	July 25, 1932 Moscow	Treaty of non-aggression	VII, 1933; 249:12
———	Nov. 23, 1932 Moscow	Convention regarding conciliation procedure	VII, 1933; 250:15

Country	Date and Place of Signing	Substance of Treaty or Agreement	Russian Source: Sborn. Deistv. Dogov. Vol.,Yr.; No.,Page
Poland	May 5, 1934 Moscow	Protocol extending the treaty of July 25, 1932	VIII, 1935; 288:16
Turkey	Dec. 17, 1925 Paris	Political treaty	III, 1927; 129:9
———	Dec. 17, 1929 Ankara	Protocol extending the political treaty of December 17, 1925	VI, 1931; 223:11
———	March 7, 1931 Ankara	Protocol regarding the amendment of §2 of the protocol of December 17, 1929	VIII, 1935; 290:20
———	Oct. 30, 1931 Ankara	Protocol regarding extension of the terms of §2 of the protocol of December 17, 1929	VII, 1933; 252:20
———	Nov. 7, 1935 Ankara	Protocol on the extension of the Treaty of friendship and neutrality between U.S.S.R. and Turkey	SZiR SSSR, 1936, II, No. 17, §140

4. Agreements Relating to Other Political Questions

Country	Date and Place of Signing	Substance of Treaty or Agreement	Russian Source
China	Dec. 22, 1929 Khaborovsk	Protocol regarding the settlement of the conflict over the Chinese-Eastern Railway	VI, 1931; 222:9
Czechoslovakia	Dec. 7, 1934 Geneva	Exchange of notes relating to questions concerning the Eastern Pact	VIII, 1935; 294
———	May 16, 1935 Praha	Treaty of mutual assistance	SZiR SSSR, 1935 II, Nos. 14–15 §130
France	Dec. 5, 1934 Geneva	Protocol on questions concerning the Eastern Pact	VIII, 1935; 292:22
Roumania	March 5–9, 1918 Odessa	Agreement regarding political and military matters	I, 1921; 15:74
Turkey	Nov. 25 (Dec. 25), 1930 Ankara	Exchange of notes regarding the classification of visits of men-of-war	VII, 1933; 251:19

PART II

AGREEMENTS CONCERNING LEGAL PROBLEMS

Country	Date and Place of Signing	Substance of Treaty or Agreement	*Russian Source: Sborn. Deistv. Dogov. Vol., Yr.; No., Page*
		1. CONSULAR AGREEMENTS	
Czecho-slovakia	Nov. 16, 1935 Moscow	Consular convention	*SZiR SSSR,* 1936 II, No. 35, §319
Finland	Jan. 2–4, 1923 Helsinki	Exchange of notes regarding consular matters	III, 1927; 135:61
Germany	Oct. 12, 1925 Moscow	Consular treaty	III, 1927; 131:19
Poland	June 18, 1924 Moscow	Consular convention	III, 1927; 133:39
Sweden	Feb. 2, 1927 Moscow	Exchange of notes regarding consular matters	IV, 1928; 163:35
		2. AGREEMENTS REGARDING PROBLEMS OF ARBITRATION IN COMMERCIAL AND CIVIL MATTERS	
Germany	Oct. 12, 1925 Moscow	Agreement regarding legal assistance in civil matters	III, 1927; 133:74
Latvia	Oct. 10, 1927 Riga	Convention regarding arbitral tribunals in commercial and civil cases	V, 1930; 193:14
———	May 18, 1928 Riga	Supplementary protocol to the convention regarding arbitration tribunals in commercial and civil cases	V, 1930; 194:19
		3. AGREEMENTS REGARDING PROBLEMS OF MUTUAL LEGAL ASSISTANCE IN CIVIL CASES	
Austria	Sept. 19, 1924 Moscow	Agreement regarding legal assistance in civil matters	II, 1925; 113:32

Country	Date and Place of Signing	Substance of Treaty or Agreement	Russian Source: Sborn. Deistv. Dogov. Vol., Yr.; No., Page
Estonia	Jan. 20, 1930 Tallinn	Agreement regarding legal assistance in civil matters	VI, 1931; 225:15
————	Dec. 22, 1930 (Jan. 8, 1931)	Exchange of notes regarding the amendment of the agreement of January 20, 1930	VII, 1933; 261:39
France	July 11, 1936	Exchange of notes extending the agreement of July 13, 1935, on commercial and mutual relations between U.S.S.R. and U.S.A.	SZiR SSSR, 1936 II, No. 35, §320
Germany	Oct. 12, 1925 Moscow	Agreement regarding legal assistance in civil matters	III, 1927; 132:35
————	Feb. 7, (Mar. 7, 1931) Berlin	Exchange of notes regarding the amendment of the agreement of October 12, 1925	SZiR SSSR, 1931, II, §114, p. 417
Latvia	June 2, 1927 Moscow	Agreement regarding legal assistance in civil matters	IV, 1928; 161:31
————	Dec. 17, 1930 (Jan. 4, 1931) Riga	Exchange of notes regarding the amendment of the agreement of June 2, 1927, on legal assistance in civil matters	VII, 1933; 260:38

4. Agreements on Other Legal Problems

Country	Date and Place of Signing	Substance of Treaty or Agreement	Russian Source
Finland	July 7, 1922 Moscow	Agreement regarding the amendment of Article 22 of the treaty of peace	IV, 1923; 114:27
————	Aug. 12, 1922 Helsinki	Convention regarding repatriation	IV, 1923; 115:28
————	Oct. 28, 1922 Helsinki	Agreement regarding floating of timber in watercourses	V, 1923; 121:9
Italy	July 26, 1930 Rome	Exchange of notes regarding the arrest of property belonging to a foreign state	VI, 1931; 224:14

Country	Date and Place of Signing	Substance of Treaty or Agreement	Russian Source: Sborn. Deistv. Dogov. Vol.,Yr.;No.,Page
Roumania	Nov. 20, 1923 Tiraspol	Agreement regarding means and measures for prevention and settlement of conflicts that may arise concerning the Dniester River	II, 1925; 112:28
U.S.A.	Nov. 22, 1935 Moscow	Exchange of notes regarding the order of execution of judicial decrees	*SZiR SSSR,* 1935, II, No. 2, §10

PART III

Country	Date and Place of Signing	Substance of Treaty or Agreement	Russian Source: Sborn. Deistv. Dogov. Vol.,Yr.;No.,Page
1. AGREEMENTS RELATING TO GENERAL PROBLEMS OF THE BOUNDARIES			
Finland	June 1, 1922 Helsinki	Convention regarding protection and inviolability of the frontiers	III, 1922; 90:61
———	July 28, 1923 Helsinki	Agreement regarding the maintenance [care] of the Gulf of Finland outside territorial waters, and pilot service	II, 1925; 126:110
———	April 13, 1929 Moscow	Convention regarding customs supervision in the Gulf of Finland	V, 1930; 199:41
———	April 13, 1929 Moscow	Protocol extending the convention regarding customs control in the Gulf of Finland with the agreement of July 28, 1923, on maintenance [care] of the Gulf of Finland outside territorial waters	V, 1930; 200:45
Poland	April 10, 1932 Moscow	Agreement regarding legal problems in the boundary zones	VIII, 1935; 299:49
2. AGREEMENTS REGARDING THE ORDER OF SETTLEMENT OF BOUNDARY INCIDENTS			
Afghanistan	Sept. 13, 1932 Kabul	Exchange of notes on amicable settlement of disputes in boundary zones	VII, 1933; 263:54
Estonia	Aug. 8, 1927 Tallinn	Agreement regarding the settlement of frontier disputes	IV, 1928; 168:49
———	Oct. 22, 1931 Tallinn	Protocol amending the protocol attached to the agreement of August 8, 1927	VII, 1933; 264:62
Finland	Sept. 24, 1928 Helsinki	Exchange of notes regarding prevention of conflicts on the Isthmus of Karelia	V, 1930; 198:38
Latvia	July 19, 1926 Riga	Agreement regarding the inquiry into and settlement of conflicts in the frontier zone	IV, 1928; 164:38

325

Country	Date and Place of Signing	Substance of Treaty or Agreement	Russian Source: Sborn. Deistv. Dogov. Vol.,Yr.;No.,Page
Poland	June 3, 1933 Moscow	Convention regarding investigation and settlement of conflicts in the boundary zones	VIII, 1935; 300:79
Turkey	Aug. 6, 1928 Ankara	Convention regarding the settlement of conflicts in the boundary zones	VI, 1931; 228:29

3. AGREEMENTS RELATING TO BOUNDARY COMMISSION

Country	Date and Place	Substance	Source
Iran	Aug. 14, 1927 Teheran	Exchange of notes regarding special commissaries in the boundary zone	IV, 1928; 165:43
———	Oct. 15 (Nov. 20, 1928 Teheran	Exhange of notes regarding frontier commissaries	V, 1930; 195:19

4. AGREEMENTS REGARDING THE ORDER OF CROSSING FRONTIERS BY BORDER INHABITANTS

Country	Date and Place	Substance	Source
Iran	May 31, 1928 Teheran	Convention regarding the crossing of frontiers by the inhabitants of adjacent districts	VI, 1931; 226:19
Turkey	Aug. 6, 1928 Ankara	Convention regarding the crossing of the boundary line by the inhabitants of the boundary zones	VI, 1931; 227:24

5. AGREEMENTS RELATING TO THE USE OF WATER FROM WATER SYSTEMS

Country	Date and Place	Substance	Source
Iran	Feb. 20, 1926 Ashkhabad	Convention regarding mutual use of water from frontier rivers and waterways	III, 1927; 136:64
———	Aug. 27, 1935 Teheran	Treaty with Iran regarding settlement on the land	SZiR SSSR, 1936, II, No. 7, §36
Turkey	Jan. 8, 1927 Ankara	Convention regarding using water from the boundary rivers and waterways	V, 1930; 196:26

6. AGREEMENTS RELATING TO PROBLEMS OF CROSSING THE BORDERS BY ANIMALS

Country	Date and Place	Substance	Source
Afghanistan	May 6, 1935 Kabul	Agreement between U.S.S.R. and Afghanistan on measures against locusts on their respective territories	SZiR SSSR, 1935, II, No. 16, §135

APPENDIX 327

Country	Date and Place of Signing	Substance of Treaty or Agreement	Russian Source: Sborn. Deistv. Dogov. Vol.,Yr.;No.,Page
Finland	July 4, 1933 Helsinki	Convention regarding deer	VIII, 1935; 301:91
Iran	Aug. 27, 1935 Teheran	Sanitary-veterinary convention	*SZiR SSSR,* 1936 II, No. 7, §36
Turkey	Aug. 6, 1928 Ankara	Convention regarding the prevention of the spread of epizootics over the Georgian-Turkish boundary line	VI, 1931; 234:59
———	Aug. 6, 1928 Ankara	Convention regarding the use of pastures	V, 1930; 197:32

PART IV

AGREEMENTS REGARDING ECONOMIC PROBLEMS

Country	Date and Place of Signing	Substance of Treaty or Agreement	*Russian Source:* *Sborn.* *Deistv. Dogov.* *Vol., Yr.; No., Page*
		1. COMMERCIAL TREATIES AND CUSTOM AGREEMENTS	
Belgium	Nov. 5, 1937 Brussels	Exchange of notes regarding amendment of certain paragraphs of the provisional agreement of the commercial convention of September 5, 1935	*SZiR SSSR*, 1938, II, No. 25, §174
Czechoslovakia	June 5, 1922 Praha	Provisional agreement [on establishment of trade relations]	I, 1924; 28:188
———	June 6, 1922 Praha	Provisional agreement [*idem.*]	I, 1924; 29:192
———	March 25, 1935 Praha	Treaty of commerce and navigation	*SZiR SSSR*, 1935, II, No. 14–15, §131
Estonia	May 17, 1929 Tallinn	Treaty of commerce	VI, 1931; 235:69
France	Jan. 11, 1934 Paris	Provisional commercial treaty	VIII, 1935; 310:158
———	Jan. 6, 1936 (Jan. 21, 1936) Paris	Agreement regarding the extension of the provisional trade agreement	*SZiR SSSR*, 1936, No. 20, §20 and 1936, No. 4, §43 and No. 6, §60
———	Feb. 4, 1936 Paris	Agreement between U.S.S.R. and France concerning the collection of importation duties on Russian products and on the transit of French merchandise through the territory of the U.S.S.R.	*SZiR SSSR*, 1936, II, No. 12, §112

Country	Date and Place of Signing	Substance of Treaty or Agreement	Russian Source: Sborn. Deistv. Dogov. Vol., Yr.; No., Page
Germany	Oct. 12, 1925 Moscow	Treaty comprising the following agreements: 1. Conditions of residence and business; and legal protection; 2. Economics; 3. Railways; 4. Navigation; 5. Fiscal; 6. Commercial Courts of Arbitration; 7. Legal protection of industrial property	III, 1927; 133:74
———	Dec. 21, 1928 Moscow	Protocol regarding annexes supplementary to treaty of October 12, 1925	V, 1930; 204:56
———	May 28, 1932 Berlin	Protocol regarding customs and tariff problems	VII, 1933; 265:65
Great Britain	Feb. 16, 1934 London	Provisional commercial treaty	VIII, 1935; 302:103
Greece	June 11, 1929 Athens	Convention regarding commerce and navigation	VI, 1931; 231:45
Iceland	May 25, 1927 Moscow	Exchange of notes regarding the régime of the most-favored nation	IV, 1928; 172:59
Iran	March 10, 1929 Teheran	Customs convention	VI, 1931; 233:52
———	Oct. 27, 1931 Teheran	Convention regarding migration, commerce and navigation	VII, 1933; 270:75
———	Oct. 27, 1935 Teheran	Treaty regarding settlement on the land, and of commerce and navigation; convention regarding campaign against locusts, plant diseases and parasites; and sanitary-veterinary convention	SZiR SSSR, 1937, II No. 7, §36
Italy	Feb. 7, 1924 Rome-Moscow	Treaty of commerce and navigation	II, 1925; 114:35
———	May 6, 1933 Rome	Customs convention	VIII, 1935; 303:113

Country	Date and Place of Signing	Substance of Treaty or Agreement	Russian Source: Sborn, Deistv. Dogov. Vol., Yr.; No., Page
Latvia	Dec. 4, 1933 Moscow	Commercial treaty	VIII, 1935; 304:116
Lithuania	Sept. 4, 1928 Kaunas	Exchange of notes regarding the most-favored-nation régime for customs and tariff	V, 1930; 205:70
——	Aug. 29, 1931 Kaunas	Protocol regarding the legal status of the Soviet Trade Representation in Lithuania	VII, 1933; 269:71
Norway	Dec. 15, 1925 Moscow	Treaty of commerce and navigation	III, 1927; 139:115
Sweden	March 15, 1924 Stockholm	Commercial agreement	I, 1925; 116:68
——	Oct. 8, 1927 Moscow	Convention regarding the legal status of the Soviet Trade Representation in Sweden	V, 1930; 209:85
Turkey	March 16, 1931 Ankara	Treaty of commerce and navigation	VII, 1933; 271:95
U.S.A.	July 11, 1936	Exchange of notes regarding the extension of agreement of July 13, 1935, on commercial relations	SZiR SSSR, 1936, II, No. 35, §320
——	Aug. 4, 1937 Moscow	Exchange of notes on commercial relations	Ibid., 1937, II, No. 35, §296
Yemen	Nov. 1, 1928 Sanaa	Treaty of friendship and commerce	VI, 1931; 220:6

2. Agreements Regarding Financial Problems

Country	Date and Place of Signing	Substance of Treaty or Agreement	Russian Source
Turkey	Jan. 1, 1934 Ankara	Protocol regarding the realization of the credit of eight million dollars (U.S.)	VIII, 1935; 307:133

3. Agreements Regarding Protection of Industrial Property

Country	Date and Place of Signing	Substance of Treaty or Agreement	Russian Source
Austria	April 26, 1927 Moscow	Exchange of notes on registration of trademarks	IV, 1928; 169:56

Country	Date and Place of Signing	Substance of Treaty or Agreement	Russian Source: Sborn. Deistv. Dogov. Vol.,Yr.;No.,Page
Czecho-slovakia	March 25, 1935 Praha	Treaty of commerce and navigation	SZiR SSSR, 1935, II, Nos. 14–15, §131
Denmark	Dec. 23, 1927 Moscow	Exchange of notes regarding mutual registration of trademarks	IV, 1928; 170:57
Estonia	March 3, 1928 Tallinn	Agreement regarding the mutual protection of trademarks	V, 1930; 210:88
Finland	Nov. 30, 1932 Moscow	Exchange of notes regarding mutual registration of trademarks	VII, 1933; 272:107
Germany	Oct. 12, 1925 Moscow	Treaty comprising the following agreements: 1. Conditions of residence and business; and legal protection; 2. Economics; 3. Railways; 4. Navigation; 5. Fiscal; 6. Commercial Courts of Arbitration, and 7. Legal protection of industrial property	III, 1927; 133:74
Italy	June 19, 1926 (June 15, 1927) Moscow	Exchange of notes regarding registration of trademarks	IV, 1928; 171:58
Norway	Feb. 24, 1928 Moscow	Convention regarding mutual protection of industrial property rights	V, 1930; 206:72
Sweden	July 21, 1926 Moscow	Mutual recognition of the registration of trademarks	IV, 1928; 178: 114

4. AGREEMENTS REGARDING PROBLEMS OF FISHING

Country	Date and Place of Signing	Substance of Treaty or Agreement	Russian Source
Finland	Sept. 20, 1922 Helsinki	Convention regarding fisheries in the Gulf of Finland	IV, 1924; 117:39
———	Oct. 21, 1922 Helsinki	Agreement regarding fishing and seal fisheries in the Arctic Ocean	IV, 1923; 117:39
———	Oct. 28, 1922 Helsinki	Agreement regarding the maintenance of the channel, and regarding fishing on the watercourse forming part of the frontier in the Gulf of Finland	V, 1923; 122:13

Country	Date and Place of Signing	Substance of Treaty or Agreement	Russian Source: Sborn. Deistv. Dogov. Vol.,Yr.;No.,Page
Finland	May 25, 1934 Moscow	Agreement regarding fishing and seal fisheries in Lake Ladoga	VIII, 1935; 309:150
Great Britain	May 22, 1930 London	Provisional agreement on fisheries in waters contiguous to northern coasts of U.S.S.R.	VI, 1931; 230:43
Iran	Oct. 1, 1927 Moscow	Agreement regarding fisheries in the southern part of the Caspian Sea	V, 1930; 207:74
————	Oct. 1, 1927	Exchange of notes in conformity with Article 10 of the agreement regarding fisheries	V, 1930; 208:86
Japan	Jan. 23, 1928 Moscow	Convention regarding fisheries	V, 1930; 211:89
————	May 25, 1935 Moscow	Protocol on the extension of the term of the fishing convention with Japan of January 23, 1928	SZiR SSSR, 1936, II, No. 37, §323
————	May 25, 1936 Moscow	Protocol extending through the year of 1937 the fisheries régime established by the convention of January 23, 1928	

5. AGREEMENTS ON PROBLEMS OF RAFTING TIMBER OVER THE WATERCOURSES

Estonia	May 9, 1922 Tallinn	Treaty regarding rafting the timber	I, 1924; 75:337
Finland	Oct. 28, 1922 Helsinki	Agreement regarding rafting the timber	V, 1923; 123:16
————	Oct. 15, 1933 Moscow	Convention regarding amendment of the convention of October 28, 1922	VIII, 1935; 308:139
Poland	June 19, 1933 Warsaw	Convention regarding floating of timber in frontier rivers	VIII, 1935; 305:125
————	July 9, 1933 Moscow	Protocol to the convention of June 19, 1933	VIII, 1935; 306:131

Country	Date and Place of Signing	Substance of Treaty or Agreement	*Russian Source: Sborn. Deistv. Dogov. Vol.,Yr.;No.,Page*
		6. AGREEMENTS REGARDING OTHER ECONOMIC PROBLEMS	
Italy	March 21, 1930 Moscow	Exchange of notes regarding exemption from consular visas of certificates on the origin of the goods	VI, 1931; 232:50
————	June 2, 1931 Moscow	Exchange of notes regarding certificates of origin of goods	VII, 1933; 266:68
————	Aug. 7 (Oct. 23), 1932 Moscow	Exchange of notes regarding certificates of origin of goods	VII, 1933; 267:70

PART V

AGREEMENTS ON POSTAL–TELEGRAPHIC RELATIONS

Country	Date and Place of Signing	Substance of Treaty or Agreement	Russian Source: Sborn. Deistv. Dogov. Vol.,Yr.;No.,Page
		1. GENERAL AGREEMENTS	
Latvia	March 3, 1921 Riga	Provisional postal-telegraphic agreement	II, 1921; 70: 143
Turkey	July 9, 1922 Tiflis	Postal-telegraph convention	I, 1924; 81:355
		2. GENERAL POSTAL AGREEMENTS	
Estonia	June 27, 1924 Tallinn	Postal convention	III, 1927; 142: 138
Finland	June 18, 1924 Helsinki	Postal convention	II, 1925; 120:74
——	Oct. 27, 1929 Moscow	Declaration regarding the ratification of the protocol regarding the amendment of the postal convention	VI, 1931; 237:87
Iran	April 25, 1923 Moscow	Postal convention	I, 1924; 79:350
		3. SPECIAL AGREEMENTS RELATING TO PROBLEMS OF POSTAL COMMUNICATIONS	
Bulgaria	July 10, 1935 Moscow	Agreement on the exchange of postal parcels between U.S.S.R. and Bulgaria	*SZiR SSSR*, 1936 II, No. 19, §177
Czechoslovakia	June 8, 1935 Moscow	Agreement regarding the exchange of postal parcels between U.S.S.R. and Czechoslovakia	*Ibid.*, No. 13, §127
Denmark	June 29, 1936 Moscow	Agreement regarding the exchange of postal parcels with Denmark	*Ibid.*, No. 14, §72

Country	Date and Place of Signing	Substance of Treaty or Agreement	*Russian Source: Sborn. Deistv. Dogov. Vol.,Yr.;No.,Page*
France	March 9, 1936 Moscow	Agreement regarding parcel post	*SZiR SSSR*, 1936, II., No. 36, §321
Germany	March 7, 1935 Moscow	Agreement regarding parcel post	*Ibid.*, 1935, II, No. 11, §111
Great Britain	April 19, 1934 London	Agreement regarding parcel post	VIII, 1935; 313: 189
Iran	Aug. 2, 1929 Moscow	Agreement regarding parcel post	VI, 1931; 236:80
Japan	Nov. 23, 1931 Moscow	Agreement regarding parcel post	VII, 1933; 273: 108
Latvia	Jan. 12, 1922 Moscow	Provisional agreement regarding parcel post	I, 1924; 78:346
Sweden	Sept. 12, 1924 Stockholm	Agreement regarding exchange of parcel post and letters of declared value	II, 1925; 123:98

4. AGREEMENTS REGARDING PROBLEMS OF TELEGRAPHIC AND RADIO COMMUNICATION

Country	Date and Place of Signing	Substance of Treaty or Agreement	Russian Source
Estonia	June 27, 1924 Tallinn	Radio and telegraphic convention	III, 1927; 143: 153
Finland	June 18, 1924 Helsinki	Convention regarding telegraphic communications	II, 1925; 121:89
Iran	April 27, 1923 Moscow	Telegraphic convention	I, 1924; 80:352

5. AGREEMENTS ON PROBLEMS REGARDING TELEPHONE RELATIONS

Country	Date and Place of Signing	Substance of Treaty or Agreement	Russian Source
Estonia	June 27, 1924 Tallinn	Convention regarding telephone communications	III, 1927; 144: 158

PART VI

AGREEMENTS ON PROBLEMS OF TRANSPORTATION

Country	Date and Place of Signing	Substance of Treaty or Agreement	Russian Source: Deistv. Dogov. Vol.,Yr.; No.,Page Russian Source:
1. AGREEMENTS CONCERNING PROBLEMS OF RAILWAY TRANSPORTATION			
Estonia	Oct. 25, 1925 Riga	Agreement regarding through rail passenger and freight traffic	IV, 1928; 184: 162
Finland	June 18, 1924 Helsinki	Convention regarding through railroad passenger and freight traffic	III, 1927; 152: 238
——	March 29, 1927 Helsinki	Agreement regarding the amendment of Article 7 of the Statute attached to the convention of June 18, 1924, on through passenger and freight traffic	IV, 1928; 186: 234
——	Nov. 17, 1929 Helsinki	Notes modifying the convention of June 18, 1924, on through passenger and freight traffic	VI, 1931; 241: 147
——	Jan. 5, 1933 Helsinki	Convention regarding the amendment of Articles 3–5, 9–10, and 13 of the convention of June 18, 1924, on through rail passenger and freight traffic	VIII, 1935; 318: 322
——	Feb. 11, 1936 Helsinki	Protocol amending the convention of June 18, 1924, regarding the direct railroad passenger and freight traffic	SZiR SSSR, 1936, II, No. 17, §141
Manchukuo	March 23, 1935 Tokio	Agreement regarding the transfer of the Chinese Eastern Railway	VIII, 1935; 316: 288
Poland	April 24, 1924 Warsaw	Convention regarding through railroad passenger and freight traffic	V, 1930; 215:123
——	April 24, 1924 Warsaw	Protocol altering certain rules of the convention with Poland of April 24, 1924, on the direct railroad passenger and freight transit	SZiR SSSR, 1935, II, No. 16, §134
Turkey	July 9, 1922 Tiflis	Railroad convention	V, 1930; 216: 138

Country	Date and Place of Signing	Substance of Treaty or Agreement	Russian Source: Sborn. Deistv. Dogov. Vol., Yr.; No., Page
———	July 3, 1937 Ankara	Agreement on the amendment of Articles 12 and 16 of the railway convention with Turkey of July 9, 1922	SZiR SSSR, 1937 II, No. 35, §295

2. AGREEMENTS REGARDING PROBLEMS OF TRANSPORTATION ON SEA AND RIVERS

Country	Date and Place of Signing	Substance of Treaty or Agreement	Russian Source
Czechoslovakia	March 25, 1935 Praha	Treaty with Czechoslovakia on commerce and navigation	SZir SSSR, 1935, II, Nos. 14–15, §131
Denmark	Dec. 13, 1924 (July 29, 1925) Copenhagen	Exchange of notes regarding mutual recognition of tonnage measurement certificates	III, 1927; 148: 235
Estonia	March 4, 1926 Tallinn	Exchange of notes regarding mutual recognition of tonnage certificates	III, 1927; 153: 260
Finland	June 5, 1923 Moscow	Agreement regarding the navigation of the Neva River	II, 1925; 125: 104
———	March 17, 1928 Helsinki	Agreement regarding the amendment of Article 7 of the agreement concerning the navigation of the Neva River of June 5, 1923	V, 1930; 217:145
Germany	April 16, 1929 Moscow	Exchange of notes regarding tonnage measurement certificates	VI, 1931; 240: 146
Iran	Oct. 1, 1927 Moscow	Exchange of notes regarding Port Pehlevi	IV, 1928; 176:95
Japan	Aug. 17, 1929 Tokio	Exchange of notes regarding the mutual recognition of tonnage measurement certificates	VI, 1931; 242: 148
Latvia	March 19, 1925 Riga	Exchange of declarations regarding mutual acceptance of tonnage-measurement certificates	III, 1927; 150: 236
Norway	April 9, 1926 Oslo	Declaration of mutual recognition of tonnage-measurement certificates	III, 1927; 151: 237
Poland	March 31, 1936 Moscow	Agreement with Poland on mutual recognition of tonnage certificates of merchant vessels	SZiR SSSR, 1937, II, No. 23, §157

PART VII

AGREEMENTS REGARDING PROBLEMS OF HEALTH

Country	Date and Place of Signing	Substance of Treaty or Agreement	Russian Source: Sborn. Deistv. Dogov. Vol.,Yr.;No.,Page
Estonia	June 25, 1922 Tartu	Sanitary convention	I, 1924; 95:432
Iran	Aug. 27, 1935 Teheran	Sanitary-veterinary convention	SZiR SSSR, 1937, II, No. 7, §36
Latvia	June 24, 1923 Tartu	Sanitary convention	I, 1924; 94:423
Poland	Feb. 7, 1923 Warsaw	Sanitary convention	II, 1925; 128: 118

PART VIII

INTERNATIONAL CONVENTIONS TO WHICH THE U.S.S.R. IS A PARTY

Date and Place	Substance	Russian Source:
1. POLITICAL AGREEMENTS		
Feb. 9, 1920 Paris	Treaty concerning the status of the Archipelago of Spitzbergen	*SZiR SSSR,* 1935, II, No. 17, §136
Aug. 27, 1928 Paris	Treaty for the renunciation of war as an instrument of national policy	V, 1930; 188:5
Feb. 9, 1929 Moscow	Protocol regarding putting into force the treaty for the renunciation of war	V, 1930; 189:8
July 3, 1933 London	Convention defining aggression	VIII, 1935; 296:27
July 4, 1933	Convention defining aggression	VIII, 1935; 297:31
July 20, 1936 Montreux	Convention on the régime of straits	*SZiR SSSR,* 1937, II, No. 13, §71
2. AGREEMENTS REGARDING BOUNDARY PROBLEMS		
Aug. 19, 1925 Helsinki	Convention for the suppression of the contraband traffic in alcoholic liquors	V, 1930; 201:46
Aug. 19, 1925 Helsinki	Additional agreement on the suppression of the traffic in alcoholic liquors	V, 1930; 202:53
April 22, 1926 Helsinki	Protocol to the additional agreement for the suppression of the traffic in alcoholic liquors	V, 1930; 203:54
3. AGREEMENTS ON ECONOMIC AND FINANCIAL PROBLEMS		
May 20, 1875 Paris	Convention on metric system	IV, 1928; 180:122
July 5, 1890 Brussels	Convention for the publication of customs tariffs	*SZiR SSSR,* 1936, II, No. 29, §298
July 7, 1911 Washington	Convention on preservation and protection of fur seals	III, 1927; 140:19, 140:129
Oct. 6, 1921 Sèvres	Convention modifying the convention on metric system of 1875	IV, 1928; 180:131

Date and Place	Substance	Russian Source:
April 21, 1926 Rome	Convention regarding the convention of June 7, 1905, for the establishment of the international institute of agriculture	*SZiR SSSR*, 1936, II, No. 34, §318
Nov. 22, 1928 Paris	Convention on international expositions	*Ibid.*, 1936, II, No. 16, §139
June 7, 1930 Geneva	Convention providing a uniform law for bills of exchange and promissory notes	*Ibid.*, 1937, II, No. 18, §108
June 7, 1930 Geneva	Convention for the settlement of certain conflicts of laws in connection with bills of exchange and promissory notes	*Ibid.*, 1937, II, No. 18, §109
June 7, 1930 Geneva	Convention on stamp laws in connection with bills of exchange and promissory notes	*Ibid.*, 1937, II, No. 18, §110
Sept. 5, 1935 Geneva	International agreement between customs authorities to facilitate the clearing of undischarged or lost triptychs	*Ibid.*, 1936, II, No. 4, §45
Sept. 5, 1935 Paris	Provisional convention with the Belgo-Luxembourg Economic Union	*Ibid.*, 1937, II, No. 2, §10

4. AGREEMENTS ON THE PROBLEMS OF TRANSPORT AND COMMUNICATION

Date and Place	Substance	Russian Source:
March 14, 1884 Paris	Convention for the protection of submarine cables	*SZiR SSSR*, 1926, II, No. 22, §145
Sept. 23, 1910 Brussels	International convention regarding the unification of certain rules respecting collisions between vessels	*Ibid.*, 1926, II, No. 22, §145
Sept. 23, 1910 Brussels	International convention regarding the unification of certain rules respecting assistance and salvage at sea	*Ibid.*, 1926, II, No. 22, §145
April 20, 1921 Barcelona	Declaration recognizing the right to a flag of states having no seacoast	*Ibid.*, 1935, II, No. 17, §137
April 24, 1926 Paris	Convention on motor traffic	III, 1927; 154:261
May 31, 1929 London	Convention on safety of life at sea	*SZiR SSSR*, 1936, II, No. 38, §324
Oct. 12, 1929 Warsaw	Convention for the unification of certain rules regarding international air transport	VIII, 1935; 319: 326
July 5, 1930 London	International load line convention	VII, 1933; 276:124
Oct. 23, 1930 Lisbon	Convention concerning maritime signals	VII, 1933; 275:117

Date and Place	Substance	Russian Source:
Oct. 23, 1930 Lisbon	Convention concerning manned lightships not on their stations	VII, 1933; 274:113
March 30, 1931 Geneva	Convention on the unification of the road signals	*SZiR SSSR*, 1936, II, No. 33, §316
Dec. 9, 1932 Madrid	International convention regarding tele-communication	VIII, 1935; 314: 202
March 20, 1934 Cairo	The universal postal convention	*SZiR SSSR*, 1935, II, No. 19–30, §167
March 20, 1934 Cairo	Universal postal convention. Final protocol of the provisions on the transport of regular mail by air.	*SZiR SSSR*, 1935, II, No. 19–30, §167
March 20, 1934 Cairo	Agreement regarding the exchange of letters and boxes of declared value	*SZiR SSSR*, 1935, II, No. 19–30, §167

5. AGREEMENTS ON PROBLEMS OF HEALTH

Date and Place	Substance	Russian Source:
Dec. 9, 1907 Rome	Agreement regarding the establishment of an International Office of Public Health	*SZiR SSSR*, 1926, II, No. 69, §528
Feb. 19, 1925 Geneva	Convention on traffic in opium and drugs	*Ibid.*, 1937, II, No. 17, §106
June 21, 1926 Paris	Sanitary convention	V, 1930; 218:148
Aug. 1, 1930 Paris	Convention on anti-diphtheritic serum	VII, 1933; 277:199
July 13, 1931 Geneva	Convention for limiting the manufacture and regulating the distribution of narcotic drugs	*SZiR SSSR*, 1937, II, No. 17, §107
July 25, 1934 Athens	Convention for mutual protection against dengue fever	*Ibid.*, 1936, II, No. 37, §322
Dec. 22, 1934 Paris	Agreement for dispensing with bills of health	VIII, 1935; 322: 341
Dec. 22, 1934 Paris	Agreement for dispensing with consular visas on bills of health	VIII, 1935; 322: 343

6. AGREEMENTS ON PROBLEMS OF LAWS OF WAR

Date and Place	Substance	Russian Source:
Dec. 21, 1904 The Hague	Convention regarding the exemption of hospital ships from harbor dues and taxes, and final act	I–II, 1928; 126:360
Oct. 18, 1907 The Hague	Convention for adaptation of principles of the Geneva Convention to maritime warfare	I, 1921; 38, 239

Date and Place	Substance	Russian Source:
June 17, 1925 Geneva	Protocol prohibiting the use in war of asphyxiating, poisonous or other gases and of bacteriological methods of warfare	V, 1930; 187:1
July 27, 1929 Geneva	Convention regarding the amelioration of the condition of wounded and sick in armies in the field	VII, 1933; 278:204
Dec. 27, 1936 Moscow	Declaration of rules regarding activity of submarines toward merchant ships in wartime rules added to the Protocol of London of November 6, 1936	*SZiR SSSR*, 1937, II, No. 25, §170
Sept. 14, 1937 Nyon	Agreement concerning submarine activities in connection with the Spanish civil war	*Ibid.*, 1938, No. 16, §108
Sept. 17, 1937 Geneva	Supplementary agreement to the Nyon agreement of September 14, 1937	*Ibid.*, 1938, No. 16, §109

7. AGREEMENTS ON OTHER PROBLEMS

Date and Place	Substance	Russian Source:
May 4, 1910 Paris	Convention on suppression of the circulation of traffic in obscene publications	*SZiR SSSR*, 1936, II, No. 21, §179
June 21, 1920 Paris	Convention for the establishment of the International Institute of Refrigeration	IV, 1928; 175:115
Jan. 25, 1924 Paris	Agreement regarding the creation of an International Bureau of Epizoodics	V, 1930; 213:110
Dec. 31, 1925 Helsinki	The Baltic geodetic convention	V, 1930; 212:106
April 20, 1929 Geneva	Convention on the suppression of counterfeiting currency, and protocol	VII, 1933; 262:40
Nov. 23, 1934	Agreement amending paragraphs 1, 4, 5, 6, 7, and 9 of the international convention on refrigeration of June 21, 1920	*SZiR SSSR*, 1935, II, No. 17, §136
June 22, 1936 Helsinki	Protocol extending up to January 1, 1949, the Baltic geodetic convention of December 31, 1925	*Ibid.*, 1936, II, No. 4, §45

INDEX

INDEX